CLASSICAL READINGS IN CULTURE AND CIVILIZATION

With the growing popularity of cultural studies as a degree discipline, sociologists have, in recent times, looked to the two notions of 'culture' and 'civilization' as forming the base for any analysis of Western society. This reader brings together key published essays from some of the most renowned thinkers from the mid-eighteenth century to the mid-twentieth. Major figures such as Sigmund Freud, Immanuel Kant and Friedrich Nietzsche are represented, as well as less familiar figures such as Alfred Weber and Marcel Mauss.

This wide-ranging and comprehensive survey of cultural and sociological thought features extracts from such works as Thomas Jefferson's *Notes on the State of Virginia* (1781) and Nietzsche's *On the Genealogy of Morals* (1887). 'Civilization' points to processes at the core of the development of modern societies, while 'culture' points to the way in which these processes have been criticized. A consideration of these, such as this reader provides, is thus vital, not only for a true understanding of our recent history, but also for a picture of our own culture and society.

Classical Readings in Culture and Civilization provides a significant contribution to the genealogy of the very identity of the West, at a time of increasing uncertainty. It is therefore essential reading for students of sociology and cultural studies as well as anyone interested in the history of philosophical thought, culture and civilization and their development in the last two hundred years.

John Rundell is Director of the Ashworth Centre for Social Theory at the University of Melbourne. His previous publications include *Origins of Modernity* and *Rethinking Imagination*. **Stephen Mennell** is Professor of Sociology at University College, Dublin, and is the author of *Uses and Abuses of Social Theory*, *All Manners of Food* and *Norbert Elias: Civilization and the Human Self-image*.

INTERNATIONAL LIBRARY OF SOCIOLOGY

Founded by Karl Mannheim

Editor: John Urry

Lancaster University

CLASSICAL READINGS IN CULTURE AND CIVILIZATION

Edited by
John Rundell and Stephen Mennell

London and New York

First published 1998
by Routledge
11 New Fetter Lane, London EC4P 4EE

Simultaneously published in the USA and Canada
by Routledge
29 West 35th Street, New York, NY 10001

Typeset in Baskerville by RefineCatch Limited, Bungay, Suffolk
Printed and bound in Great Britain by
TJ International Ltd, Padstow, Cornwall

British Library Cataloguing in Publication Data
A catalogue record for this book is available from the British Library

Library of Congress Cataloging in Publication Data
Classical readings in culture and civilization/
edited [by] John Rundell and Stephen Mennell
p.   cm. –– (International library of sociology)
Includes bibliographical references (p.   ) and index.
1. Culture.   2. Civilization, Modern.
I. Rundell, John F.   II. Mennell, Stephen.   III. Series.
HM101.C8948 1998   97–42944
306––dc21   CIP

ISBN 0–415–10516–1 (hbk)
ISBN 0–415–10517–X (pbk)

CONTENTS

ACKNOWLEDGEMENTS

Permission given by the following copyright holders is gratefully acknowledged:

Immanuel Kant, 'Civilisation and Enlightenment: Idea for a Universal History From a Cosmopolitan Point of View' (1784) extracted from *Kant on History*, trans. BECK, © 1963. Reprinted by permission of Prentice-Hall, Inc., Upper Saddle River, NJ. Friedrich Schiller, 'Civilisation and Romanticism' (1794) reprinted from *On the Aesthetic Education of Man*, edited and translated by Elizabeth M. Wilkinson and L. A. Willoughby, © Oxford University Press 1967. Reprinted by permission of Oxford University Press. Friedrich Nietzsche, 'Civilisation as Cruelty' (1887) reprinted from *The Birth of Tragedy and the Genealogy of Morals*, translated by Francis Golffing, © 1956 Doubleday, a division of Bantam, Doubleday, Dell Publishing Group, Inc. Used by permission of Doubleday, a division of Bantam Doubleday Dell Publishing Group, Inc. Georg Simmel, 'Culture's Inevitable Loss; The Concept of Tragedy of Culture' (1911) reprinted from *The Conflict in Modern Culture and Other Essays*, trans. K. P. Etzkorn, © 1968. Reprinted by permission of Teachers College Press, New York. Thomas Mann, 'Militarism and Culture' (1918) reprinted from *Reflections of a Nonpolitical Man*, © English translation by Walter D. Morris, 1983 Frederick Ungar Publishing Co., Inc. Reprinted with the permission of The Continuum Publishing Company. Sigmund Freud, 'Why War' (1932) reprinted from *The Standard Edition of the Complete Psychological Works of Sigmund Freud*, edited and translated by James Strachey. Published by Basic Books, Inc. by arrangement with Sigmund Freud Copyrights, The Hogarth Press and the Institute of Psycho-Analysis, London. Reprinted by permission of Basic Books, a division of HarperCollins Publishers, Inc. and Hogarth Press, London. Emile Durkheim and Marcel Mauss, 'Between Sociology and Anthropology I: Note on the Notion of Civilization' (1913) reprinted from *SR v. 38 no. 4*, © Social Research 1971, translated with an introduction by Benjamin Nelson. Reprinted by permission of Social Research, New York. Robert E. Park, 'Cities of Culture', Cities of Civilization; The Problem of Cultural Differences' (1922) reprinted from *Race and Culture*, by Robert E. Park and Everett C. Hughes, © 1950 by The Free Press; copyright renewed 1978 by Everett C. Hughes. Reprinted with the permission of The Free Press, a Division of Simon & Schuster. Norbert Elias, 'Civilization, Culture, Identity: Nationalism and State-Formation' (1989) reprinted from *The Germans: Essays on Power Struggles and the Formation Habitus*, translated/edited by Dunning and Mennell, © Blackwell Publishers. Reprinted with the permission of Blackwell Publishers, Oxford and Columbia University Press, New York. Translation of Marcel Mauss, 'Les Civilization: Éléments et Formes', *Oeuvres*, Vol. II, Paris, Minuit, pp. 473–9, by Stephen Mennell. Translation of Alfred Weber, 'Prinzipielles zur

ACKNOWLEDGEMENTS

Kultursoziologie: Gesellschaftsprozess, Zivilisationsprozess und Kulturbewegung' by G. W. Weltner and C. F. Hirshman. Translation of Lucien Febvre, 'Civilization: evolution of a word and a group of ideas' by K. Folan, first appearing in *A New Kind of History. From the writings of Febvre*, edited by Peter Burke, © Routledge and Kegan Paul 1973.

INTRODUCTION:
CIVILIZATION, CULTURE AND THE
HUMAN SELF-IMAGE

John Rundell and Stephen Mennell

Classical Readings in Culture and Civilization brings together a collection of diverse writers from the second half of the eighteenth century to the first third of the twentieth around the topic of civilization and culture. The writers are Immanuel Kant, Adam Ferguson, Thomas Jefferson, Alexis de Tocqueville, Friedrich Schiller, Friedrich Nietzsche, Georg Simmel, Thomas Mann, Sigmund Freud, Emile Durkheim, Marcel Mauss, Lucien Febvre, Alfred Weber, Robert E. Park and Norbert Elias. The book should be viewed, not so much as an anthology of essays and extracts by well-known philosophers and social theorists on the topic of civilization and culture, but more as a series of reflections on a common theme which spans at least 200 years.

However, it is more than this. The selections, overall, can be read as a genealogical guide to the development of 'culture' and 'civilization' in the context of current debates concerning the modernity or postmodernity of our current situation, not only in academic discourses – in sociology, in anthropology, in history, in cultural studies – but also in contemporary culture, generally. Thus, the book is a genealogy of concepts now broadly in use, or broadly criticized. It is, then, also a genealogical contribution to issues internal to these concepts, such as the universality or specificity of one culture against another, whether human societies progress or decline, and what a 'civilization' or 'culture' might be. More significantly, though, this book is also a contribution to the genealogy of the identity of the West at a time of its own uncertainty. However, as these contributions indicate, the identity of the West has always been a topic for criticism, and in very many registers and from competing perspectives. Looked at from a longer-term perspective, the postmodernity of our current age, as we embark on a new millennium, has affinities with the modernity of the end of the eighteenth and nineteenth centuries.

The book traces major stages in the genealogy of common themes which crystallize in their modern usages in the eighteenth century, and develop into more specialized terms in the human sciences generally – and in sociology and anthropology in particular – during the nineteenth and twentieth centuries. Between the earliest of our selections (Adam Ferguson's *The History of Civil Society*, in 1767) and the most recent (Norbert Elias's '"Civilisation" and "Culture": Nationalism and Nation-State Formation', the ideas of which evolved during the turmoil of the Second World War), the notions of civilization and culture especially evolve in the force-field between the development of generalized and *universal* categories of civilization and culture, on the one hand, and a concern with the identity of the West, on the other.

The book's geographical focus is in the main on French and German – and to a lesser extent American – intellectual orientations and interests. With the exception of the excerpt from Adam Ferguson, who was Scottish, the British experience and understanding is not represented, nor for that matter is the Italian or Spanish, though each has its own heritage of meanings. Even so, the more general theoretical problems and insights concerning the notions of civilization and culture emerge from the temporal and national contexts to which we limit ourselves. No anthology can claim to be exhaustive or definitive; ours certainly does not. In all anthologies there are bound to be omissions, either by design or by accident. None the less, the writers selected can be seen as participants in an ongoing debate. The assumption of near-synonymy between civilization and culture will be seen to be misleading. Each of these words has its own history; each grows out of, and refers initially to, a particular constellation of social forces long before it enters either popular language or, later, the specialist vocabulary of the human sciences.

The scope of the concepts of civilization and culture

In common usage, the words 'civilization' and 'culture' refer to particular levels of material and intellectual development and artistic expression. If the words are not used interchangeably, which they often are, then they are viewed as belonging to the same family of concepts that refer not only to increasingly complex forms of development and expression, but also to traditions, ideals, manners and depth of character. However, in the context of contemporary European and Anglo-American intellectual culture it may be difficult to speak of 'civilization' and 'culture' at all. From a postmodern perspective, the grand narratives of freedom, reason and progress are seen to be tied to Europe's own civilizing mission which resulted only in new forms of destruction and domination. The history of civilization is the history of brutality, and culture is its handmaiden. In the triumphalist spirit of European self-confidence, civilization is seen to have 'very positive connotations which by its logic is grammatically singular, denoting processes (and their results) which have made men (and women) more "civil", that is less "animal"-like, less savage'.[1] In other words, the notion of civilization is given a homogeneity which is forged through a preoccupation with the issue as to whether there is a single and universal civilization of the human race, and whether it is progressing in terms of morality and well-being.

However, almost at the moment of its birth the concept of civilization began to fragment. Since its inception, the concept of civilization had been constituted by an internal tension between universality and particularity that occurred in the empirical domain once the European voyages of discovery were under way, and philosophically, once other cultures became subject to philosophical speculation and reflection. The voyages beyond the Mediterranean world from the fifteenth century onwards entailed that the various Europeans – Spanish, Portuguese, English, French and Dutch – came in contact with other worlds quite different from those already known in its hinterland. Of those worlds in its hinterland prior to the voyages of discovery the Islamic one was, arguably, the most important. The concept of civilization became one way of gathering together the diversity of experiences and impressions ranging from the most power-saturated to the most naively curious. The heterogeneity of ethnically and culturally distinct societies and groups entailed that the plural forms of human association had to be acknowledged. The notion of civilization is made deeper and richer by the importation of notions of culture and *Bildung* into its orbit, particularly through the works of Johann Herder and Alexander von Humboldt. An ethnographical notion of culture emerged that became an interpretative key not only to observing, but also to admiring other cultural universes.[2] The question emerged, though: were these other cultures 'civilizations'?

In this context, the notion of civilization developed as a category under which the heterogeneous processes supposedly internal to the West, such as capitalism, nation-building, industry and democracy, could be gathered, whilst simultaneously providing a broader framework through which to interpret, in negative or positive terms, the different societies that the ones from Europe came in contact with. In a similar way, the notion of culture became a framework through which the modern processes which 'civilization' came to represent were subject to critique, as well as a category pertaining to broader anthropological concerns.

The notion of civilization, especially, became a site of tension between two opposing tendencies – one that emphasized universalistic images of the human race, and another that emphasized the plurality of cultures and societies. This tension also propelled the empirical interest in the civilizational background to Europe's own experience as well as in other civilizations that Europeans themselves confronted. This interest led to the development of comparative civilizational analysis with its distinction between the pre-civilizational and the civilizational. In terms of conventional civilizational historiography, the periods between 3000 and 900 BC became the representative origins of civilization from 'the Sumerians of Mesopotamia (*c*.3000 BC), the Egyptians of the Nile Valley (likewise *c*.3000 BC), as well as the Indus Valley civilization (after 2700 BC), the civilization of Shang China (before *c*.1500 BC), [the] Minoan Crete (*c*.2000 BC), the Olmecs of Mexico (from *c*.1000 BC) and Chavin of Peru (from *c*.900 BC)'.[3] The societal constructing processes which became civilizational ones were processes of state-formation and organized militarization, as well as the development of cities and urbanization, all of which entailed growing control and power over extended social and natural space, through the invention of institutions of rulership and administration. As one commentator has noted, a civilization must be capable of giving 'coherence either to a wide ranging empire or to a system of states for at least several centuries'.[4]

Furthermore, this type of civilizational analysis also emphasized cultural achievements. The invention of writing is viewed as a key cultural creation, along with a shift from naturalistic and mimetic art forms to symbolic abstraction and stylization.[5] Furthermore, the so-called 'Axial Age and the emergence of transcendental visions', which occurred globally during the first millennium before Christ, became the indicator of major spiritual, moral and intellectual, that is, civilizational breakthroughs. The Axial Age involved 'a kind of critical, reflexive questioning of the actual and a new vision of what lies beyond'.[6] This occurred in religious thought, although it also signified the birth of philosophy. Civilization, particularly if the Axial Age is taken as a representative example as well as a point of rupture from the pre-civilizational, is perceived as the wellspring and centre of human creativity. It, thus, 'refers to a particular concatenation of worldview, customs, structures and culture (both material culture and high culture) which forms some kind of historical whole and which co-exists (if not always simultaneously) with other varieties of this phenomenon'.[7]

In other words, civilization became variously defined in terms of power techniques of control and expansion, where empire-building is the implicit or explicit point of reference.

It has also been defined on the basis of the long-term formation of intellectual and symbolizing activity, that is, on the basis of enduring cultural products and identities. In both these aspects there is an assumption of a territorially expansive and historically enduring social form. When these currents are viewed together, civilizations can be seen as territorially expansive social forms which co-ordinate both 'sources of social power', and the sites of symbolic and intellectual creativity in the form of, again, historically enduring, expansive cultural surpluses. This comprehensive, double-sided empirically orientated notion of civilization has become the basis for comparative civilizational analysis.

However, this empirically orientated notion of civilization relies either implicitly or explicitly on a background image of humankind to orientate and ground it. In other words, civilization can also be defined in terms of anthropological assumptions concerning the self-transformation of humankind, that is, on the basis of assumptions concerning 'human universal competences which are either acquired or perfected in the course of the civilizing process'.[8] This image of self-transformation, as has been indicated above, is often tied to a notion of progress with a concomitant philosophy of history. In this context, a natural history of civilization is formulated, by such writers as Turgot, Condorcet and Comte, who posit teleologically driven development in terms of continual improvement culminating in the Enlightenment.[9] For these writers, Enlightenment refers to the discovery of the natural laws of progress, and once discovered, to their application to society and its problems in the manner of a science. This current is not uncritically present in this volume. The essays and extracts by Kant, Ferguson and Jefferson, in their own way, criticize the outright identification of civilization with progress, whilst the essays by Schiller and Nietzsche, which take their points of departure from Romanticism, not only uncouple this conceptual marriage, but also critically turn the concept of civilization against itself.

Moreover, once philosophies of history are challenged by the social theories of civilization that emerge at the end of the nineteenth century, at least two possible conceptual strategies present themselves: one which reformulates philosophy of history into theories of sociocultural evolution that presume some notion of universal human competence: and one that concentrates more centrally on the dynamics of the 'civilizing process' itself, from the development of complex institutions and cultural formations or world-views, to the relation between individuals and their social contexts. The social theorization of civilization in both these aspects occurs in the fields of academic anthropology, sociology and history, particularly the French tradition from Durkheim to Lévi-Strauss, which includes the *Annales* School which Febvre and Bloch co-founded, German sociology including Sombart to Max and Alfred Weber, and psychoanalysis, particularly in the form of Freud's more speculative writings. Separately or together, these currents have provided a rich array of concepts for critical enquiry. Within the collection of essays presented in this volume, the second strategy which emphasizes the dynamics of civilizing processes is more widely represented, especially in the works of Emile Durkheim, Alfred Weber, Sigmund Freud and Norbert Elias.[10]

Furthermore, each of the ways culture can be defined, and even used as a sub-category of civilization, can be taken up as a critical point of departure and radicalized so that it becomes the basis for a critique of civilization. For example, within the works presented in this book, the symbolizing and aesthetic dimensions, already present and often prioritized in empirical studies of 'civilizations', can become either the basis for an opposition of culture to civilization, an opposition which developed as part of Romanticism's critique of the Enlightenment (Schiller, Nietzsche, Mann), or the basis of a culturalist interpretation of civilization which emphasizes the cultural profile rather than forms of organized power (Simmel, Durkheim, Mauss, and Alfred Weber). Alternatively, the assumption of universal human competences can become the basis for either the Enlightenment's opposition of universal reason to particular civilizations (Kant, most forcefully, and Hegel, as well as the French Enlighteners), or an anthropologically motivated critique of civilization that places a pre-civilizational or ideal image of humanity prior to the intercession of civilization itself. This anthropologically motivated rejection of civilization is first voiced by Rousseau, in opposition to the predominant French Enlightenment trend, and finds its way into the work of Nietzsche and Freud.

Moreover, the notion of civilization can also be understood historically. A historically sensitive notion of civilization can become a framework for a critique based in notions of power and legitimation. Whilst not unrelated to any of the perspectives mentioned above, this historicist perspective views the notion of civilization as a product of a particular culture's attempt to understand, reconstruct and even legitimate its own societal processes, and to either dominate, or demarcate itself from, surrounding cultural and societal forms and processes. Of the works published in this book, Febvre's and Elias's are representative of this current. Febvre and Elias historicize 'civilization' and then proceed to analyse it according to distinctions between 'us' and 'them', distinctions ultimately grounded in conflicts between groups in a field of power.

The discourses on civilization, even prior to the advent of the academic disciplines of anthropology and historical sociology, already inhabited a diverse interpretive field in which even such a rich and explosive notion (as civilization) could not be limited to a pre-defined set of conceptual boundaries with taken-for-granted assumptions. Romanticism had already seen to that. The choice of selections, as well as the structure of the book into three sections – 'Civilization as Political Transformation', 'Cultural Critiques of Civilization' and 'Sociology and Anthropology: From Civilization to Civilizing Processes' – and the placement of the authors, at times chronologically, at other times thematically, indicates the competing perspectives through which the notion of civilization itself has been constituted and criticized.

Thus, the notion of civilization carries with it an accumulated heritage of meanings, perspectives and theoretical strategies that have developed throughout the course of contemporary cultural reflection which at times compete, converge and coalesce within the book, and even within some of the texts themselves. This book emphasizes three perspectives among many possible ones – one emphasizes a relation between civilization and political transformation that occurs as a tension between democratization and nation-building, another emphasizes culture as the basis for a critique of civilization, and another emphasizes images of human self-transformation that lie at the centre of any notion of civilization or civilizing project. Moreover, it should not be presumed that one perspective belongs to or is present exclusively in any of the writers presented here. Rather, points of comparison can be made within and between the authors within this frame of reference. To be sure, and to reiterate the point made above, these perspectives inhabit a conceptual force-field constituted between two poles: universalized versus particularized notions of civilization and culture, and the identity of the West.

This thematic approach is the basis for the more detailed discussion of the essays and extracts below, beginning with the concept of civilization and its relation to nation-building and historical consciousness (progress), before turning to the image of political transformation, especially its republican current and its antinomies. In a fourth section we discuss the development of the anthropological concept of culture, and its distinction from the *high cultural* before proceeding to discuss the Romantic critique of civilization, and its legacy which also spans the *fin de siècle*. We then discuss the attempts, primarily in the French and German contexts, to develop or combine sociological notions of civilization and culture, before finally turning to view civilization and culture as *processes*, rather than as static entities in the wake of typological, comparative analyses.

The concept of civilization

The concept of civilization has a longer history than that of culture. It belongs to a family of Latin words including *civilis* (civil, civilian), *civis* (citizen), *civitas* (self-governing municipality) and *civilitas* (citizenship, its rights and duties, from the Roman Republic onwards).[11] These Roman meanings are also carried into the medieval *civitabilis*, which refers to both the entitlement to citizenship (in a free city) and the activity of becoming urbanized, urbane.

In his entry in the 1931 *Encyclopædia of the Social Sciences*, Carl Brinkman gives a more nuanced view. According to him, there is only an indirect derivation from the Latin. '*Civilis* denoted general qualities connected with the citizen (*civis*) and more particularly with a certain politeness and amiability, especially when shown by superiors . . . to inferiors.'[12] Brinkman thus emphasizes rank and style of life. The contrast made between civilization and barbarism by both Greeks and Romans referred to what was proper to the development of individual human beings – that is, to their conduct, personal accomplishments and virtues. The distinction made between the citizen and the barbarian was not in terms of an idea of progress (which is modern), but rather on the basis of accomplishments that defined who was human and non-human. The barbarian was someone who was inhuman – outside of the society of accomplished citizens.

A common feature of these accounts is that the etymology of the word points to an internal tension between a meaning which is political and another that refers to style of life. However, Brinkman implies that a significant shift of meaning occurred during the seventeenth and eighteenth centuries. To be sure, an emphasis on the style of life continues, particularly in terms of manners. But this is a continuity within the context of an overall process of modernization, especially if modernization is – for once – understood in the old sense of 'progress' and 'enlightenment'. As Febvre notes in his genealogy of the concept (pp. 160–90 below), the word 'civilization' denoted a synthesis of the new sciences of nature, morals, society and humanity, which were born out of a confidence in the techniques of reason that would, through factual investigation, render the world transparent and capable of transformation towards perfection. According to Febvre the problematics of the notion of civilization were initially related to two competing pairs of words: *civilité* and *civilisé* versus *police* and *policé*.

Civilité was used on both sides of the English Channel, from the sixteenth and seventeenth centuries onwards, to denote tactfulness, sincerity and gentleness in conduct and conversation with others. It thus referred to what at an earlier stage had been commonly termed 'courtesy' or *courtoisie*. *Police* and *policé*, on the other hand, were concepts superior to *civilité*. Throughout the eighteenth century *police* accrued connotations of morality, intellect and rationality. However, *police* could not sustain the weight of the newer meanings; it was also associated with the narrower senses of law and right, and so the word 'civilization' was coined to denote not only a code of manners, but also an intellectually cultivated style of life, associated with conversation and debate within real or imagined public spheres – salons, coffee houses, journals, newspapers. Febvre draws attention to the development of the word not as the outcome of an unbroken genealogy leading directly back to the Roman world, but rather as something related to the experience of a process of modernization, though he views this experience from a particularly French viewpoint.

Gradually, according to Elias, *civilisation* came to fulfil a more general function:

> this concept expresses the self-consciousness of the West . . . It sums up everything in which Western society of the last two or three centuries believes itself superior to earlier societies or 'more primitive' contemporary ones. By this term Western society seeks to describe what constitutes its special character and what it is proud of: the level of *its* technology, the nature of *its* manners, the development of *its* scientific knowledge or view of the world, and much more.[13]

These connotations emerged, however, through prolonged polemics in the contexts of struggles between classes or strata in the long history of state-formation. In France, it was the Physiocrats and other reformers, generally of bourgeois origins, who in the late eighteenth century first associated it with ideas of progress and social improvement. It is significant that they derived the word from *civilité*, the word used by courtiers to describe their own ways of behaviour (and originally to distinguish them from the more rough and ready standards of medieval *courtoisie*). The French court was relatively more open to outsiders than was generally the case in Germany, and the French intelligentsia had taken on many of the ways and attitudes of the courtiers. So, although the word originated in the lexicon of the reformers, it eventually came to be associated with the progress and identity of the nation as a whole.

In Germany, the word *Zivilisation* took on rather different shades of meaning from its French and English equivalents (see Elias, pp. 225–40 below). The social and political context was very different. There was no single state or political centre, but numerous small courts which, in the seventeenth and eighteenth centuries, were French-speaking and relatively closed to outsiders. Princes and their courts regarded the German language as vulgar. The question of 'What is really German?' was pondered, mainly among a thinly scattered stratum of German-speaking and, again, mainly bourgeois intellectuals (the *Bildungsbürgertum*). In their hands, *Zivilisation* came to mean 'something which is indeed useful, but nevertheless only a value of the second rank, comprising only the outer appearance of human beings, the surface of human existence'.[14] In contrast, it was through the word *Kultur* that German intellectuals expressed their own pride, achievements and identity, and it came to be associated, in contrast to the *Zivilisation* of the courts – the superficiality, ceremony, polite conversation – with inwardness, depth of feeling, immersion in books, development of the individual personality, with all that was natural, real and genuine. Kant seems to have been the first to use the two concepts in contraposition in this way (see pp. 39–47 below). The idea of *Kultur*, it should be noted, was used by the German intelligentsia to demarcate and distinguish themselves and their own achievements *both* from the established courtly circles 'above', *and* from the ranks of society 'below'. So, at first, the antithesis of *Zivilisation* and *Kultur* expressed exclusion and exclusivity. As the German *Bildungsbürgertum* rose in power and prestige, however, they had less need to contrast themselves with French-speaking courtiers, and the idea of *Zivilisation* came to be associated more with France and the Western powers generally (see Thomas Mann's essay, pp. 130–8 below). In that way, the *Zivilisation/Kultur* antithesis came to play a part in German nationalism, *Kultur* carrying an inclusively German meaning, and *Zivilisation* serving to exclude the non-German.

The concept of civilization, linked as it was to questions of social identity, also raised questions of 'who are we?' and 'where are we going to?', and thus of people's awareness of historical transformation. This issue of the relation between past, present and future was first posed in the famous dispute between the ancients and moderns in the sixteenth century. It can indeed be traced as far back as the sixth century, in the context of the extinction of the western Roman Empire, when to be modern meant to rescue and to continue the knowledge of the Roman *antiquas* and render it fruitful for the new societies. The main spokesman for this movement was Cassiodorus, whose concept of the modern referred not to any break in the cultural tradition of antiquity, but explicitly to its *uninterrupted* continuity.[15] However, from our perspective today, to be modern means the opposite – not imitation, not re-creation, but replacement through a rejection of what went before, and the creation of new ways of thinking. This reconceptualization of the idea of 'the modern' began during the twelfth century in which the relation between Christian-Germanic culture and antiquity was conceptualized in terms of the translation of cultural traditions to new and different historical and social sites. However, 'at the same time . . . the image was invented of "the ancients" as "giants" on whose shoulders the "moderns" stood like dwarves'.[16]

Later, from the sixteenth century onwards, this resulted in two separate images with a tension between them: on the one hand, of respect by the moderns for the ancients, and on the other, the idea that the dwarves on the giants' shoulders could see further, and thus were superior. The participants in this debate – the so-called *République des lettres* – were divided between those who advocated that antiquity be imitated, taken as a model, and those who thought it should be rejected and forgotten.[17] The latter emphasized developments in the present and looked at the growing explosion of knowledge in the natural sciences, in particular, and the technologies derived from them.[18] For them, historical change is not only good, it was valued positively under the umbrella term of progress. However, not everyone in the seventeenth and eighteenth centuries shared this enthusiasm for and faith in science; and, as the human sciences became more clearly differentiated from the natural sciences, this difference of opinion was also reproduced in debates about modern politics.

Civilization as political transformation

One thing all these thinkers had in common was the great significance they attached to civil society – *civitas*. There was also a major division of opinion among them, about the nature of political action – was it based in the language of virtues or in a language of practical reasoning? But for all of them, civilization was a matter of *political* and not scientific transformation. This is a topic of Part I of the present book, 'Civilization as Political Transformation'.

The concern with civil society had its roots in older preoccupations not only with 'manners' but also with sovereignty and 'virtues'. Civil society thus refers not only to civil conduct, but also to two competing political traditions which have long and deep roots within European political thought, certainly from the fourteenth century onwards. J. G. A. Pocock has argued that these traditions are the *juridical*, which embodied the notion of rights, and the *republican*, which embodied the notion of virtue.[19] Seen in this way, the notion of civil society shows similar patterns of conceptual conflict to that of the notion of civilization identified by Febvre and Elias, especially in France.

A tension emerged between the juridical and the republican notions of civil society, as well as with the view of civil society as a private sphere limited to economic, religious and cultural freedoms. Within civil society in the sense of a private sphere, the notion of virtue was redefined, along with codes of manners, in terms of the refinement and enrichment of personality through the cultivation of commerce and the arts. It was their function to tame and refine the passions, and as Adam Ferguson would say, to polish manners. But gradually there came about a conceptual impoverishment of civil society to either a notion denoting private economic activity (for example in the work of Hegel and Marx), or a notion allied to public administration (for example in the work of the German legalists). According to Max Weber in 'The City', the republican concern with virtue lost ground to the juridical concern with rights, law and administration.[20]

In Britain, however, the republican current continued and found its way to North America. The significance of this is seen in Jefferson's *Notes on the State of Virginia* (pp. 61–72 below). In Kant's work too, there is a deep tension between juridical and republican notions of society. The republican current, moreover, continued to be utopian. It became a vehicle for many and varied historical and conceptual experiments including radical liberalism, socialism and anarchism, which called for either a real subordination of the state to civil society or the development of self-governing bodies independent of the state. This current provided a perspective from which a critique of bureaucratic and regulatory state power could be developed.[21] Not that the western republican model is without its own dangers and forms of tyranny: Alexis de Tocqueville, in *Democracy in America*, was perceptively to note the tendencies towards new forms of tyranny, the tyranny of the majority, associated with conditions of relative social equality (see pp. 73–82 below).

Fresh nuances also emerged from the extension and 'export' of European institutions and ideas into the new worlds of the Americas, South Asia, the Pacific and Australasia, and from Europeans' attempts to comprehend their new empires. It can be argued that the political 'mapping' of these regions occurred according to an absolutist imagination of the world, the result of which was that the empires were absolutist in structure. However, there also emerged 'creole' and 'indigenous' political structures, not just as *responses* to external forms of control but also as experiments – as in Jefferson's *Notes on Virginia*.[22] The new worlds were a perplexity, especially to European Enlighteners. The new worlds represented a test, as well as a confirmation of the Enlightenment's faith in the underlying universality of the human condition. As Holbach notes,

> Savage man and the civilized, the white man and the red man, the black man, Indian and European, Chinaman and Frenchman, Negro and Lapp have the same nature. The differences between them are only modifications of their common nature, produced by climate, government, education, opinions and the various causes which operate upon them.[23]

In its search for confirmation of the universality of 'human nature', the old world was viewed as a source of corruptibility. Thus, if the answers were not to be found in the cosmopolitan centres of the old world, they might well be found in the untouched and unsullied wildernesses of the new world, for 'if human nature was the same everywhere, and the same yesterday, today and tomorrow, then the primitive and the pastoral might reveal it in its nakedness'.[24] Thus the new worlds came to be viewed in the idyllic terms of the noble savage. However, these worlds – and for many that principally meant the Americas – could also be viewed as the dark counter-model to civilization itself: untamed, wild and degenerate. A controversy raged during the eighteenth century as to the nature, origin and condition of the still largely unexplored lands and their peoples. This debate – though it has been described as no more than the scribblings of prejudiced and uninformed minds – was widespread and very influential, for what was at issue was an attempt to account for the perceived backwardness of the new-found lands, as well as older non-European worlds, in which nothing could be cultivated – neither plants, nor people, nor civilization.[25]

Between the sixteenth and eighteenth centuries, then, the notion of civilization converged on three social processes informed either uncritically or critically by a background notion of progress: the development of stylized forms of social conduct termed manners; the development of a separate sphere of political and economic activity termed either republican or commercial civil society; and the growing conflict between civil society and the institutional forms of absolutist state power and government. It was also influenced by the increasing European exploration of, and familiarity with, the new worlds of the Americas, southern Asia and the Pacific. The essays by Kant, Ferguson and Jefferson can be interpreted in these contexts.

The contribution of Immanuel Kant (1724–1804) to the Enlightenment discussion about civilization – represented here by 'Idea for a Universal History from a Cosmopolitan Point of View', pp. 39–47 below – is the most rigorous and far-reaching of the philosophical essays included here. Kant makes a distinction between cultivation, *civilité*/civilization and maturity. Cultivation refers to the activity of higher learning, particularly in the arts and sciences; *civilité* and civilization refer to courtesy and manners (of which Kant asserts we already have enough); maturity refers to the condition of general freedom. It is not a movement from savagery to civilization that Kant has in mind, but one from barbarism to maturity. For Kant, barbarism does not refer to an image of primitivism, but quite specifically to tyranny. From a political perspective, then, maturity or self-mastery comes about by establishing a constitutional state, where civil society shapes the state, and not the other way round. These conceptual distinctions constitute his decisive contribution to the idea of civilization as an image of political transformation, and it is for this reason that his essay opens this section, rather than Ferguson's written some years earlier.

Ferguson's *An Essay on the History of Civil Society* (pp. 48–60), written in 1767, and Jefferson's *Notes on the State of Virginia* (pp. 61–72), written in 1781, partly anticipate the concerns of Kant's essay. For Adam Ferguson (1723–1816), civilization means accomplishments that result in increases in both social wealth (commerce) and culture (science and the arts). For him, the distinction between the pre-civilized and the civilized corresponds to that between the rude and the polished. The extracts which appear below – 'Of Supposed National Eminence, and of the Vicissitudes of Human Affairs', from Part Fifth ('Of the Decline of Nations'), and 'Of Rude Nations prior to the Establishment of Property', from Part Second ('On the History of Rude Nations') – show him engaging with the prejudiced interpretations of the New World. He challenges the predominant image, whether in the versions derived from Hobbes or from Rousseau, of a state of nature inhabited by pre-social and atomistic human beings. Ferguson also shows a modern society torn between conflicting forces of wealth creation and moral disintegration, both resulting from the increasing division of labour. Ferguson's legacy to sociology prefigures the works of Marx, Spencer and Durkheim. Though the title has been given to others besides him, Ferguson is often referred to as the 'father of sociology'.[26]

For Thomas Jefferson (1743–1826), civilization means the development of democratic government and culture, and he distinguishes between the civilized and the non-civilized in terms of virtue and tyranny. His views were set out in response to a series of queries posed by François Barbé, Secretary to the French Minister in Philadelphia. He rejects the image of the new world constructed in the main by Georges Buffon, replacing it with an active and fertile one. He emphasizes the particular way European Americans have developed a specific form of republican civilization with both institutional and cultural dimensions. The institutional dimensions were constituted through a balance of powers; the cultural ones through an emphasis on a cultivation of manners that enhanced a political identity. Jefferson confronted a twofold problem that has continued to haunt America (cf. the extracts and essays by de Tocqueville and Park, below): the threat of political corruption and tyranny in the context of an immigrant society that was possibly too heterogeneous and diverse to constitute an integrated political community.

Jefferson's responses are indicative of the uniqueness of the American solution (notwithstanding the unfinished issues of slavery and native Americans). In Jefferson's view, the threat posed by tyranny and corruption is addressed by the creation of multiple modes of representation, which simultaneously is viewed as multiple ways of exercising and, thus, providing a check on power. The threat posed by an amorphous mass is addressed by Jefferson in terms of a model of the cultivation of virtues and manners. In a modern, functionally and culturally diverse society, custom and tradition are not enough to guard against the formation of mass society. In Jefferson's view – and here he returns to French Enlightenment currents – education in the republican ideals and arts of ruling and being ruled can only guard against corruption. Together these place a limit on power. This can be seen in responses on 'Constitution', 'Religion' and 'Manners'.

For Alexis de Tocqueville (1805–59), like Ferguson and Jefferson, the threats to republican democracy are internal, rather than external. In his *Democracy in America* (Volume 1, 1835; Volume 2, 1840), de Tocqueville argues that the immanent trend towards the centralization of the state in modern democratic polities is countered, in the American case, by a variety of differentiated and independent public agencies, which include not only separate legislature, executive and judiciary, but also an independent press, intermediary associations and local government. In the context of the latter, de Tocqueville posits the American federalist model as one that differentiates power both normatively, through the constitution, and spatially, that is regionally, and through society as a whole. Unlike the French centralist model that he contrasts it with, a federalist model builds in a permanent tension between centrifugal and centripetal dynamics of power. In this way, if the federal model is one of a tension between political powers, then, following de Tocqueville, republican federal democracy can be viewed as a model that generalizes this tension throughout all of society, and at both organizational and cultural levels. Republican federal democracy, thus, exhibits tensions between state and civil society, public and private, equality and inequality, equality and freedom, freedom and unfreedom, the majority and the minority.

The inherent dangers to republican federal democracy reveal themselves once these tensions begin to dissolve, and one side begins to dominate the other(s). For de Tocqueville, it is not so much the anarchy of an atomized mass of individuals that is the danger to democracy. Rather, in a series of reflections (pp. 73–82 below) that foreshadow much of the critique of social democracy, he argues that the dangers lie in the development of a centralized state and pacified public and private spheres. In democracies, according to de Tocqueville, a paradox emerges in that the state is simultaneously delegated to take on more and more areas of legitimate and legal responsibility for the lives of its citizenry, and in so doing constantly makes private life into a series of public, administrative issues. In other words, the private sphere simply becomes a sphere of public administration. Moreover, the public sphere itself – the sphere of opinion – becomes subject to the dystopic emotional cultures of democracy, especially envy and indifference.[27]

The Concept of Culture

Like 'civilization', the notion of 'culture' is more complex than it appears to be at first glance.[28] The word is derived from the Latin *cultus* and refers to the cultivation of the earth, and later the human mind; it first appears much later than civilization, in the 1793 edition of a German dictionary, even though the conceptual field to which it refers had existed for much of the century. All subsequent meanings of culture go back to the German meaning of the term, rather than to its Latin root.[29] In the entries on culture in both the 1931 and 1968 encyclopædias of the social sciences, Tylor's omnibus definition of 1871 is taken as a benchmark: culture is 'that complex whole which includes knowledge, belief, art, morals, law, custom and any other capabilities and habits acquired by man as a member of society'.[30] However, this anthropological usage of the term is one aspect of a complex set of developments, issues and problems.

In Germany towards the end of the eighteenth century, *Kultur* – as we have seen – emerged as a word demarcating one stratum from another. It was also shaped through an initial sense of optimism and then through a sense of crisis as the political disasters of the French Revolution rocked this enthusiasm for the revolution by a European intelligentsia critical of absolutism. Furthermore, the growth of cities and markets and the division of labour so amply described by Ferguson and by Adam Smith, together with the organization of factory work, created a new urban mass society which was often an object of fear, awe and speculation. The Enlightenment's faith and confidence in the principles of reason came to be questioned, and the first Romantic movement emerged.

So rather more was involved in the emergence of the concept of culture than its use simply as a counterpoint to *Zivilisation*. The American anthropologists A. L. Kroeber (1876–1960) and Clyde Kluckhohn (1905–60) posit several currents in the development of the concept of culture in Germany, especially as it emerged from a concern with universal histories of human progress and improvement. One current, derived from Herder, is proto-anthropological, comparative, almost ethnographic and relativist; later anthropological usages of the term stemmed from this. A second current, contemporary with the first, identified culture with the spirit or *Geist*, and with creativity and 'high culture'; Kroeber and Kluckhohn see this second, *geistlich*, notion of culture as decreasing in significance, but in our opinion its influence continued throughout the nineteenth century and into the sociological tradition.[31]

The proto-anthropological notion of culture emerged from Herder's work, especially from his 1770 'Essay on the Origin of Language'. Culture was seen as the means through which human beings reproduced and understood themselves. Herder's arguments were aimed, *pace* Elias, not so much in aid of the self-legitimization of a class, but against Rousseau's image of the human being, born free but everywhere culturally enchained. Like Ferguson, Herder argued that human beings were not singular animals, but required social groupings to survive, and this necessitated that knowledge of their environment be gained, accumulated and passed from one generation to another. In a deeper sense, for Herder, this knowledge indicated the anthropological understanding of what human beings were. For him, they were simultaneously social and cultural animals, and language was the means through which they became such animals. Language, so Herder argued, was the collectively formed, intermediate means through which the continuity of human life from one generation to the next is assured, which was sedimented as culture. This sedimentation also assured the continuity between the present and the past as a cumulative and creative process.[32] Culture was, thus, viewed as an inherited and inheritable permanent resource to be drawn upon. The past, as culture, could be turned to inform us of our present lives, not as habit or tradition, but as a form of reflective activity, the goal of which was self-understanding and thus a critical distancing from the past.[33]

A double implication emerged from Herder's notion of culture. Culture could be viewed as something relative, the legitimacy and authenticity of which was internal to each society. Furthermore, the weight of what constituted culture fell on linguistically constituted *everyday* understandings, which prepared much of the ground for Dilthey's later notion of everyday life. In Dilthey's formulation, culture is broadened to embrace not only the interrelation of life, expression and understanding which are anchored in language, but also the way in which these are objectified in institutions. Hence, for him, culture – which is transposed into the hermeneutics of understanding – stems from an interaction between two worlds: a subjective one of human uniqueness, and an objective one of institutional forms through which culture is articulated, and in which the subject finds him/herself permanently located.[34]

The *geistlich* notion of culture emerged alongside the proto-anthropological one, often acting as a supplement to it, but also standing on its own as a working interpretation. The idea of progress and technical-rational innovation, resulting in the increasing mastery of nature, was generalized into an image of innovation, creativity and perfectibility in all areas of life. Culture in this second view refers to specific human practices – the creation of art, religion and science – which are valued as 'high culture'. It emphasizes the processes of creativity, innovation and a *break* from the past, and thus the movement and ceaseless activity of the present. The development and identification of high cultural practices depended on a pre-given hierarchic classification involving processes of social inclusion and exclusion. We should remind ourselves that in the German case 'high culture' referred not so much to *politesse*, but to the self-legitimization of an excluded stratum. Culture did not, however, 'simply codify these activities by conferring upon them a new legitimisation and label . . . [it also] implied criteria by which practices, accepted as cultural *sui generis*, were thought of as being able to satisfy'.[35] These criteria were tied to an idea of creativity.

In order to qualify as an artist (someone who created high culture), a person had to fulfil two requirements of creativity. First, the work of art – the painting, the poem, the novel – and not the artist became the source of meaning. In other words, a separation between the artist and what he or she created had to occur, with the emphasis falling on what was created, which must also represent and transmit an accumulation of insights and experiences to a wider public. The work of art, then, was no longer the specific expression of the artist's disposition or particular practice, nor was it produced for a particular audience, such as a religious one. This makes an interpretation of the work possible without knowledge of its creator's life. Art and life were separated. Second, in a strict sense, the work of art had to be novel. The ideal of an authoritative piece of work anchored in traditions and schools was replaced by the ideal of originality. The learning and practice of skills and crafts were downgraded or subordinated to this ideal, further enhancing the sense of separation between the artist, the artist's ordinary life, and the works that he or she produced. The works stand alone.[36]

It was the *geistlich* version of culture, that emphasizing the creative imagination, that became the source of the Romantic critique of civilization. In the *Critique of Judgement*, Kant stressed the role of the genius as the repository of the imaginative force, in whom elements of art and nature were combined in such a way that practical and technical knowledge were

13

mixed with blind spontaneity.[37] The early German Romantics, the first Romantic generation of the later eighteenth and early nineteenth century, followed Kant's lead. They shared a strong sense of crisis and reacted to it in two specific ways that are relevant to the understanding of the development of diverse meanings of culture.

On the one hand, they constructed a holistic image of humankind, through which the various dimensions of human experience that had been split up and broken down into discrete parts by the analytical powers of reason could be reunified. Poetry and the creative imagination would save and deliver human beings from a life that had been fragmented by the division of labour and political conflicts, and narrowed by a cognitive rationalism. Reason was to be reunited with feelings, and subordinated to the imagination. Nature and culture, or nature and humankind, would be reconciled.

On the other hand, and in the wake of the older dispute between the ancients and the moderns, ideas of time and history were also relativized during the early Romantic period against a predominant belief in progress. This provided the Romantic thinkers with the interpretative device for bringing the past into the present as a recaptured ideal against which modern civilization could be judged. As modern civilization became increasingly identified with the functional division of labour, instrumental rationalism, alienation, statism, and the corruption of democratic ideals, another counter-model (apart from that found in the New World) emerged. The Romantic generation constructed a counter-model of European Antiquity based on culture, rather than the politics emphasized by the earlier republican generation. Moreover, what was broadly termed the Orient, but generally referred to China and India, was as much romanticized as demonized in the West's imagination. China, certainly during the eighteenth century, was worshipped in French thought from Voltaire to the Physiocrats as a civilization that the Physiocrats wanted France to resemble – earthly, rationalized, enlightened. The first Romantic generation viewed India as well as Antiquity ambivalently. India was either a state of original harmony and child-like naiveté, or outside of history, static and thus not open to the change which *in itself* was championed as a hallmark of the West.[38] These counter-models provided the means through which different utopian visions could emerge, utopias emphasizing the reintegration of different spheres, and especially of art and freedom, and the reassertion of the sacred in the face of secular forces.

Civilization and violence: cultural critiques of civilization

Romanticism is central to Part II of this book, which focuses on the way in which 'culture' was mobilized as a critique of 'civilization'. The 'Romantic predicament', as it has been called, represents a cultural response to the issues to which civilization gives rise.[39] This predicament is as evident in Schiller's two letters from *On the Aesthetic Education of Man* (1794), which opens Part II, as it is in Freud's letter of 1932 to Einstein – 'Why War?' – which closes it. The same predicament or unease is also present in the second part of Nietzsche's *Genealogy of Morals* (1887), in an essay by Georg Simmel entitled 'The Concept and Tragedy of Culture' and in Thomas Mann's 'Civilization's Literary Man', written in 1918.

On the Aesthetic Education of Man (pp. 85–94 below) is a direct response by Friedrich Schiller (1759–1805) to the sense of crisis, especially the despair and loss of confidence brought about by the political crises within the French Revolution in 1793 and 1794. It is both an analysis of these political crises and an aesthetic response to them. It is also a seminal work (together with his essays entitled 'Naive and Sentimental Poetry' and 'On the Sublime') which introduces many of the ideas that were to become part of the Romantic conceptual landscape and its cultural critique of civilization. Schiller's work reveals the positive utopian vision of the first Romantic generation, in which humankind moves from a pre-civilizational, pre-reflexive relation with nature to a reflexive civilized one – from simple enjoyment of mimesis to autonomous creation. The image of unity was represented by the Athenian Greeks, whose life threw the vicissitudes of the modern period into relief. Arthur Lovejoy calls Schiller 'the spiritual grandfather of German Romanticism'. In many ways, too, he could also be called the unacknowledged grandfather of Marxism, given his description of modern civilization, and his analysis of what, for him, is its alienated condition.[40]

Another image of a foreign territory emerges alongside the ones constructed either in the past or beyond Europe's shores. It is a world within the human being, a world of creativity, imagination and energy.[41] The image of inner life permits a renewal of the critique of civilization, already incipient from Hobbes to Rousseau. It is now posed in terms of a conflict between an internal world and an external one. Broadly speaking, this anthropological critique of civilization conceptualizes an internal world that belongs primordially outside or beyond civilization, and an external one which is brought in from the outside to tame, pacify and civilize this internal world against either its own creative energies or its worst excesses. Nietzsche's *Genealogy of Morals* is representative of this current, as is Freud's 'Why War?'

In many ways, Friedrich Nietzsche (1844–1900) is the most important figure in Part II, as Kant was in Part I. Nietzsche's work has left its indelible mark on the way in which both civilization and culture have subsequently been understood, from Georg Simmel, through Thomas Mann, Sigmund Freud, Alfred and Max Weber to Norbert Elias. The core of Nietzsche's critique of civilization is published below (pp. 95–114) under the title 'Civilization as Cruelty' – which indicates the direction his critique takes.

In Nietzsche's view, civilization and culture stand in tension with one another – they can neither be reduced to one another, nor reconciled. Civilization involved the de-naturalization of the life instincts, as well as the de-intellectualization of culture. Nietzsche argues that in pre-civilizational periods – which he idealizes, at least in his early work, in the period of archaic Greece – the instincts of life were wild, expansive and joyful. The advent of civilization did not so much re-channel and narrow the life instincts; it redefined them negatively, turning them inward against themselves. According to Nietzsche, this redefinition occurred during the Greek enlightenment in the fifth and fourth centuries BC, especially in the hands of Socrates. The negative, civilizational impact upon the life instincts was given further impetus through their reinterpretation during the Christian period. Civilization, for Nietzsche, thus became synonymous with the invention of guilt and bad conscience during these two historic watersheds. Furthermore, this negative internalization was achieved by those castes and groups who envied life and creativity and championed its denial. Civilization, from this genealogical perspective, was a de-naturalization of life, brought about through a process of reversal and internalization.[42]

The reversal and internalization of the life instincts was accompanied by the de-intellectualization of culture. In pre-civilizational periods, according to Nietzsche, life and culture were marked by unrestrained creativity. In periods when the life instincts are reversed, culture itself loses its capacity for self-reflection and for the creation of meaningful content. Civilization breeds only weak cultures of *ressentiment*, which must be rejected out of hand. As he states, human beings are the 'sick animal[s]', made ill by civilization as they internalize denial, by the invention of moral categories, and in so doing they turn away from life itself.

Nietzsche thus wanted to move beyond Romanticism, which viewed creativity and art as divine and serving morality. Nietzsche desired a creativity that surpassed morals, and even art itself. He viewed creativity as an instinctive life force and not as something that came from the imagination.

Given his anthropological premises, Nietzsche writes a history of creativity and sociability as a decline into passive nihilism. His conception of civilization, and his critique of it through his own notion of culture, informs subsequent cultural critiques of civilization. His two main themes – the de-naturalization of man through civilization and the de-intellectualization of culture, both profoundly pessimistic – are repeated in the works of Simmel and Freud, as well as providing an intellectual and cultural background to the works of Mann and Elias.

The *fin de siècle*: the war of the worlds

Between Nietzsche and these later authors comes the crucial period of the *fin de siècle*. The 'hundred years peace' has thus far endured for eight decades, and there was a pervasive sense of solid stability. The sense that all was solid was profoundly shaken, and then blown apart. First it was shaken by a cultural crisis, centred in the cities. Then there was a civilizational crisis, which blew apart all sense of solidity, in the trenches of the Western Front.[43]

By the end of the nineteenth century, the metropolis had come to outweigh court society as the centre of gravity for civilization and culture.[44] As Elias points out, in the particular case of central Europe, the courtly elite and the *haute bourgeoisie* had reached an accommodation that found expression in militaristic clubs and associations.[45] There was, however, not only an accommodation with those who were familiar; there was also an unease towards the strange and the unfamiliar, and the forms of unfamiliarity and strangeness became increasingly evident and diverse. As cities expanded, and as some – such as Paris and Vienna after the 1848 revolutions – underwent redesign, classes and groups that had been more or less distant from and unfamiliar to each other came into closer contact. Thus, not only the industrial working class, which had achieved certain forms of political representation and power, but also ethnic groups like Jews and others such as the Czechs and the Hungarians, who had their own national aspirations, became increasingly visible. There was, to use an urban metaphor, an increase in social traffic, which brought both disdain and *ressentiment*, not only interaction but also the *avoidance* of interaction.[46] This social flux helped prepare the ground for a world war, as Wilhelmine Germany and the Habsburg Empire were ill-equipped to cope with the complexity and diversity of the *fin de siècle* city: anti-Semitism, nationalism, militarism and democratization. Within this constellation, new relations of inclusion and exclusion were formed and others refigured; in this process, strangers played a key role through their simultaneous closeness and remoteness. Strangeness entails that the stranger is treated not as an individual but – as Simmel said – is abstracted and characterized as a certain *type*.[47] Durkheim, Simmel, Freud and Elias all shared in this, being Jews, as were many artists, writers and intellectuals generally.[48]

Within the growing cities, morality and immorality also became more visible and more the subject of overt polemics. The *haute bourgeoisie* denounced as 'decadent' those who rejected their own tastes and codes of behaviour. As a counter to what they saw as the stultifying morality of the bourgeoisie, there were those who embraced 'decadence' as a way of life, whether in the bordello or in a bohemian lifestyle. 'Decadence' also had an aesthetic dimension as a reaction against the bourgeoisie's taste for mimetic ornamentation derived from the courtly elite, which cluttered their homes from floor to ceiling and even (in Central Europe) appeared on the faces of their young men in the form of duelling scars.[49] It is, however, incorrect to see the 'decadent' aesthetic counter-movements of the fin de siècle, such as the Secession and Jugendstil movements of Vienna and Berlin, as merely reactive. Decadence was a movement against civilization (in the Eliasian sense), but not against culture. Although the decadent movements of the *fin de siècle* attempted to criticize civilization as a way of life, and via that *haut bourgeois* culture, they did so on grounds of its perceived lack of authenticity. Instead of demolishing *high* culture, they wished to defend it from within its own visions of creativity and autonomy, in spite of the values that informed this defence.

The *fin de siècle* city, which really covers the quarter-century between 1890 and 1914, has two distinct generations – a 1890 generation to which Wilhelm Dilthey, Sigmund Freud, Georg Simmel, Max Weber, Thomas Mann and Emile Durkheim belong, and a 1905 generation to which such figures as Marcel Mauss and Lucien Febvre, August Klimt, Robert Musil, Ludwig Wittgenstein and Georg Lukács belong. The division between them is both intellectual and experiential. Intellectually, the 1890 generation positioned itself in relation to positivism and neo-Kantianism, whilst the 1905 generation positioned itself in relation to Romanticism and expressivism. Experientially, the outbreak of war in 1914 divides these two generations. For the 1890 generation it is a crisis, but one experienced from the distance of years, whilst the 1905 generation experienced it first hand.[50]

Thus, Georg Simmel (1858–1918) participated in this 1890 movement of cultural reflection through his 'sociological impressionism'. He argues, in 'The Concept and Tragedy of Culture' (pp. 115–29 below), that once culture achieves an independent existence it becomes removed from what was originally intended. The separation between life and art (as a defining characteristic of high culture) involves, for Simmel, not only a proliferation of cultural contents, but also specialization. The paradox of high culture, for him, is that what appears to be continuing enrichment is in fact continuing impoverishment.[51] Furthermore, Thomas Mann (1875–1955), in his 'Civilization's Literary Man' (pp. 130–8 below), invokes the German ideal of *Kultur* as a defence of Germany in the 'civilizational' war between Europe's national empires. 'Germany' also became the battleground – French *civilisation* versus German *Kultur*. Mann accepted the differentiation between high culture and the life of the artist/writer. This also entailed that art and politics were separate and, for Mann, art was to be defended on the basis of its greatness. All the better if aesthetic greatness and national characteristics coincided. This conjunction was, in fact, a major current within the way in which culture and civilization were deployed by many of the writers selected here.

If the close of the eighteenth century was marked by a sense of disappointment, failure and crisis among European intellectuals, the closure of the nineteenth century and the beginning of the twentieth was marked by *unease*. Sigmund Freud (1856–1939) represents this most acutely, although from an additional perspective. He used an architectural or spatial metaphor through which to explore familiar, *yet foreign and internal* territory. Internal foreign territory – the unconscious – becomes the meeting-place, for Freud, of the three dimensions of the human animal – nature, the present, and the past. Chaos and untamed nature mark this internal foreign territory. Civilization must, if not colonize it (which it cannot), then at least construct bulwarks against it, to coax, cajole and direct it for civilization *as culture* or live with its consequence, which is *war*.

Culture and anthropology, civilization and sociology

Around the turn of the century, discourses about civilization and culture underwent change, as intellectuals struggled to capture the diversity and complexity of the new worlds confronting them: in the cities, in inner mental life, and in the hitherto unfamiliar societies then coming under systematic scrutiny by anthropologists in the field. Moreover, the three axioms of nineteenth-century human science – the unity of humankind's experience, the unity and progress of humankind, and the unity of shared culture – came under increasing critical attack. Two other axioms remained stubbornly persistent: first, that societies moved from simple to more complex and differentiated forms and that this movement provided the empirical watershed between what constituted civilization and what did not; and secondly, that societies were internally functionally integrated, working as organic wholes. These developments were to have an impact on the notions of civilization and culture and the conceptual relation between them, and this is the focus of Part III, 'Sociology and Anthropology: From Civilization to Civilizing Processes'.

As a division of labour proceeded within the academy, the notion of culture secured a permanent and central place within the newly distinct discipline of anthropology by the end of the nineteenth century. The axiom that societies moved from simple to more complex ones, which provided the dividing line between non-civilizations and civilizations, did not provide the basis for another axiomatic distinction between the cultural and the non-cultural to emerge. Such a distinction, which would have resulted in a coalescence of non-civilization and non-culture, had been averted, and under the influence of Herder and more recently the German-American anthropologist Boas (1858–1942) a new axiom emerged – in anthropology at least: civilizations are cultures, but the opposite is not true.[52] All societies have culture and are, by definition, cultural.

Between the wars, the views of the Polish-British anthropologist Bronislaw Malinowski (1884–1942) were especially influential. In Malinowski's view, 'culture comprises inherited artefacts, goods, technical processes, ideas, habits and values. Social organizations cannot be really understood except as part of culture . . .'[53] Malinowski makes a distinction between culture and civilization, but civilization is reserved for a special aspect of *advanced* cultures in which the idea of *high* culture is expanded to include cognitive knowledge and not only aesthetics. The distinction he makes is not between the low, the high or the decadent, but between the human and the non-human. Humankind mediates its world through culture. Malinowski emphasizes a notion of culture which is functionally orientated to the satisfaction of the wide range of human needs. Needs, for him, are never *directly* known, experienced or satisfied. The human species, as the one that requires the longest learning period, also requires a rich or 'thick' medium of learning, and culture provides this medium.[54]

Culture for Malinowski includes material existence as well as norms, rules and knowledge, which expand humankind's outward chances of control. Malinowski termed the material condition of life 'material *culture*', which is the indispensable 'secondary environment' that moulds or conditions each generation of human beings in the way in which the body and emotions are expressed and deployed. Language, too, is 'material' culture; though rooted in a physical capacity, it is 'a body of vocal customs'.[55] Moreover, patterns of social organization are subsumed into culture – they and the activities through which they operate are a result of social rules and customs. Culture is, therefore, a catch-all term, that includes and co-ordinates all forms and dimensions of human activity. A version of this wide notion of culture is found much later, for example in Bourdieu's use of the term 'habitus'.[56] Culture is everything, even if internal distinctions can be made within it. No longer does culture denote a sphere of autonomous creation determined and signified by specific practices. In the hands of Malinowski – and a little later of Kroeber and Kluckhohn – it is turned into a theory of society and by implication a generalizable concept of identity. In many respects, this is what it always was – but now in its fully developed anthropological guise it defines the identity of the human species and not simply of a stratum, a class, or a nation. The only limit to the notion of culture is a genetic one.[57]

Yet, despite the omnibus quality of the anthropological concept of culture, the notion of civilization did not disappear. Its development in the twentieth century was subject to three major influences, which partly overlap with those on the development of the concept of culture. One has already been discussed above – the unease of the *fin de siècle*. A second is the development of the 'national' schools of sociology.[58] The third was the experience of total war and totalitarianism.

The First World War had already challenged the identification of civilization with *politesse*, virtue and peace; and then Europe erupted into war again in 1939 because it had been unable to resolve the deep problems that had issued from the end of the First World War. National Socialism in Germany, fascism in Italy, falangism in Spain, and the Leninist and then Stalinist forms of communism in Russia all challenged the idea of political democratization to its core. Rather than seeing these variants of authoritarianism and totalitarianism as *different* forms of civilization, many writers viewed them problematically as either anti-civilizing, or as the end result of a civilization made mad from its own deep structural tendencies, whether these be located at the level of institutions or at the level of culture.[59] In this way, the concept of civilization was to some extent preserved as a concept of identity, particularly of the West, rather than being used as a conceptual tool in a more general comparative sociology.

The French, German and American schools all participated in the intellectual disputes of the turn of the century. For the founding schools of sociology, especially the Durkheimian and the Weberian, their conceptual and analytic work was the most basic and fundamental task. As Lévi-Strauss said of the French school, they attempted to 'reduce the concrete complexity of the data . . . into more simple and more elementary structures'.[60] While Lévi-Strauss had mainly in mind Durkheimian sociology, the point is more general. Attempts were made to subsume a multiplicity of processes under one or two umbrella concepts, be they civilization, culture, or, more significantly, *society*. Given the axiomatic distinction between non-civilization and civilization, the discipline of sociology concentrated on Western industrial and urban societies, mainly in the present and recent past, since the nineteenth century was seen as a watershed in their development. Sociology became the representation of, and reflection about, modern society, within a conceptual field shaped by the experience of industrialization, nation-state formation, the monetarization of social relations, the subordination of wage labour to capital, and the development of democratic movements and politics. In this context a series of conceptual tensions emerged between the notions of civilization and society – civilization was either absorbed into the notion of society, or sociological categories were utilized as its conceptual framework – which meant that it was effectively subsumed into sociology. This established another academic division of labour. Anthropology looked at pre-industrial and pre-state societies, sociology investigated modern societies, and discussions of civilization were concerned with societies that had not only developed states but were usually also empires. Thus civilizations were power centres, were territorially expansive, and existed for long periods. In the context of this academic division of labour, concern with civilization was limited to the formation of Western and non-Western state societies prior to the development of the West's own modern period.

In the nineteenth century the works of Lewis Henry Morgan (1818–81), Friedrich Engels (1820–95), Herbert Spencer (1820–1903) and Emile Durkheim (1858–1917) had laid much of the groundwork for a sociological unilinear-evolutionary model of civilizations.[61] In *The Division of Labour in Society*, Durkheim is explicitly influenced by Spencer's work. Like Spencer, Durkheim emphasizes the differentiation and specialization of functions that result in increasing social distance between people. Although this idea is found in Ferguson's work, for example, it is from Spencer (along with Auguste Comte and Ferdinand Tönnies) that Durkheim draws a theoretical language which he can develop in his own way and from his own perspective, not only to conceptualize modern society, but also to draw more general conclusions. Durkheim argues that Spencer's sociology, embodying a justification of the free market unfettered by the state, and employing a conceptual framework that reduces society to a congeries of disconnected individuals, can account neither for the associations which exist within the division of labour, nor for the *increasing* activity of the state. In looking at this aspect alone, Durkheim presages much of the social democratic debate of the later part of the twentieth century, by arguing that the state increases its activities as a centre of co-ordination in the context of the increasing division of functions. His descriptions of mechanical and organic solidarity in pre-modern and modern societies contribute to the development of a unilinear-evolutionary model of civilizations in terms of functional differentiation.[62]

The unique feature of Durkheim's account, however, is that it emphasizes not only a dimension of functional differentiation, but also a cultural dimension. The *conscience collective* becomes the principle of integration. This is one of the most important features of Durkheim's work. Durkheim transposes the notion of culture into, first, the category of *conscience collective*, and then later into his more robust notion of collective representations, which becomes the core of his sociology. The early part of Durkheim's work is neither the most interesting nor the most representative of his *œuvre* and the development of his school. Nor is it far-reaching for a theory of civilization, however influential is the unilinear-evolutionary legacy.[63]

The 'Note on the Notion of Civilization', written by Durkheim and Marcel Mauss (1872–1950) in 1913, and Mauss's 'Civilizations: Elements and Forms', written in 1929, can together be seen as starting points for correctives to the two one-sided views of civilization that have emerged so far. As shown in the discussion above, a notion of civilization emerged that identified it with nation-building, the differentiation of social functions, and forms of political republicanism. Then in the discussion of culture, we have seen that this concept emerged as a device for the critique of civilization. This Romantic idea of culture emphasizes its autonomy, and places an idea of high culture at the centre of its own critique of civilization, the story of which is often represented as one of decline. In both cases notions of civilization emerged that reduced it (civilization) to 'society', and to processes of either domination or differentiation. Culture is restricted to aesthetics and its creation. For both Durkheim and Mauss, though, civilization and culture combine in a much more complex history of the West and a more complex set of theoretical strategies.

In Durkheim's later work, the concept of civilization serves a triple purpose. First, it enables him to conceptualize more deeply the relation both between society and the individual, and between the different levels of social reality. In a manner worthy of Blaise Pascal, the human animal is seen as both 'beast' and 'angel' and thus as requiring what would later be called a 'civilizing process' to humanize it. Furthermore, for Durkheim, this civilizing process does not occur at the level of everyday life, which is characterized by fragmentation and heterogeneity. It is constituted rather through a society's collective ethos, which is gathered, condensed and represented in symbolic form, and then created and recreated in effervescent practices beyond the reaches of everyday life. In this sense, civilization re-articulates social bonds as well as the symbolic forms they take; for Durkheim, humankind is a symbolizing animal, and it is through symbolization that a civilizing process takes place that anchors each individual in society. In order to argue this, Durkheim rejected the distinction between anthropology and sociology that was then becoming consolidated.[64] The insights yielded by anthropology allow him both to extend the range of sociological analysis and to re-address the problem of culture through his notion of collective representations.[65] If human beings are 'the symbolizing animal', then culture makes sense for him only in its *sacred* dimension. But the sacred as civilization cannot be contained within discrete territories and societies. Civilization thus becomes an inclusive category, integrating into itself a delimited meaning of the anthropological notion of culture – as both identity formation and symbolic creation.

The extended notion of civilization is why the 'Note on the Notion of Civilization' and its continuation in Mauss's own 'Civilizations: Elements and Forms' of 1929 are so important. Translated in part and published in English in this volume for the first time (pp. 155–9 below), Mauss's essay was a contribution to a symposium on the concept and meaning of civilization held in Paris that year, which Lucien Febvre, among others, also attended. Civilizations, in Mauss's view, are social entities in which states and cultural forms are mutually co-present and co-extensive and yet irreducible to one another. Their coherence is achieved in an unstable, yet enduring, combination of cultural factors and forms of political association, which are not contained within the parameters of state-formation only. This is particularly clear if Durkheim's *The Elementary Forms of Religious Life* and Mauss's *The Gift* are read alongside these brief essays.[66] Moreover, Mauss draws a major theoretical conclusion which is anti-evolutionist. For him, the common characteristic of all civilizations is their arbitrariness – which points the way to structuralism; this, in turn, helps explain Lévi-Strauss's admiration for his former intellectual mentor.[67]

If, for Durkheim and Mauss, the boundary between sociology and anthropology was a fluid one, for Lucien Febvre and the *Annales* School, the boundary between history and the human sciences generally was equally fluid. There are two broad currents that inform the work of Lucien Febvre, including his essay published below (pp. 160–90), '*Civilisation*: Evolution of a Word and a Group of Ideas', and the *Annales* School as a whole. Febvre wished to adapt economic, anthropological, geographical, linguistic and psychological knowledge and actions to the study of history, whilst simultaneously insisting on, and infusing, a historical orientation to the study of humankind and society in the social and human sciences. Like the boundary between these groups of knowledge, the boundary and the relation between present and past was equally fluid. These two currents, and the interdisciplinarity that emerged from it, were set against a background of a deep hostility to not only the German historiography of the nineteenth century that equated the history of states and political elites with history *per se* (a position Thomas Mann, for example, encountered in his 'unpolitical' stance in his attempt to defend culture), but also narrative or 'empirical' history that was both descriptive and sequential. This type of history also had an implicit commitment to the notion of progress.[68]

By the end of the nineteenth century and into the twentieth, this type of history was also being questioned from a number of different directions: the hermeneutic, in the wake of Dilthey, and to some extent by Alfred Weber's essay included here (pp. 191–215 below); the 'structural' and 'post-structural', with which the *Annales* School can also be identified; and the figurational, typified by the work of Norbert Elias, which also has some affinities with the *Annales* approach. Each approach emphasizes, although in varying degrees, the open-endedness of the relation between past and present, and thus grapples with the interconnected images and models of progress and historical determinism. In each approach, history is as much part of the perspectives constructed from the present, as of those derived from the past. Moreover, each approach emphasizes the heterogeneity of the domains that could come under the scrutiny of history, from manners and rituals, to commerce and family life. The heterogeneity also relativized (although did not resolve) the distinction between material and mental life (or the dispute between the materialists and the idealists). However, each became a legitimate domain of enquiry, with its own historical pattern. Each domain was forged and informed by historical processes which left their indelible mark on the present. The issues that most preoccupied the above three approaches was the nature and length of the historical processes involved, a simultaneous attempt to break from the legacy of evolutionary or historical determinism, and the relation between material and mental life.

The *Annales* School developed a twofold strategy in order to address the nineteenth-century legacy and the issues that emerged from it. It insisted on the multiple forms of human life, actions and settings that could both cohere into a meaningful pattern and intersect with other meaningful patterns. In this context, historical writing, research and practice concentrated on the locale under scrutiny which gave the site a specificity often denied by universal histories. Civilization, thus, referred to the intersection and long history (long durée) of the multiple forms of human life within specific (although often extensive) geographical settings.

Thus, whilst Febvre sees himself as part of the Durkheimian legacy, Braudel, a later member of the School, located himself in a current that begins with the image of civilization as one of 'qualities of movement' between quite heterogeneous elements that Mauss puts forward in his essay 'Civilizations: Elements and Forms'.[69] However, the second direction is more directly related to Febvre's essay published below. In order to break free from empiricism and historical determinism Febvre argued that 'historical facts' are inventions or constructs, which have their own genealogies and histories that are quite specific and local, as he demonstrates in '*Civilisation*: Evolution of a Word and a Group of Ideas'. For him, and in a similar vein to Durkheim's method, historical 'facts' are not events but abstractions, and thus historical research and practice is oriented to the problematization of these 'facts'.[70]

Notwithstanding the common ground of intellectual issues and problems being confronted, the German story was a little different. If, as Albert Salomon noted, French (as well as American) 'sociology [and the human sciences, generally, had] an objective function in the context of their respective societies as an instrument of pragmatic enlightenment and moral education', then German sociology is characterized by its heterogeneity. Germany produced sociologists and not a sociology.[71] Moreover, while the whole of the turn of the century generation felt an unease, in Germany this unease was tinged with pessimism. The history of German democratization was of increasing scepticism and then defeat. Salomon called *fin de siècle* German sociology 'a liberalism in despair', against a background of nationalism.[72]

Salomon points to a continuing tension in the development of German sociology between *Zivilisation* and *Kultur* (and between Enlightenment and Romanticism), which was played out in a number of currents. The first current consisted of revolts against the determinism of Hegel's work, typified by Burckhardt and Dilthey, and against the determinism of Marx's typified by Tönnies and Max Weber.[73] The second current was the revolt against the bureaucratization characteristic of Wilhelmine Germany, which produced not only a culture of mediocrity (as Nietzsche contended) but also an adaptation of the personality to a regime of impersonal rules and structures. This current is best typified by the work of Max Weber on the pervasive growth of purposive rationality, and by Simmel's sociological impressionism. This interest in the subordination of the personality (a motif already present in German Romantic culture from Goethe onwards) is further explored in a sociological register not only by Simmel but also by Max Scheler (1874–1928) and Alfred Schutz (1899–1959). This resulted, particularly in Schutz's case, in an expansion of the concept of culture in a manner resembling its anthropological usage: culture no longer refers only to high cultural patterns, but to the framework of everyday experience, orientations, and patterns of thinking.[74]

It was Max Weber's younger brother, Alfred Weber (1868–1958), who posited a more generalizable paradigm for the sociology of civilization, society and culture. Apart from Elias's theory of civilizing processes, his work represents the most ambitious theoretical approach to civilization and culture in the first half of the twentieth century. Alfred Weber not only drew on his brother's work but attempted a systematic conceptual synthesis of the older notions of civilization and culture. His synthesis was first outlined in a 1921 article, which is published for the first time in English in this volume under the title of 'Fundamentals of Culture-Sociology: Social Process, Civilizational Process and Culture-Movement' (pp. 191–215 below). Later he was to elaborate the model at much greater length in his book *Kulturgeschichte als Kultursoziologie*, deploying it in relation to comparable evidence from the major historic civilizations of the world.[75]

In scope, Alfred Weber's work shares some affinities with the better known and more influential works of Oswald Spengler (*The Decline of the West*, first published in 1918) and Arnold Toynbee (*A Study of History*, 1936/1939). In contrast to Spengler in particular, his essay can be viewed as one that critically engages with the morphological approach in which World History is broken down to become the continuous organic birth, growth and decline of great cultures. The contrast between Alfred Weber and Spengler revolves around the question of identity. For Spengler, because each civilization constructs its own identity and has an organic passage of time, the West is one civilization among many whose time is at an end. For Alfred Weber, this question of the particular identity of *a* civilization is suspended and, for him, the task of civilizational analysis is to identify the processes through which civilizational formation and development can be theorized.[76]

Alfred Weber also moved in the opposite direction to Malinowski and Kroeber, who absorbed the notion of society into culture. He works from the German distinction between *Kultur* and *Zivilisation*, but with an eye also on the *sociological* category of society. He attempts both to extend and delimit each and yet bring them – culture, civilization, society – into a relation in which they buttress one another in terms of an overall theoretical strategy. For him, it is essential to account for both social innovation and historical continuity without invoking a principle of *universal* history from the vantage point of the particular history of the West. Alfred Weber argues that for a theory to give up *universalistic* claims – of progress, of freedom – does not mean that it gives up claims to *generalizability*. If anything, for him, it facilitates comparisons between societies (or civilizations in the more general and less technical meaning of the term).[77]

Alfred Weber's strategy and task was first to separate a 'civilization process' from social and cultural ones. Each has its own 'logic' of development – and in an anthropological sense, each is unique historically and socially. Secondly, he wanted to assess how cultural processes are related to both in a way that does not assume a teleological or biological-evolutionary direction. By *social process*, Alfred Weber refers to the material world in which human beings work, co-operate and establish institutions which make social continuity possible. He transposes the German interpretation of high culture into a sociological register and terms it *civilization process*. While for him it still refers to art, religion and philosophy, it is none the less extended in analytical terms to refer to the intellectualization of the world, increasing domination over nature through the deployment of cognitive-rational means, and the development of practical skills. Thus, following Max Weber's notion of rationalization, civilization processes refer specifically to the internal historical development of what, more conventionally, would be called cultural forms.

Cultural movement is Alfred Weber's particular way of theorizing both the relation between social processes and *mentalités* (social process and civilization process) in a way that emphasizes their historical uniqueness and the potential for innovation and change which is common to all societies. Cultural surpluses form, which not only transform the inner horizon or vision of society, but also rupture the civilization process, counteracting its own tendencies towards historical continuity. Thus, for him, the investigation of social, cultural and civilization processes are interrelated yet separate contributions which together theorize the cosmic or global condition of humankind. In the end his is an anthropological theory, in the older philosophical meaning of the term. The 'cosmic' process is a metaphor for the self-perpetuating and self-transforming capacity of humankind. The universalism is moved from the domain of politics to that of the human self-image.

Alfred Weber's global theory is an achievement of synthesizing social theory. This is what distinguished it in the history of the notions of civilization and culture. The structure of his theory and the relation between the social and civilization processes and cultural movement influenced the development of the theory of civilization itself, especially in America.

The German sociological and French anthropological notions of civilization and culture from this period of the late 1880s to the 1930s travelled, like so many *real* emigrants, to the United States. As in other new world societies of the Americas generally and of Australasia, there was an increase in international social traffic between Europe and America, which entailed an increase in international conceptual traffic as well. Alfred Weber is important, but so too are Durkheim, Max Weber and Georg Simmel. Many European intellectuals, however, particularly the later generation of critical theorists, who were to have such an impact on the self-understanding of the West in its European and American versions, remained blind to the specificity of American culture and politics. In terms of civilization, an old prejudice, discussed earlier (pp. 9–10), was replicated. Among the writers in this volume, de Tocqueville remained almost the only European thinker who genuinely and deeply engaged with the society of the New World. The development of American sociology, which was deeply informed by a republican current which this New World society made its own, was shaped by, among other things, the experience of slavery and immigration.

Slavery was associated with absolutism, immigration with urban development. As Max Weber noted in his own study of the city, and as Simmel contended in his essay on the metropolis, *Stadtluft macht frei* – city air makes one free. But alongside its liberating qualities, the city is also a place of disaffection, alienation and violence. This is the world of Robert E. Park (1864–1944) and the Chicago School. Park's essay, 'The Problem of Cultural Differences' (pp. 216–24 below), combines Malinowski's anthropology of culture with American philosophical pragmatism. He argues that there are three things that typify American civilization: mechanical invention, mass education, and universal suffrage, to which Park adds a fourth, mobility. For him, this is what gives the American city its fluidity and restlessness. It is the benchmark of the modern world and ultimate characteristic of American civilization. The 'melting pot' referred to in American sociological theory clearly shows the conceptual peregrinations of 'civilization' and 'culture' during this formative period, their conceptual conflation, and their reliance on a background array of assumptions derived from the various deeply problematic conceptual strategies of the nineteenth century discussed above.[78]

Conclusions: from civilization to civilizing processes

In the end, it was a combination of, and thus a tension between, evolutionary-unilinear and morphological-taxonomic uses of the concept of civilization which was most widely adopted. This combination incorporated elements of both the anthropological and the 'autonomous' or 'high' versions of the concept of culture, and it was employed to denote types of societies that had undergone extensive processes of differentiation and reached high levels of complexity. Social and cultural complexity was seen as the essence of modern civilization.

Most of the writers represented in this book questioned, from a normative point of view, whether differentiation and complexity were in fact socially beneficial or disruptive. Ferguson, Schiller and Simmel are ambivalent towards modernization, Nietzsche overtly hostile.

Another, less normative, set of questions concerns causality. As Eisenstadt has pointed out, the older evolutionary models, in identifying the *trend* towards complexity, also assumed that this trend caused and explained the specific characteristics of particular civilizations as well as social change within them. In addition, these older models also assumed that the 'development of human societies is relatively cumulative and unilinear and that major "stages" of development are universal – even if there are major differences in detail and even if not all societies reach every stage of evolution'.[79]

In this context the work of Norbert Elias represents a breakthrough. Elias recognized that German sociology continued to be trapped within either ontological (particularly Hegelian) or transcendental (Kantian) assumptions. For Elias there were two escape routes – both Nietzschean: one which emphasized power, and another which entailed the examination in a sociological perspective of the Nietzschean image of humankind as the animal that undergoes a civilizing process. Power is introduced by Elias as a corrective to the functional images of civilization. Instead of civilizations *per se*, there are civilizing processes as the outcomes of power struggles and strategies of inclusion and exclusion between groups. These entail – as a long-term historical process – transformations in the regime of affects. In other words, in linking transformations of power to transformations of affects, Elias was able to develop an integrated theoretical strategy addressing the relation between what he terms the sociogenetic and the psychogenetic dimensions of human life. The outcome was *The Civilizing Process*.[80]

In *The Civilizing Process*, many issues discussed over the previous two centuries in philosophical, conceptual terms, are transformed as far as possible into sociological questions susceptible to theoretical–empirical investigation. In this sense, the scope of his work, its interdisciplinarity, and its emphasis on history, shares some affinities with the *Annales* School, discussed above. However, in a more clearly defined theoretical strategy his basic thesis is that there is a link between the long-term structural development of societies – especially state-formation – and changes in people's social character, typical personality make-up or habitus. The basic proposition is that:

> if in this or that region the power of central authority grows, if over a larger or smaller area the people are forced to live in peace with each other, the moulding of affects and the standards of the drive economy are very gradually changed as well.[81]

Elias's theory of state-formation implicitly begins from Max Weber's definition of the state as an organization which successfully upholds a claim to binding rule-making over a territory, by virtue of commanding a monopoly of the legitimate use of violence,[82] but he is more interested in the *process* through which a monopoly of the means of violence (and taxation) is established and extended, and how this in turn transforms the regime of affects and emotions. Elias outlines the processes at work during the long period of European state-formation when centripetal forces, fluctuatingly and with regressions, gained the upper hand. State-formation involved an 'elimination contest' between numerous rival territorial magnates, a violent competitive process with a compelling sequential dynamic through which successively larger territorial units emerged with more effective central monopoly apparatuses. The contest was less the result of the aggressiveness of individual warriors than the cause: more pacific rulers simply would not survive, given the structure of the contest. The other side of the process, however, is the internal pacification of larger and larger territories by the more and more effective monopoly apparatuses.

State-formation, for Elias, is only one process interweaving with others to enmesh individuals in increasingly complex webs of interdependence. It interweaves with the division of labour, the growth of trade, towns, the use of money and administrative apparatuses, together with increasing population, in a spiral process. Internal pacification of territory facilitates trade, which facilitates the growth of towns and division of labour and generates taxes, which support larger military and administrative organizations, which in turn facilitate the internal pacification of larger territories, and so on – a cumulative process experienced as a compelling force by the people caught up in it. Furthermore, according to Elias, the gradually higher standards of self-restraint engendered in people contributed in turn to the upward spiral – being necessary, for example, to the formation of gradually more effective and calculable administration. Elias did not seek single causal factor explanations, but traced how various causal strands interweave over time to produce an overall process with increasing momentum.[83]

Elias argues that as webs of interdependence become denser and more extensive, there gradually takes place a shift in the *balance* between external constraints (*Fremdzwänge* – constraints *by other people*) and self-constraints (*Selbstzwänge*) in favour of the latter. Though violence and its taming are central to Elias's concerns, *The Civilizing Process* begins rather at the development of social standards surrounding matters of outward bodily propriety:

conventions about eating, washing, spitting, blowing one's nose, urinating and defecating, undressing. He focused on these most basic, 'natural' or 'animalic' of human functions because these are things human beings cannot avoid doing, no matter what society, culture or era they live in. Moreover, infants are born in the same emotional condition everywhere, so that the *lifetime* point of departure is always the same. Therefore, if change occurs in the way these functions are handled, it can be seen rather clearly. In the European case, many of these matters came to be hidden away behind the scenes of social life, and, increasingly invested with feelings of shame, also hidden behind the scenes of mental life as constraints which one generation had painfully to learn become so deeply habituated in later generations that they are repressed into the unconscious. Something similar happened to the states' means of violence; confined literally and metaphorically to barracks, they continued to exert a steady but largely unnoticed 'civilizing' pressure on citizens.

Some of the part-processes which constitute Elias's overall model of civilizing processes – like the taming of warriors – are plainly of potential universal relevance. Research is beginning only now, however, to discover how far the model applies to historical contexts beyond Western Europe.[84] If the jury is still out on whether the theory of civilizing processes is still too inherently marked by its European origins, it can be more certainly claimed that Elias's model has been thoroughly purged of traces of 'progress', let alone of *inevitable* progress. The theory was first formulated by someone who had witnessed the decay of the state's monopoly of violence under the Weimar Republic, as well as the earlier phases of the Nazi regime, and he was always very conscious of the potential reversibility, fragility even, of civilizing processes:

> The armour of civilized conduct would crumble rapidly if, through a change in society, the degree of insecurity that existed earlier were to break in upon us again, and if the danger became as incalculable as once it was. Corresponding fears would burst the limits set to them today.[85]

A consequence of Elias's transformation of the notion of civilization into a processual concept was that *decivilizing* processes too may have a structure which may be revealed through empirical sociological research. Elias began the task in one of his last books, *The Germans*,[86] from which his essay on '"Civilisation" and "Culture": Nationalism and Nation-State Formation' (pp. 225–40 below) is taken. Moreover, this essay indicates, in the paradigmatic form already established in *The Civilizing Process*, and in a historicized way similar to Febvre's essay, that questions of identity ultimately revolve around the marking of boundaries between insiders and outsiders. For Elias, the *substantive* narrative about the civilizing process of the West, from feudalism to the twentieth century, a preoccupation shared by most of the writers in this book, centres around the fusion between state-formation and nation-building, and identity.

What overall conclusion can be drawn, looking back from the end of the second millennium at more than two hundred years of thought about the concepts of civilization and culture? One is a little surprising. The concept of 'civilization', fairly recently seen as so hopelessly encumbered with value judgements, and connotations of teleological progress, has been rescued for serious academic purposes. Even if some doubts remain about how finally and conclusively it is possible to separate a sociological conception of civilizing process from the heteronomous evaluations of 'civilization', it is undeniable that Elias's theory has opened up a rich vein of empirically orientated comparative-historical research.[87]

The concept of culture has also been paradigmatically reformulated, the result of which is a recasting of its conceptual and substantive horizons. In substantive terms, the anthropological conception of culture always involved a recognition of a plurality of cultural forms. This pluralism posed a challenge, from outside so to speak, to the unitary idea of 'high culture'. But there was also an internal challenge to 'high culture', arising from the demand for aesthetic innovation itself – to the point where the idea of a unified concept of art was destroyed. The process of a continual rupturing of style has become identified with postmodern aesthetics, which originated in the artistic movements of the 1920s; it blurs the boundaries between 'high', folk and mass cultures, as well as between styles and genres.[88]

The notion of culture has also been further opened up through conceptual explorations that occurred along the pre-existing anthropological and *geistlich* fault-lines identified by Kroeber and Kluckhohn. At a deeper level, these explorations, and the substantive challenges to high culture, mentioned above, were informed by the way in which the human self-image was portrayed, especially in the wake of Kant's transcendental legacy. Like the Eliasian reconstruction of the notion of civilization, the notion of culture became a framework through which to respond to the trap of the philosophy of the subject and consciousness. This response occurred predominantly in the inter-war period of the twentieth century in two major ways. An intersubjective framework for culture emerged that emphasized the dynamic interplay between finite, culturally situated selves and others, who, through this interplay, constituted their realities and identities. Furthermore, a linguistic turn occurred in which, following Herder's basic insight, language, rather than culture *per se*, was viewed as the repository of human creativity, self-understanding and self-reflexivity. At a more fundamental level than this culturalist perspective of language, though, *language itself* was viewed as the paradigm and the model through which the multiple processes of human and social life are made possible, and take objective form. This post-Idealist paradigm, which also challenged materialism, occurred in the work of, and conjuncturally brings together, three quite different thinkers – Saussure, and after him Lévi-Strauss; Wittgenstein, and after him Habermas; and Heidegger, and in his wake Gadamer.

Language, for Wittgenstein, devolves from its *geistlich*, totalizing concept to become an irreducible variety of pragmatic contexts or 'linguistic games' through which intersubjectivity itself is constituted. For Saussure and Lévi-Strauss, language is viewed as a homogeneous system of relations of signs, 'conceived as a unified structure that lies behind the particular speech acts . . . ', whilst for Heidegger and Gadamer, language is the continuing occurrence into which humans are born. Hence it is their permanent ontological condition, but one which only provides approximations and never truths.[89] Notwithstanding the distinct differences between these versions of language, their impact on the notion of culture has been quite profound. No longer is culture viewed as the domain of artefacts, or simply as the repository of identity. Rather, the notion of culture is extended to embrace *all* aspects through which the human world is linguistically and (*or* – depending on one's starting point) symbolically constituted, from speech acts and utterances, to signs and symbols. Thus, language is a constitutive image; it embraces the way in which culture is learnt, transmitted valued and embodied.[90]

As such, and while the anthropological notion of culture always entailed plurality, the linguistic turn provides a paradigmatic form through which this plurality can, itself, be grounded. Wittgenstein's notion of the language game opens onto the irreducibility of plural contexts, whilst Saussure's and Lévi-Strauss's notions of symbolic structures emphasize the arrangement of signs that give shape to an apparent *bricolage* of forms which were arbitrary.[91]

However, the linguistic turn has a result similar to the Malinowskian turn in the concept of culture, discussed above – 'everything is language'. However, as recent work has shown, either in the context of the neo-Heideggerian ontology of *différence* (Derrida), or the neo-Freudianism of Castoriadis's idea of imaginary significations, there is a horizon of meaning that is irreducible to both linguistification and symbolization. This horizon of meaning is conceptualized, at least in Castoriadis's work, as a domain of the creative imagination, and this formulation opens onto the *creation* of cultures (and by extension, civilizations) – and, thus, not only their context and transmission.[92]

For the key problems to which this book is addressed, the Eliasian concept of civilization and the anthropological notion of culture are the more relevant, though. Both are fundamentally connected with theoretical explorations of the human condition in its broadest sense – with the problems of an animal which inhabits both the natural and the social worlds at once, and the way in which this animal constitutes itself and its habitants by creating and mobilizing resources of both power and culture. Moreover, as Elias stressed, the intersection of the two worlds of nature and society creates inherent tensions. Furthermore, Nietzsche's genealogical approach serves to remind us that these tensions are never fully resolved: they constantly yield conflicts and transformations that are always incomplete, often unexpected and unintended. The selections in *Classical Readings in Culture and Civilization* show, and others and more contemporary ones continue to do so, that the notions of 'civilization' and 'culture' remain as tropes through which those tensions and the issues of power, the self-constitution of the human species, and the way we perceive ourselves as well as others, can be theorized.

Notes

1 I. Wallerstein, 'The Modern World System as a Civilization', *Thesis Eleven*, No. 20, 1988, p. 70.

2 See also Dmitri N. Shalin, 'Romanticism and the Rise of Sociological Hermeneutics', *Social Research*, Vol. 53, No. 1, 1986, pp. 73–123; Charles Taylor, *Hegel*, Cambridge, Cambridge University Press, 1976, especially his introductory chapter, 'The aims of the new epoch'.

3 C. Renfrey, 'The Emergence of Civilization', *The Penguin Encyclopedia of Ancient Civilizations*, ed. Arthur Cotterell, 1980, London, Penguin, p. 14.

4 Vytautas Kavolis, 'History of Consciousness and Civilizational Analysis', *Comparative Civilizations Review*, No. 17 (Fall 1987), p. 3.

5 M. Weber, *Economy and Society*, Vol. 1, 'Religious Groups', pp. 401–7. See also Section 3, 'The Role of Writing and Literacy in the Development of Social and Political Power', in *State and Society* (eds) J. Gledhill, B. Bender and M. T. Larson, 1988, London, Unwin/Hyman, pp. 173–276. See especially the chapters by Morgens Trolle Larsen, 'Introduction: Literacy and Social Complexity' (pp. 173–91); John Baines, 'Literacy, Social Organization and the Archeological Record: The Case of Early Egypt' (pp. 192–214); Michael Harbsmeier, 'Inventions of Writing' (pp. 253–76).

6 B. J. Schwarz, 'The Age of Transcendence', *Daedalus*, 1975, p. 3. This issue of *Daedalus* is a special issue on the Axial Age, and is called 'Wisdom, Revelation and Doubt: Perspectives on the First Millennium BC'. See also S. N. Eisenstadt, 'The Axial Age: The Emergence of Transcendental Visions and the Rise of the Clerics', *Archives Européennes de Sociologie*, 2, 1982, pp. 294–314.

7 Wallerstein, 'The Modern World System as a Civilization', p. 70.

8 J. P. Arnason, 'Social Theory and the Concept of Civilization', *Thesis Eleven*, No. 20, 1988, p. 88. The following discussion, in part, follows suggestive comments by J. P. Arnason concerning the conceptual tension internal to the concept of civilization.

9 See Anne Robert Jacques Turgot (1727–81), *Turgot on Progress, Sociology and Economics*, Cambridge, Cambridge University Press, 1976; Jean-Antoine-Nicoles de Caritate Condorcet (1743–94), *Sketch*

for a Historical Picture of the Progress of the Human Mind, translated by Jane Barraclough, with an Introduction by Stuart Hampshire, London, Weidenfeld & Nicolson, 1955; August Comte (1798–1857), *The Crisis of Industrial Civilization: The Early Essays of August Comte*, edited and introduced by Ronald Fletcher, London, Heinemann, 1974; *The Foundations of Sociology*, edited by Kenneth Thompson, London, Nelson, 1976.

10 For the development of the French current see H. Stuart Hughes, *The Obstructed Path: French Social Thought in the Years of Desperation 1930–1960*, 1966, New York, Harper & Row; Stephen Lukes, *Emile Durkheim: His Life and Work*, 1973, London, Penguin; Philippe Besnard (ed.), *The Sociological Domain: The Durkheimians and the Founding of French Sociology*, 1983, Cambridge, Cambridge University Press; Peter Burke (ed.), *A New Kind of History from the Writings of Febvre*, 1973, London, Routledge & Kegan Paul.

11 S. Chodorow, *The Mainstream of Civilization*, 6th edn, Fort Worth, TX, Harcourt Press, 1994, p. 9.

12 C. Brinkman, 'Civilization', *Encyclopædia of the Social Sciences*, New York, Macmillan, 1931, p. 525.

13 N. Elias, *The Civilizing Process*, Oxford, Blackwell, 1994, p. 3 (original publication, 1939).

14 Ibid., p. 4.

15 T. Schabert, 'Modernity and History I: What is Modernity?', in *The Promise of History*, ed., A. Moulakis, 1986, New York, Walter de Gruyter, p. 9; see also his 'Modernity and History II: On the Edge of Modernity?' in the same volume, and Leo Strauss, 'The Three Waves of Modernity', in *An Introduction to Political Philosophy: Ten Essays by Leo Strauss*, 1989, New York, Wayne State University Press.

16 Schabert, 'Modernity and History I', p. 10.

17 See not only Schabert, but also: R. G. Collingwood, *The Idea of History*, Oxford, Oxford University Press, 1946; H.-G. Gadamer, *Truth and Method*, London, Sheed & Ward, 1989: A. Heller, *A Theory of History*, Oxford, Blackwell, 1982; N. Elias, *The Court Society*, Oxford, Blackwell, 1983.

18 Cf. Schabert, 'Modernity and History I'; Charles Taylor, *Hegel*, Cambridge, Cambridge University Press, 1975 and *Sources of the Self*, Cambridge MA, MIT Press, 1989; Hans Blumenberg, *The Legitimacy of the Modern Age*, Cambridge MA, MIT Press, 1983. The moderns saw their task as grounding the principles for this new knowledge within the cognitive procedures and principles of rationality. For Descartes, it involved cleansing knowledge of pre-cognitive dimensions, but within the wider dispute between the ancients and moderns, all tradition is subject to the verdict of present doctrines. Ideas or theories are ranked as mere predecessors of current thinking; philosophy loses its position as the integrating discipline, and the sciences are split up into the natural and human sciences. The natural sciences take on self-appointed sovereignty with their own notion of truth against which the efficacy of the human sciences is judged.

19 Cf. J. G. A. Pocock, 'Virtues, Rights and Manners: A Model for Historians of Political Thought', in *Virtue, Commerce and History: Essays on Political Thought and History, Chiefly in the Eighteenth Century*, Cambridge, Cambridge University Press, 1985, pp. 37–50. This essay is in part a thematic elaboration of his seminal *The Machiavellian Moment: Florentine Political Thought and the Atlantic Republican Tradition*, Princeton, Princeton University Press, 1975. See also Quentin Skinner, *The Foundations of Modern Political Thought*, especially Vol. 1, 'The Renaissance', Cambridge, Cambridge University Press, 1978.

20 Max Weber, 'The City', in *Economy and Society*, Berkeley, University of California Press, 1972, Vol. 2, pp. 1212–1372.

21 See John Keane, 'Despotism and Democracy: The Origins and Development of the Distinction between Civil Society and the State, 1750–1850', in J. Keane (ed.), *Civil Society and the State*, London, Verso, 1988, especially pp. 37–9.

22 See Jeremy Smith, 'European State Formation, 800–1800', unpublished Ph.D. thesis, University of Melbourne, 1995.

23 Holbach, quoted in Henry Steele Commager, *The Empire of Reason: How Europe Imagined and America Realized the Enlightenment*, Oxford, Oxford University Press, 1972.

24 Commager, *Empire*, p. 72.

25 See Commager, *Empire*, especially ch. 4, and Commager, *Jefferson, Nationalism and the Enlightenment*, New York, George Braziller, especially ch. 2. According to Commager, the most influential argument was put forward by the Comte de Buffon in his *Histoire naturelle*. Claiming an objective basis in the biblical account of the flood, Buffon argued in philosophical and scientific terms that the New World emerged after the deluge and thus later than the Old World. This accounted for the fetid air,

the swamps, the infertility of its land and its peoples, and the sense of general decay and languor. This argument was widely accepted, even by Kant in his early anthropological lectures. See also Antonello Gerbi, *The Dispute of the New World: The History of a Polemic 1750–1900*, revised and enlarged edition translated by Jeremy Moyle, Pittsburgh, University of Pittsburgh Press, 1973.

26 See Robert Bierstedt, 'Sociological Thought in the Eighteenth Century' in T. Bottomore and R. A. Nisbet (eds), *A History of Sociological Thought*, New York, Basic Books, 1978, pp. 3–38; D. G. MacRae, 'Adam Ferguson', in T. Raison (ed.), *The Founding Fathers of Sociology*, Harmondsworth, Penguin, 1969, pp. 17–26; W. C. Lehmann's major and indispensable study *Adam Ferguson and the Beginnings of Modern Sociology*, New York, Columbia University Press, 1930; David Kettler's fine analysis, *The Social and Political Thought of Adam Ferguson*, Ohio State University Press, 1965; Alan Swingewood, *A Short History of Sociological Thought*, 2nd edn, London, Macmillan, 1991.

27 Alexis de Tocqueville, *Democracy in America*, Vols 1 and 2, New York, Vintage Books, 1990. See also G. Poggi, *Images of Society*, Stanford, Stanford University Press, 1972, especially pp. 3–61; J. Stone and S. Mennell (eds), *Alexis de Tocqueville on Democracy, Revolution and Society*, Chicago, Chicago University Press, 1979; F. Feher, 'The Evergreen Tocqueville (On the Occasion of the Hungarian Publication of *Democracy in America*)', *Thesis Eleven*, No. 42, 1995, pp. 69–86.

28 See G. Markus, 'A Society of Culture: The Constitution of Modernity', in *Rethinking Imagination: Culture and Creativity*, eds G. Robinson and J. Rundell, London, Routledge, 1994, pp. 15–29. See also A. L. Kroeber and Clyde Kluckhohn, *Culture: A Critical Review of Concepts and Definitions*, New York, Vintage Books, 1952, for an excellent discussion of the way in which this term developed in the German context, pp. 25–52.

29 Kroeber and Kluckhohn, *Culture*, pp. 12–15.

30 Edward B. Tylor, *Primitive Culture: Researches into the Development of Mythology, Philosophy, Religion, Art and Custom*, New York, Harper & Row, 1958, Vol. 1, p. 1; Bronislaw Malinowski, 'Culture', *Encyclopædia of the Social Sciences*, New York, Macmillan, 1931, Vol. 4, p. 621; Milton Singer, 'The Concept of Culture', *International Encyclopædia of the Social Sciences*, ed. David L. Sills, New York, Macmillan and Free Press, Vol. 3, 1968, pp. 527–43.

31 Kroeber and Kluckhohn, *Culture*, especially pp. 30–46. Kroeber and Kluckhohn privilege the anthropological and neo-Kantian notions of culture, particularly as they are the ones that came to be consolidated in later anthropological versions. See also Raymond Williams, *Culture and Society 1780–1950*, London, Chatto & Windus, 1967, especially ch. 2. Williams's study is concerned with the formation and the development of the English notion of culture. He makes the useful distinction between art, democracy and industrialization as three aspects which constituted the historical field of his study. These intersect and conflict with one another. As he says, 'our meaning of culture is a response to the events which our meanings of industry and culture most evidently define' (p. 295). Culture, for Williams, refers primarily to ways of life anchored in communities, including strata, that are being made and re-made, and have unknown dimensions to them.

32 J. G. Herder, 'Essay on the Origin of Language', in *J. G. Herder on Social and Political Culture*, translated, edited and with an introduction by F. M. Barnard, Cambridge, Cambridge University Press, 1969, pp. 156–7.

33 See Markus, 'Society of Culture', pp. 16–17. Apart from Herder's anthropology, hermeneutics emerged as the other main field for the interpretation of the relation between the present and the past. Schleiermacher's work is representative here, but so, too, is Droysen. See Schleiermacher, *Hermeneutics: The Hand-written Manuscripts*, ed. Heinz Kimmerle, trans. J. Duke and J. Fostman, Georgia, Scholars Press, 1977; Dmitri Shalin, 'Romanticism and the Rise of Sociological Hermeneutics', pp. 77–123; H.-G. Gadamer, *Truth and Method*, 2nd rev. edn, ed. and trans. by Joel Weinsheimer and Donald G. Marshall, London, Sheed & Ward, 1989; J. Rundell, 'Gadamer and the Circles of Hermeneutics', in *Reconstructing Theory: Gadamer, Habermas, Luhmann*, ed. David Roberts, Melbourne, Melbourne University Press, 1995.

34 See W. Dilthey, 'The Construction of the Human World in the Historical Sciences', in H. P. Rickman, (ed.) *W. Dilthey: Selected Writings*, Cambridge, Cambridge University Press, 1976.

35 Markus, 'Society of Culture', p. 18.

36 Cf. Markus, 'Society of Culture', pp. 18–19.

37 Immanuel Kant, *Critique of Judgement*, Indianapolis, Hackett Publishing Co., 1987. See also James Engell, *The Creative Imagination*, Cambridge MA, Harvard University Press, 1981; M. H. Abrams, *The Mirror and the Lamp: Romantic Theory and Critical Tradition*, Oxford, Oxford University Press, 1953;

and Richard Kearney, *The Wake of Imagination*, London, Hutchinson, 1988. The idea of an internally derived creative force focused on the imagination, which is itself no longer a source of evil or a vehicle of divine intervention or inspiration, itself has a long history. Kearney explores this, making a threefold distinction between: the classical/medieval imagination which has a theocentric paradigm of iconography, emphasizing mimesis and reproduction; the modern imagination which has an anthropological paradigm of self-portraiture, emphasizing creativity or production; and the postmodern imagination of parody.

38 Cf. J. Kahn, *Culture, Multiculture, Postculture*, London, Sage, 1995, pp. 37–43. See also T. Webb, *English Romantic Hellenism, 1700–1824*, Manchester University Press, 1982, pp. 1–32. More often than not, classical Greek antiquity was looked upon as the most favoured ideal. The emergence of the counter-model of Antiquity had a number of dimensions to it, irrespective of whether Antiquity referred to archaic or classical Greece, or Republican or Imperial Rome. One aspect was, that to be considered a member of 'polished society', familiarity with the works of Homer, Aristotle, Virgil and Ovid was viewed 'as an important part of the mental furniture of the cultured man [and woman]' (Webb, p. 17). Another aspect of the emergence of the model of Antiquity was the development of comparativist-ethnographical perspectives that emerged from the diaries of missionaries and travellers during the seventeenth century who drew comparisons between the New World Indians and the ancient Greeks – the New World Indians were ennobled and the ancient Greeks became savages. And so, like the dispute over the New World, Antiquity was viewed in either negative or positive terms: as a barbarous age which had little relevance for the modern world and whose cultural products were violent, crude and mimetic, and thus deficient, or an irresistibly attractive age in which unity was achieved between nature and the highest form of human expression. For the purposes of this Introduction the affirmative current is the more important, for it provided the point of reference for the first Romantic critique of modern civilization, especially. In this context, the classical, rather than the Homeric, period (although Sparta and either Republican or Imperial Rome also held interest) became the primary point of interest because it not only inspired a democratic form of politics, but also and more importantly came to represent an age of primal unity that was achieved culturally, that is aesthetically. While there was a realization that a return was impossible and that the loss of unity was inevitable, there were attempts to posit a 'new unity which would fully incorporate the [new] reflective [aesthetic] consciousness', (Charles Taylor, *Hegel*, p. 35). This attraction to Antiquity should not be viewed as a re-run of the dispute between the ancients and the moderns, from the side of the ancients. Rather, the sustained interest in Antiquity was prompted by a concern to solve the problems of the modern present from the vantage point of this present and not simply to replicate or mimic the ways of thinking and acting in Antiquity. This would go against not only the spirit of Enlightenment, but also the spirit of Romanticism which privileged the ideals of innovation and creativity.

39 See Geoffrey Thurley, *The Romantic Predicament*, New York, St Martin's Press, 1983.

40 Cf. Arthur O. Lovejoy, 'Schiller and the Genesis of German Romanticism', in *Essays in the History of Ideas*, Baltimore, The Johns Hopkins Press, 1948, p. 220; and Philip J. Kain, *Schiller, Hegel and Marx*, Montreal, McGill-Queens University Press, 1982. See also T. J. Reed, *Schiller*, Oxford, Oxford University Press, 1991 for an intellectual biography, and Lesley Sharpe's excellent study of Schiller's work, *Friedrich Schiller: Drama, Thought, Politics*, Cambridge, Cambridge University Press, 1991.

41 See Charles Taylor, *Sources of the Self*, Cambridge MA, MIT Press, 1989, especially Part IV.

42 P. R. Harrison, 'Friedrich Nietzsche', in P. Beilharz (ed.), *Social Theory: A Guide to Central Thinkers*, Sydney, Allen & Unwin, 1992, pp. 175–80, when he posits the distinction between denaturalization and de-intellectualization; Richard Schadt, *Nietzsche*, London, Routledge & Kegan Paul, 1981; Gilles Deleuze, *Nietzsche and Philosophy*, London, Atlantic Press, 1983.

43 David S. Luft, *Robert Musil and the Crisis of European Culture, 1880–1942*, Berkeley, University of California Press, 1980, pp. 8–9.

44 Luft, *Musil*; Allan Janick and Stephen Toulmin, *Wittgenstein's Vienna*, London, Weidenfeld & Nicolson, 1973; Carl Schorske, *Fin de Siècle Vienna*, Cambridge, Cambridge University Press, 1981; Lewis Mumford, *The City in History*, London, Secker & Warburg, 1961.

45 Norbert Elias, *The Germans: Power Struggles and the Development of Habitus in the Nineteenth and Twentieth Centuries*, trans. E. Dunning and S. J. Mennell, Oxford, Polity Press, 1996.

46 Schorske, *Vienna*, especially ch. 2, pp. 24–115; Janick and Toulmin, *Wittgenstein's Vienna*, especially

ch. 2, pp. 33–66; Luft, *Musil*, pp. 1–22; Marshall Berman, *All that is Solid Melts into Air*, New York, Simon & Schuster, 1982; Mark M. Anderson, *Kafka's Clothes: Ornamentation and Aestheticism in the Habsburg fin de siècle*, Oxford, Clarendon Press, 1992, pp. 1–73.

47 Georg Simmel, 'The Stranger', in D. N. Levine (ed.), *Georg Simmel on Individuality and Social Forms*, Chicago, University of Chicago Press, 1971, pp. 143–9.

48 Simmel, 'The Metropolis and Mental Life', in Levine (ed.), *Georg Simmel*, pp. 324–39; see also Janick and Toulmin, *Wittgenstein's Vienna*, pp. 33–66; and G. Lohmann, 'Georg Simmel's 'Metropolis and Mental Life'', *Thesis Eleven*, No. 44, 1996.

49 See Elias, *The Germans*; Janick and Toulmin, *Wittgenstein's Vienna*; and Bram Dijkstra, *Idols of Perversity: Fantasies on Feminine Evil in fin de siècle Culture*, Oxford, Oxford University Press, 1986, especially chs. 9 and 12.

50 H. Stuart Hughes, *Consciousness and Society*, 1967, London, Macgibbon and Kee, pp. 33–66 and 337–44. See also Luft, *Musil*, pp. 13–18.

51 See also David Frisby, *Sociological Impressionism*, London, Heinemann, 1981. The emphasis on Simmel's essayism is one-sided and does not take into account his attempts to posit a post-metaphysical sociology that stands between Kant and Nietzsche, an attempt that yielded many insights.

52 George W. Stocking (ed.), *Franz Boas Reader: The Shaping of American Anthropology, 1883–1911*, Chicago, University of Chicago Press, 1982.

53 Bronislaw Malinowski, 'Culture'. See Kroeber and Kluckhohn, *Culture*, and Milton Singer, 'The Concept of Culture'. By the 1920s, two different and competing strands of conceptualization marked the interpretation of culture. One perspective, articulated by Boas, Malinowski and Kroeber, emphasized cultural patterns, and was pluralistic and relativistic. The other 'structural-functional' interpretation of culture, mainly developed by Radcliffe-Brown (under the influence of Durkheim), emphasized underlying social structures, such as kinship, that were assumed to be universal and to provide a framework through which the parts of a society contributed to its organic unity. Although this latter structural-functionalist perspective is neither unimportant nor irrelevant, our remarks mainly concern the former, 'cultural pattern' perspective. The classic analysis of the assumptions underlying the various forms of functionalism is by Robert K. Merton, 'Manifest and Latent Functions', in *Social Theory and Social Structure*, New York, Free Press, 1968, pp. 73–138.

54 Malinowski, 'Culture', pp. 627 ff. The idea of a 'thick' medium is reminiscent of Clifford Geertz's idea of 'thick description' in *The Interpretation of Cultures*, New York, Basic Books, 1973, pp. 3–30. See also Geertz's essay 'The Growth of Culture and the Evolution of Mind', pp. 55–83 in the same volume; without mentioning Malinowski, Geertz states that the formation of the human brain could only have arisen within the framework of human culture.

55 Malinowski, 'Culture', p. 622.

56 Pierre Bourdieu, *Outline of a Theory of Practice*, Cambridge, Cambridge University Press, 1977; *Distinction: A Social Critique of the Judgement of Taste*, London, Routledge, 1984.

57 Kroeber and Kluckhohn, *Culture*.

58 Kroeber and Kluckhohn, *Culture*; and Hughes, *Consciousness and Society*.

59 See O. Spengler (1880–1936), *The Decline of the West*, trans. Charles Francis Atkinson, London, George Allen & Unwin, 1959; M. Horkheimer and T. W. Adorno, *Dialectic of Enlightenment*, London, Verso, 1979.

60 Claude Lévi-Strauss, 'French Sociology', in *Twentieth-Century Sociology*, ed. Georges Gurvitch and Wilbert E. Moore, New York, The Philosophical Library, 1945, p. 525; Victor Karady, 'The Prehistory of French Sociology 1917–1957', in *French Sociology: Rupture and Renewal Since 1968*, ed. Charles C. Lemert, Columbia, Columbia University Press, pp. 33–47.

61 Lewis Henry Morgan, *Ancient Society*, New York, Holt, 1877; Friedrich Engels, *The Origins of the Family, Private Property and the State*, Chicago, Charles H. Kerr, 1902 (original German, 1884); Herbert Spencer, *The Principles of Sociology*, London, Appleton, 1876; Emile Durkheim, *The Division of Labour in Society*, New York, Macmillan, 1933 (original French, 1893).

62 Emile Durkheim, *The Division of Labour in Society*, trans. George Simpson, Glencoe, IL., The Free Press, 1960, pp. 200–6 and 70–173 respectively.

63 Though this is not explicitly indicated by Lévi-Strauss in his 1945 essay on the history of the Durkheimian school, it is clear that this is what he has in mind, especially when he states,

paraphrasing Durkheim, 'society cannot exist without symbolism' (Lévi-Strauss, 'French Sociology', p. 518). This tension in Durkheim's work is further explored by Johann P. Arnason in 'Social Theory and the Concept of Civilization', pp. 87–105. The following discussion leans on Arnason's interpretation.

64 Cf. Lévi-Strauss, 'French Sociology', pp. 511–15.

65 See for example his 'Individualism and the Intellectuals', which was written at the time of the Dreyfus affair, and is not only a critique of the anti-semitism of the Third Republic, but also a statement of his version of the modern republican civilization of the West; see also 'Conclusion' to Durkheim, *The Elementary Forms of Religious Life*, London, Allen & Unwin, 1915.

66 M. Mauss, *The Gift*, London, Cohen & West, 1954.

67 See Arnason, 'Social Theory', p. 90; Lévi-Strauss, 'French Sociology' and also his interpretative essay *Marcel Mauss* in *Introduction to the Work of Marcel Mauss*, trans. Felicity Baker, London, Routledge, 1987.

68 See T. Stoianovich, *French Historical Method: The* Annales *Paradigm*, 1976, Ithaca, Cornell University Press, pp. 29 ff, and Ch. Moreze, 'The Application of Social Sciences to History', *Journal of Contemporary History*, Vol. 3, No. 2, April 1968, pp. 207–16.

69 F. Braudel, *The Mediterranean and the Mediterranean World in the Age of Philip II*, Vol. 2, 1982, London, William Collins Sons & Co., especially pp. 757–836, 'Civilizations'.

70 Whilst Braudel may agree with this, the escape from historical determinism is, for him, found in civilizational histories, in a specific meaning of this term. Braudelian historical research begins from the presupposition that history is a holistic science and, thus, heterogeneity of patterns only establish meaning in relation to other patterns within the overall scope of the enquiry. In other words, for Braudel, civilizational history is a form of historical research in which a system of realities exceeds the scope and lifespan of specific societies, as well as specific dimensions that other historical perspectives may attribute to a given society as causal. See F. Braudel, *The Mediterranean* and *Civilization and Capitalism*, in 3 vols, New York, Harper & Row, 1985, and T. Stoianovich, *French Historical Method*, chs 3–8, p. 148.

71 Albert Salomon, 'German Sociology', in Gurvitch and Moore (eds), *Twentieth-Century Sociology*, p. 587.

72 Salomon, 'German Sociology', p. 587; see also Willem Hennis, Introduction to H. H. Gerth and C. Wright Mills (eds), *From Max Weber*, New York, Oxford University Press, 1946; Hughes, *Consciousness and Society*, esp. ch. 8.

73 Jacob Burckhardt, *The Civilization of the Renaissance in Italy*, Oxford, Phaidon Press, 1945 (originally published in 1860); W. Dilthey, *Selected Writings*, Cambridge, Cambridge University Press, 1976; F. Tönnies, *Community and Association*, London, Routledge & Kegan Paul, 1955; Max Weber, *Economy and Society*, 2 vols, Berkeley, University of California Press, 1979.

74 See Salomon, 'German Sociology', pp. 587–613; and also Alfred Schutz, *The Phenomenology of the Social World*, Evanstown, IL, Northwestern University Press, 1967 (originally published in German, 1932).

75 Alfred Weber, *Kulturgeschichte als Kultursoziologie*, Munich, R. Piper, 1950 (first published in 1935).

76 Arnold Toynbee (1889–1975), *A Study of History*, London, Oxford University Press, 1947; Oswald Spengler, *Decline*, especially pp. 3–50.

77 Alfred Weber shares Dilthey's assumption that one can ultimately step outside the hermeneutic circle by developing general sociological concepts. However, following Gadamer's critique of Dilthey, as well as Elias's remarks above, this attempt can be seen to conceal from view the author's own cultural visions. See H.-G. Gadamer, *Truth and Method*.

78 On Park and the Chicago School see Martin Bulmer, *The Chicago School of Sociology*, Chicago, Chicago University Press, 1987; Roscoe C. Hinkle, *Developments in American Sociological Theory 1915-1950*, Albany, State University of New York Press, 1994, which has some useful remarks on Park's notion of culture (pp. 375–6) which are drawn on for the Preface remarks to Park's essay in this book; and Lee Harvey, *Myths of the Chicago School of Sociology*, Aldershot, Avebury, 1987. For the continuing American debate on the notion of civilization during the first half of the twentieth century, and which culminates in a colloquium on civilization, see W. R. Dennes (ed.), *Civilization*, Berkeley, University of California Press, 1942 – a series of lectures given by various authors at Berkeley in 1941.

79 S. N. Eisenstadt, 'Social Change, Differentiation and Evolution', *American Sociological Review*, 1964,

Vol. 29, No. 3, p. 375; 'Social Evolution', in Sills (ed.), *International Encyclopædia of the Social Sciences*, Vol. 5, pp. 228–34.

80 Norbert Elias, *Civilizing Process*.

81 Elias, *Civilizing Process*, p. 165.

82 Max Weber, *Economy and Society*, Vol. 1, p. 54.

83 Elias's model of explanation is a 'process model' (see Stephen Mennell, *Norbert Elias: Civilization and the Human Self-Image*, Oxford, Blackwell, 1989, pp. 177 ff.), which reveals not 'structure *and* process' but the structure *of* processes.

84 See, for example, Eiko Ikegami, *The Taming of the Samurai: Honorific Individualism and the Making of Modern Japan*, Cambridge MA, Harvard University Press, 1995; Wim Rasing, *'Too Many People': Order and Nonconformity in Iglulingmiut Social Process*, Nijmegen, Catholic University of Nijmegen, 1994.

85 Elias, *Civilizing Process*, p. 253 *n.*

86 Elias, *The Germans*, see also Z. Bauman, *Modernity and the Holocaust*, Oxford, Polity Press, 1989; Stephen Mennell, 'Decivilizing Processes: Theoretical Significance and Some Lines for Research', *International Sociology*, Vol. 5 (2), 1990, 205–23.

87 Mennell, *Norbert Elias*; Willem Kranendonk, *Society as Process: A Bibliography of Figurational Sociology in the Netherlands*, Amsterdam, Publikatiereeks Sociologisch Instituut, 1990.

88 The practical problems arising from the fractured character of the concept of culture can be seen very clearly in debates about 'cultural policy'. The abandonment by some cultural politicians of the goal of 'democratization of culture' – that is, the attempt to popularize what had been considered autonomous or 'high' culture for a wider audience – drove them to attempt to base a new policy of 'cultural democracy' on the anthropological conception of culture. But, since every human group already has 'culture' in the anthropological sense, that conception gives no basis for regarding one group's culture as being better or worse, more or less satisfying, than any other's. See Stephen Mennell, 'Theoretical Considerations on the Study of Cultural 'Needs'', *Sociology*, Vol. 13 (2), 1979, 235–57; and *Cultural Policy in Towns*, Strasbourg, Council of Europe, 1976.

89 Gyorgy Markus, 'The Paradigm of Language: Wittgenstein, Lévi-Strauss, Gadamer', in *The Structural Allegory: Reconstructive Encounters with the New French Thought*, ed. with an Introduction by John Fekete, Minneapolis, Minnesota University Press, 1984, p. 108.

90 For an overview of some contemporary ways of defining culture, especially from the vantage point of the linguistic turn, see Etienne Vermeesch, 'An Analysis of the Concept of Culture', in *The Concept and Dynamics of Culture*, ed. by Bernado Bernardi, The Hague, Mouton Publishers, pp. 9–74.

91 See L. Wittgenstein, *Philosophical Investigations*, trans. G. E. M. Anscombe, Oxford, Blackwell, 1988, and C. Lévi-Strauss, *The Savage Mind*, Chicago, Chicago University Press, 1966 for whom the Durkheimian/Maussian background is still relevant. J. Habermas attempts to unify the Wittgensteinian emphasis on the plurality of language games through a meta-theory of rationality that is simultaneously a culturally located learning theory. See his *Communication and the Evolution of Society*, trans. with an Introduction by Thomas McCarthy, London, Heinemann, 1979, and *The Theory of Communicative Action*, Vol. 1, trans. Thomas McCarthy, Boston, Beacon Press, 1984, especially pp. 43–74. The Wittgensteinian aspect also comes into play in the cultural relativist debate from an anthropological perspective between Peter Winch and Alistair MacIntyre in *Rationality*, ed. Bryan R. Wilson, Oxford, Blackwell, 1991. See P. Winch, 'Understanding a Primitive Society', and A. MacIntyre, 'The Idea of a Social Science', pp. 78–111 and 112–30, respectively. See also M. Hollis and S. Lukes (eds), *Rationality and Rationalism*, Oxford, Blackwell, 1982, especially the essay by Charles Taylor, 'Rationality', pp. 87–105. Herder's anthropological notion of culture stands behind Taylor's work, overall, as he attempts to posit a notion of rationality that is able to address both universalistic and particularistic concerns. See his *Sources of the Self*, Cambridge, Cambridge University Press, 1989, especially Part 1.

92 See C. Castoriadis, *The Imaginary Institution of Society*, trans. Kathleen Blamey, Cambridge, Cambridge University Press, 1987; J. Derrida, *Writing and Difference*, trans. Alan Bass, London, Routledge, 1978. R. Kearney's *The Wake of Imagination: Ideas of Creativity in Western Culture* explores this issue from the perspective of different conceptions of the imagination and creativity from the feudal, the modern to the postmodern.

Part I

CIVILIZATION AS POLITICAL TRANSFORMATION

1

CIVILIZATION AND ENLIGHTENMENT

'Idea for a Universal History from a Cosmopolitan Point of View'[1] (1784)

Immanuel Kant (1724–1804)

Immanuel Kant, as one of the major thinkers of the Enlightenment, argues that universal history denotes the movement of humankind from political immaturity or domination to political maturity or republicanism. Nature provides nothing but an impersonal backdrop to this story; for Kant, Enlightenment, or maturity, is a developmental or long-term process in which each generation builds on the political experience and knowledge of the previous ones. Civilization, thus, is the condition of a cumulative process of political maturity brought about by humankind using its reason.

As the title of this essay indicates, Kant writes from the vantage point of a citizen of the world. This means that the essay is written by someone who views himself as a citizen whose identity is not bounded by a nation or a state, but by a transcendental horizon which, for Kant, means the universal condition and capacity of human reason. This horizon underlies this essay – as it does all of his political writings – which begins by asking how human beings can live together in a way that minimizes the conditions of violence and tyranny. It takes concrete form in Kant's ideal-type construction of a modern republican, constitutional state. Kant's essay raises many, if not most, of the issues concerning civilization and culture to which many of the essays and extracts will return again and again.

Whatever concept one may hold, from a metaphysical point of view, concerning the freedom of the will, certainly its appearances, which are human actions, like every other natural event are determined by universal laws. However obscure their causes, history, which is concerned with narrating these appearances, permits us to hope that if we attend to the play of freedom of the human will in the large, we may be able to discern a regular movement in it, and that what seems complex and chaotic in the single individual may be seen from the standpoint of the human race as a whole to be a steady and progressive though slow evolution of its original endowment. Since the free will of man has obvious influence upon marriages, births, and deaths, they seem to be subject to no rule by which the number of them could be reckoned in advance. Yet the annual tables of them in the major countries prove that they occur according to laws as stable as [those of] the unstable weather, which we likewise cannot determine in advance, but which, in the large, maintain the growth of plants, the flow of rivers, and other natural events in an unbroken, uniform course. Individuals and even whole peoples think little on this. Each, according to his own inclination, follows his own purpose, often in opposition to others; yet each individual and people, as if following some guiding thread, go toward a natural but to each of them unknown goal; all work toward furthering it, even if they would set little store by it if they did know it.

Since men in their endeavors behave, on the whole, not just instinctively, like the brutes, nor yet like rational citizens of the world according to some agreed-on plan, no history of man conceived according to a plan seems to be possible, as it might be possible to have such a history of bees or beavers. One cannot suppress a certain indignation when one sees men's actions on the great world-stage and finds, beside the wisdom that appears here and there among individuals, everything in the large woven together from folly, childish vanity, even from childish malice and destructiveness. In the end, one does not know what to think of the human race, so conceited in its gifts. Since the philosopher cannot presuppose any [conscious] individual purpose among men in their great drama, there is no other expedient for him except to try to see if he can discover a natural purpose in this idiotic course of things human. In keeping with this purpose, it might be possible to have a history with a definite natural plan for creatures who have no plan of their own.

We wish to see if we can succeed in finding a clue to such a history; we leave it to Nature to produce the man capable of composing it, Thus Nature produced Kepler, who subjected, in an unexpected way; the eccentric paths of the planets to definite laws; and she produced Newton, who explained these laws by a universal natural cause.

First Thesis

All natural capacities of a creature are destined to evolve completely to their natural end.

Observation of both the outward form and inward structure of all animals confirms this of them. An organ that is of no use, an arrangement that does not achieve its purpose, are contradictions in the teleological theory of nature. If we give up this fundamental principle, we no longer have a lawful but an aimless course of nature, and blind chance takes the place of the guiding thread of reason.

Second Thesis

In man (as the only rational creature on earth) *those natural capacities which are directed to the use of his reason are to be fully developed only in the race, not in the individual.*

Reason in a creature is a faculty of widening the rules and purposes of the use of all its powers far beyond natural instinct; it acknowledges no limits to its projects. Reason itself does not work instinctively, but requires trial, practice, and instruction in order gradually to progress from one level of insight to another. Therefore a single man would have to live excessively long in order to learn to make full use of all his natural capacities. Since Nature has set only a short period for his life, she needs a perhaps unreckonable series of generations, each of which passes its own enlightenment to its successor in order finally to bring the seeds of enlightenment to that degree of development in our race which is completely suitable to Nature's purpose. This point of time must be, at least as an ideal, the goal of man's efforts, for otherwise his natural capacities would have to be counted as for the most part vain and aimless. This would destroy all practical principles, and Nature, whose wisdom must serve as the fundamental principle in judging all her other offspring, would thereby make man alone a contemptible plaything.

Third Thesis

Nature has willed that man should, by himself, produce everything that goes beyond the mechanical ordering of his animal existence, and that he should partake of no other happiness or perfection than that which he himself, independently of instinct, has created by his own reason.

Nature does nothing in vain, and in the use of means to her goals she is not prodigal. Her giving to man reason and the freedom of the will which depends upon it is clear indication of her purpose. Man accordingly was not to be guided by instinct, not nurtured and instructed with ready-made knowledge; rather, he should bring forth everything out of his own resources. Securing his own food, shelter, safety and defense (for which Nature gave him neither the horns of the bull, nor the claws of the lion, nor the fangs of the dog, but hands only), all amusement which can make life pleasant, insight and intelligence, finally even goodness of heart – all this should be wholly his own work, In this, Nature seems to have moved with the strictest parsimony, and to have measured her animal gifts precisely to the most stringent needs of a beginning existence, just as if she had willed that, if man ever did advance from the lowest barbarity to the highest skill and mental perfection and thereby worked himself up to happiness (so far as it is possible on earth), he alone should have the credit and should have only himself to thank – exactly as if she aimed more at his rational self-esteem than at his well-being. For along this march of human affairs, there was a host of troubles awaiting him. But it seems not to have concerned Nature that he should live well, but only that he should work himself upward so as to make himself, through his own actions, worthy of life and of well-being.

It remains strange that the earlier generations appear to carry through their toilsome labor only for the sake of the later, to prepare for them a foundation on which the later generations could erect the higher edifice which was Nature's goal, and yet that only the latest of the generations should have the good fortune to inhabit the building on which a long line of their ancestors had (unintentionally) labored without being permitted to partake of the fortune they had prepared. However puzzling this may be, it is necessary if one assumes that a species of animals should have reason, and, as a class of rational beings each of whom dies while the species is immortal, should develop their capacities to perfection.

Fourth Thesis

The means employed by Nature to bring about the development of all the capacities of men is their antagonism in society, so far as this is, in the end, the cause of a lawful order among men.

By "antagonism" I mean the unsocial sociability of men, i.e., their propensity to enter into society, bound together with a mutual opposition which constantly threatens to break up the society. Man has an inclination to associate with others, because in society he feels himself to be more than man, i.e., as more than the developed form of his natural capacities. But he also has a strong propensity to isolate himself from others, because he finds in himself at the same time the unsocial characteristic of wishing to have everything go according to his own wish. Thus he expects opposition on all sides because, in knowing himself, he knows that he, on his own part, is inclined to oppose others. This opposition it is which awakens all his powers, brings him to conquer his inclination to laziness and, propelled by vainglory, lust for power, and avarice, to achieve a rank among his fellows whom he cannot tolerate but from whom he cannot withdraw. Thus are taken the first true steps from barbarism to culture, which consists in the social worth of man; thence gradually develop all talents, and taste is refined; through continued enlightenment the beginnings are laid for a way of thought which can in time convert the coarse, natural disposition for moral discrimination into definite practical principles, and thereby change a society of men driven together by their natural feelings into a moral whole. Without those in themselves unamiable characteristics of unsociability from whence opposition springs – characteristics each man must find in his own selfish pretensions – all talents would remain hidden, unborn in an Arcadian shepherd's life, with all its concord, contentment, and mutual affection. Men, good-natured as the sheep they herd, would hardly reach a higher worth than their beasts; they would not fill the empty place in creation by achieving their end, which is rational nature. Thanks be to Nature, then, for the incompatibility, for heartless competitive vanity, for the insatiable desire to possess and to rule! Without them, all the excellent natural capacities of humanity would forever sleep, undeveloped. Man wishes concord; but Nature knows better what is good for the race; she wills discord, He wishes to live comfortably and pleasantly; Nature wills that he should be plunged from sloth and passive contentment into labor and trouble, in order that he may find means of extricating himself from them. The natural urges to this, the sources of unsociableness and mutual opposition from which so many evils arise, drive men to new exertions of their forces and thus to the manifold development of their capacities. They thereby perhaps show the ordering of a wise Creator and not the hand of an evil spirit, who bungled in his great work or spoiled it out of envy.

Fifth Thesis

The greatest problem for the human race, to the solution of which Nature drives man, is the achievement of a universal civic society which administers law among men.

The highest purpose of Nature, which is the development of all the capacities which can be achieved by mankind, is attainable only in society, and more specifically in the society with the greatest freedom. Such a society is one in which there is mutual opposition among the members, together with the most exact definition of freedom and fixing of its limits so that it may be consistent with the freedom of others. Nature demands that humankind should itself achieve this goal like all its other destined goals. Thus a society in which freedom under external laws is associated in the highest degree with irresistible power, i.e., a perfectly just civic constitution, is the highest problem Nature assigns to the human race; for Nature can achieve her other purposes for mankind only upon the solution and completion of this assignment. Need forces men, so enamored otherwise of their boundless freedom, into this state of constraint. They are forced to it by the greatest of all needs, a need they themselves occasion inasmuch as their passions keep them from living long together in wild freedom. Once in such a preserve as a civic union, these same passions subsequently do the most good. It is just the same with trees in a forest: each needs the others, since each in seeking to take the air and sunlight from others must strive upward, and thereby each realizes a beautiful, straight stature, while those that live in isolated freedom put out branches at random and grow stunted, crooked, and twisted. All culture, art which adorns mankind, and the finest social order are fruits of unsociableness, which forces itself to discipline itself and so, by a contrived art, to develop the natural seeds to perfection.

Sixth Thesis

This problem is the most difficult and the last to be solved by mankind.

The difficulty which the mere thought of this problem puts before our eyes is this. Man is an animal which, if it lives among others of its kind, requires a master. For he certainly abuses his freedom with respect to other men, and although as a reasonable being he wishes to have a law which limits the freedom of all, his selfish animal impulses tempt him, where possible, to exempt himself from them. He thus requires a master, who will break his will and force him to obey a will that is universally valid, under which each can be free. But whence does he get this master? Only from the human race. But then the master is himself an animal, and needs a master. Let him begin it as he will, it is not to be seen how he can procure a magistracy which can maintain public justice and which is itself just, whether it be a single person or a group of several elected persons. For each of them will always abuse his freedom if he has none above him to exercise force in accord with the laws. The highest master should be just in himself, and yet a man. This task is therefore the hardest of all; indeed, its complete solution is impossible, for from such crooked wood as man is made of, nothing perfectly straight can be built.[2] That it is the last problem to be solved follows also from this: it requires that there be a correct conception of a possible constitution, great experience gained in many paths of life, and – far beyond these – a good will ready to accept such a constitution. Three such things are very hard, and if they are ever to be found together, it will be very late and after many vain attempts.

Seventh Thesis

The problem of establishing a perfect civic constitution is dependent upon the problem of a lawful external relation among states and cannot be solved without a solution of the latter problem.

What is the use of working toward a lawful civic constitution among individuals, i.e., toward the creation of a commonwealth? The same unsociability which drives man to this causes any single commonwealth to stand in unrestricted freedom in relation to others; consequently, each of them must expect from another precisely the evil which oppressed the individuals and forced them to enter into a lawful civic state. The friction among men, the inevitable antagonism, which is a mark of even the largest societies and political bodies, is used by Nature as a means to establish a condition of quiet and security. Through war, through the taxing and never-ending accumulation of armament, through the want which any state, even in peacetime, must suffer internally, Nature forces them to make at first inadequate and tentative attempts; finally, after devastations, revolutions, and even complete exhaustion, she brings them to that which reason could have told them at the beginning and with far less sad experience, to wit, to step from the lawless condition of savages into a league of nations. In a league of nations, even the smallest state could expect security and justice, not from its own power and by its own decrees, but only from this great league of nations (*Foedus Amphictyonum*[3]), from a united power acting according to decisions reached under the laws of their united will. However fantastical this idea may seem – and it was laughed at as fantastical by the Abbé de St. Pierre[4] and by Rousseau,[5] perhaps because they believed it was too near to realization – the necessary outcome of the destitution to which each man is brought by his fellows is to force the states to the same decision (hard though it be for them) that savage man also was reluctantly forced to take, namely, to give up their brutish freedom and to seek quiet and security under a lawful constitution.

All wars are accordingly so many attempts (not in the intention of man, but in the intention of Nature) to establish new relations among states, and through the destruction or at least the dismemberment of all of them to create new political bodies, which, again, either internally or externally, cannot maintain themselves and which must thus suffer like revolutions; until finally, through the best possible civic constitution and common agreement and legislation in external affairs, a state is created which, like a civic commonwealth, can maintain itself automatically.

[There are three questions here, which really come to one.] Would it be expected from an Epicurean concourse of efficient causes that states, like minute particles of matter in their chance contacts, should form all sorts of unions which in their turn are destroyed by new impacts, until once, finally, by chance a structure should arise which could maintain its existence – a fortunate accident that could hardly occur? Or are we not rather to suppose that Nature here follows a lawful course in gradually lifting our race from the lower levels of animality to the highest level of humanity, doing this by her own secret art, and developing in accord with her law all the original gifts of man in this apparently chaotic disorder? Or perhaps we should prefer to conclude that, from all these actions and counteractions of men in the large, absolutely nothing, at least nothing wise, is to issue? That everything should remain as it always was, that we cannot therefore tell but that discord, natural to our race, may not prepare for us a hell of evils, however civilized we may now be, by annihilating civilization and all cultural progress through barbarous devastation? (This is the fate we may well have to suffer under the rule of blind chance – which is in fact identical with lawless freedom – if there is no secret wise guidance in Nature.) These three questions, I say, mean about the same as this: Is it reasonable to assume a purposiveness in all the parts of nature and to deny it to the whole?

Purposeless savagery held back the development of the capacities of our race; but finally, through the evil into which it plunged mankind, it forced our race to renounce this condition and to enter into a civic order in which those capacities could be developed. The same is done by the barbaric freedom of established states. Through wasting the powers of the commonwealths in armaments to be used against each other, through devastation brought on by war, and even more by the necessity of holding themselves in constant readiness for war, they stunt the full development of human nature. But because of the evils which thus arise, our race is forced to find, above the (in itself healthy) opposition of states which is a consequence of their freedom, a law of equilibrium and a united power to give it effect. Thus it is forced to institute a cosmopolitan condition to secure the external safety of each state.

Such a condition is not unattended by the danger that the vitality of mankind may fall asleep; but it is at least not without a principle of balance among men's actions and counteractions, without which they might be altogether destroyed. Until this last step to a union of states is taken, which is the halfway mark in the development of mankind, human nature must suffer the cruelest hardships under the guise of external well-being; and Rousseau was not far wrong in preferring the state of savages, so long, that is, as the last stage to which the human race must climb is not attained.

To a high degree we are, through art and science, *cultured*. We are *civilized* – perhaps too much for our own good – in all sorts of social grace and decorum. But to consider ourselves as having reached *morality* – for that, much is lacking. The ideal of morality belongs to culture; its use for some simulacrum of morality in the love of honor and outward decorum constitutes mere civilization. So long as states waste their forces in vain and violent self-expansion, and thereby constantly thwart the slow efforts to improve the minds of their citizens by even withdrawing all support from them, nothing in the way of a moral order is to be expected. For such an end, a long internal working of each political body toward the education of its citizens is required. Everything good that is not based on a morally good disposition, however, is nothing but pretense and glittering misery. In such a condition the human species will no doubt remain until, in the way I have described, it works its way out of the chaotic conditions of its international relations.

Eighth Thesis

The history of mankind can be seen, in the large, as the realization of Nature's secret plan to bring forth a perfectly constituted state as the only condition in which the capacities of mankind can be fully developed, and also bring forth that external relation among states which is perfectly adequate to this end.

This is a corollary to the preceding. Everyone can see that philosophy can have her belief in a millenium, but her millenarianism is not Utopian, since the Idea can help, though only from afar, to bring the millenium to pass. The only question is: Does Nature reveal anything of a path to this end? And I say: She reveals something, but very little. This great revolution seems to require so long for its completion that the short period during which humanity has been following this course permits us to determine its path and the relation of the parts to the whole with as little certainty as we can determine, from all previous astronomical observation, the path of the sun and his host of satellites among the fixed stars. Yet, on the fundamental premise of the systematic structure of the cosmos and from the little that has been observed, we can confidently infer the reality of such a revolution.

Moreover, human nature is so constituted that we cannot be indifferent to the most remote epoch our race may come to, if only we may expect it with certainty. Such indifference is even less possible for us, since it seems that our own intelligent action may hasten this happy time for our posterity. For that reason, even faint indications of approach to it are very important to us. At present, states are in such an artificial relation to each other that none of them can neglect its internal cultural development without losing power and influence among the others. Therefore the preservation of this natural end [culture], if not progress in it, is fairly well assured by the ambitions of states. Furthermore, civic freedom can hardly be infringed without the evil consequences being felt in all walks of life, especially in commerce, where the effect is loss of power of the state in its foreign relations. But this freedom spreads by degrees. When the citizen is hindered in seeking his own welfare in his own way, so long as it is consistent with the freedom of others, the vitality of the entire enterprise is sapped, and therewith the powers of the whole are diminished. Therefore limitations on personal actions are step by step removed, and general religious freedom is permitted. Enlightenment comes gradually, with intermittent folly and caprice, as a great good which must finally save men from the selfish aggrandizement of their masters, always assuming that the latter know their own interest. This enlightenment, and with it a certain commitment of heart which the enlightened man cannot fail to make to the good he clearly understands, must step by step ascend the throne and influence the principles of government.

Although, for instance, our world rulers at present have no money left over for public education and for anything that concerns what is best in the world, since all they have is already committed to future wars, they will still find it to their own interest at least not to hinder the weak and slow, independent efforts of their peoples in this work. In the end, war itself will be seen as not only so artificial, in outcome so uncertain for both sides, in after-effects so painful in the form of an ever-growing war debt (a new invention) that cannot be met, that it will be regarded as a most dubious undertaking. The impact of any revolution on all states on our continent, so closely knit together through commerce, will be so obvious that the other states, driven by their own danger but without any legal basis, will offer themselves as arbiters, and thus they will prepare the way for a distant international government for which there is no precedent in world history. Although this government at present exists only as a rough outline, nevertheless in all the members there is rising a feeling which each has for the preservation of the whole. This gives hope finally that after many reformative revolutions, a universal cosmopolitan condition, which Nature has as her ultimate purpose, will come into being as the womb wherein all the original capacities of the human race can develop.

Ninth Thesis

A philosophical attempt to work out a universal history according to a natural plan directed to achieving the civic union of the human race must be regarded as possible and, indeed, as contributing to this end of Nature.

It is strange and apparently silly to wish to write a history in accordance with an Idea of how the course of the world must be if it is to lead to certain rational ends. It seems that with such an Idea only a romance could be written. Nevertheless, if one may assume that Nature, even in the play of human freedom, works not without plan or purpose, this Idea could still be of use. Even if we are too blind to see the secret mechanism of its workings, this Idea may still serve as a guiding thread for presenting as a system, at least in broad outlines, what would otherwise be a planless conglomeration of human actions. For if one starts with Greek history, through which every older or contemporaneous history has been handed down or at least certified;[6] if one follows the influence of Greek history on the construction and misconstruction of the Roman state which swallowed up the Greek, then the Roman influence on the barbarians who in turn destroyed it, and so on down to our times; if one adds episodes from the national histories of other peoples insofar as they are known from the history of the enlightened nations, one will discover a regular progress in the constitution of states on our continent (which will probably give law, eventually, to all the others). If, further, one concentrates on the civic constitutions and their laws and on the relations among states, insofar as through the good they contained they served over long periods of time to elevate and adorn nations and their arts and sciences, while through the evil they contained they destroyed them, if only a germ of enlightenment was left to be further developed by this overthrow and a higher level was thus prepared – if, I say, one carries through this study, a guiding thread will be revealed. It can serve not only for clarifying the confused play of things human, and not only for the art of prophesying later political changes (a use which has already been made of history even when seen as the disconnected effect of lawless freedom), but for giving a consoling view of the future (which could not be reasonably hoped for without the presupposition of a natural plan) in which there will be exhibited in the distance how the human race finally achieves the condition in which all the seeds planted in it by Nature can fully develop and in which the destiny of the race can be fulfilled here on earth.

Such a justification of Nature – or, better, of Providence – is no unimportant reason for choosing a standpoint toward world history. For what is the good of esteeming the majesty and wisdom of Creation in the realm of brute nature and of recommending that we contemplate it, if that part of the great stage of supreme wisdom which contains the purpose of all the others – the history of mankind – must remain an unceasing reproach to it? If we are forced to turn our eyes from it in disgust, doubting that we can ever find a perfectly rational purpose in it and hoping for that only in another world?

That I would want to displace the work of practicing empirical historians with this Idea of world history, which is to some extent based upon an a priori principle, would be a misinterpretation of my intention. It is only a suggestion of what a philosophical mind (which would have to be well versed in history) could essay from another point of view. Otherwise the notorious complexity of a history of our time must naturally lead to serious doubt as to how our descendants will begin to grasp the burden of the history we shall leave to them after a few centuries. They will naturally value the history of earlier times, from which the documents may long since have disappeared, only from the point of view of what interests them, i.e., in answer to the question of what the various nations and governments have contributed to the goal of world citizenship, and what they have done to damage it. To consider this, so as to direct the ambitions of sovereigns and their agents to the only means by which their fame can be spread to later ages: this can be a minor motive for attempting such a philosophical history.

Notes

Translation and Notes by Lewis White Beck.

1 A statement in the "Short Notices" or the twelfth number of the *Gothaische Gelehrte Zeitung* of this year [1784], which no doubt was based on my conversation with a scholar who was traveling through, occasions this essay, without which that statement could not be understood.

    [The notice said: "A favorite idea of Professor Kant's is that the ultimate purpose of the human race is to achieve the most perfect civic constitution, and he wishes that a philosophical historian might undertake to give us a history of humanity from this point of view, and to show to what extent humanity in various ages has approached or drawn away from this final purpose and what remains to be done in order to reach it."]

2 The role of man is very artificial. How it may be with the dwellers on other planets and their nature we do not know. If, however, we carry out well the mandate given us by Nature, we can perhaps flatter ourselves that we may claim among our neighbors in the cosmos no mean rank. Maybe among them each individual can perfectly attain his destiny in his own life. Among us, it is different: only the race can hope to attain it.

3 [An allusion to the Amphictyonic League, a league of Greek tribes originally for the protection of a religious shrine, which later gained considerable political power.]

4 [Charles-Irénée Castel, Abbé de Saint Pierre (1658–1743), in his *Projet de paix perpetuelle* (Utrecht, 1713). Trans. H. H. Bellot (London, 1927).]

5 [In his *Extrait du projet de paix perpetuelle de M. l'Abbé de St. Pierre* (1760). Trans. C. E. Vaughn, *A Lasting Peace through the Federation of Europe* (London, 1917).]

6 Only a learned public, which has lasted from its beginning to our own day, can certify ancient history. Outside it, everything else is *terra incognita*; and the history of peoples outside it can only be begun when they come into contact with it. This happened with the Jews in the time of the Ptolemies through the translation of the Bible into Greek, without which we would give little credence to their isolated narratives. From this point, when once properly fixed, we can retrace their history. And so with all other peoples. The first page of Thucydides, says Hume, is the only beginning of all real history (David Hume, "Of the Populousness of Ancient Nations," in *Essays Moral, Political, and Literary*, eds. T. H. Green and T. H. Grose (London, Longmans, 1875), Vol. I, p. 414).

2

NATIONS AND CIVILIZATIONS

Extracts from *An Essay on the History of Civil Society* (1767)

Adam Ferguson (1723–1816)

Adam Ferguson was a member of the Scottish Enlightenment, whose other members included David Hume, Adam Smith, John Miller and Henry Home (Lord Kames). He was one of the Enlighteners who drew on societies of the New World by way of the anthropology of his day – travelogues and diaries. He argued that there was no natural basis for the distinctions that were made between societies, nor was social development inevitable or fixed. His theory of civilization emphasizes contingency and reversibility, and is thus a critique of teleological versions with their images of birth, maturity and progress. Furthermore, his theory of civilization is developed as a means for critiquing the present state of affairs.

In order to highlight these two sides of Ferguson's theory of civilization, the extracts chosen have been placed in reverse order. In 'Of Supposed National Eminence, and of the Vicissitudes of Human Affairs' Ferguson argues that all societies move from rude to polished, and part of this movement is their capacity to develop distinctions between insiders and outsiders, distinctions which are usually based in ignorance. Civilizations, too, for him are in constant danger of political corruption and disintegration and it is this danger which makes them contingent and reversible. This aspect comes to the fore in the second extract published below, 'Of Rude Nations prior to the Establishment of Property'. In Ferguson's view, democracy first appears in societies that are resistant to the development of institutions and thus differentiation. In smaller and undifferentiated societies power given over to a leader can always be revoked. This problem is further pursued in his *History of the Progress and Termination of the Roman Republic* (1783).

Part Fifth

Of the Decline of Nations

Section I
Of supposed National Eminence, and of the Vicissitudes of Human Affairs

No nation is so unfortunate as to think itself inferior to the rest of mankind: few are even willing to put up with the claim to equality. The greater part having chosen themselves, as at once, the judges and the models of what is excellent in their kind, are first in their own opinion, and give to others consideration or eminence, so far only as they approach to their own condition. One nation is vain of the personal character, or of the learning, of a few of its members; another, of its policy, its wealth, its tradesmen, its gardens, and its buildings; and they who have nothing to boast, are vain, because they are ignorant. The Russians, before the reign of Peter the Great, thought themselves possessed of every national honour, and held the *Nenei*, or *dumb nations*, (the name which they bestowed on their western neighbours of Europe), in a proportional degree of contempt. The map of the world, in China, was a square plate, the greater part of which was occupied by the provinces of this great empire, leaving on its skirts a few obscure corners, into which the wretched remainder of mankind were supposed to be driven. 'If you have not the use of our letters, nor the knowledge of our books,' said the learned Chinese to the European missionary, 'what literature, or what science, can you have?'

The term *polished*, if we may judge from its etymology, originally referred to the state of nations in respect to their laws and government. In its later applications, it refers no less to their proficiency in the liberal and mechanical arts, in literature, and in commerce. But whatever may be its application, it appears, that if there were a name still more respectable than this, every nation, even the most barbarous, or the most corrupted, would assume it; and bestow its reverse where they conceived a dislike, or apprehended a difference. The names of *alien*, or *foreigner*, are seldom pronounced without some degree of intended reproach. That of *barbarian*, in use with one arrogant people, and that of *gentil*, with another, only served to distinguish the stranger, whose language and pedigree differed from theirs.

Even where we pretend to found our opinions on reason, and to justify our preference of one nation to another, we frequently bestow our esteem on circumstances which do not relate to national character, and which have little tendency to promote the welfare of mankind. Conquest, or great extent of territory, however peopled, and great wealth, however distributed or employed, are titles upon which we indulge our own, and the vanity of other nations, as we do that of private men on the score of their fortunes and honours. We even sometimes contend, whose capital is the most overgrown; whose king has the most absolute power; and at whose court the bread of the subject is consumed in the most senseless riot. These indeed are the notions of vulgar minds; but it is impossible to determine, how far the notions of vulgar minds may lead mankind.

There have certainly been very few examples of states, who have, by arts or policy, improved the original dispositions of human nature, or endeavoured, by wise and effectual precautions, to prevent its corruption. Affection, and force of mind, which are the band and the strength of communities, were the inspiration of God, and original attributes in the nature of man. The wisest policy of nations, except in a very few instances, has tended, we may suspect, rather to maintain the peace of society, and to repress the external effects of bad passions, than to strengthen the disposition of the heart itself to justice and goodness. It has tended, by introducing a variety of arts, to exercise the ingenuity of men, and by engaging them in a variety of pursuits, inquiries, and studies, to inform, but frequently to corrupt the mind. It has tended to furnish matter of distinction and vanity; and by incumbering the individual with new subjects of personal care, to substitute the anxiety he entertains for himself, instead of the confidence and the affection he should entertain for his fellow-creatures.

Whether this suspicion be just or no, we are come to point at circumstances tending to verify, or to disprove it: and if to understand the real felicity of nations be of importance, it is certainly so likewise, to know what are those weaknesses, and those vices, by which men not only mar this felicity, but in one age forfeit all the external advantages they had gained in a former.

The wealth, the aggrandizement and power of nations, are commonly the effects of virtue; the loss of these advantages, is often a consequence of vice.

Were we to suppose men to have succeeded in the discovery and application of every art by which states are preserved, and governed; to have attained, by efforts of wisdom and magnanimity, the admired establishments and advantages of a civilized and flourishing people; the subsequent part of their history, containing, according to vulgar apprehension, a full display of those fruits in maturity, of which they had till then carried only the blossom, and the first formation, should, still more than the former, merit our attention, and excite our admiration.

The event, however, has not corresponded to this expectation. The virtues of men have shone most during their struggles, not after the attainment of their ends. Those ends themselves, though attained by virtue, are frequently the causes of corruption and vice. Mankind, in aspiring to national felicity, have substituted arts which increase their riches, instead of those which improve their nature. They have entertained admiration of themselves, under the titles of *civilized* and of *polished*, where they should have been affected with shame; and even where they have for a while acted on maxims tending to raise, to invigorate, and to preserve the national character, they have, sooner or later, been diverted from their object, and fallen a prey to misfortune, or to the neglects which prosperity itself had encouraged.

War, which furnishes mankind with a principal occupation of their restless spirit, serves, by the variety of its events, to diversify their fortunes. While it opens to one tribe or society, the way to eminence, and leads to dominion, it brings another to subjection, and closes the scene of their national efforts. The celebrated rivalship of Carthage and Rome was, in both parties, the natural exercise of an ambitious spirit, impatient of opposition, or even of equality. The conduct and the fortune of leaders, held the balance for some time in suspense; but to whichever side it had inclined, a great nation was to fall; a seat of empire, and of policy, was to be removed from its place; and it was then to be determined, whether the Syriac or the Latin should contain the erudition that was, in future ages, to occupy the studies of the learned.

States have been thus conquered from abroad, before they gave any signs of internal decay, even in the midst of prosperity, and in the period of their greatest ardour for national objects. Athens, in the height of her ambition, and of her glory, received a fatal wound, in striving to extend her maritime power beyond the Grecian seas. And nations of every description, formidable by their rude ferocity, respected for their discipline and military experience, when advancing, as well as when declining, in their strength, fell a prey, by turns, to the ambition and arrogant spirit of the Romans. Such examples may excite and alarm the jealousy and caution of states; the presence of similar dangers may exercise the talents of politicians and statesmen; but mere reverses of fortune are the common materials of history, and must long since have ceased to create our surprise.

Did we find, that nations advancing from small beginnings, and arrived at the possession of arts which lead to dominion, became secure of their advantages, in proportion as they were qualified to gain them; that they proceeded in a course of uninterrupted felicity, till they were broke by external calamities; and that they retained their force, till a more fortunate or vigorous power arose to depress them; the subject in speculation could not be attended with many difficulties, nor give rise to many reflections. But when we observe among nations a kind of spontaneous return to obscurity and weakness; when, in spite of perpetual admonitions of the danger they run, they suffer themselves to be subdued, in one period, by powers which could not have entered into competition with them in a former, and by forces which they had often baffled and despised; the subject becomes more curious, and its explanation more difficult.

The fact itself is known in a variety of different examples. The empire of Asia was, more than once, transferred from the greater to the inferior power. The states of Greece, once so warlike, felt a relation of their vigour, and yielded the ascendant they had disputed with the monarchs of the east, to the forces of an obscure principality, become formidable in a few years, and raised to eminence under the conduct of a single man. The Roman empire, which stood alone for ages; which had brought every rival under subjection, and saw no power from whom a competition could be feared, sunk at last before an artless and contemptible enemy. Abandoned to inroad, to pillage, and at last to conquest, on her frontier, she decayed in all her extremities, and shrank on every side. Her territory was dismembered, and whole provinces gave way, like branches fallen down with age, not violently torn by superior force. The spirit with which Marius had baffled and repelled the attacks of barbarians in a former age, the civil and military force with which the consul and his legions had extended this empire, were now no more. The Roman greatness, doomed to sink as it rose, by slow degrees, was impaired in every encounter. It was reduced to its original dimensions, within the compass of a single city; and depending for its preservation on the fortune of a siege, it was extinguished at a blow; and the brand, which had filled the world with its flames, sunk like a taper in the socket.

Such appearances have given rise to a general apprehension, that the progress of societies to what we call the heights of national greatness, is not more natural, than their return to weakness and obscurity is necessary and unavoidable. The images of youth, and of old age, are applied to nations; and communities, like single men, are supposed to have a period of life, and a length of thread, which is spun by the fates in one part uniform and strong, in another weakened and shattered by use; to be cut, when the destined æra is come, and to make way for a renewal of the emblem in the case of those who arise in succession. Carthage, being so much older than Rome, had felt her decay, says Polybius, so much the sooner: and the survivor too, he foresaw, carried in her bosom the seeds of mortality.

The image indeed is apposite, and the history of mankind renders the application familiar. But it must be obvious, that the ease of nations, and that of individuals, are very different. The human frame has a general course; it has, in every individual, a frail contexture, and a limited duration; it is worn by exercise, and exhausted by a repetition of its functions. But in a society, whose constituent members are renewed in every generation, where the race seems to enjoy perpetuated youth, and accumulating advantages, we cannot, by any parity of reason, expect to find imbecilities connected with mere age and length of days.

The subject is not new, and reflections will croud upon every reader. The notions, in the mean time, which we entertain, even in speculation, upon a subject so important, cannot be entirely fruitless to mankind; and however little the labours of the speculative may influence the conduct of men, one of the most pardonable errors a writer can commit, is to believe that he is about to do a great deal of good. But leaving the care of effects to others, we proceed to consider the grounds of inconstancy among mankind, the sources of internal decay, and the ruinous corruptions to which nations are liable, in the supposed condition of accomplished civility.

[. . .]

Part Second

On the History of Rude Nations

Section II
Of Rude Nations prior to the Establishment of Property

From one to the other extremity of America; from Kamschatka westward to the river Oby, and from the Northern Sea, over that length of country, to the confines of China, of India, and Persia from the Caspian to the Red sea, with little exception, and from thence over the inland continent and the western shores of Africa; we every where meet with nations on whom we bestow the appellations of barbarous or savage. That extensive tract of the earth, containing so great a variety of situation, climate, and soil, should, in the manners of its inhabitants, exhibit all the diversities which arise from the unequal influence of the sun, joined to a different nourishment and manner of life. Every question, however, on this subject is premature, till we have first endeavoured to form some general conception of our species in its rude state, and have learned to distinguish mere ignorance from dullness, and the want of arts from the want of capacity.

Of the nations who dwell in those, or any other of the less cultivated parts of the earth, some intrust their subsistence chiefly to hunting, fishing, or the natural produce of the soil. They have little attention to property, and scarcely any beginnings of subordination or government. Others having possessed themselves of herds, and depending for their provision on pasture, know what it is to be poor and rich. They know the relations of patron and client, of servant and master, and suffer themselves to be classed according to their measures of wealth. This distinction must create a material difference of character, and may furnish two separate heads, under which to consider the history of mankind in their rudest state; that of the savage, who is not yet acquainted with property; and that of the barbarian, to whom it is, although not ascertained by laws, a principal object of care and desire.

It must appear very evident, that property is a matter of progress. It requires, among other particulars which are the effects of time, some method of defining possession. The very desire of it proceeds from experience; and the industry by which it is gained, or improved, requires such a habit of acting with a view to distant objects, as may overcome the present disposition either to sloth or to enjoyment. This habit is slowly acquired, and is in reality a principal distinction of nations in the advanced state of mechanic and commercial arts.

In a tribe which subsists by hunting and fishing, the arms, the utensils, and the fur, which the individual carries, are to him the only subjects of property. The food of to-morrow is yet wild in the forest, or hid in the lake; it cannot be appropriated before it is caught; and even then, being the purchase of numbers, who fish or hunt in a body, it accrues to the community, and is applied to immediate use, or becomes an accession to the stores of the public.

Where savage nations, as in most parts of America, mix with the practice of hunting some species of rude agriculture, they still follow, with respect to the soil and the fruits of the earth, the analogy of their principal object. As the men hunt, so the women labour together; and, after they have shared the toils of the seed-time, they enjoy the fruits of the harvest in common. The field in which they have planted, like the district over which they are accustomed to hunt, is claimed as a property by the nation, but is not parcelled in lots to its members. They go forth in parties to prepare the ground, to plant, and to reap. The harvest is gathered into the public granary, and from thence, at stated times, is divided into shares for the maintenance of separate families. Even the returns of the market, when they trade with foreigners are brought home to the stock of the nation.

As the fur and the bow pertain to the individual, the cabbin and its utensils are appropriated to the family; and as the domestic cares are committed to the women, so the property of the household seems likewise to be vested in them. The children are considered as pertaining to the mother, with little regard to descent on the father's side. The males, before they are married, remain in the cabbin in which they are born; but after they have formed a new connection with the other sex, they change their habitation, and become an accession to the family in which they have found their wives. The hunter and the warrior are numbered by the matron as a part of her treasure; they are reserved for perils and trying occasions; and in the recess of public councils, in the intervals of hunting or war, are maintained by the cares of the women, and loiter about in mere amusement or sloth.

While one sex continue to value themselves chiefly on their courage, their talent for policy, and their warlike atchievements, this species of property which is bestowed on the other, is in reality a mark of subjection not, as some writers alledge, of their having acquired an ascendant. It is the care and trouble of a subject with which the warrior does not chuse to be embarrassed. It is a servitude, and a continual toil, where no honours are won; and they whose province it is, are in fact the slaves and the helots of their country. If in this destination of the sexes, while the men continue to indulge themselves in the contempt of sordid and mercenary arts, the cruel establishment of slavery is for some ages deferred; if in this tender, though unequal alliance, the affections of the heart prevent the severities practised on slaves; we have in the custom itself, as perhaps in many other instances, reason to prefer the first suggestions of nature, to many of her after refinements.

If mankind, in any instance, continue the article of property on the footing we have now represented, we may easily credit what is farther reported by travellers, that they admit of no distinctions of rank or condition; and that they have in fact no degree of subordination different from the distribution of function, which follows the differences of age, talents, and dispositions. Personal qualities give an ascendant in the midst of occasions which require their exertion; but in times of relaxation, leave no vestige of power or prerogative. A warrior who has led the youth of his nation to the slaughter of their enemies, or who has been foremost in the chace, returns upon a level with the rest of his tribe; and when the only business is to sleep, or to feed, can enjoy no pre-eminence; for he sleeps and he feeds no better than they.

Where no profit attends dominion, one party is as much averse to the trouble of perpetual command, as the other is to the mortification of perpetual submission: 'I love victory, I love great actions,' says Montesquieu in the character of Sylla; 'but have no relish for the languid detail of pacific government, or the pageantry of high station.' He has touched perhaps what is a prevailing sentiment in the simplest state of society, when the weakness of motives suggested by interest, and the ignorance of any elevation not founded on merit, supplies the place of disdain.

The character of the mind, however, in this state, is not founded on ignorance alone. Men are conscious of their equality, and are tenacious of its rights. Even when they follow a leader to the field, they cannot brook the pretensions to a formal command: they listen to no orders; and they come under no military engagements, but those of mutual fidelity, and equal ardour in the enterprise.

This description, we may believe, is unequally applicable to different nations, who have made unequal advances in the establishment of property. Among the Caribbees, and the other natives of the warmer climates in America, the dignity of chieftain is hereditary, or elective, and continued for life: the unequal distribution of property creates a visible subordination. But among the Iroquois, and other nations of the temperate zone, the titles of *magistrate* and *subject*, of *noble* and *mean*, are as little known as those of *rich* and *poor*. The old men, without being invested with any coercive power, employ their natural authority in advising or in prompting the resolutions of their tribe: the military leader is pointed out by the superiority of his manhood and valour: the statesman is distinguished only by the attention with which his counsel is heard; the warrior by the confidence with which the youth of his nation follow him to the field: and if their concerts must be supposed to constitute a species of political government, it is one to which no language of ours can be applied. Power is no more than the natural ascendency of the mind; the discharge of office no more than a natural exercise of the personal character; and while the community acts with an appearance of order, there is no sense of disparity in the breast of any of its members.

In these happy, though informal, proceedings, where age alone gives a place in the council; where youth, ardour, and valour in the field, give a title to the station of leader; where the whole community is assembled on any alarming occasion, we may venture to say, that we have found the origin of the senate, the executive power, and the assembly of the people; institutions for which ancient legislators have been so much renowned. The senate among the Greeks, as well as the Latins, appears, from the etymology of its name, to have been originally composed of elderly men. The military leader at Rome, in a manner not unlike to that of the American warrior, proclaimed his levies, and the citizen prepared for the field, in consequence of a voluntary engagement. The suggestions of nature, which directed the policy of nations in the wilds of America, were followed before on the banks of the Eurotas and the Tyber; and Lycurgus and Romulus found the model of their institutions where the members of every rude nation find the earliest mode of uniting their talents, and combining their forces.

Among the North-American nations, every individual is independent; but he is engaged by his affections and his habits in the cares of a family. Families, like so many separate tribes, are subject to no inspection or government from abroad; whatever passes at home, even bloodshed and murder, are only supposed to concern themselves. They are, in the mean time, the parts of a canton; the women assemble to plant their maize; the old men go to council; the huntsman and the warrior joins the youth of his village in the field. Many such cantons assemble to constitute a national council, or to execute a national enterprise. When the Europeans made their first settlements in America, six such nations had formed a league, had their amphyctiones or states-general, and, by the firmness of their union, and the ability of their councils, had obtained an ascendant from the mouth of the St Laurence to that of the Missisippi. They appeared to understand the objects of the confederacy, as well as those of the separate nation; they studied a balance of power; the statesman of one country watched the designs and proceedings of another; and occasionally threw the weight of his tribe into a different scale. They had their alliances and their treaties, which, like the nations of Europe, they maintained, or they broke, upon reasons of state; and remained at peace from a sense of necessity or expediency, and went to war upon any emergence of provocation or jealousy.

Thus, without any settled form of government, or any bond of union, but what resembled more the suggestion of instinct, than the invention of reason, they conducted themselves with the concert, and the force, of nations. Foreigners, without being able to discover who is the magistrate, or in what manner the senate is composed, always find a council with whom they may treat, or a band of warriors with whom they may fight. Without police or compulsory laws, their domestic society is conducted with order, and the absence of vicious dispositions, is a better security than any public establishment for the suppression of crimes.

Disorders, however, sometimes occur, especially in times of debauch, when the immoderate use of intoxicating liquors, to which they are extremely addicted, suspends the ordinary caution of their demeanour, and inflaming their violent passions, engages them in quarrels and bloodshed. When a person is slain, his murderer is seldom called to an immediate account: but he has a quarrel to sustain with the family and the friends; or, if a stranger, with the countrymen of the deceased; sometimes even with his own nation at home, if the injury committed be of a kind to alarm the society. The nation, the canton, or the family, endeavour, by presents, to atone for the offence of any of their members; and, by pacifying the parties aggrieved, endeavour to prevent what alarms the community more than the first disorder, the subsequent effects of revenge and animosity. The shedding of blood, however, if the guilty person remain where he has committed the crime, seldom escapes unpunished: the friend of the deceased knows how to disguise, though not to suppress, his resentment; and even after many years have elapsed, is sure to repay the injury that was done to his kindred or his house.

These considerations render them cautious and circumspect, put them on their guard against their passions, and give to their ordinary deportment an air of phlegm and composure superior to what is possessed among polished nations. They are, in the mean time, affectionate in their carriage, and in their conversations pay a mutual attention and regard, says Charlevoix, more tender and more engaging, than what we profess in the ceremonial of polished societies.

This writer has observed, that the nations among whom he travelled in North America, never mentioned acts of generosity or kindness under the notion of duty. They acted from affection, as they acted from appetite, without regard to its consequences. When they had done a kindness, they had gratified a desire; the business was finished, and passed from the memory. When they received a favour, it might, or it might not, prove the occasion of friendship: if it did not, the parties appeared to have no apprehensions of gratitude, as a duty by which the one was bound to make a return, or the other intitled to reproach the person who had failed in his part. The spirit with which they give or receive presents, is the same which Tacitus observed among the ancient Germans: They delight in them, but do not consider them as matter of obligation. Such gifts are of little consequence, except when employed as the seal of a bargain or treaty.

It was their favourite maxim, That no man is naturally indebted to another; that he is not, therefore, obliged to bear with any imposition, or unequal treatment. Thus, in a principle apparently sullen and inhospitable, they have discovered the foundation of justice, and observe its rules, with a steadiness and candour which no cultivation has been found to improve. The freedom which they give in what relates to the supposed duties of kindness and friendship, serves only to engage the heart more entirely, where it is once possessed with affection. We love to chuse our object without any restraint, and we consider kindness itself as a task, when the duties of friendship are exacted by rule. We therefore, by our demand for attentions, rather corrupt than improve the system of morality; and by our exactions of gratitude, and our frequent proposals to inforce its observance, we only shew, that we have mistaken its nature; we only give symptoms of that growing sensibility to interest, from which we measure the expediency of friendship and generosity itself; and by which we would introduce the spirit of traffic into the commerce of affection. In consequence of this proceeding, we are often obliged to decline a favour with the same spirit that we throw off a servile engagement, or reject a bribe. To the unrefining savage every favour is welcome, and every present received without reserve or reflection.

The love of equality, and the love of justice, were originally the same: and although, by the constitution of different societies, unequal privileges are bestowed on their members; and although justice itself requires a proper regard to be paid to such privileges; yet he who has forgotten that men were originally equal, easily degenerates into a slave; or in the capacity of a master, is not to be trusted with the rights of his fellow-creatures. This happy principle gives to the mind its sense of independence, renders it indifferent to the favours which are in the power of other men, checks it in the commision of injuries, and leaves the heart open to the affections of generosity and kindness. It gives to the untutored American that air of candour, and of regard to the welfare of others, which, in some degree, softens the arrogant pride of his carriage, and in times of confidence and peace, without the assistance of government or law, renders the approach and commerce of strangers secure.

Among this people, the foundations of honour are eminent abilities and great fortitude; not the distinctions of equipage and fortune: The talents in esteem are such as their situation leads them to employ, the exact knowledge of a country, and stratagem in war. On these qualifications, a captain among the Caribbees underwent an examination. When a new leader was to be chosen, a scout was sent forth to traverse the forests which led to the enemy's country, and, upon his return, the candidate was desired to find the track in which he had travelled. A brook, or a fountain, was named to him on the frontier, and he was desired to find the nearest path to a particular station, and to plant a stake in the place. They can, accordingly, trace a wild beast, or the human foot, over many leagues of a pathless forest, and find their way across a woody and uninhabited continent, by means of refined observations, which escape the traveller who has been accustomed to different aids. They steer in slender canoes, across stormy seas, with a dexterity equal to that of the most experienced pilot. They carry a penetrating eye for the thoughts and intentions of those with whom they have to deal; and when they mean to deceive, they cover themselves with arts which the most subtile can seldom elude. They harangue in their public councils with a nervous and figurative elocution; and conduct themselves in the management of their treaties with a perfect discernment of their national interests.

Thus being able masters in the detail of their own affairs, and well qualified to acquit themselves on particular occasions, they study no science, and go in pursuit of no general principles. They even seem incapable of attending to any distant consequences, beyond those they have experienced in hunting or war. They intrust the provision of every season to itself; consume the fruits of the earth in summer and, in winter, are driven in quest of their prey, through woods, and over deserts covered with snow. They do not form in one hour those maxims which may prevent the errors of the next; and they fail in those apprehensions, which, in the intervals of passion, produce ingenuous shame, compassion, remorse, or a command of appetite. They are seldom made to repent of any violence; nor is a person, indeed, thought accountable in his sober mood, for what he did in the heat of a passion, or in a time of debauch.

Their superstitions are groveling and mean: and did this happen among rude nations alone, we could not sufficiently admire the effects of politeness; but it is a subject on which few nations are intitled to censure their neighbours. When we have considered the superstitions of one people, we find little variety in those of another. They are but a repetition of similar weaknesses and absurdities, derived from a common source, a perplexed apprehension of invisible agents, that are supposed to guide all precarious events to which human foresight cannot extend.

In what depends on the known or the regular course of nature, the mind trusts to itself; but in strange and uncommon situations, it is the dupe of its own perplexity, and, instead of relying on its prudence or courage, has recourse to divination, and a variety of observances, that, for being irrational, are always the more revered. Superstition being founded in doubts and anxiety, is fostered by ignorance and mystery. Its maxims, in the mean time, are not always confounded with those of common life; nor does its weakness or folly always prevent the watchfulness, penetration, and courage, men are accustomed to employ in the management of common affairs. A Roman consulting futurity by the pecking of birds, or a King of Sparta inspecting the intrails of a beast, Mithridates consulting his women on the interpretation of his dreams, are examples sufficient to prove, that a childish imbecility on this subject is consistent with the greatest military and political talents.

Confidence in the effect of superstitious observances is not peculiar to any age or nation. Few, even of the accomplished Greeks and Romans, were able to shake off this weakness. In their case, it was not removed by the highest measures of civilization. It has yielded only to the light of true religion, or to the study of nature, by which we are led to substitute a wise providence operating by physical causes, in the place of phantoms that terrify or amuse the ignorant.

The principal point of honour among the rude nations of America, as indeed in every instance where mankind are not greatly corrupted, is fortitude. Yet their way of maintaining this point of honour, is very different from that of the nations of Europe. Their ordinary method of making war is by ambuscade; and they strive, by over-reaching an enemy, to commit the greatest slaughter, or to make the greatest number of prisoners, with the least hazard to themselves. They deem it a folly to expose their own persons in assaulting an enemy, and do not rejoice in victories which are stained with the blood of their own people. They do not value themselves, as in Europe, on defying their enemy upon equal terms. They even boast, that they approach like foxes, or that they fly like birds, not less than that they devour like lions. In Europe, to fall in battle is accounted an honour; among the natives of America, it is reckoned disgraceful. They reserve their fortitude for the trials they abide when attacked by surprise, or when fallen into their enemies hands; and when they are obliged to maintain their own honour, and that of their nation, in the midst of torments that require efforts of patience more than of valour.

On these occasions, they are far from allowing it to be supposed that they wish to decline the conflict. It is held infamous to avoid it, even by a voluntary death; and the greatest affront which can be offered to a prisoner, is to refuse him the honours of a man, in the manner of his execution: 'With-hold,' says an old man, in the midst of his torture, 'the stabs of your knife; rather let me die by fire, that those dogs, your allies, from beyond the seas, may learn to suffer like men.' With terms of defiance, the victim, in those solemn trials, commonly excites the animosity of his tormentors, as well as his own; and whilst we suffer for human nature, under the effect of its errors, we must admire its force.

The people with whom this practice prevailed, were commonly desirous of repairing their own losses, by adopting prisoners of war into their families: and even in the last moment, the hand which was raised to torment, frequently gave the sign of adoption, by which the prisoner became the child or the brother of his enemy, and came to share in all the privileges of a citizen. In their treatment of those who suffered, they did not appear to be guided by principles of hatred or revenge: they observed the point of honour in applying as well as in bearing their torments; and, by a strange kind of affection and tenderness, were directed to be most cruel where they intended the highest respect: the coward was put to immediate death by the hands of women: the valiant was supposed to be intitled to all the trials of fortitude that men could invent or employ: 'It gave me joy,' says an old man to his captive, 'that so gallant a youth was allotted to my share: I proposed to have placed you on the couch of my nephew, who was slain by your countrymen; to have transferred all my tenderness to you; and to have solaced my age in your company: but maimed and mutilated as you now appear, death is better than life: prepare yourself therefore to die like a man.'

It is perhaps with a view to these exhibitions, or rather in admiration of fortitude, the principle from which they proceed, that the Americans are so attentive, in their earliest years, to harden their nerves. The children are taught to vie with each other in bearing the sharpest torments; the youth are admitted into the class of manhood, after violent proofs of their patience; and leaders are put to the test, by famine, burning, and suffocation.

It might be apprehended, that among rude nations, where the means of subsistence are procured with so much difficulty, the mind could never raise itself above the consideration of this subject; and that man would, in this condition, give examples of the meanest and most mercenary spirit. The reverse, however, is true. Directed in this particular by the desires of nature, men, in their simplest state, attend to the objects of appetite no further than appetite requires; and their desires of fortune extend no further than the meal which gratifies their hunger: they apprehend no superiority of rank in the possession of wealth, such as might inspire any habitual principle of covetousness, vanity, or ambition: they can apply to no task that engages no immediate passion, and take pleasure in no occupation that affords no dangers to be braved, and no honours to be won.

It was not among the ancient Romans alone that commercial arts, or a sordid mind, were held in contempt. A like spirit prevails in every rude and independent society. 'I am a warrior, and not a merchant,' said an American to the governor of Canada, who proposed to give him goods in exchange for some prisoners he had taken; 'your cloaths and utensils do not tempt me but my prisoners are now in your power, and you may seize them: if you do, I must go forth and take more prisoners, or perish in the attempt; and if that chance should befal me, I shall die like a man; but remember, that our nation will charge you as the cause of my death.' With these apprehensions, they have an elevation, and a stateliness of carriage, which the pride of nobility, where it is most revered by polished nations, seldom bestows.

They are attentive to their persons, and employ much time, as well as endure great pain, in the methods they take to adorn their bodies, to give the permanent stains with which they are coloured, or preserve the paint, which they are perpetually repairing, in order to appear with advantage.

Their aversion to every sort of employment which they hold to be mean, makes them pass great part of their time in idleness or sleep; and a man who, in pursuit of a wild beast, or to surprise his enemy, will traverse a hundred leagues on snow, will not, to procure his food, submit to any species of ordinary labour. 'Strange,' says Tacitus, 'that the same person should be so much averse to repose, and so much addicted to sloth.'

Games of hazard are not the invention of polished ages; men of curiosity have looked for their origin, in vain, among the monuments of an obscure antiquity; and it is probable that they belonged to times too remote and too rude even for the conjectures of antiquarians to reach. The very savage brings his furs, his utensils, and his beads, to the hazard-table: he finds here the passions and agitations which the applications of a tedious industry could not excite: and while the throw is depending, he tears his hair, and beats his breast, with a rage which the more accomplished gamester has sometimes learned to repress: he often quits the party naked, and stripped of all his possessions; or where slavery is in use, stakes his freedom to have one chance more to recover his former loss.

With all these infirmities, vices, or respectable qualities, belonging to the human species in its rudest state; the love of society, friendship, and public affection, penetration, eloquence, and courage, appear to have been its original properties, not the subsequent effects of device or invention. If mankind are qualified to improve their manners, the subject was furnished by nature; and the effect of cultivation is not to inspire the sentiments of tenderness and generosity, nor to bestow the principal constituents of a respectable character, but to obviate the casual abuses of passion; and to prevent a mind, which feels the best dispositions in their greatest force, from being at times likewise the sport of brutal appetite and ungovernable violence.

Were Lycurgus employed anew to operate on the materials we have described, he would find them, in many important particulars, prepared by nature herself for his use. His equality in matters of property being already established, he would have no faction to apprehend from the opposite interests of the poor and the rich; his senate, his assembly of the people, is constituted; his discipline is in some measure adopted; and the place of his helots is supplied by the task allotted to one of the sexes. With all these advantages, he would still have had a very important lesson for civil society to teach, that by which a few learn to command, and the many are taught to obey: he would have all his precautions to take against the future intrusion of mercenary arts, the admiration of luxury, and the passion for interest: he would still perhaps have a more difficult task than any of the former, in teaching his citizens the command of appetite, and an indifference to pleasure, as well as contempt of pain; in teaching them to maintain, in the field, the formality of uniform precautions, and as much to avoid being themselves surprised, as they endeavour to surprise their enemy.

For want of these advantages, rude nations in general, though they are patient of hardship and fatigue, though they are addicted to war, and are qualified by their stratagem and valour to throw terror into the armies of a more regular enemy; yet, in the course of a continued struggle, always yield to the superior arts, and the discipline of more civilized nations. Hence the Romans were able to over-run the provinces of Gaul, Germany, and Britain; and hence the Europeans have a growing ascendency over the nations of Africa and America.

On the credit of a superiority which certain nations possess, they think that they have a claim to dominion; and even Caesar appears to have forgotten what were the passions, as well as the rights of mankind, when he complained, that the Britons, after having sent him a submissive message to Gaul, perhaps to prevent his invasion, still pretended to fight for their liberties, and to oppose his descent on their island.

There is not, perhaps, in the whole description of mankind, a circumstance more remarkable than that mutual contempt and aversion which nations, under a different state of commercial arts, bestow on each other. Addicted to their own pursuits, and considering their own condition as the standard of human felicity all nations pretend to the preference, and in their practice give sufficient proof of sincerity. Even the savage still less than the citizen, can be made to quit that manner of life in which he is trained: he loves that freedom of mind which will not be bound to any task, and which owns no superior: however tempted to mix with polished nations, and to better his fortune, the first moment of liberty brings him back to the woods again; he droops and he pines in the streets of the populous city; he wanders dissatisfied over the open and the cultivated field; he seeks the frontier and the forest, where, with a constitution prepared to undergo the hardships and the difficulties of the situation, he enjoys a delicious freedom from care, and a seducing society, where no rules of behaviour are prescribed, but the simple dictates of the heart.

3

CIVILIZATION, ENLIGHTENMENT AND THE NEW WORLD

Extracts from *Notes on the State of Virginia* (1781)

Thomas Jefferson (1743–1826)

Thomas Jefferson's *Notes on the State of Virginia*, although written in 1781, was published in English only in 1787, after being first published in French in 1785. It is recognized as a founding classic of the American Enlightenment, written by an encyclopedist and politician whose interests covered not only the political structure and practices of the American New World, but also agriculture, education, trade and commerce. This work is a confident portrayal of a New World society, against its portrayal as backward and infertile, violent and uncivilized by its European critics. Four major themes combine in *Notes on the State of Virginia* – nation-building, civilization, democracy and culture.

Jefferson portrays a nation in the making that draws on its own natural and cultural resources. In this context, civilization does not refer to a political legacy or a critical perspective. It refers to a political image of a state that must combat its own tendencies towards corruption, dependence and tyranny. In Jefferson's view, the mark of a civilization occurs with the division between force and law. According to him, it is only civilization that can limit power and replace inequality with equality. Jefferson also argues that political republicanism requires a cultural republicanism of tolerance, diversity of opinion and disagreement, and education into the arts of rulership. These two aspects – political and cultural republicanism – are the keys to understanding Jefferson's response, in civilizational terms, to the Old World's prejudice against the New, and are represented by the extracts published below.

Query XIII

Constitution

. . . This constitution was formed when we were new and unexperienced in the science of government. It was the first too which was formed in the whole United States. No wonder then that time and trial have discovered very capital defects in it.

1. The majority of the men in the state, who pay and fight for its support, are unrepresented in the legislature, the roll of freeholders intitled to vote, not including generally the half of those on the roll of the militia, or of the tax-gatherers.

2. Among those who share the representation, the shares are very unequal. Thus the county of Warwick, with only one hundred fighting men, has an equal representation with the county of Loudon, which has 1746. So that every man in Warwick has as much influence in the government as 17 men in Loudon. But lest it should be thought that an equal interspersion of small among large counties, through the whole state, may prevent any danger of injury to particular parts of it, we will divide it into districts, and shew the proportions of land, of fighting men, and of representation in each.

	Square miles.	Fighting men.	Dele-gates	Sena-tors.
Between the sea-coast and falls of the rivers	11,205	19,012	71	12
Between the falls of the rivers and the Blue ridge of mountains	18,759	18,828	46	8
Between the Blue ridge and the Alleghaney	11,911	7,673	16	2
Between the Alleghaney and Ohio	79,650	4,458	16	2
Total	121,525	49,971	149	24

An inspection of this table will supply the place of commentaries on it. It will appear at once that nineteen thousand men, living below the falls of the rivers, possess half the senate, and want four members only of possessing a majority of the house of delegates; a want more than supplied by the vicinity of their situation to the seat of government, and of course the greater degree of convenience and punctuality with which their members may and will attend in the legislature. These nineteen thousand, therefore, living in one part of the country, give law to upwards of thirty thousand, living in another, and appoint all their chief officers executive and judiciary. From the difference of their situation and circumstances, their interests will often be very different.

3. The senate is, by its constitution, too homogeneous with the house of delegates. Being chosen by the same electors, at the same time, and out of the same subjects, the choice falls of course on men of the same description. The purpose of establishing different houses of legislation is to introduce the influence of different interests or different principles. Thus in Great-Britain it is said their constitution relies on the house of commons for honesty, and the lords for wisdom; which would be a rational reliance if honesty were to be bought with money, and if wisdom were hereditary. In some of the American states the delegates and senators are so chosen, as that the first represent the persons, and the second the property of the state. But with us, wealth and wisdom have equal chance for admission into both houses. We do not therefore derive from the separation of our legislature into two houses, those benefits which a proper complication of principles is capable of producing, and those which alone can compensate the evils which may be produced by their dissensions.

4. All the powers of government, legislative, executive, and judiciary, result to the legislative body. The concentrating [of] these in the same hands is precisely the definition of despotic government. It will be no alleviation that these powers will be exercised by a plurality of hands, and not by a single one. 173 despots would surely be as oppressive as one. Let those who doubt it turn their eyes on the republic of Venice. As little will it avail us that they are chosen by ourselves. An *elective despotism* was not the government we fought for;

but one which should not only be founded on free principles, but in which the powers of government should be so divided and balanced among several bodies of magistracy, as that no one could transcend their legal limits, without being effectually checked and restrained by the others. For this reason that convention, which passed the ordinance of government, laid its foundation on this basis, that the legislative, executive and judiciary department should be separate and distinct, so that no person should exercise the powers of more than one of them at the same time. But no barrier was provided between these several powers. The judiciary and executive members were left dependant on the legislative, for their subsistence in office, and some of them for their continuance in it. If therefore the legislature assumes executive and judiciary powers, no opposition is likely to be made; nor, if made, can it be effectual; because in that case they may put their proceedings into the form of an act of assembly, which will render them obligatory on the other branches. They have accordingly, in many instances, decided rights which should have been left to judiciary controversy: and the direction of the executive, during the whole time of their session, is becoming habitual and familiar. And this is done with no ill intention. The views of the present members are perfectly upright. When they are led out of their regular province, it is by art in others, and inadvertence in themselves. And this will probably be the case for some time to come. But it will not be a very long time. Mankind soon learn to make interested uses of every right and power which they possess, or may assume. The public money and public liberty, intended to have been deposited with three branches of magistracy, but found inadvertently to be in the hands of one only, will soon be discovered to be sources of wealth and dominion to those who hold them; distinguished too by this tempting circumstance, that they are the instrument, as well as the object of acquisition. With money we will get men, said Cæsar, and with men we will get money. Nor should our assembly be deluded by the integrity of their own purposes, and conclude that these unlimited powers will never be abused, because themselves are not disposed to abuse them. They should look forward to a time, and that not a distant one, when corruption in this, as in the country from which we derive our origin, will have seized the heads of government, and be spread by them through the body of the people; when they will purchase the voices of the people, and make them pay the price. Human nature is the same on every side of the Atlantic, and will be alike influenced by the same causes. The time to guard against corruption and tyranny, is before they shall have gotten hold on us. It is better to keep the wolf out of the fold, than to trust to drawing his teeth and talons after he shall have entered. To render these considerations the more cogent, we must observe in addition,

5. That the ordinary legislature may alter the constitution itself. On the discontinuance of assemblies, it became necessary to substitute in their place some other body, competent to the ordinary business of government, and to the calling forth the powers of the state for the maintenance of our opposition to Great-Britain. Conventions were therefore introduced, consisting of two delegates from each county, meeting together and forming one house, on the plan of the former house of Burgesses, to whose places they succeeded. These were at first chosen anew for every particular session. But in March 1775, they recommended to the people to chuse a convention, which should continue in office a year. This was done accordingly in April 1775, and in the July following that convention passed an ordinance for the election of delegates in the month of April annually. It is well known, that in July 1775, a separation from Great-Britain and establishment of Republican government had never yet entered into any person's mind. A convention therefore, chosen under that ordinance, cannot be said to have been chosen for purposes which certainly did not exist in

the minds of those who passed it. Under this ordinance, at the annual election in April 1776, a convention for the year was chosen. Independance, and the establishment of a new form of government, were not even yet the objects of the people at large. One extract from the pamphlet called Common Sense had appeared in the Virginia papers in February, and copies of the pamphlet itself had got into a few hands. But the idea had not been opened to the mass of the people in April, much less can it be said that they had made up their minds in its favor. So that the electors of April 1776, no more than the legislators of July 1775, not thinking of independance and a permanent republic, could not mean to vest in these delegates powers of establishing them, or any authorities other than those of the ordinary legislature. So far as a temporary organization of government was necessary to render our opposition energetic, so far their organization was valid. But they received in their creation no powers but what were given to every legislature before and since. They could not therefore pass an act transcendant to the powers of other legislatures. If the present assembly pass any act, and declare it shall be irrevocable by subsequent assemblies, the declaration is merely void, and the act repealable, as other acts are. So far, and no farther authorized, they organized the government by the ordinance entitled a Constitution or Form of government. It pretends to no higher authority than the other ordinances of the same session; it does not say, that it shall be perpetual; that it shall be unalterable by other legislatures; that it shall be transcendant above the powers of those, who they knew would have equal power with themselves. Not only the silence of the instrument is a proof they thought it would be alterable, but their own practice also: for this very convention, meeting as a House of Delegates in General Assembly with the new Senate in the autumn of that year, passed acts of assembly in contradiction to their ordinance of government; and every assembly from that time to this has done the same. I am safe therefore in the position, that the constitution itself is alterable by the ordinary legislature. Though this opinion seems founded on the first elements of common sense, yet is the contrary maintained by some persons. 1. Because, say they, the conventions were vested with every power necessary to make effectual opposition to Great-Britain. But to complete this argument, they must go on, and say further, that effectual opposition could not be made to Great-Britain, without establishing a form of government perpetual and unalterable by the legislature; which is not true. An opposition which at some time or other was to come to an end, could not need a perpetual institution to carry it on: and a government, amendable as its defects should be discovered, was as likely to make effectual resistance, as one which should be unalterably wrong. Besides, the assemblies were as much vested with all powers requisite for resistance as the conventions were. If therefore these powers included that of modelling the form of government in the one case, they did so in the other. The assemblies then as well as the conventions may model the government; that is, they may alter the ordinance of government. 2. They urge, that if the convention had meant that this instrument should be alterable, as their other ordinances were, they would have called it an ordinance: but they have called it a *constitution*, which *by force of the term* means "an act above the power of the ordinary legislature." I answer, that *consitutio, constitutum, statutum, lex*, are convertible terms. "A *constitution* is called that which is made by the ruler. An *ordinance*, that which is rewritten by emperors or ordained. A *statute* is called the same as law." *Constitution* and *statute* were originally terms of the civil law, and from thence introduced by Ecclesiastics into the English law. Thus in the statute 25. Hen. 8. c. 19. §1. "*Constitutions* and *ordinances*" are used as synonimous. The term *constitution* has many other significations in physics and in politics; but in Jurisprudence, whenever it is applied to any act of the legislature, it invariably means a statute, law, or ordinance, which is the present case. No inference then of a different meaning can be drawn from the adoption of this title: on the contrary, we might conclude, that, by their affixing to it a term synonimous with ordinance, or statute, they meant it to be an ordinance or statute. But of what consequence is their meaning, where their power is denied? If they meant to do more than they had power to do, did this give them power? It is not the name, but the authority which renders an act obligatory. Lord Coke says, "an article of the statute 11 R. 2. c. 5. that no person should attempt to revoke any ordinance then made, is repealed, for that such restraint is against the jurisdiction and power of the parliament." 4. inst. 42. and again, "though divers parliaments have attempted to restrain subsequent parliaments, yet could they never effect it"; for the latter parliament hath ever power to abrogate, suspend, qualify, explain, or make void the former in the whole or in any part thereof, notwithstanding any words of restraint, prohibition, or penalty, in the former: for it is a maxim in the laws of the parliament, "*because subsequent laws nullify earlier laws which are contrary.*" 4. inst. 43. – To get rid of the magic supposed to be in the word *constitution*, let us translate it into its definition as given by those who think it above the power of the law; and let us suppose the convention instead of saying, "We, the ordinary legislature, establish a *constitution*," had said, "We, the ordinary legislature, establish an act *above the power of the ordinary legislature.*" Does not this expose the absurdity of the attempt? 3. But, say they, the people have acquiesced, and this has given it an authority superior to the laws. It is true, that the people did not rebel against it: and was that a time for the people to rise in rebellion? Should a prudent acquiescence, at a critical time, be construed into a confirmation of every illegal thing done during that period? Besides, why should they rebel? At an annual election, they had chosen delegates for the year, to exercise the ordinary powers of legislation, and to manage the great contest in which they were engaged. These delegates thought the contest would be best managed by an organized government. They therefore, among others, passed an ordinance of government. They did not presume to call it perpetual and unalterable. They well knew they had no power to make it so; that our choice of them had been for no such purpose, and at a time when we could have no such purpose in contemplation. Had an unalterable form of government been meditated, perhaps we should have chosen a different set of people. There was no cause then for the people to rise in rebellion. But to what dangerous lengths will this argument lead? Did the acquiescence of the colonies under the various acts of power exercised by Great-Britain in our infant state, confirm these acts, and so far invest them with the authority of the people as to render them unalterable, and our present resistance wrong? On every unauthoritative exercise of power by the legislature, must the people rise in rebellion, or their silence be construed into a surrender of that power to them? If so, how many rebellions should we have had already? One certainly for every session of assembly. The other states in the Union have been of opinion, that to render a form of government unalterable by ordinary acts of assembly, the people must delegate persons with special powers. They have accordingly chosen special conventions to form and fix their governments. The individuals then who maintain the contrary opinion in this country, should have the modesty to suppose it possible that they may be wrong and the rest of America right. But if there be only a possibility of their being wrong, if only a plausible doubt remains of the validity of the ordinance of government, is it not better to remove that doubt, by placing it on a bottom which none will dispute? If they be right, we shall only have the unnecessary trouble of meeting once in convention. If they be wrong, they expose us to the hazard of having no fundamental rights at all. True it is, this is no time for deliberating on forms of government. While an enemy is within our bowels, the first object is to expel him. But when this shall be done, when peace shall be established, and leisure given us for intrenching within good forms, the rights for which we have bled, let no man be found indolent enough to decline a little more trouble for placing them beyond the reach of question. If any thing more be requisite to produce a conviction of the expediency of calling a convention, at a proper season, to fix our form of government, let it be the reflection,

6. That the assembly exercises a power of determining the Quorum of their own body which may legislate for us. After the establishment of the new form they adhered to the *Law of the majority*, founded in common law as well as common right. It is the natural law of every assembly of men, whose numbers are not fixed by any other law. They continued for some time to require the presence of a majority of their whole number, to pass an act. But the British parliament fixes its own quorum: our former assemblies fixed their own quorum: and one precedent in favour of power is stronger than an hundred against it. The house of delegates therefore have lately voted that, during the present dangerous invasion, forty members shall be a house to proceed to business? They have been moved to this by the fear of not being able to collect a house. But this danger could not authorize them to call that a house which was none: and if they may fix it at one number, they may at another, till it loses its fundamental character of being a representative body. As this vote expires with the present invasion, it is probable the former rule will be permitted to revive: because at present no ill is meant. The power however of fixing their own quorum has been avowed, and a precedent set. From forty it may be reduced to four, and from four to one: from a house to a committee, from a committee to a chairman or speaker, and thus an oligarchy or monarchy be substituted under forms supposed to be regular. "All bad examples are derived from good ones; but when power comes to the ignorant or the less good, the new example is transferred from the worthy and fit to the unworthy and unfit." When therefore it is considered, that there is no legal obstacle to the assumption by the assembly of all the powers legislative, executive, and judiciary, and that these may come to the hands of the smallest rag of delegation, surely the people will say, and their representatives, while yet they have honest representatives, will advise them to say, that they will not acknowledge as laws any acts not considered and assented to by the major part of their delegates.

In enumerating the defects of the constitution, it would be wrong to count among them what is only the error of particular persons. In December 1776, our circumstances being much distressed, it was proposed in the house of delegates to create a *dictator*, invested with every power legislative, executive and judiciary, civil and military, of life and of death, over our persons and over our properties: and in June 1781, again under calamity, the same proposition was repeated, and wanted a few votes only of being passed. One who entered into this contest from a pure love of liberty, and a sense of injured rights, who determined to make every sacrifice, and to meet every danger, for the re-establishment of those rights on a firm basis, who did not mean to expend his blood and substance for the wretched purpose of changing this master for that, but to place the powers of governing him in a plurality of hands of his own choice, so that the corrupt will of no one man might in future oppress him, must stand confounded and dismayed when he is told, that a considerable portion of that plurality had meditated the surrender of them into a single hand, and, in lieu of a limited monarch, to deliver him over to a despotic one! How must we find his efforts and sacrifices abused and baffled, if he may still by a single vote be laid prostrate at the feet of one man! In God's name, from whence have they derived this power? Is it from our ancient laws? None such can be produced. Is it from any principle in our new constitution, expressed or implied? Every lineament of that expressed or implied, is in full opposition to it. Its fundamental principle is, that the state shall be governed as a commonwealth. It provides a republican organization, proscribes under the name of *prerogative* the exercise of all powers undefined by the laws; places on this basis the whole system of our laws; and, by consolidating them together, chuses that they shall be left to stand or fall together, never providing for any circumstances, nor admitting that such could arise, wherein either should be suspended, no, not for a moment. Our antient laws expressly declare, that those who are but delegates themselves shall not delegate to others powers which require judgment and integrity in their exercise. – Or was this proposition moved on a supposed right in the movers of abandoning their posts in a moment of distress? The same laws forbid the abandonment of that post, even on ordinary occasions; and much more a transfer of their powers into other hands and other forms, without consulting the people. They never admit the idea that these, like sheep or cattle, may be given from hand to hand without an appeal to their own will. – Was it from the necessity of the case? Necessities which dissolve a government, do not convey its authority to an oligarchy or a monarchy. They throw back, into the hands of the people, the powers they had delegated, and leave them as individuals to shift for themselves. A leader may offer, but not impose himself, nor be imposed on them. Much less can their necks be submitted to his sword, their breath be held at his will or caprice. The necessity which should operate these tremendous effects should at least be palpable and irresistible. Yet in both instances, where it was feared, or pretended with us, it was belied by the event. It was belied too by the preceding experience of our sister states, several of whom had grappled through greater difficulties without abandoning their forms of government. When the proposition was first made, Massachusetts had found even the government of committees sufficient to carry them through an invasion. But we at the time of that proposition were under no invasion. When the second was made, there had been added to this example those of Rhode-Island, New-York, New-Jersey, and Pennsylvania, in all of which the republican form had been found equal to the task of carrying them through the severest trials. In this state alone did there exist so little virtue, that fear was to be fixed in the hearts of the people, and to become the motive of their exertions and the principle of their government? The very thought alone was treason against the people; was treason against mankind in general; as rivetting for ever the chains which bow down their necks, by giving to their oppressors a proof, which they would have trumpeted through the universe, of the imbecility of republican government, in times of pressing danger, to shield them from harm. Those who assume the right of giving away the reins of government in any case, must be sure that the herd, whom they hand on to the rods and hatchet of the dictator, will lay their necks on the block when he shall nod to them. But if our assemblies supposed such a resignation in the people, I hope they mistook their character. I am of opinion, that the government, instead of being braced and invigorated for greater exertions under their difficulties, would have been thrown back upon the bungling machinery of county committees for administration, till a convention could have been called, and its wheels again set into regular motion. What a cruel moment was this for creating such an embarrassment, for putting to the proof the attachment of our countrymen to republican government! Those who meant well, of the advocates for this measure, (and most of them meant well, for I know them personally, had been their fellow-labourers in the common cause, and had often proved the purity of their principles), had been seduced in their judgment by the example of an ancient republic, whose constitution and circumstances were fundamentally different. They had sought this precedent in the history of Rome, where alone it was to be found, and where at length too it had proved fatal. They had taken it from a republic, rent by the most bitter factions and tumults, where the government was of a heavy-handed unfeeling aristocracy, over a people ferocious, and rendered desperate by poverty and wretchedness; tumults which could not be allayed under the most trying circumstances, but by the omnipotent hand of a single despot. Their constitution therefore allowed a temporary tyrant to be erected, under the name of a Dictator; and that temporary tyrant, after a few examples, became perpetual. They misapplied this precedent to a people, mild in their dispositions, patient under their trial, united for the public liberty, and affectionate to their leaders. But if from the constitution of the Roman government there resulted to their Senate a power of submitting all their rights to the will of one man, does it follow, that the assembly of Virginia have the same authority? What clause in our constitution has substituted that of Rome, by way of residuary provision, for all cases not otherwise provided for? Or if they may step ad libitum into any other form of government for precedents to rule us by, for what oppression may not a precedent be found in this world of the *war of all people against all things?* – Searching for the foundations of this proposition, I can find none which may pretend a colour of right or reason, but the defect before developed, that there being no barrier between the legislative, executive, and judiciary departments, the legislature may seize the whole: that having seized it, and possessing a right to fix their own quorum, they may reduce that quorum to one, whom they may call a chairman, speaker, dictator, or by any other name they please. – Our situation is indeed perilous, and I hope my countrymen will be sensible of it, and will apply, at a proper season, the proper remedy; which is a convention to fix the constitution, to amend its defects, to bind up the several branches of government by certain laws, which when they transgress their acts shall become nullities; to render unnecessary an appeal to the people, or in other words a rebellion, on every infraction of their rights, on the peril that their acquiescence shall be construed into an intention to surrender those rights.

Query XVII

Religion

The different religions received into that state?

The first settlers in this country were emigrants from England, of the English church, just at a point of time when it was flushed with complete victory over the religious of all other persuasions. Possessed, as they became, of the powers of making, administering, and executing the laws, they shewed equal intolerance in this country with their Presbyterian brethren, who had emigrated to the northern government. The poor Quakers were flying from persecution in England. They cast their eyes on these new countries as asylums of civil and religious freedom; but they found them free only for the reigning sect. Several acts of the Virginia assembly of 1659, 1662, and 1693, had made it penal in parents to refuse to have their children baptized; had prohibited the unlawful assembling of Quakers; had made it penal for any master of a vessel to bring a Quaker into the state; had ordered those already here, and such as should come thereafter, to be imprisoned till they should abjure the country; provided a milder punishment for their first and second return, but death for their third; had inhibited all persons from suffering their meetings in or near their houses, entertaining them individually, or disposing of books which supported their tenets. If no capital execution took place here, as did in New-England, it was not owing to the moderation of the church, or spirit of the legislature, as may be inferred from the law itself; but to historical

circumstances which have not been handed down to us. The Anglicans retained full possession of the country about a century. Other opinions began then to creep in, and the great
care of the government to support their own church, having begotten an equal degree of
indolence in its clergy, two-thirds of the people had become dissenters at the commencement of the present revolution. The laws indeed were still oppressive on them, but the spirit
of the one party had subsided into moderation, and of the other had risen to a degree of
determination which commanded respect.

The present state of our laws on the subject of religion is this. The convention of May
1776, in their declaration of rights, declared it to be a truth, and a natural right, that the
exercise of religion should be free; but when they proceeded to form on that declaration the
ordinance of government, instead of taking up every principle declared in the bill of rights,
and guarding it by legislative sanction, they passed over that which asserted our religious
rights, leaving them as they found them. The same convention, however, when they met as a
member of the general assembly in October 1776, repealed all *acts of parliament* which had
rendered criminal the maintaining any opinions in matters of religion, the forbearing to
repair to church, and the exercising any mode of worship; and suspended the laws giving
salaries to the clergy, which suspension was made perpetual in October 1779. Statutory
oppressions in religion being thus wiped away, we remain at present under those only
imposed by the common law, or by our own acts of assembly. At the common law, *heresy* was
a capital offence, punishable by burning. Its definition was left to the ecclesiastical judges,
before whom the conviction was, till the statute of the 1 El. c. 1. circumscribed it, by
declaring, that nothing should be deemed heresy, but what had been so determined by
authority of the canonical scriptures, or by one of the four first general councils, or by some
other council having for the grounds of their declaration the express and plain words of the
scriptures. Heresy, thus circumscribed, being an offence at the common law, our act of
assembly of October 1777, c. 17. gives cognizance of it to the general court, by declaring,
that the jurisdiction of that court shall be general in all matters at the common law. The
execution is by the writ *De hæretico comburendo*. By our own act of assembly of 1705, c. 30, if a
person brought up in the Christian religion denies the being of a God, or the Trinity, or
asserts there are more Gods than one, or denies the Christian religion to be true, or the
scriptures to be of divine authority, he is punishable on the first offence by incapacity to
hold any office or employment ecclesiastical, civil, or military; on the second by disability to
sue, to take any gift or legacy, to be guardian, executor, or administrator, and by three
years imprisonment, without bail. A father's right to the custody of his own children being
founded in law on his right of guardianship, this being taken away, they may of course be
severed from him, and put, by the authority of a court, into more orthodox hands. This is a
summary view of that religious slavery, under which a people have been willing to remain,
who have lavished their lives and fortunes for the establishment of their civil freedom.

The error seems not sufficiently eradicated, that the operations of the mind, as well as the
acts of the body, are subject to the coercion of the laws. But our rulers can have authority
over such natural rights only as we have submitted to them. The rights of conscience we
never submitted, we could not submit. We are answerable for them to our God. The legitimate powers of government extend to such acts only as are injurious to others. But it does
me no injury for my neighbour to say there are twenty gods, or no god. It neither picks my
pocket nor breaks my leg. If it be said, his testimony in a court of justice cannot be relied
on, reject it then, and be the stigma on him. Constraint may make him worse by making
him a hypocrite, but it will never make him a truer man. It may fix him obstinately in his

errors, but will not cure them. Reason and free enquiry are the only effectual agents against error. Give a loose to them, they will support the true religion, by bringing every false one to their tribunal, to the test of their investigation. They are the natural enemies of error, and of error only. Had not the Roman government permitted free enquiry, Christianity could never have been introduced. Had not free enquiry been indulged, at the æra of the reformation, the corruptions of Christianity could not have been purged away. If it be restrained now, the present corruptions will be protected, and new ones encouraged. Was the government to prescribe to us our medicine and diet, our bodies would be in such keeping as our souls are now. Thus in France the emetic was once forbidden as a medicine, and the potatoe as an article of food. Government is just as infallible too when it fixes systems in physics. Galileo was sent to the inquisition for affirming that the earth was a sphere: the government had declared it to be as flat as a trencher, and Galileo was obliged to abjure his error. This error however at length prevailed, the earth became a globe, and Descartes declared it was whirled round its axis by a vortex. The government in which he lived was wise enough to see that this was no question of civil jurisdiction, or we should all have been involved by authority in vortices. In fact, the vortices have been exploded, and the Newtonian principle of gravitation is now more firmly established, on the basis of reason, than it would be were the government to step in, and to make it an article of necessary faith. Reason and experiment have been indulged, and error has fled before them. It is error alone which needs the support of government. Truth can stand by itself. Subject opinion to coercion: whom will you make your inquisitors? Fallible men; men governed by bad passions, by private as well as public reasons. And why subject it to coercion? To produce uniformity. But is uniformity of opinion desireable? No more than of face and stature. Introduce the bed of Procrustes then, and as there is danger that the large men may beat the small, make us all of a size, by lopping the former and stretching the latter. Difference of opinion is advantageous in religion. The several sects perform the office of a Censor morum over each other. Is uniformity attainable? Millions of innocent men, women, and children, since the introduction of Christianity, have been burnt, tortured, fined, imprisoned; yet we have not advanced one inch towards uniformity. What has been the effect of coercion? To make one half the world fools, and the other half hypocrites. To support roguery and error all over the earth. Let us reflect that it is inhabited by a thousand millions of people. That these profess probably a thousand different systems of religion. That ours is but one of that thousand. That if there be but one right, and ours that one, we should wish to see the 999 wandering sects gathered into the fold of truth. But against such a majority we cannot effect this by force. Reason and persuasion are the only practicable instruments. To make way for these, free enquiry must be indulged; and how can we wish others to indulge it while we refuse it ourselves. But every state, says an inquisitor, has established some religion. No two, say I, have established the same. Is this a proof of the infallibility of establishments? Our sister states of Pennsylvania and New York, however, have long subsisted without any establishment at all. The experiment was new and doubtful when they made it. It has answered beyond conception. They flourish infinitely. Religion is well supported; of various kinds, indeed, but all good enough; all sufficient to preserve peace and order: or if a sect arises, whose tenets would subvert morals, good sense has fair play, and reasons and laughs it out of doors, without suffering the state to be troubled with it. They do not hang more malefactors than we do. They are not more disturbed with religious dissensions. On the contrary, their harmony is unparalleled, and can be ascribed to nothing but their unbounded tolerance, because there is no other circumstance in which they differ from every nation on earth. They have made the happy discovery, that the way to silence religious disputes, is to take no notice of them. Let us too give this experiment fair play, and get rid, while we may, of those tyrannical laws. It is true, we are as yet secured against them by the spirit of the times. I doubt whether the people of this country would suffer an execution for heresy, or a three years imprisonment for not comprehending the mysteries of the Trinity. But is the spirit of the people an infallible, a permanent reliance? Is it government? Is this the kind of protection we receive in return for the rights we give up? Besides, the spirit of the times may alter, will alter. Our rulers will become corrupt, our people careless. A single zealot may commence persecutor, and better men be his victims. It can never be too often repeated, that the time for fixing every essential right on a legal basis is while our rulers are honest, and ourselves united. From the conclusion of this war we shall be going down hill. It will not then be necessary to resort every moment to the people for support. They will be forgotten, therefore, and their rights disregarded. They will forget themselves, but in the sole faculty of making money, and will never think of uniting to effect a due respect for their rights. The shackles, therefore, which shall not be knocked off at the conclusion of this war, will remain on us long, will be made heavier and heavier, till our rights shall revive or expire in a convulsion.

Query XVIII

Manners

The particular customs and manners that may happen to be received in that state?

It is difficult to determine on the standard by which the manners of a nation may be tried, whether *catholic*, or *particular*. It is more difficult for a native to bring to that standard the manners of his own nation, familiarized to him by habit. There must doubtless be an unhappy influence on the manners of our people produced by the existence of slavery among us. The whole commerce between master and slave is a perpetual exercise of the most boisterous passions, the most unremitting despotism on the one part, and degrading submissions on the other. Our children see this, and learn to imitate it; for man is an imitative animal. This quality is the germ of all education in him. From his cradle to his grave he is learning to do what he sees others do. If a parent could find no motive either in his philanthropy or his self-love, for restraining the intemperance of passion towards his slave, it should always be a sufficient one that his child is present. But generally it is not sufficient. The parent storms, the child looks on, catches the lineaments of wrath, puts on the same airs in the circle of smaller slaves, gives a loose to his worst of passions, and thus nursed, educated, and daily exercised in tyranny, cannot but be stamped by it with odious peculiarities. The man must be a prodigy who can retain his manners and morals undepraved by such circumstances. And with what execration should the statesman be loaded, who permitting one half the citizens thus to trample on the rights of the other, transforms those into despots, and these into enemies, destroys the morals of the one part, and the amor patriæ of the other. For if a slave can have a country in this world, it must be any other in preference to that in which he is born to live and labour for another: in which he must lock up the faculties of his nature, contribute as far as depends on his individual endeavours to the evanishment of the human race, or entail his own miserable condition on the endless generations proceeding from him. With the morals of the people, their industry also is destroyed. For in a warm climate, no man will labour for himself who can make another labour for him. This is so true, that of the proprietors of slaves a very small proportion indeed are ever seen to labour. And can the liberties of a nation be thought secure when we have removed their only firm basis, a conviction in the minds of the people that these liberties are of the gift of God? That they are not to be violated but with his wrath? Indeed I tremble for my country when I reflect that God is just: that his justice cannot sleep for ever: that considering numbers, nature and natural means only, a revolution of the wheel of fortune, an exchange of situation, is among possible events: that it may become probable by supernatural interference! The Almighty has no attribute which can take side with us in such a contest. – But it is impossible to be temperate and to pursue this subject through the various considerations of policy, of morals, of history natural and civil. We must be contented to hope they will force their way into every one's mind. I think a change already perceptible, since the origin of the present revolution. The spirit of the master is abating, that of the slave rising from the dust, his condition mollifying, the way I hope preparing, under the auspices of heaven, for a total emancipation, and that this is disposed, in the order of events, to be with the consent of the masters, rather than by their extirpation.

4

DEMOCRACY AND DESPOTISM

Extracts from *Democracy in America*, Vol. 2 (1840)

Alexis de Tocqueville (1805–1859)

Between 11 May 1831 and 20 February 1832 Alexis de Tocqueville tra-velled the United States of America, ostensibly to investigate the Ameri-can penal system. What developed from his travels when he returned to Paris was an ethnography of the system and culture of American dem-ocracy written in two stages – the first volume was published in 1835, and concentrates on the structural features of American democracy, whilst the second was published in 1840 and concentrates on its cultural aspects, as well as those features which can transform a republican democracy into a despotic one.

If Jefferson gives an optimistic view of America as the new world repub-lican civilization (and his optimism is modified by a sense of the schisms of this new world), Alexis de Tocqueville is less sanguine. His *Democracy in America* – especially the passage 'That the Notions of Democratic Nations on Government are Naturally Favourable to the Concentration of Power' – draws attention to the dialectic of new world republicanism. De Tocqueville's importance is that he recognizes not only the tyranny of the few or of one person in what he calls 'aristocratic society', but also the tyranny of the many under a more democratic society. He detects the danger of the 'tyranny of equality' not only in the domain of politics, through the administration by the democratic state of more and more aspects of private life, but also (in the second part of *Democracy in America*, published in 1840) in the whole area of social life, in its culture, taste and intellectual affairs.

Book IV

Chapter I

That equality naturally gives men a taste for free institutions

The principle of equality, which makes men independent of each other, gives them a habit and a taste for following, in their private actions, no other guide but their own will. This complete independence, which they constantly enjoy towards their equals and in the inter-course of private life, tends to make them look upon all authority with a jealous eye, and speedily suggests to them the notion and the love of political freedom. Men living at such times have a natural bias to free institutions. Take any one of them at a venture, and search if you can his most deep-seated instincts; you will find that of all governments he will soonest conceive and most highly value that government, whose head he has himself elected, and whose administration he may control.

Of all the political effects produced by the equality of conditions, this love of independence is the first to strike the observing, and to alarm the timid; nor can it be said that their alarm is wholly misplaced, for anarchy has a more formidable aspect in democratic countries than elsewhere. As the citizens have no direct influence on each other, as soon as the supreme power of the nation fails, which kept them all in their several stations, it would seem that disorder must instantly reach its utmost pitch, and that, every man drawing aside in a different direction, the fabric of society must at once crumble away.

I am however persuaded that anarchy is not the principal evil which democratic ages have to fear, but the least. For the principle of equality begets two tendencies; the one leads men straight to independence, and may suddenly drive them into anarchy; the other conducts them by a longer, more secret, but more certain road, to servitude. Nations readily discern the former tendency, and are prepared to resist it; they are led away by the latter, without perceiving its drift; hence it is peculiarly important to point it out.

For myself, I am so far from urging as a reproach to the principle of equality that it renders men untractable, that this very circumstance principally calls forth my approbation. I admire to see how it deposits in the mind and heart of man the dim conception and instinctive love of political independence, thus preparing the remedy for the evil which it engenders: it is on this very account that I am attached to it.

Chapter II

That the notions of democratic nations on government are naturally favourable to the concentration of power

The notion of secondary powers, placed between the sovereign and his subjects, occurred naturally to the imagination of aristocratic nations, because those communities contained individuals or families raised above the common level, and apparently destined to command by their birth, their education, and their wealth. This same notion is naturally wanting in the minds of men in democratic ages, for converse reasons; it can only be introduced artificially, it can only be kept there with difficulty; whereas they conceive, as it were without thinking upon the subject, the notion of a sole and central power which governs the whole community by its direct influence. Moreover in politics, as well as in philosophy and in religion, the intellect of democratic nations is peculiarly open to simple and general notions. Complicated systems are repugnant to it, and its favourite conception is that of a great nation composed of citizens all resembling the same pattern, and all governed by a single power.

The very next notion to that of a sole and central power, which presents itself to the minds of men in the ages of equality, is the notion of uniformity of legislation. As every man sees that he differs but little from those about him, he cannot understand why a rule which is applicable to one man should not be equally applicable to all others. Hence the slightest privileges are repugnant to his reason; the faintest dissimilarities in the political institutions of the same people offend him, and uniformity of legislation appears to him to be the first condition of good government.

I find, on the contrary, that this same notion of a uniform rule, equally binding on all the members of the community, was almost unknown to the human mind in aristocratic ages; it was either never entertained, or it was rejected.

These contrary tendencies of opinion ultimately turn on either side to such blind instincts and such ungovernable habits, that they still direct the actions of men, in spite of particular exceptions. Notwithstanding the immense variety of conditions in the middle ages, a certain number of persons existed at that period in precisely similar circumstances; but this did not prevent the laws then in force from assigning to each of them distinct duties and different rights. On the contrary, at the present time all the powers of government are exerted to impose the same customs and the same laws on populations which have as yet but few points of resemblance.

As the conditions of men become equal amongst a people, individuals seem of less importance, and society of greater dimensions; or rather, every citizen, being assimilated to all the rest, is lost in the crowd, and nothing stands conspicuous but the great and imposing image of the people at large. This naturally gives the men of democratic periods a lofty opinion of the privileges of society, and a very humble notion of the rights of individuals; they are ready to admit that the interests of the former are everything, and those of the latter nothing. They are willing to acknowledge that the power which represents the community has far more information and wisdom than any of the members of that community; and that it is the duty, as well as the right, of that power to guide as well as govern each private citizen.

If we closely scrutinize our contemporaries, and penetrate to the root of their political opinions, we shall detect some of the notions which I have just pointed out, and we shall perhaps be surprised to find so much accordance between men who are so often at variance.

The Americans hold, that in every state the supreme power ought to emanate from the people; but when once that power is constituted, they can conceive, as it were, no limits to it, and they are ready to admit that it has the right to do whatever it pleases. They have not the slightest notion of peculiar privileges granted to cities, families, or persons: their minds appear never to have foreseen that it might be possible not to apply with strict uniformity the same laws to every part, and to all the inhabitants.

These same opinions are more and more diffused in Europe; they even insinuate themselves amongst those nations which most vehemently reject the principle of the sovereignty of the people. Such nations assign a different origin to the supreme power, but they ascribe to that power the same characteristics. Amongst them all, the idea of intermediate powers is weakened and obliterated: the idea of rights inherent in certain individuals is rapidly disappearing from the minds of men; the idea of the omnipotence and sole authority of society at large rises to fill its place. These ideas take root and spread in proportion as social conditions become more equal, and men more alike; they are engendered by equality, and in turn they hasten the progress of equality.

In France, where the revolution of which I am speaking has gone further than in any other European country, these opinions have got complete hold of the public mind. If we listen attentively to the language of the various parties in France, we shall find that there is not one which has not adopted them. Most of these parties censure the conduct of the government, but they all hold that the government ought perpetually to act and interfere in everything that is done. Even those which are most at variance are nevertheless agreed upon this head. The unity, the ubiquity, the omnipotence of the supreme power, and the uniformity of its rules, constitute the principal characteristics of all the political systems which have been put forward in our age. They recur even in the wildest visions of political regeneration: the human mind pursues them in its dreams.

If these notions spontaneously arise in the minds of private individuals, they suggest themselves still more forcibly to the minds of princes. Whilst the ancient fabric of European society is altered and dissolved, sovereigns acquire new conceptions of their opportunities and their duties; they learn for the first time that the central power which they represent may and ought to administer by its own agency, and on a uniform plan, all the concerns of the whole community. This opinion, which, I will venture to say, was never conceived before our time by the monarchs of Europe, now sinks deeply into the minds of kings, and abides there amidst all the agitation of more unsettled thoughts.

Our contemporaries are therefore much less divided than is commonly supposed; they are constantly disputing as to the hands in which supremacy is to be vested, but they readily agree upon the duties and the rights of that supremacy. The notion they all form of government is that of a sole, simple, providential, and creative power.

All secondary opinions in politics are unsettled; this one remains fixed, invariable, and consistent. It is adopted by statesmen and political philosophers; it is eagerly laid hold of by the multitude; those who govern and those who are governed agree to pursue it with equal ardour; it is the foremost notion of their minds, it seems connatural with their feelings. It originates therefore in no caprice of the human intellect, but it is a necessary condition of the present state of mankind.

Chapter III

That the sentiments of democratic nations accord with their opinions in leading them to concentrate political power

If it be true that, in ages of equality, men readily adopt the notion of a great central power, it cannot be doubted on the other hand that their habits and sentiments predispose them to recognize such a power and to give it their support. This may be demonstrated in a few words, as the greater part of the reasons, to which the fact may be attributed, have been previously stated.

As the men who inhabit democratic countries have no superiors, no inferiors, and no habitual or necessary partners in their undertakings, they readily fall back upon themselves and consider themselves as beings apart. I had occasion to point this out at considerable length in treating of individualism. Hence such men can never, without an effort, tear themselves from their private affairs to engage in public business; their natural bias leads them to abandon the latter to the sole visible and permanent representative of the interests of the community, that is to say, to the State. Not only are they naturally wanting in a taste for public business, but they have frequently no time to attend to it. Private life is so busy in democratic periods, so excited, so full of wishes and of work, that hardly any energy or leisure remains to each individual for public life. I am the last man to contend that these propensities are unconquerable, since my chief object in writing this book has been to combat them. I only maintain that at the present day a secret power is fostering them in the human heart, and that if they are not checked they will wholly overgrow it.

I have also had occasion to show how the increasing love of well-being, and the fluctuating character of property cause democratic nations to dread all violent disturbance. The love of public tranquillity is frequently the only passion which these nations retain, and it becomes more active and powerful amongst them in proportion as all other passions droop and die. This naturally disposes the members of the community constantly to give or to surrender additional rights to the central power, which alone seems to be interested in defending them by the same means that it uses to defend itself.

As in ages of equality no man is compelled to lend his assistance to his fellow-men, and none has any right to expect much support from them, every one is at once independent and powerless. These two conditions, which must never be either separately considered or confounded together, inspire the citizen of a democratic country with very contrary propensities. His independence fills him with self-reliance and pride amongst his equals; his debility makes him feel from time to time the want of some outward assistance, which he cannot expect from any of them, because they are all impotent and unsympathizing. In this predicament he naturally turns his eyes to that imposing power which alone rises above the level of universal depression. Of that power his wants and especially his desires continually remind him, until he ultimately views it as the sole and necessary support of his own weakness.[1]

This may more completely explain what frequently takes place in democratic countries, where the very men who are so impatient of superiors patiently submit to a master, exhibiting at once their pride and their servility.

The hatred which men bear to privilege increases in proportion as privileges become more scarce and less considerable, so that democratic passions would seem to burn most fiercely at the very time when they have least fuel. I have already given the reason of this phenomenon. When all conditions are unequal, no inequality is so great as to offend the eye; whereas the slightest dissimilarity is odious in the midst of general uniformity: the more complete is this uniformity, the more insupportable does the sight of such a difference become. Hence it is natural that the love of equality should constantly increase together with equality itself, and that it should grow by what it feeds upon.

This never-dying ever-kindling hatred, which sets a democratic people against the smallest privileges, is peculiarly favourable to the gradual concentration of all political rights in the hands of the representative of the State alone. The sovereign, being necessarily and incontestably above all the citizens, excites not their envy, and each of them thinks that he strips his equals of the prerogative which he concedes to the crown.

The man of a democratic age is extremely reluctant to obey his neighbour who is his equal; he refuses to acknowledge in such a person ability superior to his own; he mistrusts his justice, and is jealous of his power; he fears and he contemns him; and he loves continually to remind him of the common dependence in which both of them stand to the same master.

Every central power which follows its natural tendencies courts and encourages the principle of equality; for equality singularly facilitates, extends, and secures the influence of a central power.

In like manner it may be said that every central government worships uniformity: uniformity relieves it from inquiry into an infinite number of small details which must be attended to if rules were to be adapted to men, instead of indiscriminately subjecting men to rules: thus the government likes what the citizens like, and naturally hates what they hate. These common sentiments, which, in democratic nations, constantly unite the sovereign and every member of the community in one and the same conviction, establish a secret and lasting sympathy between them. The faults of the government are pardoned for the sake of its tastes; public confidence is only reluctantly withdrawn in the midst even of its excesses and its errors, and it is restored at the first call. Democratic nations often hate those in whose hands the central power is vested; but they always love that power itself.

Thus, by two separate paths, I have reached the same conclusion. I have shown that the principle of equality suggests to men the notion of a sole, uniform, and strong government: I have now shown that the principle of equality imparts to them a taste for it. To governments of this kind the nations of our age are therefore tending. They are drawn thither by the natural inclination of mind and heart; and in order to reach that result, it is enough that they do not check themselves in their course.

I am of opinion, that, in the democratic ages which are opening upon us, individual independence and local liberties will ever be the produce of artificial contrivance; that centralization will be the natural form of government.

[. . .]

Chapter VI

What sort of despotism democratic nations have to fear

I had remarked during my stay in the United States, that a democratic state of society, similar to that of the Americans, might offer singular facilities for the establishment of despotism; and I perceived, upon my return to Europe, how much use had already been made by most of our rulers, of the notions, the sentiments, and the wants engendered by this same social condition, for the purpose of extending the circle of their power. This led me to think that the nations of Christendom would perhaps eventually undergo some sort of oppression like that which hung over several of the nations of the ancient world.

A more accurate examination of the subject, and five years of further meditations, have not diminished my apprehensions, but they have changed the object of them.

No sovereign ever lived in former ages so absolute or so powerful as to undertake to administer by his own agency, and without the assistance of intermediate powers, all the parts of a great empire: none ever attempted to subject all his subjects indiscriminately to strict uniformity of regulation, and personally to tutor and direct every member of the community. The notion of such an undertaking never occurred to the human mind; and if any man had conceived it, the want of information, the imperfection of the administrative system, and above all, the natural obstacles caused by the inequality of conditions, would speedily have checked the execution of so vast a design.

When the Roman emperors were at the height of their power, the different nations of the empire still preserved manners and customs of great diversity; although they were subject to the same monarch, most of the provinces were separately administered; they abounded in powerful and active municipalities; and although the whole government of the empire was centred in the hands of the emperor alone, and he always remained, upon occasions, the supreme arbiter in all matters, yet the details of social life and private occupations lay for the most part beyond his control. The emperors possessed, it is true, an immense and unchecked power, which allowed them to gratify all their whimsical tastes, and to employ for that purpose the whole strength of the State. They frequently abused that power arbitrarily to deprive their subjects of property or of life: their tyranny was extremely onerous to the few, but it did not reach the greater number; it was fixed to some few main objects, and neglected the rest; it was violent, but its range was limited.

But it would seem that if despotism were to be established amongst the democratic nations of our days, it might assume a different character; it would be more extensive and more mild; it would degrade men without tormenting them. I do not question, that in an age of instruction and equality like our own, sovereigns might more easily succeed in collecting all political power into their own hands, and might interfere more habitually and decidedly within the circle of private interests, than any sovereign of antiquity could ever do. But this same principle of equality which facilitates despotism, tempers its rigour. We have seen how the manners of society become more humane and gentle in proportion as men become more equal and alike. When no member of the community has much power or much wealth, tyranny is, as it were, without opportunities and a field of action. As all fortunes are scanty, the passions of men are naturally circumscribed, – their imagination limited, their pleasures simple. This universal moderation moderates the sovereign himself, and checks within certain limits the inordinate stretch of his desires.

Independently of these reasons drawn from the nature of the state of society itself, I might add many others arising from causes beyond my subject; but I shall keep within the limits I have laid down to myself.

Democratic governments may become violent and even cruel at certain periods of extreme effervescence or of great danger; but these crises will be rare and brief. When I consider the petty passions of our contemporaries, the mildness of their manners, the extent of their education, the purity of their religion, the gentleness of their morality, their regular and industrious habits, and the restraint which they almost all observe in their vices no less than in their virtues, I have no fear that they will meet with tyrants in their rulers, but rather guardians.

I think then that the species of oppression by which democratic nations are menaced is unlike anything which ever before existed in the world: our contemporaries will find no prototype of it in their memories. I am trying myself to choose an expression which will accurately convey the whole of the idea I have formed of it, but in vain; the old words despotism and tyranny are inappropriate: the thing itself is new; and since I cannot name it, I must attempt to define it.

I seek to trace the novel features under which despotism may appear in the world. The first thing that strikes the observation is an innumerable multitude of men all equal and alike, incessantly endeavouring to procure the petty and paltry pleasures with which they glut their lives. Each of them, living apart, is as a stranger to the fate of all the rest, – his children and his private friends constitute to him the whole of mankind; as for the rest of his fellow-citizens, he is close to them, but he sees them not; – he touches them, but he feels them not; he exists but in himself and for himself alone; and if his kindred still remain to him, he may be said at any rate to have lost his country.

Above this race of men stands an immense and tutelary power, which takes upon itself alone to secure their gratifications, and to watch over their fate. That power is absolute, minute, regular, provident, and mild. It would be like the authority of a parent, if, like that authority, its object was to prepare men for manhood; but it seeks on the contrary to keep them in perpetual childhood: it is well content that the people should rejoice, provided they think of nothing but rejoicing. For their happiness such a government willingly labours, but it chooses to be the sole agent and the only arbiter of that happiness: it provides for their security, foresees and supplies their necessities, facilitates their pleasures, manages their principal concerns, directs their industry, regulates the descent of property, and subdivides their inheritances – what remains, but to spare them all the care of thinking and all the trouble of living?

Thus it every day renders the exercise of the free agency of man less useful and less frequent; it circumscribes the will within a narrower range, and gradually robs a man of all the uses of himself. The principle of equality has prepared men for these things: it has predisposed men to endure them, and oftentimes to look on them as benefits.

After having thus successively taken each member of the community in its powerful grasp, and fashioned them at will, the supreme power then extends its arm over the whole community. It covers the surface of society with a network of small complicated rules, minute and uniform, through which the most original minds and the most energetic characters cannot penetrate, to rise above the crowd. The will of man is not shattered, but softened, bent, and guided: men are seldom forced by it to act, but they are constantly restrained from acting: such a power does not destroy, but it prevents existence; it does not tyrannize, but it compresses, enervates, extinguishes, and stupefies a people, till each nation is reduced to be nothing better than a flock of timid and industrious animals, of which the government is the shepherd.

I have always thought that servitude of the regular, quiet, and gentle kind which I have just described, might be combined more easily than is commonly believed with some of the outward forms of freedom; and that it might even establish itself under the wing of the sovereignty of the people.

Our contemporaries are constantly excited by two conflicting passions; they want to be led, and they wish to remain free: as they cannot destroy either one or the other of these contrary propensities, they strive to satisfy them both at once. They devise a sole, tutelary, and all-powerful form of government, but elected by the people. They combine the principle of centralization and that of popular sovereignty; this gives them a respite: they console themselves for being in tutelage by the reflection that they have chosen their own guardians. Every man allows himself to be put in leading-strings, because he sees that it is not a person or a class of persons, but the people at large that holds the end of his chain.

By this system the people shake off their state of dependence just long enough to select their master, and then relapse into it again. A great many persons at the present day are quite contented with this sort of compromise between administrative despotism and the sovereignty of the people; and they think they have done enough for the protection of individual freedom when they have surrendered it to the power of the nation at large. This does not satisfy me: the nature of him I am to obey signifies less to me than the fact of extorted obedience.

I do not however deny that a constitution of this kind appears to me to be infinitely preferable to one, which, after having concentrated all the powers of government, should vest them in the hands of an irresponsible person or body of persons. Of all the forms which democratic despotism could assume, the latter would assuredly be the worst.

When the sovereign is elective, or narrowly watched by a legislature which is really elective and independent, the oppression which he exercises over individuals is sometimes greater, but it is always less degrading; because every man, when he is oppressed and disarmed, may still imagine, that whilst he yields obedience it is to himself he yields it, and that it is to one of his own inclinations that all the rest give way. In like manner I can under-stand that when the sovereign represents the nation, and is dependent upon the people, the rights and the power of which every citizen is deprived, not only serve the head of the state, but the state itself; and that private persons derive some return from the sacrifice of their independence which they have made to the public. To create a representation of the people in every centralized country is, therefore, to diminish the evil which extreme centralization may produce, but not to get rid of it.

I admit that by this means room is left for the intervention of individuals in the more important affairs; but it is not the less suppressed in the smaller and more private ones. It must not be forgotten that it is especially dangerous to enslave men in the minor details of life. For my own part, I should be inclined to think freedom less necessary in great things than in little ones, if it were possible to be secure of the one without possessing the other.

Subjection in minor affairs breaks out every day, and is felt by the whole community indiscriminately. It does not drive men to resistance, but it crosses them at every turn, till they are led to surrender the exercise of their will. Thus their spirit is gradually broken and their character enervated; whereas that obedience, which is exacted on a few important but rare occasions, only exhibits servitude at certain intervals, and throws the burden of it upon a small number of men. It is in vain to summon a people, which has been rendered so dependent on the central power, to choose from time to time the representatives of that power; this rare and brief exercise of their free choice, however important it may be, will not prevent them from gradually losing the faculties of thinking, feeling, and acting for themselves, and thus gradually falling below the level of humanity.

I add that they will soon become incapable of exercising the great and only privilege which remains to them. The democratic nations which have introduced freedom into their political constitution, at the very time when they were augmenting the despotism of their administrative constitution, have been led into strange paradoxes. To manage those minor affairs in which good sense is all that is wanted, – the people are held to be unequal to the task; but when the government of the country is at stake, the people are invested with immense powers: they are alternately made the playthings of their ruler, and his masters – more than kings, and less than men. After having exhausted all the different modes of election, without finding one to suit their purpose, they are still amazed, and still bent on seeking further; as if the evil they remark did not originate in the constitution of the country far more than in that of the electoral body.

It is, indeed, difficult to conceive how men who have entirely given up the habit of self-government should succeed in making a proper choice of those by whom they are to be governed; and no one will ever believe that a liberal, wise, and energetic government can spring from the suffrages of a subservient people.

A constitution, which should be republican in its head and ultra-monarchical in all its other parts, has ever appeared to me to be a short-lived monster. The vices of rulers and the ineptitude of the people would speedily bring about its ruin; and the nation, weary of its representatives and of itself, would create freer institutions, or soon return to stretch itself at the feet of a single master.

Notes

1 In democratic communities nothing but the central power has any stability in its position or any permanence in its undertakings. All the members of society are in ceaseless stir and transformation. Now it is in the nature of all governments to seek constantly to enlarge their sphere of action; hence it is almost impossible that such a government should not ultimately succeed, because it acts with a fixed principle and a constant will, upon men, whose position, whose notions, and whose desires are in continual vacillation.

It frequently happens that the members of the community promote the influence of the central power without intending it. Democratic ages are periods of experiment, innovation, and adventure.

At such times there are always a multitude of men engaged in difficult or novel undertakings, which they follow alone, without caring for their fellow-men. Such persons may be ready to admit, as a general principle, that the public authority ought not to interfere in private concerns; but, by an exception to that rule, each of them craves for its assistance in the particular concern on which he is engaged, and seeks to draw upon the influence of the government for his own benefit, though he would restrict it on all other occasions. If a large number of men apply this particular exception to a great variety of different purposes, the sphere of the central power extends insensibly in all directions, although each of them wishes it to be circumscribed.

Thus a democratic government increases its power simply by the fact of its permanence. Time is on its side; every incident befriends it; the passions of individuals unconsciously promote it; and it may be asserted, that the older a democratic community is, the more centralized will its government become.

Part II

CULTURAL CRITIQUES OF CIVILIZATION

5

CIVILIZATION AND ROMANTICISM

Extracts from *On the Aesthetic Education of Man*, in a Series of Letters (1794)

Friedrich Schiller (1759–1805)

The 'Romantic predicament', which still continues today, occurred first, approximately, between 1780 and 1850 and embraces such names as Byron, Coleridge, Shelley, Blake, Scott and Wordsworth in literature, especially poetry, Mendelssohn, Schubert and Schumann in music, and Schiller, Schelling, Novalis, and August and Friedrich Schlegel in philosophy. All, in their own way, were critical of a modern world which they viewed as alienating, corrupt or empty. Culture was deployed as the weapon against civilization. In this context, other cultures apart from the modern European one were invoked as idealized counterpoints to modern civilization – the Middle Ages (Scott and Novalis), the American New World (Coleridge) and an Athenian poetic republicanism (the Schlegels).

In *On the Aesthetic Education of Man*, barbarism is used by Schiller as a modern category to denote the pathologies of modern, Western civilization. In Schiller's understanding, it has nothing to do with the presumed savagery of so-called primitive peoples. It is a modern condition in which the division of labour and political democratization and state-formation result in the fragmentation of the human world. Schiller's response is a pedagogical one based on an ideal of aesthetic play. In a manner similar to much of Romantic criticism, Schiller's aesthetics refers to the Athenian world through the image of a lost, undistorted human nature in contrast to modern, fragmented life. This lost, undistorted condition cannot be regained, according to Schiller, but he sees it as a precondition for a new humankind which is transformed by an aesthetic revolution that unites desire and freedom, sentiment and reason.

Sixth Letter

1. Have I not perhaps been too hard on our age in the picture I have just drawn? That is scarcely the reproach I anticipate. Rather a different one: that I have tried to make it prove too much. Such a portrait, you will tell me, does indeed resemble mankind as it is today; but does it not also resemble any people caught up in the process of civilization, since all of them, without exception, must fall away from Nature by the abuse of Reason before they can return to her by the use of Reason?

2. Closer attention to the character of our age will, however, reveal an astonishing

contrast between contemporary forms of humanity and earlier ones, especially the Greek. The reputation or culture and refinement, on which we otherwise rightly pride ourselves *vis-à-vis* humanity in its merely natural state, can avail us nothing against the natural humanity of the Greeks. For they were wedded to all the delights of art and all the dignity of wisdom, without however, like us, falling a prey to their seduction. The Greeks put us to shame not only by a simplicity to which our age is a stranger; they are at the same time our rivals, indeed often our models, in those very excellences with which we are wont to console ourselves for the unnaturalness of our manners. In fullness of form no less than of content, at once philosophic and creative, sensitive and energetic, the Greeks combined the first youth of imagination with the manhood of reason in a glorious manifestation of humanity.

3. At that first fair awakening of the powers of the mind, sense and intellect did not as yet rule over strictly separate domains; for no dissension had as yet provoked them into hostile partition and mutual demarcation of their frontiers. Poetry had not as yet coquetted with wit, nor speculation prostituted itself to sophistry. Both of them could, when need arose, exchange functions, since each in its own fashion paid honour to truth. However high the mind might soar, it always drew matter lovingly along with it; and however fine and sharp the distinctions it might make it never proceeded to mutilate. It did indeed divide human nature into its several aspects, and project these in magnified form into the divinities of its glorious pantheon; but not by tearing it to pieces; rather by combining its aspects in different proportions, for in no single one of their deities was humanity in its entirety ever lacking. How different with us Moderns! With us too the image of the human species is projected in magnified form into separate individuals – but as fragments, not in different combinations, with the result that one has to go the rounds from one individual to another in order to be able to piece together a complete image of the species. With us, one might almost be tempted to assert, the various faculties appear as separate in practice as they are distinguished by the psychologist in theory, and we see not merely individuals, but whole classes of men, developing but one part of their potentialities, while of the rest, as in stunted growths, only vestigial traces remain.

4. I do not underrate the advantages which the human race today, considered as a whole and weighed in the balance of intellect, can boast in the face of what is best in the ancient world. But it has to take up the challenge in serried ranks, and let whole measure itself against whole. What individual Modern could sally forth and engage, man against man, with an individual Athenian for the prize of humanity?

5. Whence this disadvantage among individuals when the species as a whole is at such an advantage? Why was the individual Greek qualified to be the representative of his age, and why can no single Modern venture as much? Because it was from all-unifying Nature that the former, and from the all-dividing Intellect that the latter, received their respective forms.

6. It was civilization itself which inflicted this wound upon modern man. Once the increase of empirical knowledge, and more exact modes of thought, made sharper divisions between the sciences inevitable, and once the increasingly complex machinery of State necessitated a more rigorous separation of ranks and occupations, then the inner unity of human nature was severed too, and a disastrous conflict set its harmonious powers at variance. The intuitive and the speculative understanding now withdrew in hostility to take up positions in their respective fields, whose frontiers they now began to guard with jealous mistrust; and with this confining of our activity to a particular sphere we have given ourselves a

master within, who not infrequently ends by suppressing the rest of our potentialities. While in the one a riotous imagination ravages the hard-won fruits of the intellect, in another the spirit of abstraction stifles the fire at which the heart should have warmed itself and the imagination been kindled.

7. This disorganization, which was first started within man by civilization and learning, was made complete and universal by the new spirit of government. It was scarcely to be expected that the simple organization of the early republics should have survived the simplicity of early manners and conditions; but instead of rising to a higher form of organic existence it degenerated into a crude and clumsy mechanism. That polypoid character of the Greek States, in which every individual enjoyed an independent existence but could, when need arose, grow into the whole organism, now made way for an ingenious clockwork, in which, out of the piecing together of innumerable but lifeless parts, a mechanical kind of collective life ensued. State and Church, laws and customs, were now torn asunder; enjoyment was divorced from labour, the means from the end, the effort from the reward. Everlastingly chained to a single little fragment of the Whole, man himself develops into nothing but a fragment; everlastingly in his ear the monotonous sound of the wheel that he turns, he never develops the harmony of his being, and instead of putting the stamp of humanity upon his own nature, he becomes nothing more than the imprint of his occupation or of his specialized knowledge. But even that meagre, fragmentary participation, by which individual members of the State are still linked to the Whole, does not depend upon forms which they spontaneously prescribe for themselves (for how could one entrust to their freedom of action a mechanism so intricate and so fearful of light and enlightenment?); it is dictated to them with meticulous exactitude by means of a formulary which inhibits all freedom of thought. The dead letter takes the place of living understanding, and a good memory is a safer guide than imagination and feeling.

8. When the community makes his office the measure of the man; when in one of its citizens it prizes nothing but memory, in another a mere tabularizing intelligence, in a third only mechanical skill; when, in the one case, indifferent to character, it insists exclusively on knowledge, yet is, in another, ready to condone any amount of obscurantist thinking as long as it is accompanied by a spirit of order and law-abiding behaviour; when, moreover, it insists on special skills being developed with a degree of intensity which is only commensurate with its readiness to absolve the individual citizen from developing himself in extensity – can we wonder that the remaining aptitudes of the psyche are neglected in order to give undivided attention to the one which will bring honour and profit? True, we know that the outstanding individual will never let the limits of his occupation dictate the limits of his activity. But a mediocre talent will consume in the office assigned him the whole meagre sum of his powers, and a man has to have a mind above the ordinary if, without detriment to his calling, he is still to have time for the chosen pursuits of his leisure. Moreover, it is rarely a recommendation in the eyes of the State if a man's powers exceed the tasks he is set, or if the higher needs of the man of parts constitute a rival to the duties of his office. So jealously does the State insist on being the sole proprietor of its servants that it will more easily bring itself (and who can blame it?) to share its man with the Cytherean, than with the Uranian, Venus.

9. Thus little by little the concrete life of the Individual is destroyed in order that the abstract idea of the Whole may drag out its sorry existence, and the State remains for ever a stranger to its citizens since at no point does it ever make contact with their feeling. Forced to resort to classification in order to cope with the variety of its citizens, and never to get an

impression of humanity except through representation at second hand, the governing section ends up by losing sight of them altogether, confusing their concrete reality with a mere construct of the intellect; while the governed cannot but receive with indifference laws which are scarcely, if at all, directed to them as persons. Weary at last of sustaining bonds which the State does so little to facilitate, positive society begins (this has long been the fate of most European States) to disintegrate into a state of primitive morality, in which public authority has become but one party *more*, to be hated and circumvented by those who make authority necessary, and only obeyed by such as are capable of doing without it.

10. With this twofold pressure upon it, from within and from without, could humanity well have taken any other course than the one it actually took? In its striving after inalienable possessions in the realm of ideas, the spirit of speculation could do no other than become a stranger to the world of sense, and lose sight of matter for the sake of form. The practical spirit, by contrast, enclosed within a monotonous sphere of material objects, and within this uniformity still further confined by formulas, was bound to find the idea of an unconditioned Whole receding from sight, and to become just as impoverished as its own poor sphere of activity. If the former was tempted to model the actual world on a world conceivable by the mind, and to exalt the subjective conditions of its own perceptual and conceptual faculty into laws constitutive of the existence of things, the latter plunged into the opposite extreme of judging all experience whatsoever by one particular fragment of experience, and of wanting to make the rules of its own occupation apply indiscriminately to all others. The one was bound to become the victim of empty subtilties, the other of narrow pedantry; for the former stood too high to discern the particular, the latter too low to survey the Whole. But the damaging effects of the turn which mind thus took were not confined to knowledge and production; it affected feeling and action no less. We know that the sensibility of the psyche depends for its intensity upon the liveliness, for its scope upon the richness, of the imagination. The preponderance of the analytical faculty must, however, of necessity, deprive the imagination of its energy and warmth, while a more restricted sphere of objects must reduce its wealth. Hence the abstract thinker very often has a *cold* heart, since he dissects his impressions, and impressions can move the soul only as long as they remain whole; while the man of practical affairs often has a *narrow* heart, since his imagination, imprisoned within the unvarying confines of his own calling, is incapable of extending itself to appreciate other ways of seeing and knowing.

11. It was part of my procedure to uncover the disadvantageous trends in the character of our age and the reasons for them, not to point out the advantages which Nature offers by way of compensation. I readily concede that, little as individuals might benefit from this fragmentation of their being, there was no other way in which the species as a whole could have progressed. With the Greeks, humanity undoubtedly reached a maximum of excellence, which could neither be maintained at that level nor rise any higher. Not maintained, because the intellect was unavoidably compelled by the store of knowledge it already possessed to dissociate itself from feeling and intuition in an attempt to arrive at exact discursive understanding; not rise any higher, because only a specific degree of clarity is compatible with a specific fullness and warmth. This degree the Greeks had attained; and had they wished to proceed to a higher stage of development, they would, like us, have had to surrender their wholeness of being and pursue truth along separate paths.

12. If the manifold potentialities in man were ever to be developed, there was no other way but to pit them one against the other. This antagonism of faculties and functions is the great instrument of civilization – but it is only the instrument; for as long as it persists, we

are only on the way to becoming civilized. Only through individual powers in man becoming isolated, and arrogating to themselves exclusive authority, do they come into conflict with the truth of things, and force the Common Sense, which is otherwise content to linger with indolent complacency on outward appearance, to penetrate phenomena in depth. By pure thought usurping authority in the world of sense, while empirical thought is concerned to subject the usurper to the conditions of experience, both these powers develop to their fullest potential, and exhaust the whole range of their proper sphere. And by the very boldness with which, in the one case, imagination allows her caprice to dissolve the existing world-order, she does, in the other, compel Reason to rise to the ultimate sources of knowing, and invoke the law of Necessity against her.

13. One-sidedness in the exercise of his powers must, it is true, inevitably lead the individual into error; but the species as a whole to truth. Only by concentrating the whole energy of our mind into a *single* focal point, contracting our whole being into a single power, do we, as it were, lend wings to this individual power and lead it, by artificial means, far beyond the limits which Nature seems to have assigned to it. Even as it is certain that all individuals taken together would never, with the powers of vision granted them by Nature alone, have managed to detect a satellite of Jupiter which the telescope reveals to the astronomer, so it is beyond question that human powers of reflection would never have produced an analysis of the Infinite or a Critique of Pure Reason, unless, in the individuals called to perform such feats, Reason had separated itself off, disentangled itself, as it were, from all matter, and by the most intense effort of abstraction armed their eyes with a glass for peering into the Absolute. But will such a mind, dissolved as it were into pure intellect and pure contemplation, ever be capable of exchanging the rigorous bonds of logic for the free movement of the poetic faculty, or of grasping the concrete individuality of things with a sense innocent of preconceptions and faithful to the object? At this point Nature sets limits even to the most universal genius, limits which he cannot transcend; and as long as philosophy has to make its prime business the provision of safeguards against error, truth will be bound to have its martyrs.

14. Thus, however much the world as a whole may benefit through this fragmentary specialization of human powers, it cannot be denied that the individuals affected by it suffer under the curse of this cosmic purpose. Athletic bodies can, it is true, be developed by gymnastic exercises; beauty only through the free and harmonious play of the limbs. In the same way the keying up of individual functions of the mind can indeed produce extraordinary human beings; but only the equal tempering of them all, happy and complete human beings. And in what kind of relation would we stand to either past or future ages, if the development of human nature were to make such sacrifice necessary? We would have been the serfs of mankind; for several millenia we would have done slaves' work for them, and our mutilated nature would bear impressed upon it the shameful marks of this servitude. And all this in order that a future generation might in blissful indolence attend to the care of its moral health, and foster the free growth of its humanity!

15. But can Man really be destined to miss himself for the sake of any purpose whatsoever? Should Nature, for the sake of her own purposes, be able to rob us of a completeness which Reason, for the sake of hers, enjoins upon us? It must, therefore, be wrong if the cultivation of individual powers involves the sacrifice of wholeness. Or rather, however much the law of Nature tends in that direction, it must be open to us to restore by means of a higher Art the totality of our nature which the arts themselves have destroyed.

Twenty-Seventh Letter

1. You need have no fear for either reality or truth if the lofty conception of aesthetic semblance which I put forward in the last Letter were to become universal. It will not become universal as long as man is still uncultivated enough to be in a position to misuse it; and should it become universal, this could only be brought about by the kind of culture which would automatically make any misuse of it impossible. To strive after autonomous semblance demands higher powers of abstraction, greater freedom of heart, more energy of will, than man ever needs when he confines himself to reality; and he must already have left this reality behind if he would arrive at that kind of semblance. How ill-advised he would be, then, to take the path towards the ideal in order to save himself the way to the real! From semblance as here understood we should thus have little cause to fear for reality; all the more to be feared, I would suggest, is the threat from reality to semblance. Chained as he is to the material world, man subordinates semblance to ends of his own long before he allows it autonomous existence in the ideal realm of art. For this latter to happen a complete revolution in his whole way of feeling is required, without which he would not even find himself *on the way* to the ideal. Wherever, then, we find traces of a disinterested and unconditional appreciation of pure semblance, we may infer that a revolution of this order has taken place in his nature, and that he has started to become truly human. Traces of this kind are, however, actually to be found even in his first crude attempts at *embellishing* his existence, attempts made even at the risk of possibly worsening it from the material point of view. As soon as ever he starts preferring form to substance, and jeopardizing reality for the sake of semblance (which he must, however, recognize as such), a breach has been effected in the cycle of his animal behaviour, and he finds himself set upon a path to which there is no end.

2. Not just content with what satisfies nature, and meets his instinctual needs, he demands something over and above this: to begin with admittedly, only a superfluity *of material things*, in order to conceal from appetite the fact that it has limits, and ensure enjoyment beyond the satisfaction of immediate needs; soon, however, a superfluity *in material things*, an aesthetic surplus, in order to satisfy the formal impulse too, and extend enjoyment beyond the satisfaction of every need. By merely gathering supplies around him for future use, and enjoying them in anticipation, he does, it is true, transcend the present moment – but without transcending time altogether. He enjoys *more*, but he does not enjoy *differently*. But when he also lets form enter into his enjoyment, and begins to notice the outward appearance of the things which satisfy his desires, then he has not merely enhanced his enjoyment in scope and degree, but also ennobled it in kind.

3. It is true that Nature has given even to creatures without reason more than the bare necessities of existence, and shed a glimmer of freedom even into the darkness of animal life. When the lion is not gnawed by hunger, nor provoked to battle by any beast of prey, his idle strength creates an object for itself: he fills the echoing desert with a roaring that speaks defiance, and his exuberant energy enjoys its *self* in purposeless display. With what enjoyment of life do insects swarm in the sunbeam; and it is certainly not the cry of desire that we hear in the melodious warbling of the songbird. Without doubt there is freedom in these activities; but not freedom from compulsion altogether, merely from a certain kind of compulsion, compulsion from without. An animal may be said *to be at work*, when the stimulus to activity is some lack; it may be said *to be at play*, when the stimulus is sheer plenitude of vitality, when superabundance of life is its own incentive to action. Even inanimate nature

exhibits a similar luxuriance of forces, coupled with a laxity of determination which, in that material sense, might well be called play. The tree puts forth innumerable buds which perish without ever unfolding, and sends out far more roots, branches, and leaves in search of nourishment than are ever used for the sustaining of itself or its species. Such portion of its prodigal profusion as it returns, unused and unenjoyed, to the elements, is the overplus which living things are entitled to squander in a movement of carefree joy. Thus does Nature, even in her material kingdom, offer us a prelude of the Illimitable, and even here remove *in part* the chains which, in the realm of form, she casts away entirely. From the compulsion of want, or *physical earnestness*, she makes the transition via the compulsion of superfluity, or *physical play*, to aesthetic play; and before she soars, in the sublime freedom of beauty, beyond the fetters of ends and purposes altogether, she makes some approach to this independence, at least from afar, in that kind of *free activity* which is at once its own end and its own means.

4. Like the bodily organs in man, his imagination, too, has its free movement and its material play, an activity in which, without any reference to form, it simply delights in its own absolute and unfettered power. Inasmuch as form does not yet enter this fantasy play at all, its whole charm residing in a free association of images, such play – although the prerogative of man alone – belongs merely to his animal life, and simply affords evidence of his liberation from all external physical compulsion, without as yet warranting the inference that there is any autonomous shaping power within him.[1] From this play of *freely associated ideas*, which is still of a wholly material kind, and to be explained by purely natural laws, the imagination, in its attempt at a *free form*, finally makes the leap to aesthetic play. A leap it must be called, since a completely new power now goes into action; for here, for the first time, mind takes a hand as lawgiver in the operations of blind instinct, subjects the arbitrary activity of the imagination to its own immutable and eternal unity, introduces its own autonomy into the transient, and its own infinity into the life of sense. But as long as brute nature still has too much power, knowing no other law but restless hastening from change to change, it will oppose to that necessity of the spirit its own unstable caprice, to that stability its own unrest, to that autonomy its own subservience, to that sublime self-sufficiency its own insatiable discontent. The aesthetic play-drive therefore, will in its first attempts be scarcely recognizable, since the physical play-drive, with its wilful moods and its unruly appetites, constantly gets in the way. Hence we see uncultivated taste first seizing upon what is new and startling – on the colourful, fantastic, and bizarre, the violent and the savage – and shunning nothing so much as tranquil simplicity. It fashions grotesque shapes, loves swift transitions, exuberant forms, glaring contrasts, garish lights, and a song full of feeling. At this stage what man calls beautiful is only what excites him, what offers him material – but excites him to a resistance involving autonomous activity, but offers him material for *possible shaping*. Otherwise it would not be beauty – even for him. The form of his judgements has thus undergone an astonishing change: he seeks these objects, not because they give him something to enjoy passively, but because they provide an incentive to respond actively. They please him, not because they meet a need, but because they satisfy a law which speaks, though softly as yet, within his breast.

5. Soon he is no longer content that things should please him; he himself wants to please. At first, indeed, only through that which is *his*; finally through that which *he* is. The things he possesses, the things he produces, may no longer bear upon them the marks of their use, their form no longer be merely a timid expression of their function; in addition to the service they exist to render, they must at the same time reflect the genial mind which

conceived them, the loving hand which wrought them, the serene and liberal spirit which chose and displayed them. Now the ancient German goes in search of glossier skins, statelier antlers, more elaborate drinking horns; and the Caledonian selects for his feasts the prettiest shells. Even weapons may no longer be mere objects of terror; they must be objects of delight as well, and the cunningly ornamented sword-belt claims no less attention than the deadly blade of the sword. Not content with introducing aesthetic superfluity into objects of necessity, the play-drive as it becomes ever freer finally tears itself away from the fetters of utility altogether, and beauty in and for itself alone begins to be an object of his striving. Man *adorns* himself. Disinterested and undirected pleasure is now numbered among the necessities of existence, and what is in fact unnecessary soon becomes the best part of his delight.

6. And as form gradually comes upon him from without – in his dwelling, his household goods, and his apparel – so finally it begins to take possession of him himself, transforming at first only the outer, but ultimately the inner, man too. Uncoordinated leaps of joy turn into dance, the unformed movements of the body into the graceful and harmonious language of gesture; the confused and indistinct cries of feeling become articulate, begin to obey the laws of rhythm, and to take on the contours of song. If the Trojan host storms on to the battlefield with piercing shrieks like a flock of cranes, the Greek army approaches it in silence, with noble and measured tread. In the former case we see only the exuberance of blind forces; in the latter, the triumph of form and the simple majesty of law.

7. Now compulsion of a lovelier kind binds the sexes together, and a communion of hearts helps sustain a connexion but intermittently established by the fickle caprice of desire. Released from its dark bondage, the eye, less troubled now by passion, can apprehend the form of the beloved; soul looks deep into soul, and out of a selfish exchange of lust there grows a generous interchange of affection. Desire widens, and is exalted into love, once humanity has dawned in its object; and a base advantage over sense is now disdained for the sake of a nobler victory over will. The need to please subjects the all-conquering male to the gentle tribunal of taste; lust he can steal, but love must come as a gift. For this loftier prize he can only contend by virtue of form, never by virtue of matter. From being a force impinging upon feeling, he must become a form confronting the mind; he must be willing to concede freedom, because it is freedom he wishes to please. And even as beauty resolves the conflict between opposing natures in this simplest and clearest paradigm, the eternal antagonism of the sexes, so too does it resolve it – or at least aims at resolving it – in the complex whole of society, endeavouring to reconcile the gentle with the violent in the moral world after the pattern of the free union it there contrives between the strength of man and the gentleness of woman. Now weakness becomes sacred, and unbridled strength dishonourable; the injustice of nature is rectified by the magnanimity of the chivalric code. He whom no violence may alarm is disarmed by the tender blush of modesty, and tears stifle a revenge which no blood was able to assuage. Even hatred pays heed to the gentle voice of honour; the sword of the victor spares the disarmed foe, and a friendly hearth sends forth welcoming smoke to greet the stranger on that dread shore where of old only murder lay in wait for him.

8. In the midst of the fearful kingdom of forces, and in the midst of the sacred kingdom of laws, the aesthetic impulse to form is at work, unnoticed, on the building of a third joyous kingdom of play and of semblance, in which man is relieved of the shackles of circumstance, and released from all that might be called constraint, alike in the physical and in the moral sphere.

9. If in the *dynamic* State of rights it is as force that one man encounters another, and imposes limits upon his activities; if in the *ethical* State of duties Man sets himself over against man with all the majesty of the law, and puts a curb upon his desires: in those circles where conduct is governed by beauty, in the *aesthetic* State, none may appear to the other except as form, or confront him except as an object of free play. *To bestow freedom by means of freedom* is the fundamental law of this kingdom.

10. The dynamic State can merely make society possible, by letting one nature be curbed by another; the ethical State can merely make it (morally) necessary, by subjecting the individual will to the general; the aesthetic State alone can make it real, because it consummates the will of the whole through the nature of the individual. Though it may be his needs which drive man into society, and reason which implants within him the principles of social behaviour, beauty alone can confer upon him a *social character*. Taste alone brings harmony into society, because it fosters harmony in the individual. All other forms of perception divide man, because they are founded exclusively either upon the sensuous or upon the spiritual part of his being; only the aesthetic mode of perception makes of him a whole, because both his natures must be in harmony if he is to achieve it. All other forms of communication divide society, because they relate exclusively either to the private receptivity or to the private proficiency of its individual members, hence to that which distinguishes man from man; only the aesthetic mode of communication unites society, because it relates to that which is common to all. The pleasures of the senses we enjoy merely as individuals, without the genus which is immanent within us having any share in them at all; hence we cannot make the pleasures of sense universal, because we are unable to universalize our own individuality. The pleasures of knowledge we enjoy merely as genus, and by carefully removing from our judgement all trace of individuality; hence we cannot make the pleasures of reason universal, because we cannot eliminate traces of individuality from the judgements of others as we can from our own. Beauty alone do we enjoy at once as individual and as genus, i.e., as *representatives* of the human genus. The good of the Senses can only make *one* man happy, since it is founded on appropriation, and this always involves exclusion; and it can only make this *one* man one-sidedly happy, since his Personality has no part in it. Absolute good can only bring happiness under conditions which we cannot presume to be universal; for truth is the prize of abnegation alone, and only the pure in heart believe in the pure will. Beauty alone makes the whole world happy, and each and every being forgets its limitations while under its spell.

11. No privilege, no autocracy of any kind, is tolerated where taste rules, and the realm of aesthetic semblance extends its sway. This realm stretches upwards to the point where reason governs with unconditioned necessity, and all that is mere matter ceases to be. It stretches downwards to the point where natural impulse reigns with blind compulsion, and form has not yet begun to appear. And even at these furthermost confines, where taste is deprived of all legislative power, it still does not allow the executive power to be wrested from it. A-social appetite must renounce its self-seeking, and the Agreeable, whose normal function is to seduce the senses, must cast toils of Grace over the mind as well. Duty, stern voice of Necessity, must moderate the censorious tone of its precepts – a tone only justified by the resistance they encounter – and show greater respect for Nature through a nobler confidence in her willingness to obey them. From within the Mysteries of Science, taste leads knowledge out into the broad daylight of Common Sense, and transforms a monopoly of the Schools into the common possession of Human Society as a whole. In the kingdom of taste even the mightiest genius must divest itself of its majesty, and stoop in all humility to

the mind of a little child. Strength must allow itself to be bound by the Graces, and the lion have its defiance curbed by the bridle of a Cupid. In return, taste throws a veil of decorum over those physical desires which, in their naked form, affront the dignity of free beings; and, by a delightful illusion of freedom, conceals from us our degrading kinship with matter. On the wings of taste even that art which must cringe for payment can lift itself out of the dust; and, at the touch of her wand, the fetters of serfdom fall away from the lifeless and the living alike. In the Aesthetic State everything – even the tool which serves – is a free citizen, having equal rights with the noblest; and the mind, which would force the patient mass beneath the yoke of its purposes, must here first obtain its assent. Here, therefore, in the realm of Aesthetic Semblance, we find that ideal of equality fulfilled which the Enthusiast would fain see realized in substance. And if it is true that it is in the proximity of thrones that fine breeding comes most quickly and most perfectly to maturity, would one not have to recognize in this, as in much else, a kindly dispensation which often seems to be imposing limits upon man in the real world, only in order to spur him on to realization in an ideal world?

12. But does such a State of Aesthetic Semblance really exist? And if so, where is it to be found? As a need, it exists in every finely attuned soul; as a realized fact, we are likely to find it, like the pure Church and the pure Republic, only in some few chosen circles, where conduct is governed, not by some soulless imitation of the manners and morals of others, but by the aesthetic nature we have made our own; where men make their way, with undismayed simplicity and tranquil innocence, through even the most involved and complex situations, free alike of the compulsion to infringe the freedom of others in order to assert their own, as of the necessity to shed their Dignity in order to manifest Grace.

Note

1 Most of the imaginative play which goes on in everyday life is either entirely based on this feeling for free association of ideas, or at any rate derives therefrom its greatest charm. This may not in itself be proof of a higher nature, and it may well be that it is just the most flaccid natures who tend to surrender to such unimpeded flow of images; it is nevertheless this very independence of the fantasy from external stimuli, which constitutes at least the negative condition of its creative power. Only by tearing itself free from reality does the formative power raise itself up to the ideal; and before the imagination, in its productive capacity, can act according to its own laws, it must first, in its reproductive procedures, have freed itself from alien laws. From mere lawlessness to autonomous law-giving from within, there is, admittedly, still a big step to be taken; and a completely new power, the faculty for ideas, must first be brought into play. But this power, too, can now develop with greater ease, since the senses are not working against it, and the indefinite does, at least negatively, border upon the infinite.

6

CIVILIZATION AS CRUELTY

Extract from *On the Genealogy of Morals*, Second essay (1887)

Friedrich Nietzsche (1844–1900)

Nietzsche's critique of civilization has some affinities with Schiller's, but is coloured not only by Schopenhauer's philosophy of life and the will, but also by a more pessimistic attitude. His critique and rejection of civilization are based on an anthropological motif and premise – for him, humans are the 'sick animal', made sick by the brutality and sanctions that are required to civilize them.

Nietzsche's vehemence towards civilization is directed at the two millennia of the history of the West from Socrates to the Enlightenment. According to him, the moral revolutions in manners and civility during the eighteenth century especially had resulted in a deadly combination of sentimentality, conscience and utility, which had also shaped the contemporary political landscape. Social democratization, bureaucratization, and the ethics of utility, none of which can be divorced from the others, says Nietzsche, simply produce a modern nihilistic culture of mediocrity.

On the Genealogy of Morals explores the formation of this modern civilization, and in it two of the images of civilization – the positive transformations of human nature and society – find their most impassioned critique. In response to civilization, Nietzsche argues that culture must only be grounded in a creativity that surpasses morals and even art. In Nietzsche's view, creativity follows its own energy and value – life.

Second Essay

"Guilt," "bad conscience," and related matters

I

To breed an animal with the right to make promises – is not this the paradoxical problem nature has set itself with regard to man? and is it not man's true problem? That the problem has in fact been solved to a remarkable degree will seem all the more surprising if we do full justice to the strong opposing force, the faculty of oblivion. Oblivion is not merely a *vis inertiae*, as is often claimed, but an active screening device, responsible for the fact that what we experience and digest psychologically does not, in the stage of digestion, emerge into consciousness any more than what we ingest physically does. The role of this active oblivion is that of a concierge: to shut temporarily the doors and windows of consciousness; to protect us from the noise and agitation with which our lower organs work for or against one another; to introduce a little quiet into our consciousness so as to make room for the nobler functions and functionaries of our organism which do the governing and planning. This concierge maintains order and etiquette in the household of the psyche; which immediately suggests that there can be no happiness, no serenity, no hope, no pride, no *present*, without oblivion. A man in whom this screen is damaged and inoperative is like a dyspeptic (and not merely *like* one): he can't be done with anything. . . . Now this naturally forgetful animal, for whom oblivion represents a power, a form of strong health, has created for itself an opposite power, that of remembering, by whose aid, in certain cases, oblivion may he suspended – specifically in cases where it is a question of promises. By this I do not mean a purely passive succumbing to past impressions, the indigestion of being unable to be done with a pledge once made, but rather an active not wishing to be done with it, a continuing to will what has once been willed, a veritable "memory of the will"; so that, between the original determination and the actual performance of the thing willed, a whole world of new things, conditions, even volitional acts, can he interposed without snapping the long chain of the will. But how much all this presupposes! A man who wishes to dispose of his future in this manner must first have learned to separate necessary from accidental acts; to think causally; to see distant things as though they were near at hand; to distinguish means from ends. In short, he must have become not only calculating but himself calculable, regular even to his own perception, if he is to stand pledge for his own future as a guarantor does.

II

This brings us to the long story of the origin or genesis of responsibility. The task of breeding an animal entitled to make promises involves, as we have already seen, the preparatory task of rendering man up to a certain point regular, uniform, equal among equals, calculable. The tremendous achievement which I have referred to in *Daybreak* as "the custom character of morals," that labor man accomplished upon himself over a vast period of time, receives its meaning and justification here – even despite the brutality, tyranny, and stupidity associated with the process. With the help of custom and the social strait-jacket, man was, in fact, made calculable. However, if we place ourselves at the terminal point of this great process, where society and custom finally reveal their true aim, we shall find the ripest fruit of that tree to be the sovereign individual, equal only to himself, all moral custom left far behind. This autonomous, more than moral individual (the terms *autonomous* and *moral* are mutually exclusive) has developed his own, independent, long-range will, which dares to make promises; he has a proud and vigorous consciousness of what he has achieved, a sense of power and freedom, of absolute accomplishment. This fully emancipated man, master of his will, who dares make promises – how should he not be aware of his superiority over those who are unable to stand security for themselves? Think how much trust, fear, reverence he inspires (all three fully *deserved*), and how, having that sovereign rule over himself, he has mastery too over all weaker-willed and less reliable creatures! Being truly free and possessor of a long-range, pertinacious will, he also possesses a scale of values. Viewing others from the center of his own being, he either honors or disdains them. It is natural to him to honor his strong and reliable peers, all those who promise like sovereigns: rarely and reluctantly; who are chary of their trust; whose trust is a mark of distinction; whose promises are binding because they know that they will make them good in spite of all accidents, in spite of destiny itself. Yet he will inevitably reserve a kick for those paltry windbags who promise irresponsibly and a rod for those liars who break their word even in uttering it. His proud awareness of the extraordinary privilege responsibility confers has penetrated deeply and become a dominant instinct. What shall he call that dominant instinct, provided he ever feels impelled to give it a name? Surely he will call it his *conscience*.

III

His conscience? It seems a foregone conclusion that this conscience, which we encounter here in its highest form, has behind it a long history of transformations. The right proudly to stand security for oneself, to approve oneself, is a ripe but also a late fruit; how long did that fruit have to hang green and tart on the tree! Over an even longer period there was not the slightest sign of such a fruit; no one had a right to predict it, although the tree was ready for it, organized in every part to the end of bringing it forth. "How does one create a memory for the human animal? How does one go about to impress anything on that partly dull, partly flighty human intelligence – that incarnation of forgetfulness – so as to make it stick?" As we might well imagine, the means used in solving this age-old problem have been far from delicate: in fact, there is perhaps nothing more terrible in man's earliest history than his mnemotechnics. "A thing is branded on the memory to make it stay there; only what goes on hurting will stick" – this is one of the oldest and, unfortunately, one of the most enduring psychological axioms. In fact, one might say that wherever on earth one still finds solemnity, gravity, secrecy, somber hues in the life of an individual or a nation, one also senses a residuum of that terror with which men must formerly have promised, pledged, vouched. It is the past – the longest, deepest, hardest of pasts – that seems to surge up whenever we turn serious. Whenever man has thought it necessary to create a memory for himself, his effort has been attended with torture, blood, sacrifice. The ghastliest sacrifices and pledges, including the sacrifice of the first-born; the most repulsive mutilations, such as castration; the cruelest rituals in every religious cult (and all religions are at bottom systems of cruelty) – all these have their origin in that instinct which divined pain to be the strongest aid to mnemonics. (All asceticism is really part of the same development: here too the object is to make a few ideas omnipresent, unforgettable, "fixed," to the end of hypnotizing the entire nervous and intellectual system; the ascetic procedures help to effect the dissociation of those ideas from all others.) The poorer the memory of mankind has been, the more terrible have been its customs. The severity of all primitive penal codes gives us some idea how difficult it must have been for man to overcome his forgetfulness and to drum into these slaves of momentary whims and desires a few basic requirements of communal living. Nobody can say that we Germans consider ourselves an especially cruel and brutal nation, much less a frivolous and thriftless one; but it needs only a glance at our ancient penal codes to impress on us what labor it takes to create a nation of thinkers. (I would even say that we are the one European nation among whom is still to be found a maximum of trust, seriousness, insipidity, and matter-of-factness, which should entitle us to breed a mandarin caste for all of Europe.) Germans have resorted to ghastly means in order to triumph over their plebeian instincts and brutal coarseness. We need only recount some of our ancient forms of punishment: stoning (even in earliest legend millstones are dropped on the heads of culprits); breaking on the wheel (Germany's own contribution to the techniques of punishment); piercing with stakes, drawing and quartering, trampling to death with horses, boiling in oil or wine (these were still in use in the fourteenth and fifteenth centuries), the popular flaying alive, cutting out of flesh from the chest, smearing the victim with honey and leaving him in the sun, a prey to flies. By such methods the individual was finally taught to remember five or six "I won'ts" which entitled him to participate in the benefits of society; and indeed, with the aid of this sort of memory, people eventually "came to their senses." What an enormous price man had to pay for reason, seriousness, control over his emotions – those grand human prerogatives and cultural showpieces! How much blood and horror lies behind all "good things"!

IV

But how about the origin of that other somber phenomenon, the consciousness of guilt, "bad conscience"? Would you turn to our genealogists of morals for illumination? Let me say once again, they are worthless. Completely absorbed in "modern" experience, with no real knowledge of the past, no desire even to understand it, no historical instinct whatever, they presume, all the same, to write the history of ethics! Such an undertaking must produce results which bear not the slightest relation to truth. Have these historians shown any awareness of the fact that the basic moral term *Schuld* (guilt) has its origin in the very material term *Schulden* (to be indebted)? Of the fact that punishment, being a *compensation*, has developed quite independently of any ideas about freedom of the will – indeed, that a very high level of humanization was necessary before even the much more primitive distinctions, "with intent," "through negligence," "by accident," *compos mentis*, and their opposites could be made and allowed to weigh in the judgments of cases? The pat and seemingly natural notion (so natural that it has often been used to account for the origin of the notion of justice itself) that the criminal deserves to be punished *because* he could have acted otherwise, is in fact a very late and refined form of human reasoning; whoever thinks it can be found in archaic law grossly misconstrues the psychology of uncivilized man. For an unconscionably long time culprits were not punished because they were felt to be responsible for their actions; not, that is, on the assumption that only the guilty were to be punished; rather, they were punished the way parents still punish their children, out of rage at some damage suffered, which the doer must pay for. Yet this rage was both moderated and modified by the notion that for every damage there could somehow be found an equivalent, by which that damage might be compensated – if necessary in the pain of the doer. To the question how did that ancient, deep-rooted, still firmly established notion of an equivalency between damage and pain arise, the answer is, briefly: it arose in the contractual relation between creditor and debtor, which is as old as the notion of "legal subjects" itself and which in its turn points back to the basic practices of purchase, sale, barter, and trade.

V

As we contemplate these contractual relationships we may readily feel both suspicion and repugnance toward the older civilizations which either created or permitted them. Since it was here that promises were made, since it was here that a memory had to be fashioned for the promiser, we must not be surprised to encounter every evidence of brutality, cruelty, pain. In order to inspire the creditor with confidence in his promise to repay, to give a guarantee for the stringency of his promise, but also to enjoin on his own conscience the duty of repayment, the debtor pledged by contract that in case of non-payment he would offer another of his possessions, such as his body, or his wife, or his freedom, or even his life (or, in certain theologically oriented cultures, even his salvation or the sanctity of his tomb; as in Egypt, where the debtor's corpse was not immune from his creditor even in the grave). The creditor, moreover, had the right to inflict all manner of indignity and pain on the body of the debtor. For example, he could cut out an amount of flesh proportionate to the amount of the debt, and we find, very early, quite detailed legal assessments of the value of individual parts of the body. I consider it already a progress, proof of a freer, more generous, more *Roman* conception of law, when the Twelve Tables decreed that it made no difference how much or little, in such a case, the creditor cut out – *si plus minusve secuerunt, ne fraude esto*. Let us try to understand the logic of this entire method of compensations; it is strange enough. An equivalence is provided by the creditor's receiving, in place of material compensation such as money, land, or other possessions, a kind of *pleasure*. That pleasure is induced by his being able to exercise his power freely upon one who is powerless, by the pleasure of *faire le mal pour le plaisir de le faire*, the pleasure of rape. That pleasure will be increased in proportion to the lowliness of the creditor's own station; it will appear to him as a delicious morsel, a foretaste of a higher rank. In "punishing" the debtor, the creditor shares a seignorial right. For once he is given a chance to bask in the glorious feeling of treating another human being as lower than himself – or, in case the actual punitive power has passed on to a legal "authority," of seeing him despised and mistreated. Thus compensation consists in a legal warrant entitling one man to exercise his cruelty on another.

VI

It is in the sphere of contracts and legal obligations that the moral universe of guilt, conscience, and duty, ("sacred" duty) took its inception. Those beginnings were liberally sprinkled with blood, as are the beginnings of everything great on earth. (And may we not say that ethics has never lost its reek of blood and torture – not even in Kant, whose categorical imperative smacks of cruelty?) It was then that the sinister knitting together of the two ideas *guilt* and *pain* first occurred, which by now have become quite inextricable. Let us ask once more: in what sense could pain constitute repayment of a debt? In the sense that to make someone suffer was a supreme pleasure. In exchange for the damage he had incurred, including his displeasure, the creditor received an extraordinary amount of pleasure; something which he prized the more highly the more it disaccorded with his social rank. I am merely throwing this out as a suggestion, for it is difficult, and embarrassing as well, to get to the bottom of such underground developments. To introduce crudely the concept of vengeance at this point would obscure matters rather than clarify them, since the idea of vengeance leads us straight back to our original problem: how can the infliction of pain provide satisfaction? The delicacy – even more, the *tartufferie* – of domestic animals like ourselves shrinks from imagining clearly to what extent cruelty constituted the collective delight of older mankind, how much it was an ingredient of all their joys, or how naïvely they manifested their cruelty, how they considered disinterested malevolence (Spinoza's *sympathia malevolens*) a normal trait, something to which one's conscience could assent heartily. Close observation will spot numerous survivals of this oldest and most thorough human delight in our own culture. In both *Daybreak* and *Beyond Good and Evil* I have pointed to that progressive sublimation and apotheosis of cruelty which not only characterizes the whole history of higher culture, but in a sense constitutes it. Not so very long ago, a royal wedding or great public celebration would have been incomplete without executions, tortures, or *autos da fé*; a noble household without some person whose office it was to serve as a butt for everyone's malice and cruel teasing. (Perhaps the reader will recall Don Quixote's sojourn at the court of the Duchess. *Don Quixote* leaves a bitter taste in our mouths today; we almost quail in reading it. This would have seemed very strange to Cervantes and to his contemporaries, who read the work with the dearest conscience in the world, thought it the funniest of books, and almost died laughing over it.) To behold suffering gives pleasure, but to cause another to suffer affords an even greater pleasure. This severe statement expresses an old, powerful, human, all too human sentiment – though the monkeys too might endorse it, for it is reported that they heralded and preluded man in the devising of bizarre cruelties. There is no feast without cruelty, as man's entire history attests. Punishment, too, has its festive features.

VII

These ideas, by the way, are not intended to add grist to the pessimist's mill of *taedium vitae*. On the contrary, it should be clearly understood that in the days when people were unashamed of their cruelty life was a great deal more enjoyable than it is now in the heyday of pessimism. The sky overhead has always grown darker in proportion as man has grown ashamed of his fellows. The tired, pessimistic look, discouragement in face of life's riddle, the icy *no* of the man who loathes life are none of them characteristic of mankind's evilest eras. These phenomena are like marsh plants; they presuppose a bog – the bog of morbid finickiness and moralistic drivel which has alienated man from his natural instincts. On his way to becoming an "angel" man has acquired that chronic indigestion and coated tongue which makes not only the naïve joy and innocence of the animal distasteful to him, but even life itself; so that at times he stops his nose against himself and recites with Pope Innocent III the catalogue of his unsavorinesses ("impure conception, loathsome feeding in the mother's womb, wretchedness of physical substance, vile stench, discharge of spittle, urine, and faeces"). Nowadays, when suffering is invariably quoted as the chief argument against existence, it might be well to recall the days when matters were judged from the opposite point of view; when people would not have missed for anything the pleasure of inflicting suffering, in which they saw a powerful agent, the principal inducement to living. By way of comfort to the milksops, I would also venture the suggestion that in those days pain did not hurt as much as it does today; at all events, such is the opinion of a doctor who has treated Negroes for complicated internal inflammations which would have driven the most stoical European to distraction – the assumption here being that the negro represents an earlier phase of human development. (It appears, in fact, that the curve of human susceptibility to pain drops abruptly the moment we go below the top layer of culture comprising ten thousand or ten million individuals. For my part, I am convinced that, compared with one night's pain endured by a hysterical bluestocking, all the suffering of all the animals that have been used to date for scientific experiments is as nothing.) Perhaps it is even legitimate to allow the possibility that pleasure in cruelty is not really extinct today; only, given our greater delicacy, that pleasure has had to undergo a certain sublimation and subtilization, to be translated into imaginative and psychological terms in order to pass muster before even the tenderest hypocritical conscience. ("Tragic empathy" is one such term; another is *les nostalgies de la croix*.) What makes people rebel against suffering is not really suffering itself but the senselessness of suffering; and yet neither the Christian, who projected a whole secret machinery of salvation into suffering, nor the naïve primitive, who interpreted all suffering from the standpoint of the spectator or the dispenser of suffering, would have conceived of it as senseless. In order to negate and dispose of the possibility of any secret, unwitnessed suffering, early man had to invent gods and a whole apparatus of intermediate spirits, invisible beings who could also see in the dark, and who would not readily let pass unseen any interesting spectacle of suffering. Such were the inventions with which life, in those days, performed its perennial trick of justifying itself, its "evil"; nowadays a different set of inventions would be needed, e.g., life as a riddle or an epistemological problem. According to the primitive logic of feeling (but is our own so very different?) any evil was justified whose spectacle proved edifying to the gods. We need only study Calvin and Luther to realize how far the ancient conception of the gods as frequenters of cruel spectacles has penetrated into our European humanism. But one thing is certain: the Greeks could offer their gods no more pleasant condiment than the joys of cruelty. With what eyes did Homer's gods regard the destinies of men? What, in the last analysis, was the meaning of the Trojan War and similar tragic atrocities? There can be no doubt that they were intended as festivals for the gods, and, insofar as poets in this respect are more "divine" than other men, as festivals for the poets. In much the same manner the moral philosophers of Greece, at a later date, let the eyes of God dwell on the moral struggles, the heroism, and the self-mortification of the virtuous man. The "Heracles" of stern virtue was on stage and was fully aware of it; to that nation of actors, unwitnessed virtue was inconceivable. Might not the audacious invention, by philosophers of that era, of man's free will, his absolute spontaneity in the doing of good or ill, have been made for the express purpose of insuring that the interest of the gods in the spectacle of human virtue could never be exhausted? This earthly stage must never be bare of truly novel, truly unprecedented suspense, complications, catastrophes. A truly deterministic world, whose movements the gods might readily foresee, must soon pall on them: reason enough why those friends of the gods, the philosophers, would not foist such a world on them. Ancient humanity, an essentially public and visual world, unable to conceive of happiness without spectacles and feasts, was full of tender regard for the "spectator." And, as we have said before, punishment too has its festive features.

VIII

We have observed that the feeling of guilt and personal obligation had its inception in the oldest and most primitive relationship between human beings, that of buyer and seller, creditor and debtor. Here, for the first time, individual stood and measured himself against individual. No phase of civilization, no matter how primitive, has been discovered in which that relation did not to some extent exist. The mind of early man was preoccupied to such an extent with price making, assessment of values, the devising and exchange of equivalents, that, in a certain sense, this may be said to have constituted his thinking. Here we find the oldest variety of human acuteness, as well as the first indication of human pride, of a superiority over other animals. Perhaps our word *man* (*manas*) still expresses something of that pride: man saw himself as the being that measures values, the "assaying" animal. Purchase and sale, together with their psychological trappings, antedate even the rudiments of social organization and covenants. From its rudimentary manifestation in interpersonal law, the incipient sense of barter, contract, guilt, right, obligation, compensation was projected into the crudest communal complexes (and their relations to other such complexes) together with the habit of measuring power against power. The eye had been entirely conditioned to that mode of vision; and with the awkward consistency of primitive thought, which moves with difficulty but, when it does move, moves inexorably in one direction, early mankind soon reached the grand generalization that everything has its price, everything can be paid for. Here we have the oldest and naïvest moral canon of justice, of all "fair play," "good will," and "objectivity." Justice, at this level, is good will operating among men of roughly equal power, their readiness to come to terms with one another, to strike a compromise – or, in the case of others less powerful, to *force* them to accept such a compromise.

IX

Keeping within the primeval frame of reference (which, after all, is not so very different from our own) we may say that the commonwealth stood to its members in the relation of creditor to debtor. People lived in a commonwealth, enjoying its privileges (which we are, perhaps, inclined to underestimate). They lived sheltered, protected, in peace and confidence, immune from injuries and hostilities to which the man "outside" was continually exposed, since they had pledged themselves to the community in respect of such injury and hostility. But supposing that pledge is violated? The disappointed creditor – the community – will get his money back as best he can, you may be sure. It is not so much a question of the actual damage done; primarily, the offender has broken his contract, his pledge to the group, thus forfeiting all the benefits and amenities of the community which he has hitherto enjoyed. The criminal is a debtor who not only refuses to repay the advantages and advances he has received but who even dares lay hands on his creditor. Hence he is not only stripped of his advantages, as is only just, but drastically reminded what these advantages were worth. The rage of the defrauded creditor, the community, returns him to the wild and outlawed condition from which heretofore he had been protected. It rejects him, and henceforth every kind of hostility may vent itself on him. Punishment, at this level of morality, simply mimics the normal attitude toward a hated enemy who has been conquered and disarmed, who forfeits not only every right and protection but all mercy as well. The offender is treated according to the laws of war and victory celebrations, brutally, without consideration; which may explain why war, including the martial custom of ritual sacrifice, has provided all the modes under which punishment appears in history.

X

As the commonwealth grew stronger, it no longer took the infractions of the individual quite so seriously. The individual no longer represented so grave a danger to the group as a whole. The offender was no longer outlawed and exposed to general fury. Rather, he was carefully shielded by the community against popular indignation, and especially against the indignation of the one he had injured. The attempt to moderate the rage of the offended party; to obviate a general disturbance by localizing the case; to find equivalents, "arrange things," (the Roman *compositio*); but most of all the attempt, ever more determined, to fix a price for every offense, and thus to dissociate, up to a certain point, the offender from his offense – these are the traits which characterize with increasing clarity the development of penal law. Whenever a community gains in power and pride, its penal code becomes more lenient, while the moment it is weakened or endangered the harsher methods of the past are revived. The humanity of creditors has always increased with their wealth; until finally the degree to which a creditor can tolerate impairment becomes the measure of his wealth. It is possible to imagine a society flushed with such a sense of power that it could afford to let its offenders go unpunished. What greater luxury is there for a society to indulge in? "Why should I bother about these parasites of mine?" such a society might ask. "Let them take all they want. I have plenty." Justice, which began by setting a price on everything and making everyone strictly accountable, ends by blinking at the defaulter and letting him go scot free. Like every good thing on earth, justice ends by suspending itself. The fine name this self-canceling justice has given itself is *mercy*. But mercy remains, as goes without saying, the prerogative of the strongest, his province beyond the law.

XI

A word should be said here against certain recent attempts to trace the notion of justice to a different source, namely rancor. But first of all, let me whisper something in the ear of psychologists, on the chance that they might want to study rancor at close range: that flower now blooms most profusely among anarchists and anti-Semites – unseen, like the violet, though with a different odor. And as the like spirit begets the like result, we must not be surprised if we see these recent attempts hark back to certain shady efforts, discussed earlier, to dignify vengeance by the name of justice (as though justice were simply an outgrowth of the sense of injury) and to honor the whole gamut of *reactive* emotions. I am the last person to object to the latter notion: in view of the long neglected relationship between our biological needs and our emotional reactions, it is a consideration of the utmost importance. Yet I want to draw attention to the fact that precisely out of the spirit of rancor has this new nuance of scientific "equity" sprung to the service of hatred, envy, malevolence, and distrust. For "scientific equity" ceases immediately, giving way to accents of mortal enmity and the crassest bias, the moment another group of emotions comes into play whose biological value seems to me even greater and for that reason even more deserving of scientific appraisal and esteem. I am speaking of the truly *active* emotions, such as thirst for power, avarice, and the like (*vide* E. Dühring, *The Value of Existence, A Course in Philosophy*, and elsewhere). So much for the general tendency. Against Dühring's specific proposition that the native soil of justice is in the reactive emotions, it must be urged that the exact opposite is the case: the soil of the reactive emotions is the very last to be conquered by the spirit of justice. Should it actually come to pass that the just man remains just even toward his despoiler (and not simply cool, moderate, distant, indifferent: to be just is a positive attitude), and that even under the stress of hurt, contumely, denigration the noble, penetrating yet mild objectivity of the just (the *judging*) eye does not become clouded, then we have before us an instance of the rarest accomplishment, something that, if we are wise, we will neither expect nor be too easily convinced of. It is generally true of even the most decent people that a shall dose of insult, malice, insinuation is enough to send the blood to their eyes and equity out the window. The active man, the attacker and overreacher, is still a hundred steps closer to justice than the reactive one, and the reason is that he has no need to appraise his object falsely and prejudicially as the other must. It is an historical fact that the aggressive man, being stronger, bolder, and nobler, has at all times had the better view, the clearer conscience on his side. Conversely, one can readily guess who has the invention of "bad conscience" on his conscience: the vindictive man. Simply glance through history: in what sphere, thus far, has all legislation and, indeed, all true desire for laws, developed? In the sphere of "reactive" man? Not at all. Exclusively in the sphere of the active, strong, spontaneous, and aggressive. Historically speaking, all law – be it said to the dismay of that agitator (Dühring) who once confessed: "The doctrine of vengeance is the red thread that runs through my entire investigation of justice" – is a battle waged against the reactive emotions by the active and aggressive, who have employed part of their strength to curb the excesses of reactive pathos and bring about a compromise. Wherever justice is practiced and maintained, we see a stronger power intent on finding means to regulate the senseless raging of rancor among its weaker subordinates. This is accomplished by wresting the object of rancor from vengeful hands, or by substituting for vengeance the struggle against the enemies of peace and order, or by devising, proposing, and if necessary *enforcing* compromises, or by setting up a normative scale of equivalents for damages to which all future complaints may be referred. But above all, by the establishment of a code of laws which the superior power imposes upon the forces of hostility and resentment whenever it is strong enough to do so; by a categorical declaration of what it considers to be legitimate and right, or else forbidden and wrong. Once such a body of law has been established, all acts of highhandedness on the part of individuals or groups are seen as infractions of the law, as rebellion against the supreme power. Thus the rulers deflect the attention of their subjects from the particular injury and, in the long run, achieve the opposite end from that sought by vengeance, which tries to make the viewpoint of the injured person prevail exclusively. Henceforth the eye is trained to view the deed ever more impersonally – even the eye of the offended person, though this, as we have said, is the last to be affected. It follows that only after a corpus of laws has been established can there be any talk of "right" and "wrong" (and not, as Dühring maintains, after the act of injury). To speak of right and wrong *per se* makes no sense at all. No act of violence, rape, exploitation, destruction, is intrinsically "unjust," since life itself is violent, rapacious, exploitative, and destructive and cannot be conceived otherwise. Even more disturbingly, we have to admit that from the biological point of view legal conditions are necessarily exceptional conditions, since they limit the radical life-will bent on power and must finally subserve, as means, life's collective purpose, which is to create greater power constellations. To accept any legal system as sovereign and universal – to accept it, not merely as an instrument in the struggle of power complexes, but as a *weapon against struggle* (in the sense of Dühring's communist cliché that every will must regard every other will as its equal) – is an anti-vital principle which can only bring about man's utter demoralization and, indirectly, a reign of nothingness.

XII

One word should be added here about the *origin* and the *purpose* of punishment, two considerations radically distinct and yet too frequently confounded. How have our genealogists of morals treated these questions? Naïvely, as always. They would discover some kind of "purpose" in punishment, such as to avenge, or to deter, and would then naïvely place this purpose at the origin of punishment as its *causa fiendi*. And this is all. Yet the criterion of purpose is the last that should ever be applied to a study of legal evolution. There is no set of maxims more important for an historian than this: that the actual causes of a thing's origin and its eventual uses, the manner of its incorporation into a system of purposes, are worlds apart; that everything that exists, no matter what its origin, is periodically reinterpreted by those in power in terms of fresh intentions; that all processes in the organic world are processes of outstripping and overcoming, and that, in turn, all outstripping and overcoming means reinterpretation, rearrangement, in the course of which the earlier meaning and purpose are necessarily either obscured or lost. No matter how well we understand the utility of a certain physiological organ (or of a legal institution, a custom, a political convention, an artistic genre, a cultic trait) we do not thereby understand anything of its origin. I realize that this truth must distress the traditionalist, for, from time immemorial, the demonstrable purpose of a thing has been considered its *causa fiendi* – the eye is made for seeing, the hand for grasping. So likewise, punishment has been viewed as an invention for the purpose of punishing. But all pragmatic purposes are simply symbols of the fact that a will to power has implanted its own sense of function in those less powerful. Thus the whole history of a thing, an organ, a custom, becomes a continuous *chain* of reinterpretations and rearrangements, which need not be causally connected among themselves, which may simply follow one another. The "evolution" of a thing, a custom, an organ is not its *progressus* towards a goal, let alone the most logical and shortest *progressus*, requiring the least energy and expenditure. Rather, it is a sequence of more or less profound, more or less independent processes of appropriation, including the resistances used in each instance, the attempted transformations for purposes of defense or reaction, as well as the results of successful counterattacks. While forms are fluid, their "meaning" is even more so. The same process takes place in every individual organism. As the whole organism develops in essential ways, the meaning of the individual organs too is altered. In some cases their partial atrophy or numerical diminution spells the increased strength and perfection of the whole. This amounts to saying that partial desuetude, atrophy and degeneration, the loss of meaning and purpose – in short, death – must be numbered among the conditions of any true *progressus*, which latter appears always in the form of the will and means to greater power and is achieved at the expense of numerous lesser powers. The scope of any "progress" is measured by all that must be sacrificed for its sake. To sacrifice humanity as mass to the welfare of a single stronger human species would indeed constitute progress. . . .

I have emphasized this point of historical method all the more strongly because it runs counter to our current instincts and fashions, which would rather come to terms with the absolute haphazardness or the mechanistic meaninglessness of event than with the theory of a will to power mirrored in all process. The democratic bias against anything that dominates or wishes to dominate, our modern *misarchism* (to coin a bad word for a bad thing) has gradually so sublimated and disguised itself that nowadays it can invade the strictest, most objective sciences without anyone's raising a word of protest. In fact it seems to me that this prejudice now dominates all of physiology and the other life sciences, to their detriment, naturally, since it has conjured away one of their most fundamental concepts, that of *activity*, and put in its place the concept of *adaptation* – a kind of second-rate activity, mere reactivity. Quite in keeping with that bias, Herbert Spencer has defined life itself as an ever more purposeful inner adaptation to external circumstances. But such a view misjudges the very essence of life; it overlooks the intrinsic superiority of the spontaneous, aggressive, over-reaching, reinterpreting and re-establishing forces, on whose action adaptation gradually supervenes. It denies, even in the organism itself, the dominant role of the higher functions in which the vital will appears active and shaping. The reader will recall that Huxley strongly objected to Spencer's "administrative nihilism." But here it is a question of much more than simply "administration."

XIII

To return to the issue of punishment, we must distinguish in it two separate aspects: first its relatively permanent features: custom, the act, the *drama*, a certain strict sequence of procedures; and second, all that is fluid in it: its meaning, its purpose, the expectations attending on the execution of such procedures. In keeping with the views I have stated earlier, I presuppose here that the procedure itself antedates its use for purposes of punishment and that the latter has only been projected into the procedure, which had existed all along, though in a different framework. In short, I absolutely part company with the naïve view which would see the procedure as having been invented for punitive purposes, as earlier the hand for prehensile purposes. Concerning that other, fluid, "meaning" aspect of punishment, I would say that in a very late culture such as our present-day European culture the notion "punishment" has not one but a great many meanings. The whole history of punishment and of its adaptation to the most various uses has finally crystallized into a kind of complex which it is difficult to break down and quite impossible to define. (It is impossible to say with certainty today *why* people are punished. All terms which semiotically condense a whole process elude definition; only that which has no history can be defined.) However, at an earlier stage that synthesis of "meanings" must have been more easily soluble, its components more easily disassociated. We can still see how, from one situation to the next, the elements of the synthesis changed their valence and reorganized themselves in such a way that now this element, now that, predominated at the expense of the others. It might even happen that in certain situations a single element (the purpose of *deterring*, for example) absorbed the rest. To give the reader some idea how uncertain, secondary, and accidental the "meaning" of punishment really is, and how one and the same procedure may be used for totally different ends, I shall furnish him with a schema abstracted from the relatively small and random body of material at my disposal.

1 Punishment administered with the view of rendering the offender harmless and preventing his doing further damage.
2 Punishment consisting of the payment of damages to the injured party, including affect compensation.
3 Punishment as the isolation of a disequilibrating agent, in order to keep the disturbance from spreading further.
4 Punishment as a means of inspiring fear of those who determine and execute it.
5 Punishment as cancellation of the advantages the culprit has hitherto enjoyed (as when he is put to work in the mines).
6 Punishment as the elimination of a degenerate element (or, as in Chinese law, a whole stock; a means of keeping the race pure, or of maintaining a social type).
7 Punishment as a "triumph," the violating and deriding of an enemy finally subdued.
8 Punishment as a means of creating memory, either for the one who suffers it – so-called "improvement" – or for the witnesses.
9 Punishment as the payment of a fee, exacted by the authority which protects the evil-doer from the excesses of vengeance.
10 Punishment as a compromise with the tradition of vendetta, to the extent that this is still maintained and invoked as a privilege by powerful clans.
11 Punishment as a declaration of war, a warlike measure, against an enemy of peace, order and authority.

XIV

However incomplete, this list will serve to show that punishment is rife with utilitarian purposes of every kind. All the more reason why we should delete from it a fictitious usefulness which looms very large in popular thought these days, and which reckless writers are using freely to buttress our tottering belief in punishment. Punishment, these men claim, is valuable because it awakens a sense of guilt in the culprit; we should therefore view it as the true instrument of the psychological reaction called "remorse," "pangs of conscience." But this is a blunder, even as far as modern man and his psychology are concerned; applied to early man the notion becomes wholly absurd. True remorse is rarest among criminals and convicts: prisons and penitentiaries are not the breeding places of this gnawer. All conscientious observers are agreed here, though the fact may disappoint their innermost hopes and wishes. By and large, punishment hardens and freezes; it concentrates; it sharpens the sense of alienation; it strengthens resistance. If it should happen that now and again it breaks the will and brings about a miserable prostration and self-abasement, we find that psychological effect even less gratifying than the one which is most common, i.e., a dry, self-absorbed gloom. But if we stop to consider the millennia of prehistory, we may say with some assurance that it is precisely punishment that has most effectively retarded the development of guilt feeling, at any rate in the hearts of the victims of punitive authority. For we must not underestimate the extent to which the criminal is prevented, by the very witnessing of the legal process, from regarding his deed as intrinsically evil. He sees the very same actions performed in the service of justice with perfectly clear conscience and general approbation: spying, setting traps, outsmarting, bribing, the whole tricky, cunning system which chiefs of police, prosecutors, and informers have developed among themselves; not to mention the cold-blooded legal practices of despoiling, insulting, torturing, murdering the victim. Obviously none of these practices is rejected and condemned *per se* by his judges, but only under certain conditions. "Bad conscience," that most uncanny and interesting plant of our vegetation, has definitely not sprung from this soil, indeed for a very long time the notion that he was punishing a "culprit" never entered a judge's mind. He thought he had to do with a mischief-maker, an unaccountable piece of misfortune. And in his turn the man whose lot it was to be punished considered his punishment a misfortune. He no more felt a moral pang than if some terrible unforeseen disaster had occurred, if a rock had fallen and crushed him.

XV

Spinoza once, with some embarrassment, perceived this fact (to the annoyance of some of his commentators, like Kuno Fischer, who have gone out of their way to misconstrue his meaning). Teased one afternoon by heaven knows what memory, he was pondering the question of what really remained to him of that famous *morsus conscientiae*. Had he not relegated both good and evil to the realm of figments and grimly defended the honor of his "free" God against those blasphemers who would have God invariably act *sub ratione boni* ("But this would mean subordinating God to fate, and result in the worst absurdity")? The world for Spinoza had returned to that state of innocence which it had known before the invention of bad conscience – but what, in the process, had become of the sting of conscience? "It is the opposite of joy," he says finally, "a sadness attended by the memory of some past event which disappointed our expectations," (*Ethics* III, Propos. 18, Schol. 1. 2.). In much the same way for thousands of years, all evil-doers overtaken by punishment would think, "Something has unexpectedly gone wrong here," and not, "I should never have done that." They would undergo punishment as one undergoes sickness or misfortune or death, with that stout, unrebellious fatalism which still gives the Russians an advantage over us Westerners in the management of their lives. If actions were "judged" at all in those days, it was solely from the prudential point of view. There can be no doubt that we must look for the real effect of punishment in a sharpening of man's wits, an extension of his memory, a determination to proceed henceforth more prudently, suspiciously, secretly, a realization that the individual is simply too weak to accomplish certain things; in brief, an increase of self-knowledge. What punishment is able to achieve, both for man and beast, is increase of fear, circumspection, control over the instincts. Thus man is *tamed* by punishment, but by no means *improved*; rather the opposite. (It is said that misfortune sharpens our wits, but to the extent that it sharpens our wits it makes us worse; fortunately it often simply dulls them.)

XVI

I can no longer postpone giving tentative expression to my own hypothesis concerning the origin of "bad conscience." It is one that may fall rather strangely on our ears and that requires close meditation. I take bad conscience to be a deep-seated malady to which man succumbed under the pressure of the most profound transformation he ever underwent – the one that made him once and for all a sociable and pacific creature. Just as happened in the case of those sea creatures who were forced to become land animals in order to survive, these semi-animals, happily adapted to the wilderness, to war, free roaming, and adventure, were forced to change their nature. Of a sudden they found all their instincts devalued, unhinged. They must walk on legs and carry themselves, where before the water had carried them: a terrible heaviness weighed upon them. They felt inapt for the simplest manipulations, for in this new, unknown world they could no longer count on the guidance of their unconscious drives. They were forced to think, deduce, calculate, weigh cause and effect – unhappy people, reduced to their weakest, most fallible organ, their consciousness! I doubt that there has ever been on earth such a feeling of misery, such a leaden discomfort. It was not that those old instincts had abruptly ceased making their demands; but now their satisfaction was rare and difficult. For the most part they had to depend on new, covert satisfactions. All instincts that are not allowed free play turn inward. This is what I call man's interiorization; it alone provides the soil for the growth of what is later called man's *soul*. Man's interior world, originally meager and tenuous, was expanding in every dimension, in proportion as the outward discharge of his feelings was curtailed. The formidable bulwarks by means of which the polity protected itself against the ancient instincts of freedom (punishment was one of the strongest of these bulwarks) caused those wild, extravagant instincts to turn in upon man. Hostility, cruelty, the delight in persecution, raids, excitement, destruction all turned against their begetter. Lacking external enemies and resistances, and confined within an oppressive narrowness and regularity, man began rending, persecuting, terrifying himself, like a wild beast hurling itself against the bars of its cage. This languisher, devoured by nostalgia for the desert, who had to turn *himself* into an adventure, a torture chamber, an insecure and dangerous wilderness – this fool, this pining and desperate prisoner, became the inventor of "bad conscience." Also the generator of the greatest and most disastrous of maladies, of which humanity has not to this day been cured: his sickness of himself, brought on by the violent severance from his animal past, by his sudden leap and fall into new layers and conditions of existence, by his declaration of war against the old instincts that had hitherto been the foundation of his power, his joy, and his awesomeness. Let me hasten to add that the phenomenon of an animal soul turning in upon itself, taking arms against itself, was so novel, profound, mysterious, contradictory, and pregnant with possibility, that the whole complexion of the universe was changed thereby. This spectacle (and the end of it is not yet in sight) required a divine audience to do it justice. It was a spectacle too sublime and paradoxical to pass unnoticed on some trivial planet. Henceforth man was to figure among the most unexpected and breathtaking throws in the game of dice played by Heracleitus' great "child," be he called Zeus or Chance. Man now aroused an interest, a suspense, a hope, almost a conviction – as though in him something were heralded, as though he were not a goal but a way, an interlude, a bridge, a great promise. . . .

XVII

My hypothesis concerning the origin of bad conscience presupposes that this change was neither gradual nor voluntary, that it was not an organic growing into new conditions but rather an abrupt break, a leap, a thing compelled, an ineluctable disaster, which could neither be struggled against nor even resented. It further presupposes that the fitting of a hitherto unrestrained and shapeless populace into a tight mold, as it had begun with an act of violence, had to be brought to conclusion by a series of violent acts; that the earliest commonwealth constituted a terrible despotism, a ruthless, oppressive machinery for not only kneading and suppling a brutish populace but actually shaping it. I have used the word "commonwealth," but it should be clearly understood what I mean: a pack of savages, a race of conquerors, themselves organized for war and able to organize others, fiercely dominating a population perhaps vastly superior in numbers yet amorphous and nomadic. Such was the beginning of the human polity; I take it we have got over that sentimentalism that would have it begin with a contract. What do men who can command, who are born rulers, who evince power in act and deportment, have to do with contracts? Such beings are unaccountable; they come like destiny, without rhyme or reason, ruthlessly, bare of pretext. Suddenly they are here, like a stroke of lightning, too terrible, convincing, and "different" for hatred even. Their work is an instinctive imposing of forms. They are the most spontaneous, most unconscious artists that exist. They appear, and presently something entirely new has arisen, a live dominion whose parts and functions are delimited and interrelated, in which there is room for nothing that has not previously received its meaning from the whole. Being natural organizers, these men know nothing of guilt, responsibility, consideration. They are actuated by the terrible egotism of the artist, which is justified by the work he must do, as the mother by the child she will bear. Bad conscience certainly did not originate with these men, yet, on the other hand, that unseemly growth could not have developed *without* them, without their hammer blows, their artist's violence, which drove a great quantity of freedom out of sight and made it latent. In its earliest phase bad conscience is nothing other than the instinct of freedom forced to become latent, driven underground, and forced to vent its energy upon itself.

XVIII

We should guard against taking too dim a view of this phenomenon simply because it is both ugly and painful. After all, the same will to power which in those violent artists and organizers created polities, in the "labyrinth of the heart" – more pettily, to be sure, and in inverse direction – created negative ideals and humanity's bad conscience. Except that now the material upon which this great natural force was employed was man himself, his old animal self – and not, as in that grander and more spectacular phenomenon – his fellow man. This secret violation of the self, this artist's cruelty, this urge to impose on recalcitrant matter a form, a will, a distinction, a feeling of contradiction and contempt, this sinister task of a soul divided against itself, which makes itself suffer for the pleasure of suffering, this most energetic "bad conscience" – has it not given birth to a wealth of strange beauty and affirmation? Has it not given birth to beauty itself? Would beauty exist if ugliness had not first taken cognizance of itself, not said to itself, "I am ugly"? This hint will serve, at any rate, to solve the riddle of why contradictory terms such as *selflessness, self-denial, self-sacrifice* may intimate an ideal, a beauty. Nor will the reader doubt henceforth that the joy felt by the self-denying, self-sacrificing, selfless person was from the very start a *cruel* joy. – So much for the origin of altruism as a moral value. Bad conscience, the desire for self-mortification, is the wellspring of all altruistic values.

XIX

There can be no doubt that bad conscience is a sickness, but so, in a sense, is pregnancy. We shall presently describe the conditions which carried that "sickness" to its highest and most terrible peak. But first let us return for a moment to an earlier consideration. The civil-law relationship of debtor to creditor has been projected into yet another context, where we find it even more difficult to understand today, namely into the relationship between living men and their forebears. Among primitive tribes, each new generation feels toward the preceding ones, and especially toward the original founders of the tribe, a *juridical* obligation (rather than an *emotional* obligation, which seems to be of relatively recent origin). Early societies were convinced that their continuance was guaranteed solely by the sacrifices and achievements of their ancestors and that these sacrifices and achievements required to be paid back. Thus a debt was acknowledged which continued to increase, since the ancestors, surviving as powerful spirits, did not cease to provide the tribe with new benefits out of their store. Gratuitously? But nothing was gratuitous in those crude and "insensitive" times. Then how could they be repaid? By burnt offerings (to provide them with food), by rituals, shrines, customs, but above all, by obedience – for all rites, having been established by the forebears, were also permanently enjoined by them. But could they ever be *fully* repaid? An anxious doubt remained and grew steadily, and every so often there occurred some major act of "redemption," some gigantic repayment of the creditor (the famous sacrifice of the first-born, for example; in any case blood, human blood). Given this primitive logic, the fear of the ancestor and his power and the consciousness of indebtedness increase in direct proportion as the power of the tribe itself increases, as it becomes more successful in battle, independent, respected and feared. Never the other way round. Every step leading to the degeneration of the tribe, every setback, every sign of imminent dissolution, tends to diminish the fear of the ancestral spirits, to make them seem of less account, less wise, less provident, less powerful. Following this kind of logic to its natural term, we arrive at a situation in which the ancestors of the most powerful tribes have become so fearful to the imagination that they have receded at last into a numinous shadow: the ancestor becomes a god. Perhaps this is the way all gods have arisen, out of *fear*. . . . And if anyone should find it necessary to add, "But also out of piety," his claim would scarcely be justified for the longest and earliest period of the human race. But it would certainly hold true for that intermediate period during which the noble clans emerged, of whom it may justly be said that they paid back their ancestors (heroes or gods) with interest all those noble properties which had since come to reside abundantly in themselves. We shall have an opportunity later on of dealing with this "ennoblement" of the ancestral spirits (which is not the same thing as their "consecration"), but first, let us bring to a conclusion the story of man's consciousness of guilt.

XX

Man's firm belief that he was indebted to the gods did not cease with the decline of tribal organization. Just as man has inherited from the blood aristocracies the concepts *good* and *bad*, together with the psychological penchant for hierarchies, so he has inherited from the tribes, together with the tribal gods, a burden of outstanding debt and the desire to make final restitution. (The bridge is provided by those large populations of slaves and serfs, who, either perforce or through servile mimicry, had adopted the cults of their overlords. The heritage spreads out from them in all directions.) The sense of indebtedness to the gods continued to grow through the centuries, keeping pace with the evolution of man's concept of the deity. (The endless tale of ethnic struggle, triumph, reconciliation, and fusion, in short, whatever precedes the final hierarchy of racial strains in some great synthesis, is mirrored in the welter of divine genealogies and legends dealing with divine battles, victories, and reconciliations. Every progress toward universal empire has also been a progress toward a universal pantheon. Despotism, by overcoming the independent nobles, always prepares the way for some form of monotheism.) The advent of the Christian god, the "highest potency" god yet conceived by man, has been accompanied by the widest dissemination of the sense of indebtedness, guilt. If we are right in assuming that we have now entered upon the inverse development, it stands to reason that the steady decline of belief in a Christian god should entail a commensurate decline in man's guilt consciousness. It also stands to reason – doesn't it? – that a complete and definitive victory of atheism might deliver mankind altogether from its feeling of being indebted to its beginnings, its *causa prima*. Atheism and a kind of "second innocence" go together.

XXI

So much, for the moment, about the connection of "guilt" and "duty" with religious presuppositions. I have deliberately left on one side the "moralization" of these terms (their pushing back into conscience, the association of the notion of bad conscience with a deity), and even wrote at the end of the last paragraph as though such a moralization had never taken place; as though with the notion of a divine creditor falling into disuse those notions too were doomed. Unfortunately this is far from being the case. The modern moralization of the ideas of guilt and duty – their relegation to a purely subjective "bad conscience" – represents a determined attempt to invert the normal order of development, or at least to stop it in its tracks. The object now is to close the prospect of final deliverance and make man's gaze rebound from an iron barrier; to force the ideas of guilt and duty to face about and fiercely turn on – whom? Obviously on the "debtor," first of all, who, infested and eaten away by bad conscience, which spreads like a polyp, comes to view his debt as unredeemable by any act of atonement (the notion of "eternal penance"). But eventually the "creditor" too is turned on in the same fashion. Now the curse falls upon man's *causa prima* ("Adam," "original sin," the "bondage of the will"); or upon nature, which gave birth to man and which is now made the repository of the evil principle (nature as the instrument of the devil); or upon universal existence, which now appears as absolute non-value (nihilistic turning away from life, a longing for nothingness or for life's "opposite," for a different sort of "being" – Buddhism, etc.). Then suddenly we come face to face with that paradoxical and ghastly expedient which brought temporary relief to tortured humanity, that most brilliant stroke of Christianity: God's sacrifice of himself for man. God makes himself the ransom for what could not otherwise be ransomed; God alone has power to absolve us of a debt we can no longer discharge; the creditor offers himself as a sacrifice for his debtor out of sheer love (can you believe it?), out of love for his debtor. . . .

XXII

By now the reader will have guessed what has really been happening behind all these façades. Man, with his need for self-torture, his sublimated cruelty resulting from the cooping up of his animal nature within a polity, invented bad conscience in order to hurt himself, after the blocking of the more natural outlet of his cruelty. Then this guilt-ridden man seized upon religion in order to exacerbate his self-torment to the utmost. The thought of being in God's debt became his new instrument of torture. He focused in God the last of the opposites he could find to his true and inveterate animal instincts, making these a sin against God (hostility, rebellion against the "Lord," the "Father," the "Creator"). He stretched himself upon the contradiction "God" and "Devil" as on a rack. He projected all his denials of self, nature, naturalness out of himself as affirmations, as true being, embodiment, reality, as God (the divine Judge and Executioner), as transcendence, as eternity, as endless torture, as hell, as the infinitude of guilt and punishment. In such psychological cruelty we see an insanity of the *will* that is without parallel: man's will to find himself guilty, and unredeemably so; his will to believe that he might be punished to all eternity without ever expunging his guilt: his will to poison the very foundation of things with the problem of guilt and punishment and thus to cut off once and for all his escape from this labyrinth of obsession; his will to erect an ideal (God's holiness) in order to assure himself of his own absolute unworthiness. What a mad, unhappy animal is man! What strange notions occur to him; what perversities, what paroxysms of nonsense, what bestialities of idea burst from him, the moment he is prevented ever so little from being a beast of action! . . . All this is exceedingly curious and interesting, but dyed with such a dark, somber, enervating sadness that one must resolutely tear away one's gaze. Here, no doubt, is sickness, the most terrible sickness that has wasted man thus far. And if one is still able to hear – but how few these days have ears to hear it! – in this night of torment and absurdity the cry *love* ring out, the cry of rapt longing, of redemption in love, he must turn away with a shudder of invincible horror. . . . Man harbors too much horror; the earth has been a lunatic asylum for too long.

XXIII

This should take care, once for all, of the origin of "Our Holy Lord." – A single look at the Greek gods will convince us that a belief in gods need not result in morbid imaginations, that there are nobler ways of creating divine figments – ways which do not lead to the kind of self-crucifixion and self-punishment in which Europe, for millennia now, has excelled. The Hellenic gods reflected a race of noble and proud beings, in whom man's animal self had divine status and hence no need to lacerate and rage against itself. For a very long time the Greeks used their gods precisely to keep bad conscience at a distance, in order to enjoy their inner freedom undisturbed; in other words, they made the opposite use of them that Christianity has made of *its* god. They went very far in that direction, these splendid and lionhearted children, and no less an authority than the Homeric Zeus gives them to understand, now and again, that they make things a little too easy for themselves. "How strange," he says once (the case is that of Aegisthus, a *very* bad case indeed): "How strange that the mortals complain so loudly of us gods! They claim that we are responsible for all their evils. But they are the ones who create their own misery, by their folly, even in the teeth of fate." Yet the reader notices at once that even this Olympian spectator and judge is far from holding a grudge against them or thinking ill of them therefore. "How foolish they are!" he thinks as he watches the misdeeds of mortals; and the Greeks, even during the heyday of their prosperity and strength, allowed that foolishness, lack of discretion, slight mental aberrations might be the source of much evil and disaster. Foolishness, not sin. . . . But even those mental aberrations were a problem. "How can such a thing happen to people like us, nobly bred, happy, virtuous, well educated?" For many centuries noble Greeks would ask themselves this question whenever one of their number had defiled himself by one of those incomprehensible crimes. "Well, he must have been deluded by a god," they would finally say, shaking their heads. This was a typically Greek solution. It was the office of the gods to justify, up to a certain point, the ill ways of man, to serve as "sources" of evil. In those days they were not agents of punishment but, what is nobler, repositories of guilt.

XXIV

It is clear that I am concluding this essay with three unanswered questions. It may occur to some reader to ask me, "Are you constructing an ideal or destroying one?" I would ask him, in turn, whether he ever reflected upon the price that had to be paid for the introduction of every new ideal on earth? On how much of reality, in each instance, had to be slandered and misconceived, how much of falsehood ennobled, how many consciences disturbed, how many gods sacrificed? For the raising of an altar requires the breaking of an altar: this is a law – let anyone who can prove me wrong. We moderns have a millennial heritage of conscience-vivisection and cruelty to the animals in ourselves. This is our most ancient habit, our most consummate artistry perhaps, in any case our greatest refinement, our special fare. Man has looked for so long with an evil eye upon his natural inclinations that they have finally become inseparable from "bad conscience." A converse effort can be imagined, but who has the strength for it? It would consist of associating all the *unnatural* inclinations – the longing for what is unworldly, opposed to the senses, to instinct, to nature, to the animal in us, all the anti-biological and earth-calumniating ideals – with bad conscience. To whom, today, may such hopes and pretensions address themselves? The *good* men, in particular, would be on the other side; and of course all the comfortable, resigned, vain, moony, weary people. Does anything give greater offense and separate one more thoroughly from others than to betray something of the strictness and dignity with which one treats oneself? But how kind and accommodating the world becomes the moment we act like all the rest and let ourselves go! To accomplish that aim, different minds are needed than are likely to appear in this age of ours: minds strengthened by struggles and victories, for whom conquest, adventure, danger, even pain, have become second nature. Minds accustomed to the keen atmosphere of high altitudes, to wintry walks, to ice and mountains in every sense. Minds possessed of a sublime kind of malice, of that self-assured recklessness which is a sign of strong health. What is needed, in short, is just superb health. Is such health still possible today?

But at some future time, a time stronger than our effete, self-doubting present, the true Redeemer will come, whose surging creativity will not let him rest in any shelter or hiding place, whose solitude will be misinterpreted as a flight from reality, whereas it will in fact be a dwelling *on*, a dwelling *in* reality – so that when he comes forth into the light he may bring with him the redemption of that reality from the curse placed upon it by a lapsed ideal. This man of the future, who will deliver us both from a lapsed ideal and from all that this ideal has spawned – violent loathing, the will to extinction, nihilism – this great and decisive stroke of midday, who will make the will free once more and restore to the earth its aim, and to man his hope; this anti-Christ and anti-nihilist, conqueror of both God and Unbeing – *one day he must come.* . . .

XXV

But why go on? I've reached the term of my speech; to continue here would be to usurp the right of one younger, stronger, more pregnant with future than I am – the right of Zarathustra, *impious* Zarathustra. . . .

7

CULTURE'S INEVITABLE LOSS
'On the Concept and Tragedy of Culture' (1911)

Georg Simmel (1858–1918)

Georg Simmel's essay 'On the Concept and Tragedy of Culture' displays many of the issues that preoccupy his major works, especially his *Philosophy of Money*. For him, the products that modern societies produce, and the lives that people lead, are tied to specialization and differentiation, the result of which is social fragmentation. None the less, this fragmentation not only produces the experience of alienation, it also provides the condition for an experience of distance and detachment which can be interpreted as the possibility for further cultural creativity. The two issues of cultural alienation and creativity with which Simmel is preoccupied also concern German intellectuals from Hegel, Schiller and Marx, to Nietzsche, Max Weber and Lukács.

   Simmel's analysis of the concept and tragedy of culture begins from the German 'anthropological' understanding of the term. Culture, in Simmel's view, is the meeting-point and synthesis of subjective and object-ive aspects: the creative subject on the one hand, and the way in which the products of this creativity are externalized and become independent as cultural artefacts on the other. The tragedy all culture confronts – and, for Simmel, modern culture built on the experience of alienation is a specific instance of a more general problem – is a tendency for culture to be reduced to one of its sides only. According to Simmel, a culture which emphasizes the creative, inner world of the artist dislocates him or her from a broader setting and understanding; and cultural products which become anonymous indicate the reduction of cultural creations only to the end-products of specialized techniques and production lines.

Man, unlike the animals does not allow himself simply to be absorbed by the naturally given order of the world. Instead, he tears himself loose from it, places himself in opposition to it, making demands of it, overpowering it, then overpowered by it. From this first great dual-ism springs the never-ending contest between subject and object, which finds its second round within the realm of spirit itself. The spirit engenders innumerable structures which keep on existing with a peculiar autonomy independently of the soul that has created them, as well as of any other that accepts or rejects them. Thus, man sees himself as confronting art as well as law, religion as well as technology, science as well as custom. Now he is attracted, now repelled by their contents, now fused with them as if they were part of himself, now estranged and untouched by them. In the form of stability, coagulation, persistent existence, the spirit becomes object, places itself over against the streaming life, the intrinsic responsibility and the variable tensions of the soul. Spirit, most deeply tied to spirit, for this very reason experiences innumerable tragedies over this radical contrast: between subjective life, which is restless but finite in time, and its contents, which, once they are created, are fixed but timelessly valid.

The concept of culture is lodged in the middle of this dualism. It is based on a situation which in its totality can only be expressed opaquely, through an analogy, as the path of the soul to itself. A soul is never only what it represents at a given moment, it is always "more," a higher and more perfect manifestation of itself, unreal, and yet somehow eternally present. We do not here refer to an ideal mode of being which can be named or fixed at some place within the intellectual world; we mean, rather, the freeing of its self-contained forces of tension, and the development of its innermost core which obeys the intrinsic drive towards form. Just as life – and especially its intensification in consciousness – contains its past history within itself in a more immediate form than does any morsel of the inorganic world. At the same time, this historical element circumscribes its future . . . in a manner which is without analogy in the inorganic realm. The later form of an organism which is capable of growth and procreation is contained in every single phase of organic life. The inner necessity of organic evolution is far profounder than the necessity that a wound-up spring will be released. While everything inorganic contains only the present moment, living matter extends itself in an incomparable way over history and future.

Spiritual movements like *will, duty, hope, the calling* represent psychic expressions of the fundamental destiny of life: to contain its future in its present in a special form which exists only in the life process. Thus the personality as a whole and a unit carries within itself an image, traced as if with invisible lines. This image is its potentiality; to free the image in it would be to attain its full actuality. The ripening and the proving of man's spiritual powers may be accomplished through individual tasks and interests; yet somehow, beneath or above, there stands the demand that through all of these tasks and interests a transcendent promise should be fulfilled, that all individual expressions should appear only as a multitude of ways by which the spiritual life comes to itself. This demand expresses a metaphysical precondition of our practical and emotional existence, however remote it may seem from our real life in the world. It symbolizes a unity which is not simply a formal bond that circumscribes the unfolding of individual powers in an always equal manner, but rather a process of unified development which all individuals go through together. The goal of perfection intrinsically guides the unified development for which all individual capacities and perfections are means.

Here we see the source of the concept of culture, which, however, at this point follows only our linguistic feeling. We are not yet cultivated by having developed this or that individual bit of knowledge or skill; we become cultivated only when all of them serve a psychic unity which depends on but does not coincide with them. Our conscious endeavors aim towards particular interests and potentialities. The development of every human being, when it is examined in terms of identifiable items, appears as a bundle of developmental lines which expand in different directions and quite different lengths. But man does not cultivate himself through their isolated perfections, but only insofar as they help to develop his indefinable personal unity. In other words: Culture is the way that leads from the closed unity through the unfolded multiplicity to the unfolded unity.

This cannot refer only to a development towards something pre-arranged in the germinating forces of personality, sketched out within itself, as a kind of ideal plan. Linguistic usage provides secure guidance here. We will call a garden fruit cultivated which was perfected through the work of a gardener from an inedible tree fruit. Alternately, we might say that this wild tree has been cultivated into a garden fruit tree. But if we were to manufacture a sail mast from the very same tree, even though equally purposive work might be expended upon it, we would not say that the tree had been cultivated into a mast. This nuance of linguistic usage points out that, although the fruit could not have developed from the indigenous powers of the tree without human effort, it only fulfilled the potentialities which were already sketched out in its constitution. This contrasts with the form of the mast, which is superimposed upon the trunk of the tree by a completely alien system of purpose and without any predisposition of its own. It is in this sense that we will not credit a man with genuine culture on the basis of knowledge, virtuosity, or refinements which only act as additives which come to his personality from an external realm of value. In such a case, then, man is the possessor of traits of culture, but he is not cultivated. A man becomes cultivated only when cultural traits develop that aspect of his soul which exists as its most indigenous drive and as the inner predetermination of its subjective perfection.

In this context the conditions finally emerge through which culture resolves the subject–object dualism. We deny the applicability of the concept in the absence of self-development of a psychic center. Nor does the concept apply when this self-development does not depend upon objective and extrinsic means and stations. A multitude of movements can lead the soul to itself. But whereas the soul readies this precept purely from within – in religious ecstasies, moral self-devotion, dominating intellectuality, and harmony of total life – it can still lack the specific property of being cultivated. Not only because it may be lacking that external perfection which in ordinary language is depreciated as mere "civilization." This wouldn't matter at all. The state of being cultivated, however, is not given its purest and deepest meaning when the soul transverses the path from itself to itself, from its potentiality to its realization, exclusively on the strength of its subjective powers. Admittedly, when viewed from the highest perspective these processes of perfection are perhaps the most valuable. But this only proves that culture is not the only value for the soul. Its specific meaning, however, is fulfilled only when man includes in this development something which is extrinsic to him, when the path of the soul leads over values which are not themselves of psychic quality. There are objective spiritual forms – art and morality, science and purposively formed objects, religion and law, technology and social norms – stations, as it were, through which the subject has to go in order to gain that special individual value (*Eigenwert*) which is called culture. It is the paradox of culture that subjective life which we feel in its continuous stream and which drives itself towards inner perfection cannot by itself reach the perfection of culture. It can become truly cultivated only through forms which have become completely alien and crystallized into self-sufficient independence. The most decisive way of making this point is to say that culture comes into being by a meeting of the two elements, neither of which contain culture by itself: the subjective soul and the objective spiritual product.

This is the root of the metaphysical significance of historical phenomena. A number of decisive human activities build bridges between subject and object which cannot be completed or which, if completed, are again and again torn down. Some of these are: cognition; above all, work; and in certain of their meanings, also art and religion. The spirit sees itself confronted with an object towards which it is driven by the force as well as spontaneity of its nature. It remains condemned, however, in its own motion, as if in a circle which only touches the object, and which, whenever it is about to penetrate it, is abruptly forced back into its self-contained orbit by the immanent force of its law. The longing for resolution of this intransigent, final dualism is already expressed by the very derivation of the concepts subject–object as correlates, each of which gains its meaning only from the other. Work, art, law, religion, and so forth, transpose the dualism into special atmospheric layers in which its radical sharpness is reduced and certain fusions are permitted. But since these fusions are possible only under special atmospheric conditions, they are unable to overcome the basic estrangement of the parties, and remain finite attempts to solve an infinite task. Our relationship, however, to those objects through which we cultivate ourselves is different, since they themselves are spirit objectified in ethical and intellectual, social and aesthetic, religious and technical forms. The dualism in which a subject restricted to its own boundaries is confronted with an object existing only for itself takes on an incomparable form whenever both parties are spiritual. Thus the subjective spirit has to leave its subjectivity, but not its spirituality, in order to experience the object as a medium for cultivation. This is the only way by which the form of dual existence which is immediately posited with the existence of the subject organizes itself into an inner unified set of mutual relations. Here the subject becomes objective and the object becomes subjective. This is the specific attribute of the process of culture. This process, however, reveals its metaphysical form by transcending its individual contents. In order to understand this more deeply, a further-reaching analysis is required of the objectification of the spirit.

These pages took as their starting point the deep estrangement or animosity which exists between the organic and creative processes of the soul and its contents and products: the vibrating, restless life of the creative soul, which develops toward the infinite contrasts with its fixed and ideally unchanging product and its uncanny feedback effect, which arrests and indeed rigidifies this liveliness. Frequently it appears as if the creative movement of the soul was dying from its own product. Herein lies one fundamental form of our suffering from our own past, our own dogma, and our own fantasies. The discrepancy which exists between the normal states of our inner life and its contents becomes rationalized and somewhat less palpable whenever man, through his theoretical or practical work, confronts himself with these spiritual products, and views them as a sphere of the internal, independent cosmos of the objective spirit. The external or non-material work in which the spiritual life is condensed is perceived as a value of a special kind. Life often goes astray by streaming into it (as if in a blind alley), or continues to roll in its floods and deposits a rejected item at its place. Nevertheless, it is an illustration of the specifically human richness that the products of objective life belong to a stable substantive order of values which is logical or moral, religious or artistic, technical or legal. As carriers of values, their mutual interlocking and systemization frees them from the rigid isolation that alienated them from the rhythms of the processes of life. Thereby this process has gained a significance in its own right which could not have been learned from the steady progression of its course.

Extra value is added to the objectification of the spirit which, although derived in the subjective consciousness, implies by this consciousness something which transcends itself. The value itself does not always need to be positive, in the sense of something good. On the contrary, the merely formal fact that the subject has produced something objective, that its life has become embodied from itself, is perceived as something significant, because the independence of the object thus formed by the spirit can only resolve the basic tension between the process and content of consciousness. Spatially natural ideas attenuate the uncanny fact – that within the flowing process of consciousness something acquires a wholly fixed form – by legitimizing this stability in their relation to an objectively extrinsic world.

Objectivity provides the corresponding service for the spiritual world. We feel the very life of our thought tied to the unchangeability of logical norms, the full spontaneity of our actions, to moral norms. The whole process of our consciousness is filled with insights, traditions, and impressions of an environment somehow formed by the spirit. All this rigidity points to a problematic dualism opposed to the restless rhythm of this subjective psychic process within which it is generated as imagination and as subjectively psychic content. Insofar as this contrast belongs to an idealized world beyond the (realm of) individual consciousness, it will be reduced to one level and law. It is certainly decisive for the cultural meaning of the object with which we are here concerned that will and intelligence, individuality and feelings, powers and emotions of individual souls and also of their collectivity are gathered in it. But only where this does go on are those spiritual meanings brought to their destination.

In the happiness of a creator with his work, as great or insignificant as it may be, we find, beyond a discharge of inner tensions, the proof of his subjective power, his satisfaction over a fulfilled challenge, a sense of contentment that the work is completed, that the universe of valuable items is now enriched by this individual piece. Probably there is no higher sublime personal satisfaction for the creator than when we apperceive his work in all its impersonality, apart from our subjectivity. Just as the objectifications of the spirit are valuable apart from the subjective processes of life which have produced them, so, too, they have value apart from the other life processes which as their consequences depend on them.

As widely and deeply as we look for the influences of the organization of society, the technical demands of natural phenomena, works of art, and the scientific recognition of truth, custom, and morality, we imply our recognition that these phenomena exist, and that the world also includes this formulation of the spirit. This is a directive, as it were, for our processes of evaluation. It stops with the unique quality of the spiritually objective without questioning spiritual consequences beyond the definition of these items themselves.

In addition to all subjective enjoyments by which a work of art enters into us, we recognize as a value of special kind the fact that the spirit created this vessel for itself. Just as there is at least one line running between the artist's will and the individual property of the work of art, which intertwines his objective evaluation of the work with an enjoyment of his own actively creative force, we find a similarly oriented line in the attitudes of the spectator. These attitudes differ remarkably from our responses to natural phenomena. Ocean and flowers, alpine mountains and the stars in the sky derive what we call their value entirely from their reflections in the subjective souls. As soon as we disregard the mystic and fantastic anthropomorphizing of nature, it appears as a continuous contiguous whole, whose undifferentiated character denies its individual parts any special emphasis, any existence which is objectively delimited from others. It is only human categories, that cut out individual parts, to which we ascribe meaning and value. Ironically, we then construct poetic fictions which create a natural beauty that is holy within itself. In reality, however, nature has no other holiness than the one which it evokes in us.

While the product of objective forces can only be subjectively valuable, the product of subjective forces attains for us a kind of objective value. Material and non-material structures which have been invested with human will, artistry, knowledge, and emotions, represent such objective items. We recognize their significance for, and enrichment of, existence, even if we completely disregard the fact that they are being viewed, used, or consumed. Although value and importance, meaning and significance are produced exclusively in the human soul, they must affirm themselves continuously by contrast with the given nature;

but this does not harm the objective value of those structures in which those creative human powers and values already have been invested.

A sunrise which is not seen by any human eyes does not increase the value of this world or make it more sublime, since this objective fact by itself is without relevance to the categories of value. As soon, however, as a painter invests his emotion, his sense for form and color and his power of expression, in a picture of this sunrise, then we consider this work an enrichment, an increase in the value of existence as a whole. The world seems to us somehow more deserving of its existence, closer to its ultimate meaning, whenever the human soul, the source of all value has expressed itself in something which has become part of the objective world. It does not matter now whether a later soul will redeem the magic value from the canvas and dissolve it in the stream of his own subjective sensations. Both the sunrise in nature and the painting exist as realities. But where the sunrise attains value only if it lives on in individuals, the painting has already absorbed such life and made it into an object; hence our sense of value stops before it as before something definite which has no need of subjectivization.

If we expand these arguments into a spectrum, one end will show purely subjective life as the source and the locus of all meaning and value. The other extreme will equate value with objectification. It will insist that human life and action are valuable only insofar as they have something tangible to contribute to the idealistic, historical, materialistic cosmos of the spirit. According to this view, even Kant's moral will gets its value not in itself, not just by being psychologically "there," but from being embodied in a form which exists in an objectively ideal state. Even sentiments and the personality obtain their significance, in a good or a bad sense, by belonging to a realm of the super-personal.

The subjective and objective spirit are opposed to one another; culture asserts its unity by interpenetrating both. It implies a form of personal perfection which can only be completed through the mediation of a super-personal form which lies outside the subject itself. The specific value being cultivated is inaccessible to the subject unless it is reached through a path of objectively spiritual realities. These again represent *cultural* values only to the extent that they interpenetrate the path of the soul from itself to itself, from what might be called its natural state to its cultivated state.

Hence one can express the structure of the concept of culture in the following terms. There is no cultural value which would be an exclusively cultural value. On the contrary, it must first be a value within some other context, promoting some interest or some capacity of our being. It becomes a cultural value only when this partial development raises our total self one step closer to its perfected unity. It is only in this way that two corresponding situations in intellectual history become intelligible. The first is that men of low cultural interest frequently show remarkable indifference to individual elements of culture, and even reject them – insofar as they fail to discover how these elements can contribute to the fulfillment of their total personalities. (While there is probably no human product which *must* contribute to culture, on the other hand there is probably nothing human that *could not* contribute.) Second, there are phenomena (such as certain formalities and refinements of life) which appear as cultural values only in epochs that have become overripe and tired out. For whenever life itself has become empty and meaningless, developments towards its apex, which are based on the will or its potential, are merely schematic, and not capable of deriving nourishment and promotion from the substantive content of the things and ideas. This is analogous to a sick body which cannot assimilate those substances from food which a healthy body uses for growth and strength. In such a case individual development is capable of deriving from social norms only the socially correct form of conduct, from the arts only unproductive passive pleasures, and from technological progress only the negative aspect of the reduction of effort and the smoothness of daily conduct. The sort of culture that develops is formally subjective, but devoid of interweaving with those substantive elements so essential to culture. On the one hand, there is such an emotionally centralized accentuation of culture that the substantive content of objective factors becomes too much and too diverting, since it thus neither will nor can involve itself into cultural function. On the other hand, there is such a weakness and emptiness of culture that it is not at all capable of including objective factors according to their substantive content. Both these phenomena, which first appear as instances opposed to the link between personal culture and impersonal conditions, thus on closer examination only confirm their connection.

That the final and most decisive factors in life are united in culture becomes especially obvious insofar as the development of each of these factors can occur completely independently, not only without the motivation by the ideal of culture but indeed by denying it. For the view towards one or the other direction would be diverted from the unity of its goal if it were to be determined by a synthesis between these two. The men who produce the constant contents, the objective elements of culture, would probably refuse to borrow the motives and values of their efforts directly from the idea of culture. In their case the following inner situation exists: a twofold force is at work in the founder of a religion and in an artist, in a statesman and in an inventor, in a scholar and in a legislator. On the one hand, there is the expression of his essential powers, the exuberation of his nature to such a high level that it frees by itself the contents of cultural life. And on the other hand, there is the passionate dedication to the cause with its immanent laws demanding perfection, so that the creative individual becomes indifferent to himself and is extinguished. Within genius these two streams are unified. To the genius, the development of the subjective spirit for its own sake and compelled by its own forces is indistinguishable from the completely self-negating devotion to an objective task. Culture, as we have demonstrated, is always a synthesis. A synthesis, however, is not the only and most immediate form of unity, since it always presupposes the divisibility of elements as an antecedent or as a correlative.

Viewing synthesis as the most sublime of formal relationships between spirit and world could occur only during an age which is as analytical as the modern. For insofar as the analytic elements are developed in it in ways similar to an organic germ's branching out into a multiplicity of differentiated limbs, this stands beyond analysis and synthesis. This may be so because these two develop from an interaction where each, on every level, presupposes the other, or else because the analytically separated elements are later transformed through synthesis into a unity which, however, is completely different from that which existed prior to the separation. The creative genius possesses such an original unity of the subjective and the objective, which has first to be divided so that it can be resuscitated in synthetic form in the process of cultivation. This is why man's interest in culture does not lie on the same level with pure self-development of the subjective spirit or with pure dedication to a cause; instead cultural interests are attached to a cause, occasionally as something secondary, reflex-like, as an abstract generality which reads beyond the innermost and immediate value impulses of the soul. Even when the path of the soul to itself – one of the primary factors in culture – carries the other factors along, culture stays out of the game as long as the path of the soul transverses only its own domain and perfects itself in the pure self-development of its own essence.

If we consider the other factor of culture in its self-sufficient isolation – those products of

the spirit which have grown into an ideal existence independent of all psychological movements – even its most indigenous meaning and value does not coincide with its cultural
value. Its cultural meaning is completely independent. A work of art is supposed to be
perfect in terms of artistic norms. They do not ask for anything else but themselves, and
would give or deny value to the work even if there were nothing else in the world but this
particular work. The result of research should be truth and absolutely nothing further.
Religion exhausts its meaning with the salvation which it brings to the soul. The economic
product wishes to be economically perfect, and does not recognize for itself any other than
the economic scale of values. All these sequences operate within the confines of purely
internal laws. Whether and to what extent they can be substituted in the development of
subjective souls has nothing to do with its importance, which is measured through purely
objective norms which are valid for it alone. On the basis of this state of affairs it becomes
clear why we frequently meet with an apparent indifference and even aversion to culture
among people who are primarily directed only towards subjects as well as among those who
are only directed towards objects. A person who asks only for the salvation of the soul, or for
the ideal of personal power, or for purely individual growth which will not be affected by
any exterior force, will find that his evaluations miss the single *integrating* factor of culture.
The other cultural factor will be absent from a person who strives only for the purely
material completion of his works, so that they fulfill only their idea and no other that is only
tangentially connected. The extreme representative of the first type is the *stylite*, of the
other, the specialist who is entrapped by the fanaticism for his specialty. At first sight it is
somewhat startling to observe that the supporters of such undoubted "cultural values" as
religiosity, personality formation, and technologies of every kind should despise or fight the
concept of culture. However, this becomes immediately explicable when we consider that
culture always only means the *synthesis* of a subjective development with an objectively
spiritual value. It follows then, that the representation of either one of these elements must
endanger their mutual interweaving.

   This dependence of cultural values on other indigenous value-scales suggests why an
object may reach a different point on the scale of cultural values than on that of the merely
material. There are a variety of works, which remain far below the artistic, technical,
intellectual level of what has already been accomplished, yet which, nevertheless have the
capacity to join most efficiently the developmental paths of many people as developers of
their latent forces, as a bridge to their next higher station. Just as we do not derive a
completely satisfying fulfillment from only the dynamically most forceful or aesthetically
most complete impressions of nature (from which we derive the emotional feelings by
which stark and unresolved elements suddenly became clear and harmonic to us – which
we often owe to a quite simple scene or the playing of shadows on a summer afternoon),
so we cannot immediately infer from the importance of the intellectual product, as high
or low as it may be in its native dimension, what this work will accomplish for us in the
development of culture. Everything depends here on the special significance of the work,
which serves as a secondary contribution to the general development of personalities.
And this contribution may even be inversely proportional to the unique or intrinsic value
of the work.

   There are human products of almost ultimate perfection to which we have no access, or
they no access to us, because of their perfect integration. Such a work stays in its place, from
which it cannot be transplanted to our street as an isolated perfect item. Maybe we can go to
it, but we cannot take it along with us in order to raise ourselves through it to our own

perfection. For the modern feeling of life this self-contained degree of perfection is, perhaps, represented by antiquity, which denies itself the acceptance of the pulsations and restlessness of our developmental tempo. Many a person may, therefore, be induced today to search for some other fundamental factor especially for our culture. It is similar with certain ethical ideals. Products of the objective intellect which have been so designated are, perhaps, destined more than any others to carry the development from the mere possibility to the highest perfection of our totality and to give it direction.

However, there are some ethical imperatives which contain an ideal of such rigid perfection that it is impossible to draw energies from them which we could include in our development. Despite their high position within the sequence of ethical ideas, as cultural elements they will easily be subordinated to others which from their lower ethical position more readily assimilate themselves into the rhythm of our development. Another reason for the disproportion between the substantive and cultural values of a phenomenon may be found in the one-sided benefits they confer on us. Various things may make us more knowledgeable or better, happier or more adept, without actually helping to develop *us*, but only an independently objective side or quality which is attached to us. In this case we are naturally dealing with gradual and infinitely subtle differences which empirically are hard to grasp, and which are tied to the mysterious relationship between our unified total self and our individual energies and perfections.

The completely closed reality which we call our subject can be designated only by the sum of such individual phenomena, without actually being composed by them. This peculiar relationship is not at all exhausted by reference to the only logical category which is available, the parts and the whole. In isolation it could objectively exist in any number of diverse subjects. It gains the characteristics of our own subjectivity at its inside, where it fosters the growth of the unity of our own being. With these characteristics, however, it somehow builds a bridge to the value of objectivity. It is situated on our periphery by which we are wedded to the objective, exterior, intellectual world. But as soon as this function, which is directed to and nourished by the outside, is severed from its meaning, which flows into our own center, this discrepancy will be created. We will become instructed, we will act more purposively, we will become richer in satisfactions and skills, and perhaps even more educated – our process of cultivation, however, does not keep in step. Although we come from a lower level of having and knowing to a higher level, we do not come from ourselves as lower beings to ourselves as higher beings.

I have stressed the possible discrepancy between the substantive and cultural meaning of an object in order to bring out more emphatically the fundamental duality of elements which through their interweaving produce culture. This interweaving is unique because personal development, although it pertains to the subject, can be reached only through the mediation of objects. For this reason, to be cultivated becomes a task of infinite dimensions, since the number of objects that a subject can make its own is inexhaustible. Nuances of linguistic usage describe this situation most exactly: the word "culture," when it is tied to particular objects, as in religious culture, artistic culture, and so forth, usually designates not the personal qualities of individuals, but rather a general spirit. This means that in any given epoch, there is an especially large number of impressive spiritual products available through which individuals are cultivated. But this plenitude of cultural possibilities may actually constitute a threat to culture, if it leads to over-specialization. A person may acquire a remarkable degree of skill or knowledge concerning a certain substantive content – an "artistic culture" or a "religious culture" – without becoming truly cultivated. On the other hand, it is still possible that substantive perfection of a particular kind may help bring about the completion of the person as a total being.

Within this structure of culture there now develops a cleavage which, of course, is already prepared in its foundation. It makes of the subject–object-synthesis a paradox, even a tragedy. The profound dualism between subject and object survives their synthesis. The inner logic by which each member develops independently does not necessarily coincide with that of the other. Knowledge, for example, whose forms are so greatly determined by the *a priori* dimensions of our spirit, is constantly becoming completed by items which can be only accepted and not anticipated. But it does not seem to be guaranteed that these items will serve the completion of the soul. It is similar with our practical and technical relationships to things; although we form them according to our purposes, they do not yield to us completely, but have a logic and a power of their own. And it is highly doubtful that our use of them will always coincide with the unique direction of our central development. Indeed, everything objective possesses its own individual logic. Once certain themes of law, of art, of morals have been created – even if they have been created by most individual and innermost spontaneity – we cannot control the directions in which they will develop. Although we generate them, they must follow the guidelines of their own inner necessity, which is no more concerned with our individuality than are physical forces and their laws.

It is true that language rhymes and reasons for us; it collects the fragmentary impulses of our own essence and leads them to a perfection which we would not have reached on our own. Nevertheless, there is no necessity in the parallel between objective and subjective developments. Indeed, we sometimes even perceive language as a strange natural force which deflects and mutilates not only our expressions, but also our most intimate intentions. And religion, which originated in the search of the soul for itself, analogous to wings that carry the indigenous forces of the soul to their own height – it, too, has certain formative laws, which having once come into existence, unfold with a necessity that does not always coincide with our own. The anti-cultural spirit with which religion is often reproached is not only its occasional animosity toward intellectual, aesthetic, or moral values. It also refers to the deeper issue that religion proceeds on its own course, which is determined by immanent logic, and into which it drags life along. Whatever transcendental fulfillment the soul may find on this course, religion rarely leads to that perfection of its totality which is called culture.

Insofar as the logic of impersonal cultural forms is loaded with dynamic tensions, harsh frictions develop between these forms and the inner drives and norms of personality which fulfill themselves in culture. From the moment that man began to say "I" to himself, and became an object beyond and in comparison with himself, from the same moment in which the contents of the soul were formed together into a center point – from that time and based on that central form the ideal had to grow according to which everything connected with the center point formed a unit, self-contained and self-sufficient. But the contents with which the "I" must organize itself into its own unified world do not belong to it alone. They are given to it from some spatially, temporarily idealized realm outside; they are simultaneously the contents of different social and metaphysical, conceptual and ethical worlds.

In these they possess forms and relationships among one another that do not wish to dissolve into those of the "I." Through those contents the exterior worlds grasp the "I" and seek to draw it into them. They aim to break up the centralization of cultural contents around the "I" and reconstitute them according to *their* demands. Thus, in religious conflicts between the self-sufficiency or freedom of man and his subordination under divine order, and again in social conflicts between man as a rounded individual and man as a mere member of a social organism, we are entangled because our life ideals are inevitably subsumed under other circles than those of our own "I."

Man often finds himself at the point of intersection of two circles of objective forces and values, each of which would like to drag him along. Often he feels himself to be the center who orders all life contents around himself harmonically according to the logic of his personality. Thus he feels solidarity with each of these circles, insofar as each belongs to a different circle, and is claimed by another law of motion, his own. Thus our own essence forms an intersecting point of itself with an alien circle of postulates. The process of culture, however, compresses the parties of this collision into extremely close contact by making the development of the subject conditional on the assimilation of objective material. Thus the metaphysical dualism of subject and object, which seemed to have been overcome by the formation of culture, reappears in the conflict between subjective and objective developments. It is possible, moreover, that the object can step outside its mediating role in an even more basic manner, and break up the bridges over which the course of cultivation has been leading. At first it isolates and alienates itself from the working subject through the division of labor. Objects which have been produced by many persons can be arranged in a scale according to the extent to which their unity stems from the unified intellectual intention of one person, or from the partial contributions of cooperating but uncomprehending individuals. The latter pole is occupied by a city: it may strike us now as a meaningful self-contained and organically connected whole; in fact, however, it was not constructed according to any pre-existing plan, but arose out of the accidental needs and desires of individuals. The former pole is exemplified by the products of a manufacturing plant in which twenty workers have cooperated without knowledge of or interest in one another's separate work processes – while the whole, nevertheless, has been guided by a personal central will and intellect. An intermediary position is taken by a newspaper, insofar as its overall appearance can somehow be traced to a leading personality, and yet it grows because of mutually accidental contributions of the most diverse form and of diverse individuals who are complete strangers to one another. Through the cooperative effort of different persons, then, a cultural object often comes into existence which as a total unit is *without a producer*, since it did not spring forth from the total self of any individual. The elements are coordinated as if by a logic and formal intention inherent in them as objective realities; their creators have not endowed them with any such logic and intention. The objectivity of the spiritual content, which makes it independent of its acceptance or non-acceptance can be attributed here to the production process. Regardless of whether they were or were not intended by individuals, the finished product contains contents which can be transmitted through the cultural process. This is different only in degree from a little child who, in playing with letters of the alphabet, may order them accidentally into good sense. The meaning exists objectively and concretely, no matter how naively it may have been produced.

If examined more closely, this appears as an extremely radical case of an otherwise general human-spiritual fate. Most products of our intellectual creation contain a certain quota which was not produced by ourselves. I do not mean unoriginality or the inheritance of values or dependence on traditional examples. Even despite of all these, a given work in its total content could still be born in our own consciousness although the consciousness would thus only hand on what it had already received. On the contrary, there is always something significant in most of our objective efforts which other people can extract even though we were not aware of having deposited it there. In some sense it is valid to say that the weaver doesn't know what he weaves. The finished effort contains emphases, relationships, values which the worker did not intend. It is mysterious but unquestionably true: a material object takes on a spiritual meaning not put into it but integral to the object's form. Nature does not present this sort of problem. It is not the will of any artist that has given purity of style to the southern mountains, or gripping symbolism to a stormy ocean. The realm of the purely natural is endowed with the potential for meaning: it has or can have a part in all intellectual creations. The possibility of gaining a subjectively intellectual content is invested in them as an objective form. In an extreme example, a poet may have coined a puzzle with the intention of a certain solution. If, now, a different solution is found for it which fits as well, as meaningfully, as the intended one, then it will be exactly as "right" even though it was absolutely alien to his creative processes. It is contained within the created product as an idealized objectivity exactly as is the first word for which the puzzle originally had been created.

These potentialities of the objective spirit show that it possesses an independent validity, an independent chance of becoming re-subjectivized after its successful objectification, even when it was created by a subjective spirit. This chance, however, does not need to be realized: in the previous example, the second solution to the puzzle rightfully exists in its objective meaning even before it is found, indeed, even if it is never found. This peculiarity of the contents of culture is the metaphysical foundation for the ominous independence by which the realm of cultural products grows and grows as if an inner necessity were producing one member after another. Frequently this happens almost without relation to the will and personality of the producer and independent of the acceptance by consumers.

The "fetishism" which Marx assigned to economic commodities represents only a special case of this general fate of contents of culture. With the increase in culture these contents more and more stand under a paradox: they were originally created by subjects and for subjects: but in their intermediate form of objectivity, which they take on in addition to the two extreme instances, they follow an immanent logic of development. In so doing they estrange themselves from their origin as well as from their purpose. They are impelled not by physical necessities, but by truly cultural ones (which, however, cannot pass over the physical conditions). What drives forth the products of the spirit is the cultural and not the natural scientific logic of the objects. Herein lies the fatefully immanent drive of all technology, as soon as it has moved beyond the range of immediate consumption. Thus the industrial production of a variety of products generates a series of closely related by-products for which, properly speaking, there is no need. It is only the compulsion for full utilization of the created equipment that calls for it. The technological process demands that it be completed by links which are not required by the psychic process. Thus vast supplies of products come into existence which call forth an artificial demand that is senseless from the perspective of the subjects' culture.

In several branches of the sciences it is no different. On one hand, for example, philological techniques have developed to an unsurpassable finesse and methodological perfection. On the other hand, the study of subject matter which would be of genuine interest to intellectual culture does not replenish itself as quickly. Thus, the philological effort frequently turns into micrology, pedantic efforts, and an elaboration of the unessential into a method that runs on for its own sake, an extension of substantive norms whose independent path no longer coincides with that of culture as a completion of life. The same problem arises in the development of fine arts, where technical skills have developed to such an extent that they are emancipated from serving the cultural total purpose of art. By obeying only the indigenous material logic, the technique at this point develops refinement after refinement. However, these refinements represent only *its* perfection, no longer the cultural meaning of art. That extreme and total specialization – of which there are complaints nowadays in all areas of labor, but which nevertheless subordinates their progress under its laws with demonical rigor – is only a special form of this very general cultural predicament. Objects, in their development, have a logic of their own – not a conceptual one, nor a natural one, but purely as cultural works of man; bound by their own laws, they turn away from the direction by which they could join the personal development of human souls. This is not that old familiar intrusion of the realm of ultimate ends, not the primacy of technique so often lamented in advanced cultures. That is something purely psychological, without any firm relationship to the objective order of things. Here, however, we are dealing with the immanent logic of cultural phenomena. Man becomes the mere carrier of the force by which this logic dominates their development and leads them on as if in the tangent of the course through which they would return to the cultural development of living human beings – this is similar to the process by which because of strict adherence to logic our thoughts are led into theoretical consequences which are far removed from those originally intended. This is the real tragedy of culture.

In general we call a relationship tragic – in contrast to merely sad or extrinsically destructive – when the destructive forces directed against some being spring forth from the deepest levels of this very being; or when its destruction has been initiated in itself, and forms the logical development of the very structure by which a being has built its own positive form. It is the concept of culture that the spirit creates an independent objectivity by which the development of the subject takes its path. In this process the integrating and culturally conditioning element is restricted to a unique evolution which continues to use up the powers of other subjects, and to pull them into its course without thereby raising them to their own apex. The development of subjects cannot take the same path which is taken by that of the objects. By following the latter, it loses itself either in a dead end alley or in an emptiness of its innermost and most individual life. Cultural development places the subject even more markedly outside of itself through the formlessness and boundlessness which it imparts to the objective spirit, because of the infinite number of its producers. Everybody can contribute to the supply of objectified cultural contents without any consideration for other contributors. This supply may have a determined color during individual cultural epochs – that is, from within there may be a qualitative but not likewise quantitative boundary. There is no reason why it should not be multiplied in the direction of the infinite, why not book should be added to book, work of art to work of art, or invention to invention. The form of objectivity as such possesses a boundless capacity for fulfillment. This voracious capacity for accumulation is most deeply incompatible with the forms of personal life. The receptive capacity of the self is limited not only by the force and length of life, but also through a certain unity and relative compactness of its form. Therefore, the self selects, with determined limits from among the contents which offer themselves as means for its individual development. The individual might pass by what his self-development cannot assimilate, but this does not always succeed so easily. The infinitely growing supply of objectified spirit places demands before the subject, creates desires in him, hits him with feelings of individual inadequacy and helplessness, throws him into total relationships from whose impact he cannot withdraw, although he cannot master their particular contents. Thus, the typically problematic situation of modern man comes into being: his sense of being surrounded by an innumerable number of cultural elements which are neither mean-ingless to him nor, in the final analysis, meaningful. In their mass they depress him, since he is not capable of assimilating them all, nor can he simply reject them, since after all, they do belong *potentially* within the sphere of his cultural development This could be characterized with the exact reversal of the words that refer to the first Franciscan monks in their spiritual poverty, their absolute freedom from all things which wanted to divert the path of their souls: *Nihil habentes, omnia possidentes* (those who have nothing own everything). Instead man has become richer and more overloaded: *Cultures omnia habentes, nihil possidentes* (cultures which have everything own nothing).

These experiences have already been discussed in various forms. (I have elaborated them in my *Philosophy of Money* for a larger number of concrete historical fields.) What we want to bring out here is their deep roots in the concept of culture. The total wealth of this concept consists in the fact that objective phenomena are included in the process of development of subjects, as ways or means, without thereby losing their objectivity.. Whether this does in fact bring the subject to the highest degree of perfection may remain an open question. In any case, the metaphysical intention which attempts to unify the principles of the subject and of the object finds here a guarantee of its success: the metaphysical question finds an historical answer. In cultural forms, the spirit reaches an objectivity which makes it at once independent of all accidents of subjective reproductions, and yet usable for the central purpose of subjective perfection. While the metaphysical answers to this question in general tend to cut it off by somehow demonstrating that the subject–object contrast is unimport-ant, culture insists on the full opposition of the parties, on the super-subjective logic of spiritually formed objects through which the subject raises itself beyond itself to itself.

One of the basic capacities of the spirit is to separate itself from itself – to create forms, ideas and values that oppose it, and only in this form to gain consciousness of itself. This capacity has reached its widest extent in the process of culture. Here the spirit has pressed the object most energetically towards the subject, in order to lead it back into the subject. But this liaison dissolves because of the object's indigenous logic, through which the subject regains itself as more adequate and perfected. The tendency of creative people to think not about the cultural value of their work, but about its substantive meaning which is circum-scribed by its unique idea, develops logically but almost imperceptibly into caricature, into a form of specialization which is secluded from life, into a purely technical (and technological) self-satisfaction which does not find its path back to man. This objectivity makes possible the division of labor, which collects the energies of a whole complex of personalities in a single product, without considering whether individuals will be able to use it for their own devel-opment, or whether it will satisfy only extrinsic and peripheral needs. Herein lies the deeper rationale for the ideals of Ruskin to replace all factory labor by the artistic labor of individuals.

The division of labor separates the product as such from each individual contributor. Standing by itself, as an independent object, it is suitable to subordinate itself into an order of phenomena, or to serve an individual's purposes. Thereby, however, it loses that inner animation which can only be given to a total work by a complete human being, which carries its usefulness into the spiritual center of other individuals. A work of art is such an immeasurable cultural value precisely because it is inaccessible to any division of labor, because the created product preserves the creator to the innermost degree.

What in Ruskin's work might appear as a hatred of culture in reality is a passion for culture. He wants to reverse the division of labor which, by emptying cultural content of its subject, and giving it an inanimate objectivity, tears it from the genuinely cultural process. The tragic development which ties culture to the objectivity of contents, but charges the contents with a logic of their own, and thus withdraws them from cultural assimilation by subjects, is now evident to everyone who observes the infinite potential for multiplying the contents of the objective spirit at random. Since culture does not possess a concrete unity of form for its contents, and since each creator places his product as if in an unbounded space next to that of the other, the mass character of phenomena comes into existence. Everything claims with a certain right to be of cultural value, and creates in us a wish thus to utilize it. The lack of unity in the objectified spirit permits it a developmental tempo behind which the subjective spirit must increasingly lag. The subjective spirit, meanwhile, does not know how it can completely protect its unity of form from the touch and the temptation of all these "things." The superior force of the object over the subject, so general in the course of the world, temporarily checked by the fortunate balance we call culture, can once again be felt as the objective spirit develops unboundedly. The adornment and over-loading of our lives with a thousand superfluous items, from which, however, we cannot liberate ourselves; the continuous "stimulation" of civilized man who in spite of all this is not stimulated to expressions of individual creativity; the more acquaintance with or enjoyment of a thousand things which our development cannot include and which stay in it only as ballast – all these long-lamented cultural ills are nothing more than reflections of the emancipation of the objectified spirit. Thus cultural contents are bound to follow a logic which eventually is independent of their *cultural purpose*, and which continuously leads them further away from it. The situation is tragic: even in its first moments of existence, culture carries something within itself which, as if by an intrinsic fate, is determined to block, to burden, to obscure and divide its innermost purpose, the transition of the soul from its incomplete to its complete state.

The great enterprise of the spirit succeeds innumerable times in overcoming the object as such by making an object of itself, returning to itself enriched by its creation. But the spirit has to pay for this self-perfection with the tragic potential that a logic and dynamic is inevitably created by the unique laws of its own world which increasingly separates the contents of culture from its essential meaning and value.

8

MILITARISM AND CULTURE

An extract from *Reflections of a Non-political Man* (1918)

Thomas Mann (1875–1955)

In the early part of the twentieth century, up to and including the First World War, the limits of culture – language, form, style – were being explored, and criticized, as seen in the essay by Georg Simmel. This exploration also occurred, for example, in music by Schoenberg, in painting by Klimt, in architecture by Loos, and in philosophy by Wittgenstein. In the area of literature, the novel moved away from the story and the sense of immediate totality and closure in the direction of essayism and interpretation which emphasized ironic reflection and fragmentation. This attitude and essayistic style typifies the work of Franz Kafka, Robert Musil, and during this period, Thomas Mann.

In 'Civilization's Literary Man' – the essay published from *Reflections of a Non-political Man* – Thomas Mann married this essayism to a short-lived and Nietzschean-inspired hatred of democracy which became the basis for a reflection on German identity. Mann favoured the greatness of *Kultur* against politics of the *Zivilisation*. In Mann's essay, neither culture nor civilization can be separated from the issue of national identity. Civilization, for Mann, like Nietzsche, refers to the shallow society of progress and democracy (France), whilst culture refers to the fraught intellectual soul of Germany. The phrase 'civilization's literary man' is a rhetorical device with which Thomas Mann rebukes those Germans (particularly his brother Heinrich who wrote an essay in reply) who criticized the German militaristic stance from the vantage point of 'literary humanism', that is, from the vantage point of 'French' civilization. The irony for Thomas Mann, however, was that literature belonged to civilization, and he himself was a *littérateur*. This essay is a fine example of the divisions and confusions between civilization and culture when these terms are deployed as criteria of national identity.

Civilization's literary man

It was thought that the ideal of the Slavophiles was: "To eat radishes and to write denunciations." Yes, denunciations! They astonished everyone so much by their appearance and their views that the liberals had second thoughts and began to be afraid: What, did these strange people intend finally to denounce them, too?

Dostoevsky, *Works*

The great communities, however, do *not* possess – and it would be almost boring if they did – that spiritual unity that they seem to have, and then only temporarily, in time of war. The task of investigating the extent to which this applies to other countries cannot tempt us here. We must concern ourselves with Germany – and here the word "concern" must be taken somewhat etymologically, for it can be stated without any chauvinism that all intellectual concern for Germany has constantly proven to be particularly rewarding. We will now tell how, in our humble opinion, things stand with Germany.

The antitheses that loosen and call in question the inner intellectual unity and homogeneity of the large European communities are generally the same everywhere: they are basically European, but they are still strongly differentiated nationally among the various peoples, and they are united under the national synthesis, so that, for example, a radical-republican Frenchman is just as much a genuine, correct, complete and unquestionable Frenchman as is a clerical royalist. A liberal Englishman is as English as his conservative countryman; finally, the Frenchman comes to an understanding with the Frenchman, the Englishman with the Englishman best of all and for the best. There is, however, a country and people in which the situation is different: a people that is not and probably never can be a nation in that definite sense that France and England are nations, because her cultural history and her idea of humanity are against it; a country whose internal unity and homogeneity are not only complicated, but almost abolished by intellectual antitheses; a country where these antitheses are more violent, fundamental, more malicious and less open to compromise than anywhere else; because there they are scarcely, or only loosely, enclosed in a national bond, scarcely combined on a grand scale as the contradictory wills of every other country always are. This country is Germany. Germany's internal, intellectual antitheses are scarcely national; they are almost purely European, opposing one another almost completely without national coloration, without national synthesis. In Germany's soul, *Europe*'s intellectual antitheses are carried to the end – "carried to the end" in a maternal and in a warlike sense. This truly is her real national destiny. No longer physically – she has recently learned how to prevent this – but intellectually, Germany is still the battlefield of Europe. And when I say, "the German soul," I do not just mean the collective national soul, but quite specifically the soul, the mind, and the heart of the individual German. I even mean myself as well. To be the spiritual battleground for European antitheses: this is German; but it is not German to make matters easy for oneself and to manifest the national weakness, the – as Nietzsche says – "secret infinity" of one's people, by simply acting like a Frenchman. Whoever would aspire to transform Germany into a middle-class democracy in the Western-Roman sense and spirit would wish to take away from her all that is best and complex, to take away the problematic character that really makes up her nationality: he would make her dull, shallow, stupid, and un-German, and he would therefore be an anti-nationalist who insisted that Germany become a nation in a foreign sense and spirit.

A strange endeavor! Nevertheless, there are such Germans; and it would be quite wrong to believe that things were as simple in Germany as the great formula of the "protesting kingdom" would make it appear. Those who do not yet know, must certainly learn – for it is very important and interesting – that there are German intellects who not only do not join in the "protest" of their own community against the Roman West, but who even see their true mission and destiny to be part of a passionate protest *against* this protest, and who promote with all the power of their talents the intimate union of Germany with the imperium of civilization. But while the domestic opponents of the officials, of the spokesmen – oh, yes, of the spokesmen of France during the war, are still completely and decisively for their country, our antiprotestors give their struggling country no support and sympathy but enthusiastically confess themselves, as far as such a confession is permissible today, to be for the enemy, for the world of the West, of the *entente*, and especially of France, and why especially France will soon be explained. I will be careful not to call these people un-German. The concept "German" is an abyss, bottomless, and one should be extremely careful with its negative, the judgment of "un-German," so that one is not tripped up and hurt. Therefore, even though it may seem pussyfooting, I will certainly not call these people unpatriotic. I only say that their patriotism is manifested in such a way that they see the prerequisite of the greatness, or, if not of greatness, at least of the happiness and of the beauty of their country, not in its disturbing hate-provoking, "special nature," but, to repeat, in its unconditional union with the world of civilization, of literature, of elevating, rhetorical democracy that is worthy of a human being – with the world that indeed would become fulfilled by the overthrow of Germany: its empire would be complete and all-encompassing: there would be no more opposition to it.

The German proponent of this literary civilization is obviously our *radical literary man*, the one I have become accustomed to call "civilization's literary man" – and I do so because the radical literary man, the representative of the literarized, politicized, in short, of the democratized spirit, is a child of the Revolution, spiritually at home in its sphere, in its country. Actually, the phrase, "civilization's literary man," is no doubt a pleonasm. For I have, of course, already noted that civilization and literature are one and the same thing. One is not a literary man without instinctively despising Germany's "special nature" and feeling oneself bound to the imperium of civilization. To put it more precisely, being a literary man is almost the same as being a Frenchman, indeed, a classical Frenchman, a revolutionary Frenchman; for the literary man receives his greatest traditions from the France of the Revolution. His paradise lies there, his golden age. France is his country; the Revolution is his grand period. He was quite well off then, when he was still called a *philosophe*, and when he actually mediated, spread, and politically prepared the new philosophy of humanitarianism, freedom, and reason.

When I speak of the German radical literary man, for whom the national adjective seems so strange, I am not speaking of that ragtag, bobtail group that one honors far too much by any study one makes of them; not, then, of that scribbling, agitating pack of rascals that is propagating international civilization and whose radicalism is mischievousness, whose literary world is without roots and significance – these literary scum, as leaven and national ferment, may be of some value to progress, but their *lack* of any personal rank or humaneness makes them only worthy of being handled with fire tongs. I am speaking of the *noble* representatives of this type – for there are some. Generally speaking, there is no doubt a degree of innate merit, of intellect and art, that cannot be subjected to criticism on the basis of the national idea. On the contrary, people of this rank define, and perhaps redefine and correct this idea – I will not forget this. I will not fail to consider that with such high rank one is a factor and an element of the nation's fate – an unfortunate factor, perhaps – so much the worse for the nation! So much the worse for it, I say – for it is the nation's misfortune, it is its own fault, it lies in the nation, in its character, if it is left in the lurch in its most difficult hour by some of its best intellects. And not just left in the lurch. By fighting against such intellects, against their opinions in spite of their rank, one ceases to be an artist, for as an artist one was accustomed to respect rank and not to pay much attention to its opinions. One temporarily becomes a politician – and one must therefore guard oneself all the more carefully against political vices such as, for instance, attributing anti-intellectual, that is, base motives, to one's opponent, even if the reverse has already happened. The conviction of having "progress" on one's side obviously produces a moral certainty and self-assurance that borders on callousness, until one finally believes that one is ennobling vulgarity simply by making use of it. This is an excuse. We who feel ourselves less morally secure are necessarily more apprehensive. But let us get to the point!

Germany's radical literary man belongs, then, body and soul, to the *entente*, to the imperium of civilization. Not that he has had to struggle with himself, that the times have torn him in painful spiritual conflict; not that his heart is bound here *and* there, that he is trying by admonishing, punishing, appeasing, and preaching to pacify both sides, placing himself, like gentle Romain Rolland, above the fray. With full passion he thrusts himself *into* the fray – but on the side of the enemy. From the first moment he automatically took the *entente*'s side – naturally, for it had always been his own. With unerring accuracy he felt, thought and said exactly what *entente* journalists or ministers said simultaneously or later. He was courageous, he was original, but only in German terms, only relatively. I believe he has shown signs of making his own isolation appear tragic – not quite justifiably so, for it only existed within Germany. He did not exactly think lonely thoughts; what he thought was not particularly sublime, superior, or lovingly all-embracing: it could have appeared in every *entente* newspaper, and it did appear there. In short, he thought as did every Tom, Dick, and Harry among our enemies abroad, and I do not call this tragic isolation. One can say he was well off during those first weeks and months of the war, times his compatriots who are not radical literary men will remember all their lives – the time when the world, the democratic public opinion of the world, was let loose upon Germany, when filth rained upon her: he was really quite well off, I say, for everything that this "great, proud and special" people had to suffer then and later, both in word and deed – did not matter to him, did not make him hot or cold, did not touch or affect him – he excepted himself, of course; he said the others were right: what they said he had already said for a long time, word for word. Un-German? With all my strength I will resist calling him un-German, and I will not cease resisting it as long as my powers do not fail me. One can be extremely German and, at the same time, extremely anti-German. What is German is an abyss: let us stick to that. No, then! He is not un-German. He is merely an amazing, remarkable example of how alienated and disgusted with himself, how devoted to cosmopolitan ideas, how beside himself, a German may become even today, in post-Bismarckian Germany. It may be permissible to say that the structure of his intellect is *unnational*, but only insofar – or rather to the degree – that it is not German-national but nationally French: so completely so, in fact, that in more peaceful times it would be a real pleasure to study in him all the aspects of magnanimity, sentimentality, childishness, and maliciousness of the classically unbroken French national character that has as yet reached no critical self-reflection, no resignation. He is one of the best French patriots. Belief carries him and at times lends his style a magnificent tremolo, an admirable drive: the belief in the idea of the glory and the mission of his – of the French – people, that they have been called once and for all to be the teachers of mankind, to bring it "justice" after they have brought it "freedom" (which, however, comes from England). He does not merely think in French syntax and grammar: he thinks in French concepts, French antitheses, French conflicts, French affairs and scandals. He sees the war in which we are engaged entirely as the *entente* does, as a struggle between "power and spirit" – this is his principal antithesis! – between the "saber" and the idea, the lie and the truth, barbarism and justice. (I do not have to add on which side, in his opinion, saber, barbarism, and lie, and on which side the antithetically corresponding ideals are to be found.) In a word: this war seems to him to be a repetition of the Dreyfus affair on a colossally magnified scale – for those who do not believe this, I will provide completely convincing documentation. According to the analogy of this case, whoever is engaged in a spiritual struggle on the side of the civilization *entente* against the forces of the "saber," against Germany, is an intellectual. Whoever feels differently, whoever, following some kind of dark instincts in this tremendous struggle, remains loyal to Germany, is lost, a traitor to the intellect who stands against justice and truth – and whether he does so in elegant or sloppy style is justifiably immaterial to the moralist – he stands against them, and every suspicion of his motives is henceforth not only permissible but also imperative: eagerness for applause, acquisitiveness, the neat gift of profiting from the situation, probably also the only too human desire to seize the opportunity to outshine and to silence an opponent who is condemned to silence or to intrigue, to ambiguity – there is no guilelessness that civilization's literary man will not seize upon with a grimace to present siding with "the saber" in the correct psychological light. But since, however (certainly a point against Germany), it is a much more ticklish and complicated matter to speak for Germany than for "civilization," where only a good bit of dash and tremolo are necessary and the job is done – since to speak for Germany one must try, for better or worse, to dig a bit deeper, civilization's literary man refers in such a case, with marked disdain, to his opponent's "deep chatter."

This is the way civilization's literary man looks at things. His sympathy with the enemies of the protesting kingdom is intellectual solidarity. His love and passion are with the troops of the Western allies, of France and England, and probably also of Italy; he sees in them the armies of the spirit with which civilization marches. His heart goes out to them – to Germany his heart goes out quite indirectly: that is, in the sense that he yearns from the bottom of his heart for Germany's defeat. That his motives are of a more spiritual and therefore of a more noble sort is a matter of course. He wishes a German defeat because of its spiritual significance, because of the spiritual consequences it would entail for Germany and for Europe. He wants it for "domestic" reasons – as a substitute, as it were, for the revolution that Germany has of course lacked until today: for 1848 was a failure, and the unification of Germany did not result from the democratic revolution but from the worst and most unpardonable circumstance possible: from France's humiliation. To be sure, France's defeat blossomed into her greatest fortune, for it brought her the republic, that is: truth and justice. But if the only explanation of Germany's victory at that time is that providence smiled upon France (for from an intellectual viewpoint, according to civilization's literary man, Germany could never triumph under Bismarck, such a totally unintellectual man, such an anti-intellectual man of power), this is still no excuse for Germany. I do not know, it is hard to guess, what our radical literary man would have wished for at that time: today he wishes for Germany to be beaten *and converted* by the *entente* – its victory would be the victory of literature for Germany and for Europe, it would be *his* victory, just as its defeat would be his: so much has he made the cause of rhetorical democracy his own. He wishes, therefore, the physical humiliation of Germany because it would include her spiritual defeat: he wishes the collapse – but one says it more correctly in French: the *débâcle* of the *Kaiserreich* because such a physical and moral *débâcle* would – the moral one, by the way, may come before the physical one – finally, finally bring the warmly wished for, palpable, and catastrophic proof that Germany has lived in lies and brutality rather than in truth and spirit. Yes, if it could still be hoped for today, with all his heart he would certainly wish for the democratic invasion of Germany: he would not wish to let matters rest at any Marne-Valmy (it was, however, more like a Marne-Kolin), but to have civilization's troops march into Berlin with a full band – how his heart would welcome them! How he would find ways and means to give ambiguous expression to the triumph of his soul! Alas, this will not happen. It is a thankless business to play the blaspheming prophet in a country where consequences do not follow, in the country of half-measures, which is at best only overtaken by half-catastrophes and which is not capable of a tidy, novelistic fate! Civilization's literary man will not have the *débâcle* of the German *second empire* to write. Not at all. He will have to be content if Germany does not win far too impressively.

I ask you to believe me that if anything like scorn or bitterness may have forced itself into my lines, it has happened against my will. I have no desire at all to speak bitterly or scornfully; on the contrary, my efforts in this study are – let us say: to maintain a popular-scholarly style and to characterize a literary-political type. With this in mind, I hasten to make the following observation. The logical, psychological equation of the concepts, "beaten," and "converted," the equation of the physical and spiritual humiliation of a nation, proves that civilization's literary man is not really an opponent of war, not absolutely a pacifist, that he acknowledges incontestable intellectual validity in the decision to wage war, and that he sees in war an *ultima ratio*, yes, something like God's judgment. Striking, but true. Here we see a type of irrationalism that in truth is a spiritualized rationalism in which one proclaims war to be God's judgment as long as there is the slightest chance that Germany may in any way be beaten, even if only by economic suffocation. But on no account longer! For as soon as this prospect disappears, war becomes injustice and raw power, its outcome without spiritual significance. But this must not stop us from insisting that "spirit" is not necessarily pacifistic – as Italy's example teaches, where "spirit" actually made war: for is it not true, the republicans, Freemasons, radicals and literati of Italy who have waged the war represent "spirit" in that country – and certainly not the Social Democrats, who have resisted the war and who are really pacifists. The truth is that civilization's literary man does not denigrate war when it is waged in the service of civilization. Here he follows Voltaire's example, who, though disgusted by Frederick the Great's wars, could flatly demand a war (against the Turks, with whom Frederick had instead almost allied himself) for the sake of civilization. How, then, could the disciple of the Revolution – not to say: its epigone – condemn on principle the spilling of blood for the good cause, for truth, for spirit? "Resolute love of humanity" – the phrase belongs to civilization's literary man – resolute love of humanity is not fearful of shedding blood. The guillotine, just as much as the literary word, is one of its tools, just as the stake was earlier, which, to be sure, was not bloody. We do not need Gabriele d'Annunzio's lewd estheticism at all to point out where civilization's literary man is on principle *not* an opponent of war. He finds fault with *this* war because he sees it as a German war, an historical enterprise of Germany, as an outburst of the German "protest," because this war carries a German stamp, its activity, its great deeds, are German. He does *not* find fault with it to the extent that he sees it as a war of civilization against the barbaric stubbornness of Germany. In this sense, for the other side, he sees it as good. In short, he does not so much find fault with the war as with Germany, and only herein lies the solution to all the contradictions of which civilization's literary man seems guilty, and which would truly seem amazing without this key. His attitude toward the war vacillates between humanitarian disgust and the greatest admiration for the military accomplishments of the enemies. On the one hand, he sees in the *entente* something tender, fragile, precious, nobly-weak, which is naturally in great danger of being brutalized by barbaric Germany. On the other hand, however, he has only the utmost contempt for those of his countrymen who underestimated the *entente*'s military virtues and powers, or who even still underestimate them. He is delighted by the accomplishments of the powers of civilization; he admires their war mat-eriel, their armor plate, concrete fortifications, aircraft formations, and poison and choking gas bombs, without asking how this fits the image of noble weakness, while he finds the same things on the German side disgusting. A French cannon seems venerable to him, a German one, criminal, repulsive, and idiotic. Here, too, he agrees with all the *entente* minis-ters and journalists that every German victory is only the result and proof of long-standing, sneaky preparation, while every *entente* success is a triumph of spirit over matter. On the other hand, however, his love cannot even abide the idea that an *entente* power, particularly France, could be poorly prepared or insufficiently armed. Armed? They are *splendidly* armed! Again, the logic of all this is not obvious. But who would be such a pedant as to demand logic of love!

As I have said, I want to remain scholarly and informative. But my sketch of civilization's literary man reveals that I do not quite agree with him. My position on the events – a position that I certainly did not "choose," a position that was at first quite unreflected and naively obvious – everything I said about it from the very beginning has embittered him. If I had not done so before, I have now ruined my relationship with him forever. With "pain and anger," he says, he has turned from me, but his pain did not prevent his anger from making ambiguous, half-public statements to me that may be excellent in a political sense, but that are, from a human point of view, simply outright meanness – clearly a nod that the "politics of humanitarianism" is still politics and not exactly conducive to humaneness. But this external estrangement is all the more regrettable because we are basically of one opinion – not of one feeling, but of one opinion on this war. He also agrees with Dostoevsky's con-cept. He, too, recognizes in the war the ancient rebellion of Germany against the Western spirit, against his own spirit, that of the radical literary man – and the intervention of Rome (Western Rome, allied with Eastern Rome) against this rebellion; a war of intervention, then, of European civilization against stubborn Germany: for when the London *Times* announced one day that this war was being waged by the allies "in the interest of Germany's domestic affairs," this is assuredly almost exactly what one means by the words, "shameless audacity," but it was spoken completely in accord with the feeling of civilization's literary man who is also waging it for the sake of European interest in the domestic "conditions" of his country, and, like every Frenchman, after he suffered a period of demoralization in the first few weeks of the war, he has been convinced, since the miracle of the Marne, of the final victory. "Germany will have to conform," he said then, and his eyes glowed. Germany will finally have to be well behaved, he said, and she will then be happy, like a child that cries to be spanked, and, afterward is grateful that its stubbornness has been broken, that it has been helped over its inhibitions, saved, liberated. By beating Germany, by throwing her over our knee, by breaking her evil stubbornness for her own good, and by forcing her to accept reason and to become an honorable member of the democratic society of states, we are saving and freeing her.

I have already admitted that I cannot quite follow this train of thought. I will go further and admit that I find it quite unpleasant, that it somehow *personally* insults and angers me, touches my innermost honor, yes, when I first heard it, worked on me quite like poison and orpiment. But whence comes all this? Whence comes the rebellion of my final and deepest personal-suprapersonal will against the feelings of a good European, who, because he is a good European, wishes for and believes in the defeat of his fatherland, in the taming of his people by the powers of Western Civilization? I was never one of those who felt that an easy and triumphant German military victory over her enemies, with drums beating and trumpets sounding, would be good for Germany or for Europe. I said this very early. But whence comes the feeling that, from the beginning of the war, has ruled my whole being to the very core that I did not want to live – although I am in no way a hero and resolute in the face of death – that I literally did not want to live anymore if Germany were beaten by the West, humbled, her belief in herself broken so that she would have to "conform" and accept the argument, the rationale of her enemies? Supposing this had happened, that the *entente*, for its part, had won a splendid and speedy victory, that the world had been liberated from the German "nightmare," the German "protest," that the empire of civilization had been fulfilled, and that it had become arrogant from lack of opposition: the result would have been a Europe that was – well, a somewhat amusing, somewhat insipidly humane, trivially depraved, femininely elegant Europe that was already all too "human," somewhat implausibly adventurous and loud-mouthed democratic, a Europe of tango and two-step manners, a Europe of business and pleasure *à la* Edward the Seventh, a Monte-Carlo Europe, literary as a Parisian cocotte – but perhaps not a Europe in which it would have been much more advantageous for the likes of me to live than in a "military" one? Perhaps not an amusing, yes, a thoroughly amusing Europe, *lack* of desire for which, in a writer, would at least not testify to selfishness? For beyond doubt it would have been extremely arty, this *entente*-Europe for human freedom and peace, and the artiste, as far as he was precisely an "artiste," would have been able to feel as happy as a lark in it. He should consider this and one should give him credit for it.

Seriously, my rejection is quite remarkable! Remarkable for me – and I have the bad habit of forcing upon others as remarkable what seems so to me. Remarkable – for the fact remains that my own being and essence are much less foreign to those of civilization's literary man than would appear from the cold, objective critique I have subjected him to. What does he want, and if I do not want it – why not? It is, of course, not at all as if he were a bad citizen and patriot who did not care about Germany. On the contrary! He cares about her with all his might. He feels himself to the highest degree responsible for her fate. He wants and supports a development – that I consider necessary, that is to say, unavoidable, and that I also have a certain involuntary part in because of my nature, but that I still cannot see any reason to cheer. With whip and spurs he is hastening a progress – that to me, not seldom at least, seems irresistible and fated, and that I for my modest part am destined to further: but to which I nevertheless, for unclear reasons, am putting up a certain conservative resistance. I want to be completely understood. What I mean is, then: one can very well regard a progress as unavoidable and destined, without in the least feeling like egging it on with cheers and shouts – in my opinion, progress does not really need this at all. Progress has everything for it, above all, the good writers. If it appears that the good writers own the future, the truth in reality is much more that the future owns the good writers. A metaphysical proof of the goodness and imminence of a cause is the good writing in its behalf. However, one can also say that as long as a cause is supported by good writing, it, too, has value and justification, even if it is not progress. I repeat: progress has everything for it. It only seems to be the opposition. It is the conservative counterwill that in truth always and everywhere forms the opposition, that finds itself on the defensive, indeed, hopelessly on the defensive, as it well knows.

What is, then, this development, this progress I have been speaking of? Well, to indicate what it is about, I need a handful of shamelessly ugly, artificial words. It is about the politicization, literarization, intellectualization, and radicalization of Germany. It aims at her "humanization" in the Latin-political sense, and her dehumanization in the German one. It aims, to use the favorite word, the battlecry and hosanna of civilization's literary man, at the *democratization* of Germany, or, to summarize everything and to bring it over a common denominator: it aims at her de-Germanization. And I should have a part in all this mischief?

9

CIVILIZATION'S *STREIT*

'Why War?' (1932)

Sigmund Freud (1856–1939)

Sigmund Freud's 'Why War?' can be viewed as a companion piece to the better-known *Civilization and its Discontents* (1930). Freud's response to the burning question put to him in a letter from Albert Einstein, and written after the carnage of the First World War, is a more sombre and reflective piece than Thomas Mann's which was written at the height of this civilizational battle (cf. chapter 8 above). In contrast with Mann's culturalist response tying culture to the issue of national identity, Freud's response is motivated by the more abstract and generalizable meta-theoretical claims of his psychoanalytic framework which assumes the permanent condition of human violence. In Freud's view, the human propensity for violence underlies all the social relations established between humans as individuals, in groups, and between individuals and society. All human beings are caught up in civilizational war fought on three fronts: between the three poles of instincts, the ego and the super-ego (society). In other words, war is part of, and fought out in, the human being's *internal* territory.

From Freud's perspective, the solution to human violence is its civilization. In this context, Freud returns to the Kantian enquiry into the condition of 'perpetual peace'. For Freud, 'perpetual peace' is both supra-individual and supra-national; it requires the civilizational transference of power to large groups and the formation of collective identities.

Vienna, September, 1932.

Dear Professor Einstein,

When I heard that you intended to invite me to an exchange of views on some subject that interested you and that seemed to deserve the interest of others besides yourself, I readily agreed. I expected you to choose a problem on the frontiers of what is knowable to-day, a problem to which each of us, a physicist and a psychologist, might have our own particular angle of approach and where we might come together from different directions upon the same ground. You have taken me by surprise, however, by posing the question of what can be done to protect mankind from the curse of war.[1] I was scared at first by the thought of my – I had almost written 'our' – incapacity for dealing with what seemed to be a practical problem, a concern for statesmen. But I then realized that you had raised the question not as a natural scientist and physicist but as a philanthropist: you were following the promptings of the League of Nations just as Fridtjof Nansen, the polar explorer, took on the work of bringing help to the starving and homeless victims of the World War. I reflected, moreover, that I was not being asked to make practical proposals but only to set out the problem of avoiding war as it appears to a psychological observer, Here again you yourself have said almost all there is to say on the subject. But though you have taken the wind out of my sails I shall be glad to follow in your wake and content myself with confirming all you have said by amplifying it to the best of my knowledge – or conjecture.

You begin with the relation between Right and Might.[2] There can be no doubt that that is the correct starting-point for our investigation. But may I replace the word 'might' by the balder and harsher word 'violence'? To-day right and violence appear to us as antitheses. It can easily be shown, however, that the one has developed out of the other; and, if we go back to the earliest beginnings and see how that first came about, the problem is easily solved. You must forgive me if in what follows I go over familiar and commonly accepted ground as though it were new, but the thread of my argument requires it.

It is a general principle, then, that conflicts of interest between men are settled by the use of violence. This is true of the whole animal kingdom, from which men have no business to exclude themselves. In the case of men, no doubt, conflicts of *opinion* occur as well which may reach the highest pitch of abstraction and which seem to demand some other technique for their settlement. That, however, is a later complication. To begin with, in a small human horde, it was superior muscular strength which decided who owned things or whose will should prevail. Muscular strength was soon supplemented and replaced by the use of tools: the winner was the one who had the better weapons or who used them the more skilfully. From the moment at which weapons were introduced, intellectual superiority already began to replace brute muscular strength; but the final purpose of the fight remained the same – one side or the other was to be compelled to abandon his claim or his objection by the damage inflicted on him and by the crippling of his strength. That purpose was most completely achieved if the victor's violence eliminated his opponent permanently – that is to say, killed him. This had two advantages: he could not renew his opposition and his fate deterred others from following his example. In addition to this, killing an enemy satisfied an instinctual inclination which I shall have to mention later. The intention to kill might be countered by a reflection that the enemy could be employed in performing useful services if he were left alive in an intimidated condition. In that case the victor's violence was content with subjugating him instead of killing him. This was a first beginning of the idea of sparing an enemy's life, but thereafter the victor had to reckon with his defeated opponent's lurking thirst for revenge and sacrificed some of his own security.

Such, then, was the original state of things: domination by whoever had the greater might – domination by brute violence or by violence supported by intellect. As we know, this régime was altered in the course of evolution. There was a path that led from violence to right or law. What was that path? It is my belief that there was only one: the path which led by way of the fact that the superior strength of a single individual could be rivalled by the union of several weak ones. '*L'union fait la force.*' Violence could be broken by union, and the power of those who were united now represented law in contrast to the violence of the single individual. Thus we see that right is the might of a community. It is still violence, ready to be directed against any individual who resists it; it works by the same methods and follows the same purposes. The only real difference lies in the fact that what prevails is no longer the violence of an individual but that of a community. But in order that the transition from violence to this new right or justice may be effected, one psychological condition must be fulfilled. The union of the majority must be a stable and lasting one. If it were only brought about for the purpose of combating a single dominant individual and were dissolved after his defeat, nothing would have been accomplished. The next person who thought himself superior in strength would once more seek to set up a dominion by violence and the game would be repeated *ad infinitum*. The community must be maintained permanently, must be organized, must draw up regulations to anticipate the risk of rebellion and must institute authorities to see that those regulations – the laws – are respected and to superintend the execution of legal acts of violence. The recognition of a community of interests such as these leads to the growth of emotional ties between the members of a united group of people – communal feelings which are the true source of its strength.

Here, I believe, we already have all the essentials: violence overcome by the transference of power to a larger unity, which is held together by emotional ties between its members. What remains to be said is no more than an expansion and a repetition of this.

The situation is simple so long as the community consists only of a number of equally strong individuals. The laws of such an association will determine the extent to which, if the security of communal life is to be guaranteed, each individual must surrender his personal liberty to turn his strength to violent uses. But a state of rest of that kind is only theoretically conceivable. In actuality the position is complicated by the fact that from its very beginning the community comprises elements of unequal strength – men and women, parents and children – and soon, as a result of war and conquest, it also comes to include victors and vanquished, who turn into masters and slaves. The justice of the community then becomes an expression of the unequal degrees of power obtaining within it; the laws are made by and for the ruling members and find little room for the rights of those in subjection. From that time forward there are two factors at work in the community which are sources of unrest over matters of law but tend at the same time to a further growth of law. First, attempts are made by certain of the rulers to set themselves above the prohibitions which apply to everyone – they seek, that is, to go back from a dominion of law to a dominion of violence. Secondly, the oppressed members of the group make constant efforts to obtain more power and to have any changes that are brought about in that direction recognized in the laws – they press forward, that is, from unequal justice to equal justice for all. This second tendency becomes especially important if a real shift of power occurs within a community, as may happen as a result of a number of historical factors. In that case right may gradually adapt itself to the new distribution of power; or, as is more frequent, the ruling class is unwilling to recognize the change, and rebellion and civil war follow, with a temporary suspension of law and new attempts at a solution by violence, ending in the establishment of a fresh rule of law. There is yet another source from which modifications of law may arise, and one of which the expression is invariably peaceful: it lies in the cultural transformation of the members of the community. This, however, belongs properly in another connection and must be considered later.

Thus we see that the violent solution of conflicts of interest is not avoided even inside a community. But the everyday necessities and common concerns that are inevitable where people live together in one place tend to bring such struggles to a swift conclusion and under such conditions there is an increasing probability that a peaceful solution will be found. Yet a glance at the history of the human race reveals an endless series of conflicts between one community and another or several others, between larger and smaller units – between cities,

141

provinces, races, nations, empires – which have almost always been settled by force of arms. Wars of this kind end either in the spoliation or in the complete overthrow and conquest of one of the parties. It is impossible to make any sweeping judgement upon wars of conquest. Some, such as those waged by the Mongols and Turks, have brought nothing but evil. Others, on the contrary, have contributed to the transformation of violence into law by establishing larger units within which the use of violence was made impossible and in which a fresh system of law led to the solution of conflicts. In this way the conquests of the Romans gave the countries round the Mediterranean the priceless *pax Romana*, and the greed of the French kings to extend their dominions created a peacefully united and flourishing France. Paradoxical as it may sound, it must be admitted that war might be a far from inappropriate means of establishing the eagerly desired reign of 'everlasting' peace, since it is in a position to create the large units within which a powerful central government makes further wars impossible. Nevertheless it fails in this purpose, for the results of conquest are as a rule short-lived: the newly created units fall apart once again, usually owing to a lack of cohesion between the portions that have been united by violence. Hitherto, moreover, the unifications created by conquest, though of considerable extent, have only been *partial*, and the conflicts between these have called out more than ever for violent solution. Thus the result of all these warlike efforts has only been that the human race has exchanged numerous, and indeed unending, minor wars for wars on a grand scale that are rare but all the more destructive.

If we turn to our own times, we arrive at the same conclusion which you have reached by a shorter path. Wars will only be prevented with certainty if mankind unites in setting up a central authority to which the right of giving judgement upon all conflicts of interest shall be handed over. There are clearly two separate requirements involved in this: the creation of a supreme agency and its endowment with the necessary power. One without the other would be useless. The League of Nations is designed as an agency of this kind, but the second condition has not been fulfilled: the League of Nations has no power of its own and can only acquire it if the members of the new union, the separate States, are ready to resign it. And at the moment there seems very little prospect of this. The institution of the League of Nations would, however, be wholly unintelligible if one ignored the fact that here was a bold attempt such as has seldom (perhaps, indeed, never on such a scale) been made before. It is an attempt to base upon an appeal to certain idealistic attitudes of mind the authority (that is, the coercive influence) which otherwise rests on the possession of power. We have seen that a community is held together by two things: the compelling force of violence and the emotional ties (identifications is the technical name) between its members. If one of the factors is absent, the community may possibly be held together by the other. The ideas that are appealed to can, of course, only have any significance if they give expression to important affinities between the members, and the question arises of how much strength such ideas can exert. History teaches us that they have been to some extent effective. For instance, the Panhellenic idea, the sense of being superior to the surrounding barbarians – an idea which was so powerfully expressed in the Amphictyonic Council, the Oracles and the Games – was sufficiently strong to mitigate the customs of war among Greeks, though evidently not sufficiently strong to prevent warlike disputes between the different sections of the Greek nation or even to restrain a city or confederation of cities from allying itself with the Persian foe in order to gain an advantage over a rival. The community of feeling among Christians, powerful though it was, was equally unable at the time of the Renaissance to deter Christian States, whether large or small from seeking the Sultan's aid in their wars with one another. Nor does any idea exist to-day which could be expected to exert a unifying authority of the sort. Indeed it is all too clear that the national ideals by which nations are at present swayed operate in a contrary direction. Some people are inclined to prophesy that it will not be possible to make an end of war until Communist ways of thinking have found universal acceptance. But that aim is in any case a very remote one to-day, and perhaps it could only be reached after the most fearful civil wars. Thus the attempt to replace actual force by the force of ideas seems at present to be doomed to failure. We shall be making a false calculation if we disregard the fact that law was originally brute violence and that even to-day it cannot do without the support of violence.

I can now proceed to add a gloss to another of your remarks. You express astonishment at the fact that it is so easy to make men enthusiastic about a war and add your suspicions that there is something at work in them – an instinct for hatred and destruction – which goes halfway to meet the efforts of the warmongers. Once again, I can only express my entire agreement. We believe in the existence of an instinct of that kind and have in fact been occupied during the last few years in studying its manifestations. Will you allow me to take this opportunity of putting before you a portion of the theory of the instincts which, after much tentative groping and many fluctuations of opinion, has been reached by workers in the field of psycho-analysis?

According to our hypothesis human instincts are of only two kinds: those which seek to preserve and unite – which we call 'erotic', exactly in the sense in which Plato uses the word 'Eros' in his *Symposium*, or 'sexual', with a deliberate extension of the popular conception of 'sexuality' – and those which seek to destroy and kill and which we group together as the aggressive or destructive instinct. As you see, this is in fact no more than a theoretical clarification of the universally familiar opposition between Love and Hate which may perhaps have some fundamental relation to the polarity of attraction and repulsion that plays a part in your own field of knowledge. But we must not be too hasty in introducing ethical judgements of good and evil. Neither of these instincts is any less essential than the other; the phenomena of life arise from the concurrent or mutually opposing action of both. Now it seems as though an instinct of the one sort can scarcely ever operate in isolation; it is always accompanied – or, as we say, alloyed – with a certain quota from the other side, which modifies its aim or is, in some cases, what enables it to achieve that aim. Thus, for instance, the instinct of self-preservation is certainly of an erotic kind, but it must nevertheless have aggressiveness at its disposal if it is to fulfil its purpose. So, too, the instinct of love, when it is directed towards an object, stands in need of some contribution from the instinct for mastery if it is in any way to obtain possession of that object. The difficulty of isolating the two classes of instinct in their actual manifestations is indeed what has so long prevented us from recognizing them.

If you will follow me a little further, you will see that human actions are subject to another complication of a different kind. It is very rarely that an action is the work of a *single* instinctual impulse (which must in itself be compounded of Eros and destructiveness). In order to make an action possible there must be as a rule a combination of such compounded motives. This was perceived long ago by a specialist in your own subject, a Professor G. C. Lichtenberg who taught physics at Göttingen during our classical age – though perhaps he was even more remarkable as a psychologist than as a physicist.[3] He invented a Compass of Motives, for he wrote: 'The motives that lead us to do anything might be arranged like the thirty-two winds and might be given names in a similar way: for instance, "bread-bread-fame" or "fame-fame-bread".' So that when human beings are incited to war they may have a whole number of motives for assenting – some noble and some base, some which are openly declared and others which are never mentioned. There is no need to enumerate them all. A lust for aggression and destruction is certainly among them: the countless cruelties in history and in our everyday lives vouch for its existence and its strength. The satisfaction of these destructive impulses is of course facilitated by their admixture with others of an erotic and idealistic kind. When we read of the atrocities of the past, it sometimes seems as though the idealistic motives served only as an excuse for the destructive appetites; and sometimes – in the case, for instance, of the cruelties of the Inquisition – it seems as though the idealistic motives had pushed themselves forward in consciousness, while the destructive ones lent them an unconscious reinforcement. Both may be true.

I fear I may be abusing your interest, which is after all concerned with the prevention of war and not with our theories. Nevertheless I should like to linger for a moment over our destructive instinct, whose popularity is by no means equal to its importance. As a result of a little speculation, we have come to suppose that this instinct is at work in every living creature and is striving to bring it to ruin and to reduce life to its original condition of inanimate matter. Thus it quite seriously deserves to be called a death instinct, while the erotic instincts represent the effort to live. The death instinct turns into the destructive instinct when, with the help of special organs, it is directed outwards, on to objects. The organism preserves its own life, so to say, by destroying an extraneous one. Some portion of the death instinct, however, remains operative *within* the organism, and we have sought to trace quite a number of normal and pathological phenomena to this internalization of the destructive instinct. We have even been guilty of the heresy of attributing the origin of conscience to this diversion inwards of aggressiveness. You will notice that it is by no means a trivial matter if this process is carried too far: it is positively unhealthy. On the other hand if these forces are turned to destruction in the external world, the organism will be relieved and the effect must be beneficial. This would serve as a biological justification for all the ugly and dangerous impulses against which we are struggling. It must be admitted that they stand nearer to Nature than does our resistance to them for which an explanation also needs to be found. It may perhaps seem to you as though our theories are a kind of mythology and, in the present case, not even an agreeable one. But does not every science come in the end to a kind of mythology like this? Cannot the same be said to-day of your own Physics?

For our immediate purpose then, this much follows from what has been said: there is no use in trying to get rid of men's aggressive inclinations. We are told that in certain happy regions of the earth, where nature provides in abundance everything that man requires, there are races whose life is passed in tranquillity and who know neither coercion nor aggression. I can scarcely believe it and I should be glad to hear more of these fortunate beings. The Russian Communists, too, hope to be able to cause human aggressiveness to disappear by guaranteeing the satisfaction of all material needs and by establishing equality in other respects among all the members of the community. That, in my opinion, is an illusion. They themselves are armed to-day with the most scrupulous care and not the least important of the methods by which they keep their supporters together is hatred of everyone beyond their frontiers. In any case, as you yourself have remarked, there is no question of getting rid entirely of human aggressive impulses; it is enough to try to divert them to such an extent that they need not find expression in war.

Our mythological theory of instincts makes it easy for us to find a formula for *indirect* methods of combating war. If willingness to engage in war is an effect of the destructive instinct, the most obvious plan will be to bring Eros, its antagonist, into play against it. Anything that encourages the growth of emotional ties between men must operate against war. These ties may be of two kinds. In the first place they may be relations resembling those towards a loved object, though without having a sexual aim. There is no need for psycho-analysis to be ashamed to speak of love in this connection, for religion itself uses the same words: 'Thou shalt love thy neighbour as thyself.' This, however, is more easily said than done. The second kind of emotional tie is by means of identification. Whatever leads men to share important interests produces this community of feeling, these identifications. And the structure of human society is to a large extent based on them.

A complaint which you make about the abuse of authority brings me to another suggestion for the indirect combating of the propensity to war. One instance of the innate and ineradicable inequality of men is their tendency to fall into the two classes of leaders and followers. The latter constitute the vast majority; they stand in need of an authority which will make decisions for them and to which they for the most part offer an unqualified submission. This suggests that more care should be taken than hitherto to educate an upper stratum of men with independent minds, not open to intimidation and eager in the pursuit of truth, whose business it would be to give direction to the dependent masses. It goes without saying that the encroachments made by the executive power of the State and the prohibition laid by the Church upon freedom of thought are far from propitious for the production of a class of this kind. The ideal condition of things would of course be a community of men who had subordinated their instinctual life to the dictatorship of reason. Nothing else could unite men so completely and so tenaciously, even if there were no emotional ties between them. But in all probability that is a Utopian expectation. No doubt the other indirect methods of preventing war are more practicable, though they promise no rapid success. An unpleasant picture comes to one's mind of mills that grind so slowly that people may starve before they get their flour.

The result, as you see, is not very fruitful when an unworldly theoretician is called in to advise on an urgent practical problem. It is a better plan to devote oneself in every particular case to meeting the danger with whatever means lie to hand. I should like, however, to discuss one more question, which you do not mention in your letter but which specially interests me. Why do you and I and so many other people rebel so violently against war? Why do we not accept it as another of the many painful calamities of life? After all, it seems to be quite a natural thing, to have a good biological basis and in practice to be scarcely avoidable. There is no need to be shocked at my raising this question. For the purpose of an investigation such as this, one may perhaps be allowed to wear a mask of assumed detachment. The answer to my question will be that we react to war in this way because everyone has a right to his own life, because war puts an end to human lives that are full of hope, because it brings individual men into humiliating situations, because it compels them against their will to murder other men, and because it destroys precious material objects which have been produced by the labours of humanity. Other reasons besides might be given, such as that in its present-day form war is no longer an opportunity for achieving the old ideals of heroism and that owing to the perfection of instruments of destruction a future war might involve the extermination of one or perhaps both of the antagonists. All this is true, and so incontestably true that one can only feel astonished that the waging of war has not yet been unanimously repudiated. No doubt debate is possible upon one or two of these points. It may be questioned whether a community ought not to have a right to dispose of individual lives; every war is not open to condemnation to an equal degree; so long as there exist countries and nations that are prepared for the ruthless destruction of others, those others must be armed for war. But I will not linger over any of these issues; they are not what you want to discuss with me, and I have something different in mind. It is my opinion that the main reason why we rebel against war is that we cannot help doing so. We are pacifists because we are obliged to be for organic reasons. And we then find no difficulty in producing arguments to justify our attitude.

No doubt this requires some explanation. My belief is this. For incalculable ages mankind has been passing through a process of evolution of culture. (Some people, I know, prefer to use the term 'civilization'.) We owe to that process the best of what we have become, as well as a good part of what we suffer from. Though its causes and beginnings are obscure and its outcome uncertain, some of its characteristics are easy to perceive. It may perhaps be leading to the extinction of the human race, for in more than one way it impairs the sexual function; uncultivated races and backward strata of the population are already multiplying more rapidly than highly cultivated ones. The process is perhaps comparable to the domestication of certain species of animals and it is undoubtedly accompanied by physical alterations; but we are still unfamiliar with the notion that the evolution of civilization is an organic process of this kind. The *psychical* modifications that go along with the process of civilization are striking and unambiguous. They consist in a progressive displacement of instinctual aims and a restriction of instinctual impulses. Sensations which were pleasurable to our ancestors have become indifferent or even intolerable to ourselves; there are organic grounds for the changes in our ethical and aesthetic ideals. Of the psychological characteristics of civilization two appear to be the most important: a strengthening of the intellect, which is beginning to govern instinctual life, and an internalization of the aggressive impulses, with all its consequent advantages and perils. Now war is in the crassest opposition to the psychical attitude imposed on us by the process of civilization, and for that reason we are bound to rebel against it; we simply cannot any longer put up with it. This is not merely an intellectual and emotional repudiation; we pacifists have a *constitutional* intolerance of war, an idiosyncrasy magnified, as it were, to the highest degree. It seems, indeed, as though the lowering of aesthetic standards in war plays a scarcely smaller part in our rebellion than do its cruelties.

And how long shall we have to wait before the rest of mankind become pacifists too? There is no telling. But it may not be Utopian to hope that these two factors, the cultural attitude and the justified dread of the consequences of a future war, may result within a measurable time in putting an end to the waging of war. By what paths or by what side-tracks this will come about we cannot guess. But one thing we *can* say: whatever fosters the growth of civilization works at the same time against war.[4]

I trust you will forgive me if what I have said has disappointed you, and I remain, with kindest regards,

Sincerely yours,
SIGM. FREUD

Notes

1 ['Das Verhängnis des Krieges.' Freud quotes Einstein's actual words.]
2 [In the original the words '*Recht*' and '*Macht*' are used throughout Freud's letter and in Einstein's. It has unfortunately been necessary to sacrifice this stylistic unity in the translation. '*Recht*' has

been rendered indifferently by 'right', 'law' and 'justice'; and '*Macht*' by 'might', 'force' and 'power'.]

3 [Georg Christoph Lichtenberg (1742–99) was a favourite author of Freud's.]

4 [The idea of a 'process of civilization' may be traced back to Freud's very early period. But he developed it still further. In rather different terms it figures prominently in the third Essay of *Moses and Monotheism* (Standard Edition, Vol. 32), especially in Section C of Part II. Its two main characteristics (as illustrated in the religion of Moses derived from Akhenaten) are the same as those mentioned here – strengthening of intellectual life and renunciation of instinct.]

Part III

SOCIOLOGY AND ANTHROPOLOGY: FROM CIVILIZATION TO CIVILIZING PROCESSES

10

BETWEEN SOCIOLOGY AND ANTHROPOLOGY I

'Note on the Notion of Civilization' (1913)

Emile Durkheim (1858–1917) and Marcel Mauss (1872–1950)

By the turn of the twentieth century national schools of sociology were being formed, as shown by journals being established specifically for sociology: in Germany, the *Archiv für Socialwissenschaft und Socialpolitik* was founded in 1904; in the United States of America, the *American Journal of Sociology*, published from Chicago, had been in existence since 1895; and in Britain the *Sociological Review* was founded in 1908. In France, two main journals emerged from its two main sociological schools – the Durkheimian with its *Année Sociologique* founded in 1896/7, and the *Revue Internationale de Sociologie*, founded by Rene Worms in 1895, which became the vehicle for anti-Durkheimian sociology. The Durkheimian School included, among others, Marcel Mauss, Maurice Halbwachs, Henri Hubert and Robert Hertz, and extended beyond sociology to inform the work of the sinologist Marcel Granet, and the historians Marc Bloch and Lucien Febvre.

Against this broad background of the professionalization of socio-logy, the concept of civilization continued to be tied to the identity of the West and its political transformations, whilst being simultaneously developed as a category that identified civilizations with states and empires, and organized religions and cultures. Emile Durkheim critic-ally engaged with both sides of the concept of civilization. As his *The Evolution of Educational Thought* makes clear, the notion of civilization refers to the relation between a cultural heritage in the form of educational models, and a civilizing process through which a national ideal is at once forged and re-made. His 'Note on the Notion of Civiliza-tion', written with Marcel Mauss, further emphasizes civilizations as extensive patterns of cultural identity. As the emphasis for civilization is a cultural one, as also seen in *The Elementary Forms of Religious Life*, rather than one that gives precedence to states and empires, it can also refer to the social formations of the Pacific, indigenous Americans and Australians, and not only to the Middle East and its European and Indian hinterlands.

One of the rules we follow here is that, in studying social phenomena in themselves and by themselves, we take care not to leave them in the air but always to relate them to a definite substratum, that is to say, to a human group occupying a determinate portion of geographically representable space. But, of all these groups, the largest – that which comprises all of the others in itself and which consequently comprises all forms of social activity – is, it would appear, that which forms the political society: tribe, clan, nation, city, state, and so on. It seems then, on first view, that collective life can develop only within political organisms having definite contours, within strictly marked limits, that is to say, that the national life is the highest form of social phenomenon and sociology cannot know one of a higher order.

There are, none the less, phenomena which do not have such well-defined limits; they pass beyond the political frontiers and extend over less easily determinable spaces. Although their complexity renders their study difficult, it none the less behooves us to acknowledge their existence and to indicate their place within the bounds of sociology.

Ethnography and prehistory, especially, have directed attention to this perspective.

The enormous work, which has been pursued for three decades in the ethnographic museums of America and Germany and in prehistoric museums of France and Sweden above all, has not remained without theoretical results. Especially on the ethnological side, scientific requirements of simplification and of cataloguing and even simple practical necessities of organization and exposition have produced classifications which are at the same time logical, geographical, and chronological: logical because, in the absence of a possible history, logic is the sole means of perceiving, at least hypothetically, historical sequences of tools, styles, and so on; chronological and geographical because these series develop in time as in space and extend to many different peoples. For a long time now American museums have displayed charts showing the extension of this or that type of art, and prehistoric museums have proposed geological schemas for the forms of certain tools.

Therefore, social phenomena that are not strictly attached to a determinate social organism do exist: they extend into areas that reach beyond the national territory or they develop over periods of time that exceed the history of a single society. They have a life which is in some ways supranational.

But these problems are not only posed by technology or esthetics. Several phenomena of the same genre have been known in linguistics for a long time. Languages spoken by different peoples have close links to one another – for example, certain verbal and grammatical forms that appear in different societies, which permit us to group these societies into families of people who are or have been in relationship with one another or who have the same origin; thus one now speaks of an Indo-European language. It is the same with institutions. The quite different Algonquin and Iroquois nations had similar sorts of totemism and a similar kind of magic or religion. Among all the Polynesian peoples one finds a similar type of political organization (power of the chief). The beginnings of the family have been identical among all peoples who speak an Indo-European language.

Moreover, it has been recognized that phenomena which present this degree of extension are not independent of one another; they are generally linked in an interdependent system. It often occurs that one of these phenomena involves the others and reveals their existence. Matrimonial classes are characteristic of an entire ensemble of beliefs and practices which appear throughout Australia. The absence of pottery is one of the distinctive traits of Polynesian industry. A certain form of the adze is an essentially Melanesian object. All peoples who speak an Indo-European language have a common fund of ideas and institutions. There exist not merely isolated instances, but also complex and interdependent systems, which without being limited to a determinate political organism are, however, localizable in time and space.

It becomes necessary to give a special name to those systems of facts that have their own unity and form of existence. Civilization seems to be the most appropriate name. Without doubt every civilization is susceptible to nationalization; it may assume particular characteristics with each people of each state; but its most essential elements are not the product of the state or of the people alone. Rather, they extend beyond these frontiers, whether they extend out from a determinate area by a power of expansion originating within them, or whether they result from relationships established among different societies and so are the common product of these societies.

For example: we speak of a Christian civilization, which, while having different centers, has been developed by all Christian peoples. There is a Mediterranean civilization common to all the people who bordered the Mediterranean coast. There is a civilization of Northwest America common to the Tlinkit, to the Tsimshian and to the Haida, even though they speak various languages and have different customs. A civilization constitutes a kind of moral milieu encompassing a certain number of nations, each national culture being only a particular form of the whole.

It is noteworthy that these very general phenomena were the first to attract the attention of sociologists; and these served as material for emerging sociology. For Comte, it was not a question of particular societies, nations or states. What he studied was the general movement of civilization, abstracting national particularities. At least, the latter interested him only insofar as they could aid in establishing successive stages of human progress.

We have often had the occasion to show how this method is inadequate to the facts, for it leaves aside the concrete reality which the observer can better and more immediately grasp, that is, the social organism, the great collective personalities which are constituted in the course of history. It is to them that the sociologist has to relate above all. He must commit himself to describe them, to arrange them in genus and in species, to analyze and to explain the elements that compose them. One might say that the human milieu, the integral humanity of which Comte hoped to make a science, is only a construction of the spirit.

None the less, it still remains that beyond these national groupings there are other wider and less clearly defined groupings, which do have individuality and which are the seat of a new sort of social life. If there does not exist one human civilization, there have been and there still are diverse civilizations which dominate and develop the collective life of each people. Here is an order of things which deserves to be studied by appropriate procedures.

All sorts of problems, neglected until now, could be connected with this subject. One could ask what are the diverse conditions which determine variations in the areas of civilizations, why have they stopped here or there, what forms have they taken and what factors determine these forms. As Ratzel has shown, these questions that are asked concerning political frontiers could be posed equally well with respect to symbolic frontiers (*frontières idéales*).

Furthermore, not all social phenomena are equally apt to internationalize themselves. Political institutions, juridical institutions, the phenomena of social morphology constitute part of the specific character of each people. On the other hand, the myths, tales, money, commerce, fine arts, techniques, tools, language, words, scientific knowledge, literary forms and ideas – all of these travel and are borrowed. In short, they result from a process involving more than a determinate society.

It is justifiable, then, to ask on what this unequal coefficient of expansion and internationalization depends. These differences are not determined solely by the intrinsic nature of the social phenomena, but also by the diverse conditions influencing the societies. A certain form of collective life, then, may or may not be susceptible to internationalization depending on these circumstances. Christianity is essentially international, but there have also been some strictly national religions. There are some languages which are spread across vast territories; there are others which serve to distinguish nationalities, as is the case with those spoken by the great peoples of Europe.

All these problems are properly sociological. Undoubtedly, they cannot be approached unless other problems, which do not pertain to sociology, are resolved. It belongs to ethnography and to history to map these areas of civilization and to link diverse civilizations to their fundamental source. But once these preliminary tasks have sufficiently advanced, other more general questions, which do relate to sociology, become possible to consider. Some of these have been indicated above. It is a matter of arriving at causes and laws by means of methodical comparisons.

Also, one might question how writers – for example, Father Schmidt – have undertaken to separate the study of civilizations from sociology, reserving it for other disciplines, notably ethnography. First of all, ethnography does not suffice for the task. History has similar studies to make with respect to historic peoples. Moreover, civilization only expresses a collective life of a special genre, the substratum of which is a plurality of interrelated political bodies acting upon one another. International life is merely social life of a higher kind, and one which sociology needs to know. The exclusion of sociology from these studies would never have been considered if it were not still too often believed that to explain a civilization one need merely ask whence it comes, from what it has borrowed, and by what means it has passed from one point to another. In reality, the true manner of understanding all this is to determine the causes of which it is the result, that is to say, what collective interactions of diverse orders produced it.

11

BETWEEN SOCIOLOGY AND ANTHROPOLOGY II

'Civilizations: Elements and Forms' (1929)

Marcel Mauss (1872–1950)

For Durkheim and Mauss, sociology and anthropology could not be separated, and in Mauss's work anthropology came to predominate. This predominance was played out in two discrete, although interconnected ways – through analyses of the dynamics and patterns of social inter-action, and in comparative analyses of civilizations. In both *The Gift* (1925) and 'Civilizations: Elements and Forms', Mauss extends the model already present in the 1913 'Note on the Notion of Civilization'.

In *The Gift*, Mauss argues that the exchanges of archaic societies – which, in his view, are civilizations – are made up of a totality which includes the economic, judicial, moral, aesthetic and religious aspects of life. Their meaning can be grasped only if their interrelation is grasped also. In 'Civilizations: Elements and Forms', Mauss distinguishes between what has become the everyday usage of 'civilization', and a more compli-cated usage which defines it as an amalgam of social processes which may include state-formation, as well as the development of cultural and religious systems of belief. The two processes may not coincide. For Mauss, civilization cannot be reduced to the political history of a particular people, in the West or elsewhere, or a form of state. From the perspective of their cultural component, civilizations are more territorially open and extensive than empires or states.

Each direction in Mauss's work is underpinned by the Durkheimian emphasis on the social facticity of collective representations. Collective representations provide the specificity that each civilization acquires, thus providing the basis for a comparison between them, even if, as Mauss seems to think, modern civilization is typified by an increasing combina-tion of nations with industrialism, the result of which is the globalization of Western industrial civilization at the expense of more diverse forms.

Everyday meanings of the word 'Civilization'

It is no great academic error to accept the popular usage [of the word 'civilization']. People correctly speak of 'French civilization', meaning by that something more than 'French nationality', because in fact it is something which spreads beyond the linguistic boundaries of French, for example into Flanders or into German-speaking parts of

Luxembourg. German culture was until recently still dominant in the Baltic states. Hellenic and hellenistic civilization – the extent of which we do not understand that we do not understand – and Byzantine civilization, about which we ought to make the same remark – conveyed many things and ideas over great distances, and incorporated many populations other than the Greeks, often in a very firm way.

Again, it is acceptable to speak of civilization when great masses of people have succeeded in creating for themselves mentalities, manners, arts and crafts, which have been spread among the whole population forming a state (whether a single state or a compound one does not much matter). The Eastern Empire, for example, was the seat of 'Byzantine civilization'. M. Granet has rightly spoken of 'Chinese civilization' within the boundaries of China; he is equally right to describe as Chinese certain traits outside those boundaries: in all the places to which have spread Chinese writing, the prestige of the Chinese classics, drama and music, artistic symbols, and that politeness and style of life which the Chinese had before Europe was polished or policed. In Vietnam, Korea, Manchuria and Japan, one is more or less in countries of Chinese civilization. India as well has two unities, not one: 'India is the Brahmin', Sir Alfred Lyall used to say, but Indian civilization still exists over and above that; through Buddhism it radiated out through perhaps the whole ancient Far East; the Sanskrit word *nâraka*, 'hell', is used in thousands of seaports in India, Indonesia, even New Guinea. Besides, India and Bhuddism are now spreading to us.

One example may give a more concrete feel to this complexity than can any simplistic, naïvely political, history: the famous friezes and immense sculptures of the Bayon in Angkor Thom, the four storeys of people, animals and things, the ornaments of creatures celestial and symbolic, terrestrial and maritime. But these great narrative tableaux, what are they? The whole thing has an indisputable Indo-Cambodian air. It already shows a magnificent and remarkable crossbreeding! But there is more to it: one of the friezes is Buddhist, another represents the Hindu – not even Vedic – epic of Vishnu and Siva. A fairly complete explanation of these two is beginning to be given by French academics. It is the largest of the friezes which poses an hitherto insoluble difficulty. An immense army of thousands of soldiers marches past before us. The priests, officers and princes are Hindus, or Indian in appearance. It is believed to be the war of Râmayana, but that is not certain. In any case, the subalterns, the troops, some of the equipment, the arms, the gait, the clothes, the gestures are from a civilization apart, otherwise unknown. The faces (and we have no reason not to believe they are faithful representations; though stylized, they bear the mark of art and truth) represent a race which does not correspond at all well, not only with any present-day race, but even with any known pure race. A last sequence represents the life and crafts of the time. Some already have an Indo-Chinese appearance. Since the end of the first millennium AD, Indochina has been a 'witch's cauldron' where races and civilizations were blended.

This example makes apparent a third sense of the word civilization: that which is applied so to speak exclusively to moral and religious matters. One can speak of 'Buddhist civilization', or more exactly of 'civilizing Buddhism', when one knows how it punctuates a large part of the moral and aesthetic life of Indochina, China, Japan and Korea, and almost the whole life – even the politics – of the Tibetans and Buryats. The use of the expression 'Islamic civilization' can be considered appropriate in so far as Islam is able to assimilate its faithful completely, from their smallest gesture to their intimate being. Even around the idea of the Caliphate it failed to form a political state, yet it has many of the traits of a state. One can also legitimately speculate about the 'Catholic' – that is, 'universal', for itself – civilization of the medieval West, even though Latin remained a common language only for Church and University. Historically, from the point of view of the members of that civilization – it is more exact to speak of it as 'Catholic civilization' than to call it European, for the notion of Europe did not as yet exist.

Finally, there remains a group of three meanings that are given – sometimes academically, and almost always popularly – to the term civilization.

Philosophers and the public understand by civilization 'culture', *Kultur*, the means of improvement, of reaching a higher level of wealth and comfort, of strength and skilfullness, of becoming a civic and civil being, of establishing law and order, of imposing civility and courtesy, of being refined, of appreciating and promoting the arts.

Linguists to some extent share the same idea when they use the word 'culture' in a comprehensible double sense. On the one hand, they see the 'languages of civilization' – Latin, English, German, etc., and now Czech, Serb, etc. – as means of education, transmission and tradition, in science and technology, in the propagation of literature *à partir de milieux assez vastes et assez anciens*. On the other hand, they contrast these with patois and dialects, the little languages of little groups and sub-groups, of less civilized nations, and especially rural speech – that is to say, with languages which are not very extensively spoken and consequently (here there is an inference which is probable but not proven) less refined. For the linguists, a language's criterion of value, expansive character, role as lingua franca, and capacity for transmission is merged with the quality of the ideas and the language transmitted. Their double definition is not very far from ours.

Finally, statesmen, philosophers, the public – and publicists still more – speak of 'Civilization' with a capital C. On the one hand, in a period of nationalism, 'Civilization' is always *their* culture, the culture of their nation, for they generally do not know about the civilization of others. And on the other hand, in a period of rationalism, one that is generally universalist and cosmopolitan in the manner of the great religions, 'Civilization' constitutes a kind of state of affairs that is at once real and ideal, rational and natural at the same time, simultaneously causal and final, which in the course of undisputed 'progress' will be brought about little by little.

Basically, both these senses correspond to an ideal state that people have dreamed about through a century and a half of political thinking. This perfect essence has never existed except as a myth, a collective representation. This simultaneously universalist and nationalist belief is a trait of our international and national Western civilizations, European and (non-Indian) North American. On the one hand some see 'Civilization' as a kind of perfect nation: the 'closed State' of Fichte, autonomous and self-sufficient, the civilization and language of which would stretch out to fill political frontiers. A few nations have realized this ideal, and some consciously pursue it – for example, the United States. Other writers and orators think about 'human civilization', in the abstract, in the future. Humanity 'progressing' is a commonplace of philosophy, as of politics. Others, finally, reconcile the two ideas: classes, nations, civilizations are seen as having historic missions only in relation to 'Civilization'. Of course, this civilization is always Western. It is raised to the level of a common ideal as well as a rational basis of human progress; and, assisted by optimism, it is made the condition of happiness. The nineteenth century mixed up the two ideas, taking *its* civilization for civilization in general. Each nation and each class did the same. That provided material for unlimited special pleading.

However, one may think that new features of our life have created something new in the order of things. It seems to us that, in our time, for once it is in the realm of facts and no longer in that of ideology that something like 'Civilization' is coming true. To begin with, without nations disappearing – indeed without them all having been fully formed – there is a growing stock of international realities and international ideas. The international nature of the facts of civilization is becoming more marked. The number of phenomena of this type is increasing; they are spreading and spawning each other. They are increasing in quality. Tools, costumes, objects may remain here and there as specific, irrational, picturesque evidence of past nations and civilizations. Machines and chemical processes cannot do that. Science dominates everything and, as Leibniz predicted, its language is necessarily that of humanity as a whole. Finally, a new form of communication, of tradition, of description, of recording things and even matters of sentiment and custom – the cinema – is becoming universal. A new way of preserving sounds – the phonograph – and another means of broadcasting them – the radio – have in less than ten years come to transmit all music, all accents, all words, all information across every barrier. We are only at the beginning.

We do not know whether some reactions might not transform certain elements of civilization – as we have seen in the case of chemistry and aviation – into means of national violence or, what is worse, national arrogance. Nations may perhaps once again unscrupulously detach themselves from the humanity from which they draw nourishment and improvement. But it is certain that in our time an unprecedented inter-permeability is becoming established; the number of common traits among existing nations and civilizations is growing; each one is coming more and more to resemble the others because the common basis is growing daily in extent, strength and quality, and spreading daily at an increasing speed. Certain elements of the new civilization even stem from populations which a few years ago existed in isolation, and even today are remote. The success of primitive art, including music, demonstrates that the history of all this may well take unexpected turns.

Let us end with this idea of a *common basis*, of *acquired general characteristics of societies and civilizations*. This is, in my opinion, the counterpart to the idea of 'Civilization': a limit to the fusion and not a principle of civilizations. The latter are nothing if they are not cherished and developed by the nations by which they are held. But just as, within nations, science, industry and the arts, and even 'distinction' are ceasing to be the property of small classes of people and are becoming in the larger nations a sort of common privilege, so the best traits of these civilizations will become the common property of more and more numerous social groups. The poet and the historian may mourn local flavours. Perhaps there will be ways of saving them. But humanity's stock of capital will grow in any case. The products and facilities of the sun and the seaside are now being more and more rationally organized, and exploited for the market, worldwide. It is not wrong to speak of this as 'civilization'. Indisputably, all nations and civilizations are at present tending towards *accretion*, becoming *stronger*, *more general* and *more rational* (the last two terms are reciprocal for, outside symbols, people come into communion with each other only in the rational and the real).

And this accretion is evidently becoming more and more widespread, better understood, and held by larger and larger numbers of people.

M. Seignobos used to say that a civilization consisted of roads, ports and quays. This jest points to the industrial capital which created civilization. The intellectual capital which has created it must also be included: 'pure reason', 'practical reason', 'the force of judgment', to use Kant's terms. This idea of a growing heritage, a growing intellectual and material wealth shared by a more and more reasonable humanity is, I sincerely believe, founded on fact. It permits sociological appreciation of civilizations, the relations of a nation to a civilization, without necessarily carrying value judgments, neither about nations, nor civilization, nor about 'Civilization'. For the latter does not, any more than 'progress', necessarily lead to wealth or happiness.

12

HISTORY AND CIVILIZATION

'Civilisation: Evolution of a Word and a Group of Ideas' (1930)

Lucien Febvre (1878–1956)

Lucien Febvre was a founding member of the *Annales* School, the name of which was taken from the journal that he and Marc Bloch jointly established in 1929. The School's other members included Henri Berr, Fernand Braudel, who joined the group in 1937, Jacques Le Goff and Emmanuel Le Roy Ladurie, both of whom are more recent members. Lucien Febvre and the *Annales* School emphasize the complex interplay between heterogeneous dimensions of social life in equally complex interplay with its natural environment.

Febvre's '*Civilisation*: Evolution of a Word and a Group of Ideas' is a detailed analysis of the emergence of the notion of civilization within the specifically French context, and of the way in which it also gained currency as a general category to describe societal types. Febvre's essay points to the unresolved tension between the two uses of the term as a category of either identity or taxonomy. The *Annales* School generally develops the category of civilization as one pertaining to identity, and yet in so doing, also makes civilization a category through which the intersection of spatial and temporal, material and cultural settings and patterns can be thematized and explored.

It is never a waste of time to study the history of a word. Such journeys, whether short or long, monotonous or varied are always instructive. But in every major language there are a dozen or so terms, never more, often less, whose past is no food for the scholar. But it is for the historian if we give the word historian all its due force.

Such terms, whose meaning is more or less crudely defined in dictionaries, never cease to evolve under the influence of human experience and they reach us pregnant, one might say, with all the history through which they have passed. They alone can enable us to follow and measure, perhaps rather slowly but very precisely (language is not a very rapid recording instrument), the transformations which took place in a group of those governing ideas which man is pleased to think of as being immobile because their immobility seems to be a guarantee of his security.[1] Constructing the history of the French word *civilisation* would in fact mean reconstituting the stages in the most profound of all the revolutions which the French spirit has achieved and undergone in the period starting with the second half of the eighteenth century and taking us up to the present day. And so it will mean embracing in its totality, but from one particular point of view, a history whose origins and influence have not been confined within the frontiers of a single state. The simple sketch which follows may make it possible to date the periods in the revolution to which we refer with more rigour than previously. And it will at least show once more that the rhythm of the waves which break upon our societies are, in the last instance, governed and determined by the progress not of a particular science and of thought that revolves within one and the same circle, but by progress in all the disciplines together and in all the branches of learning working in conjunction.

Let us clearly mark out the limits of the problem. Some months ago a thesis was defended in the Sorbonne dealing with the civilization of the Tupi-Guarani, The Tupi-Guarani are small tribes living in South America which in every respect fit the term 'savage' as used by our ancestors. But for a long time now the concept of a civilization of non-civilized people has been current. If archaeology were able to supply the means, we should see an archaeologist coolly dealing with the civilization of the Huns, who we were once told were 'the flail of civilization'.

But our newspapers and journals, and we ourselves, talk continually about the progress, conquests and benefits of civilization. Sometimes with conviction, sometimes with irony and sometimes even with bitterness. But what counts is that we talk about it. And what this implies is surely that one and the same word is used to designate two different concepts.

In the first case civilization simply refers to all the features that can be observed in the collective life of one human group, embracing their material, intellectual, moral and political life and, there is unfortunately no other word for it, their social life. It has been suggested that this should be called the 'ethnographical' conception of civilization.[2] It does not imply any value judgment on the detail or the overall pattern of the facts examined. Neither does it have any bearing on the individual in the group taken separately, or on their personal reactions or individual behaviour. It is above all a conception which refers to a group.

In the second case, when we are talking about the progress, failures, greatness and weakness of civilization we do have a value judgment in mind. We have the idea that the civilization we are talking about – ours – is in itself something great and beautiful; something too which is nobler, more comfortable and better, both morally and materially speaking, than anything outside it – savagery, barbarity or semi-civilization. Finally, we are confident that such civilization, in which we participate, which we propagate, benefit from and popularize, bestows on us all a certain value, prestige, and dignity. For it is a collective asset enjoyed by all civilized societies. It is also an individual privilege which each of us proudly boasts that he possesses.

So within a language that is said to be clear and logical, one and the same word today refers to two very different concepts which are almost contradictory. How did this come about? How and to what extent can the history of this word throw light on these problems?

Civilisation came into the language only recently, André-Louis Mazzini, on the first page of his book dated 1847, *De l'Italie dans ses rapports avec la liberté et la civilisation moderne*, writes: 'This word was created by France, by the French spirit at the end of the century.' And that straightaway calls to mind the letter from Nietzsche to Strindberg, who in 1888 was sorry that he was not a German: 'There is no other civilization than that of France. There can be no objection to this; it stands to reason; it is necessarily the true civilization.'[3] As we shall see, these statements raise but do not settle a fairly important question. At least one fact is incontestable – *civilisation* is, in the French language, a word of recent origin and usage.

Who was the first to use it or at least to have it printed? We do not know. No one will be surprised at this confession. We are very poorly equipped, in fact we are not equipped at all to write the history of words of recent origin in our language. Apart from the series of *Dictionnaires de l'Académie française* (1694, 1718, 1740, 1762, 1798, 1835, 1878), apart from the classical indexes which, from Furetière to Littré, not forgetting the *Encyclopédie*, supplement the basic collections; and finally, apart from some useful but rather summary work on the eighteenth century – Gohin's study (1903), of *Les transformations de la langue française de 1710 à 1789*, and Max Frey's study (1925) on *Les Transformations du vocabulaire français à l'époque de la Révolution, 1798–1800*, we have no material at all to work on; and if I call such works summary, I am forced to do so by the facts themselves; we do not even have twenty individual lexicons of the language of Montesquieu, Voltaire, Turgot, Rousseau, Condorcet, etc., which alone could enable us to write one of the finest and newest chapters in that general history of French thought via language whose value and usefulness have been so well shown in M. Ferdinand Brunot's monumental *Histoire de la langue française*.

Anybody who wants to write the history of a word which appeared for the first time in the eighteenth century is today forced to carry out random samples throughout an infinite amount of literature without the help of any indexes or catalogues. And so, for a rather chancy result hours and hours of work have to be wasted. For my part, throughout the course of long reading sessions which were conducted as methodically as possible, I have not been able to find the word *civilisation* used in any French text published prior to the year 1766.

I know that the use of this neologism is usually attributed to the young Turgot's Sorbonne lectures at an earlier date. Under *Civilisation* Gohin's work mentions its date of birth: 'about 1752', and there is a reference: 'Turgot, II, 674'.[4] Obviously this reference is not to the Schelle edition, which alone is taken as an authority, but to the Daire and Dussard edition, the two volumes of which (established on the basis of the Dupont de Nemours edition) appeared in the *Collection des principaux économistes* in 1844. In it we find, published, or more precisely, reproduced in vol. ii (p. 671) *Pensées et fragments qui avaient été jetés sur le papier pour être employés dans un des trois ouvrages sur l'histoire universelle ou sur les progrès et la décadence des Sciences et des Arts*. And on p. 674 we read: '*Au commencement de la civilisation les progrès peuvent être, et surtout paraître rapides*' (At the beginning of civilization progress may be, and especially, appears to be rapid). Unfortunately it was very probably not Turgot who wrote this but Dupont de Nemours who would have used it quite naturally when publishing his master's works at a much later date.[5] We do not find it in the text reproduced by M. Schelle, taken directly from the manuscripts.[6] It does not appear either in the lectures of 1750, or in the letter of 1751 to Madame de Graffigny on the *Lettres d'une Péruvienne*; or in the article on *Étymologie* in the *Encyclopédie* (1756). The meaning conveyed in all these works,[7] often conjures up for us the word which the Sorbonne prior is said to have put forward as early as 1750, but he never actually uses it; he does not even use the verb *civiliser*, or the participle *civilisé* which was then in current use; he always keeps to *police* and to *policé*, in short he is supposed to have written down on paper on one single occasion in his life a word which he then had no further truck with and, I add, which none of his contemporaries would have ventured to put forward for at least another ten years, neither Rousseau in his *Discours* which was crowned at Dijon in 1750, nor Duclos in his *Considérations sur les moeurs de ce siècle* (1751), nor Helvetius in his *Esprit* (1758); we need not go on with the list.

So the word with which we are concerned could not be found in print until 1766. At that date the firm of Rey in Amsterdam published in two forms, one quarto volume and three duodecimo volumes, the *Antiquité dévoilée par ses usages*, by the late M. Boulanger. In volume

III of the 12mo edition we read: '*Lorsqu'un peuple sauvage vient à être civilisé, il ne faut jamais mettre fin à l'acte de la civilisation en lui donnant des lois fixes et irrévocables; il faut lui faire regarder la législation qu'on lui donne comme une civilisation continuée*' (When a savage people has become civilized, we must not put an end to the act of *civilisation* by giving it rigid and irrevocable laws; we must make it look upon the legislation given to it as a form of *continuous civilisation*).[8] This original and intelligent expression is printed in italics. The *Antiquité dévoilée* is a posthumous work; the author died in 1759. So the word would go back to that date at least if we did not know that someone added to, if not rewrote, the manuscript of the late M. Boulanger, engineer of the *Ponts et Chaussées*, while preparing it for publication. And that someone was that great neologist in the face of the Eternal, Baron d'Holbach, who had, for instance, as early as 1773 written in his *Système social*: '*L'homme en société s'électrise*' (Man becomes electric in society), two years after the appearance in the bookshops of Priestley's *Histoire de l'électricité*.[9] And the striking fact is that d'Holbach used the word '*civilisation*' in his *Système social*.[10] But Boulanger never does, with the exception of the sentence quoted above. I have read the *Recherches sur l'origine du despotisme oriental*, (1761) with great care; *civilisé* does appear in it, but fairly infrequently; *civilisation* never does; *police* and *policé* are the usual terms. The example would be unique in Boulanger's work, but not in the work of d'Holbach. In any case we have the fact we want. We have an example dated 1766 of the use of the word. I do not say that it is the first example, and of course I should like other researchers to have better luck than me and depose Boulanger, or d'Holbach, and wrest from them a claim to fame which in any case is a fairly modest one.

The word does not remain alien. Between 1765 and 1775 it becomes naturalized. In 1767 we find the Abbé Baudeau using it in his turn in the *Ephémérides du citoyen*,[11] and stating that '*la propriété foncière est un pas très important vers la civilisation la plus parfaite*' (land ownership . . . constitutes a very important step towards the most perfect form of civilization); a little bit later in 1771 he used the word again in his *Première Introduction à la philosophie économique, ou analyse des états policés*.[12] Raynal, in his *Histoire, philosophie et politique des établissements et du commerce des Européens dans les deux Indes (1770)*, follows his example; the new word is used several times in his nineteenth book.[13] Diderot in turn ventures to use the word in 1773–4, in his *Réfutation suivie de l'ouvrage d'Helvétius intitulé 'l'Homme'*.[14] But it is not simply to be found everywhere. In his essay *De la félicité publique* and in his work on *Considérations sur le sort des hommes dans les différentes époques de l'histoire*, volume i of which appeared in Amsterdam in 1772, Father Jean de Chastellux uses the word *police* a great deal but never, so it appears, *civilisation*.[15] Buffon, who is a purist author, may use the verb and the participle, but he does not seem to know the substantive at all in his *Époques de la Nature* (1774–9). The same is true of Antoine-Yves Goguet in his book *De l'origine des loix, des arts et des sciences et de leurs progrès chez les anciens peuples* (1778), where one might expect to meet it. Démeunier on the other hand, in *l'Esprit des usages et des coutumes des différents peuples* (1776), talks about the '*progrès de la civilisation*'[16] and the word is getting less rare. As we approach the Revolution it begins to triumph.[17] And in 1798, for the first time, it forces its way into the *Dictionnaire de l'Académie*, which had ignored it until then, just as the *Encyclopédie* and even the *Encyclopédie méthodique* had done;[18] the *Dictionnaire de Trévoux* alone had included it, giving it simply its old legal meaning, '*Civilisation, terme de jurisprudence. C'est un jugement qui rend civil un procès criminel*'[19] (Civilisation, term used in jurisprudence. A judgment turning a criminal case into a civil case).

So between 1765 and 1798 a term which nowadays we could hardly do without was born, grew up and imposed itself in France. But here we have another problem which can only be solved through a series of lucky finds.

If we open the second volume of Murray's *New English Dictionary* and look in it for the background to the English word, which, but for one letter is a faithful replica of the French *civilisation*, we find a very expressive text by Boswell.[20] He says that on 23 March 1772 he went to see the ageing Johnson who was working on the preparation of the fourth edition of his dictionary. And he records the following: 'He [Johnson] would not admit *civilisation*, but only *civility*. With great deference to him, I thought *civilization*, from *to civilize*, better in the sense opposed to *barbarity*, than *civility*.' It is a very curious text. 1772; one knows the intellectual relations that existed at that time between the French and the English, linking the *élite* of both countries and it is impossible not to put the obvious question concerning origins. But who borrowed from whom?

Murray does not quote any English texts prior to that of Boswell giving *civilization* with the meaning of *culture*. The text is dated 1772; and Boulanger's is 1766 at least – five years between them. It is not very much. But there is a text which would appear to confirm the fact that the French word preceded the English word. In 1771 at Amsterdam the French translation appeared of Robertson's *The History of the Reign of the Emperor Charles V.*[21] Of course I wondered about the work, which might well have been able to throw some light on the problem of origins. And in the *Introduction* (p. 23, French version) I found the following sentence: '*Il est necessaire de suivre les pas rapides qu'ils (les peuples du Nord) firent de la barbarie à la civilisation*', and a bit further on I met the following sentence: '*L'état le plus corrompu de la société humaine est celui ou les hommes ont perdu . . . leur simplicité de moeurs primitives sans être arrivés à ce degré de civilisation ou un sentiment de justice et d'honnêteté sert de frein aux passions féroces et cruelles.*' At once I turned to the English text to that *View of the Progress of Society in Europe* which opens this well known book. In both cases the word which the French translator translated as *civilisation* is not the English *civilisation*, but *refinement*.

The fact is not unimportant. It certainly diminishes any role one might attribute to the Scots in introducing this new word. In France, it is true, we find it in translated works such as the *Observations sur les commencements de la société* by J. Millar, the Glasgow professor, in 1773.[22] And Grimm, who gives an account of the book in his *Correspondance littéraire*, takes the opportunity of putting *civilisation* in print.[23] But by that date it is no longer the least bit surprising. We meet it in another translated work, Robertson's *Histoire de l'Amérique*,[24] but that dates from 1780. We also find it in Roucher's translation, annotated by Condorcet in 1790, of Adam Smith's *The Wealth of Nations*.[25] These are only a few examples. But we cannot, on the basis of the examples found, conclude that there was any transfer of the word from Scotland or England to France. Until anything new comes to light Robertson's text excludes the possibility.

However that may be, English usage like French usage ushers in a new problem. On both sides of the Channel the verb *civiliser* (to civilize) and the participle *civilisé* (civilized) appear in the language long before the corresponding substantive.[26] The examples given by Murray take us back as far as the second third of the seventeenth century (1631–41). In France Montaigne uses the word in his *Essais* as early as the sixteenth century. '*Il avait,*' he writes talking of Turnebus, '*quelque façon externe qui pouvait n'estre pas civilizée à la courtisane*' (he had a certain outward manner which might not have appeared *civilizée* to a lady of the court).[27] Half a century later Descartes, in his *Discours de la Méthode*, clearly set the man who was *civilisé* against the *sauvage*.[28] In the first half of the eighteenth century, *civiliser* and *civilisé* continue to appear from time to time. And there is nothing unexpected about the process whereby a substantive ending in *-isation* is derived from a verb ending in *-iser*.[29] How was it that nobody thought of doing so? In 1740 Voltaire, in the *Avant-Propos* to the *Essai sur les moeurs*, approved Madame du Châtelet's method whereby she intended to '*passer tout d'un coup aux nations qui ont été civilisées les premières*' (go straight to the nations which were first *civilisées*); he suggests that she should consider the whole world '*en l'étudiant de la même manière qu'il paraît avoir été civilisé*' (studying it in the order in which it appears to have become *civilisé*);[30] but unless I am mistaken he never uses the word *civilisation*. Jean-Jacques Rousseau in 1762 in the *Contrat social* reproaches Peter the Great for having intended to '*civiliser son peuple quand il ne fallait que l'aguerrir*' (*Civiliser* his people when all it needed was to be hardened);[31] but he does not use the word *civilisation* either.[32] There is something surprising about this and it might give us the idea that the time was not yet ripe, and that the process whereby the substantive is derived from the verb is not simply a mechanical one.

Can we say that the words, the nouns which were in use before the appearance of *civilisation*, made its appearance superfluous and pointless? Throughout the whole of the seventeenth century French authors classified people according to a hierarchy which was both vague and very specific. At the lowest level there were the *sauvages*. A bit higher on the scale, but without much distinction being made between the two, there came the *barbares*. After which, passing on from the first stage, we come to the people who possess *civilité*, *politesse* and finally, good *police*.

We can easily imagine that the synonymists had a lot to say about the nuances of these fairly numerous words. There was a whole category of literature full of concealed plagiarisms which set out to define the correct meaning of terms which were given ingenious psychological explanations.

Civilité was a very old word. It appears in Godefroy, together with *civil* and *civilien*, with the further guarantee of a text by Nicolas Oresme which includes *policie*, *civilité* and *communité*.[33] Robert Estienne does not overlook it in his valuable *Dictionnaire françois–latin* of 1549. He includes it after *civil*, which is nicely defined as, '*qui sçait bien son entregent*' (who knows tact) and is given as *urbanus, civilis*. In 1690 Furetière, in his *Dictionnaire universel divisé en trois tomes* (in which both *civiliser* and *civilisé* appear alongside *civil*) defines *civilité*: '*Manière honnête, douce et polie d'agir, de converser ensemble*' (sincere, gentle and polite way of conducting oneself towards others and conversing with others).[34] That is to say that whereas *civil* keeps a political and legal meaning alongside its human meaning, *civilité* only conveys ideas concerning courtesy; according to Callières (1693), it in fact replaced the word *courtoisie*, which was falling out of use at that time.[35] For the subtle grammarians of the eighteenth century, *civilité* is in fact nothing but a varnish. In the 1780 edition of the amusing *Synonymes françois* by the Abbé Girard,[36] which is so packed out with worldly experience and borrowed subtlety, we learn that '*la civilité est, par rapport aux hommes, ce qu'est le culte par rapport à Dieu: un témoignage extérieur et sensible des sentiments intérieurs*' (*civilité*' is, as far as men are concerned, what public worship is in respect of God – an external and tangible witness of internal sentiments). *Politesse* on the other hand, '*ajoute à la civilité ce que la dévotion ajoute à l'exercice du culte public: les moyens d'une humanité plus affectueuse, plus occupée des autres, plus recherchée*' (adds to *civilité* what prayer adds to practice of public worship – the means of achieving a more affectionate sort of humanity, more concerned with other people, more refined). This sort of *politesse* presupposes '*une culture plus suivie*' (more intensive cultivation) than *civilité*, and '*des qualités naturelles, ou l'art difficile de les feindre*' (natural qualities or the difficult art of feigning them).[37] So the conclusion was very generally that *politesse* was superior to *civilité*. It is a paradox developed by Montesquieu, when he maintains in a passage in the *Esprit de lois* that *civilité* is worth more in certain respects than *politesse*, the latter '*flatte les vices des autres*' (flatters the vices of others) whereas the first *'nous empêche de mettre les nôtres au jour'* (prevents us from revealing our own). But Voltaire had answered him in advance in *Zaïre* in the second dedicatory epistle (1736); he thinks, along with the rest of his age, that if Frenchmen *'depuis le règne d'Anne d'Autriche ont été le peuple le plus sociable et le plus poli de la terre'* (have since the reign of Anne of Austria been the most sociable and the most polite people on earth), such politeness was not *'une chose arbitraire comme ce qu'en appelle civilité. C'est une loi de la nature qu'ils ont heureusement plus cultivée que les autres peuples'* (something arbitrary like the thing people call *civilité*. It is a law of nature which they have happily cultivated more extensively than other people).[38]

But there was something that stood above such *politesse* – it was what the old texts called *policie*, a word dear to Rousseau,[39] and modern texts call *police*. Far and away above peoples who were *civils* and far and away above peoples who were *polis*, stood incontestably those that were *polices*.

Police – the word embraced the field of law, administration and government. Every author agreed on this point, from Robert Estienne, who in 1549 in his dictionary translated *'citez bien policées'* by *'bene moratae, bene constitutae civitates'*, to Furetière writing in 1690 *'Police, loix, ordre de conduite à observer pour la subsistance et l'entretien des États et des sociétés en général, opposé à barbarie'* (police, laws, system of conduct to be observed for the subsistence and government of states and societies in general, in opposition to barbarity). And he quotes this example of the use of the word: *'Les sauvages de l'Amérique n'avaient ni loix ni police quand on en fit la découverte'* (the savages of America had neither laws nor 'police' when they were discovered). Similarly Fénelon wrote of the Cyclops:[40] *'Ils ne connaissent pas de loi, ils n'observent aucune règle de police'* (They know no law, they observe no rule of 'police'). Thirty years after Furetière, Delamare, when composing his large and valuable *Traité de la Police* (1713) devoting Section I of Book I to the definition of *'l'idée générale de la police'* (the general concept of 'police'), again recalled the very general sense which the word had had for a long time. *'On le prend quelquefois,'* he said *'pour le gouvernement général de tous les Estats et dans ce sens il se divise en Monarchie, Aristocratie, Démocratie . . . D'autres fois, il signifie le gouvernement de chaque Estat en particulier, et alors il se divise en police ecclésiastique, police civile et police militaire'* (It is sometimes taken to mean the general government of all states and in this sense it can be broken down into Monarchy, Aristocracy, Democracy . . . On other occasions it refers to the government of each particular state and then it is broken down into ecclesiastical administration, civil administration and military administration).[41] These meanings were already old and obsolete. Delamare, who had an interest in doing so, insisted forcefully on the restricted sense. After quoting Le Bret and his *Traité de la Souveraineté du Roy*: *'Ordinairement'*, he wrote, *'et dans un sens plus limité, police se prend pour l'ordre public de chaque ville, et l'usage l'a tellement attaché a cette signification que, toutes les fois qu'il est prononcé absolument et sans suite, il n'est entendu que dans ce dernier sens'* (usually and in a more restricted sense, *police* is used to refer to the public administration in any town and usage has so tied it down to this meaning that whenever it is spoken out of context it is understood only in this latter meaning).[42]

Delamare was right. And yet a tendency began to show itself some years later, among writers who were more preoccupied with general ideas than with technical accuracy, to give to the word *'policé'* a more restricted meaning which was less specifically legal and constitutional. This fact is extremely important for our purposes.

Talking in 1731 in his *Considérations sur les moeurs de ce temps* of peoples which were *policés*, Duclos noted *'qu'ils valent mieux que les peuples polis'* (that they were of greater worth than peoples which were *polis*), for *'les peuples les plus polis ne sont pas toujours les plus vertueux'* (the peoples who are most *polis* are not always the most virtuous).[43] He added that if among savages, '*la force fait la noblesse et la distinction*' (strength conferred nobility and distinction) on men, it was not the same with peoples who were *policés*. In their case, '*la force est soumise à des loix qui en préviennent et en répriment la violence*' (force is subjected to laws which forbid and repress violence) and '*la distinction réelle et personnelle la plus reconnue vient de l'esprit*' (the most widely recognized real and personal distinction comes from the mind).[44] It is an interesting remark at that date. At the very time when administrators, purists and technicians were endeavouring to banish '*l'équivoque*' (the double meaning, doubt) which made the word *police* difficult to use, Duclos was going quite the other way and adding a new moral and intel-lectual meaning to the traditional meaning of this fundamental political and constitutional word. He was not alone. We simply have to open the *Philosophie de l'histoire* (1736) which subsequently became the *Discours préliminaire* of the *Essair sur les moeurs*. When Voltaire wrote, '*Les Péruviens, étant policés, adoraient le soleil*', (the Peruvians, being *policés*, adored the sun) or, '*Les peuples les plus policés de l'Asie en deçà de l'Euphrate adoraient les astres*' (the most *policés* peoples of Asia this side of the Euphrates adored the stars), or again: '*Une question plus philosophique, dans laquelle toutes les grandes nations policées, depuis l'Inde jusqu'à la Grèce, se sont accordées, c'est l'origine du bien et de mal*' (a question of a more philosophical nature on which all the great nations who were *policées* from India to Greece have agreed is the origin of good and evil),[45] when, fourteen years later, Rousseau in his Dijon *Discours* wrote: '*Les sciences, les lettres et les arts . . . leur font aimer leur esclavage et en font ce qu'on appelle des peuples policés*' (the sciences, letters and the arts . . . make them love their bondage and make of them what we call *peuples policés*); when, in 1756, Turgot, in his article on *Étymologie* written for the *Encyclopédie*, pointed out that '*la lange du peuple policé, plus riche . . . peut seule donner les noms de toutes les idées qui manquaient au peuple sauvage*' (the language of a *peuple policé* is richer . . . and is alone able to convey the names of all the ideas lacking in savage peoples) or upheld '*l'avantage que les lumières de l'esprit donnent au peuple policé*' (the advantage which the light of the spirit gives to a *peuple policé*),[46] it is clear that all the men who took an active part in the life and philosophical activity of their age were searching for a word with which to designate, let us say, in terms that they them-selves would not have repudiated, the triumph and spread of reason not only in the consti-tutional, political and administrative field but also in the moral, religious and intellectual field.

Their language did not really provide them with such a word. As we have seen, *civilité* was no longer possible. In 1750 Turgot still remained faithful to *politesse*, that same *politesse* which Voltaire in 1736 had said was not '*une chose arbitraire, comme ce qu'on appelle civilité*' (something like the thing people call *civilité*). Just as Madame de Sévigné had formerly complained: '*Je suis une biche au bois, éloignée de toute politesse; je ne sais plus s'il y a une musique en ce monde*' (I am a deer in the forest far from all *politesse*; I no longer know if there is any music on this earth),[47] he addressed the king in solemn terms in his *Tableau philosophique* of 1750: '*O Louis! quelle majesté t'environne. Ton peuple heureux est devenue le centre de la politesse!*' (O Louis! what majesty surrounds you. Your happy people have become the centre of *politesse*!). It was a showy phrase which was not free of a certain archaic tone.[48] In fact there was no single well-adapted word to refer to what we mean today by the word *civilisé*. And as at the same time ideas were finally evolving in such a way as to confer superiority not merely on peoples equipped with a '*police*', but on peoples that were rich in philosophical, scientific, artistic and literary culture, it could only be a temporary and rather poor expedient, when referring to the new concept, to employ the word which had for so long been used to designate the old one. Especially since, as we have seen, *police*, which in spite of everything governed the meaning of *policé*, was being given an increasingly restricted and commonplace meaning. A meaning which was dictated by the character who had such growing and formidable powers – the lieutenant of police.

So people considered using the word which Descartes had already used in 1637, giving it a quite modern meaning, and which Furetière translated by '*Rendre civil et poli, traitable et courtois*' (making *civil* and *poli*, tractable and courteous), but giving examples such as the following, '*La prédication de l'Évangile a civilisé les peuples barbares les plus sauvages*' (the preaching of the Gospel has *civilisé* the most savage barbarous peoples), or '*Les paysans ne sont pas civilisés comme les bourgeois, et les bourgeois comme les courtisans*' (peasants are not as *civilisés* as town-dwellers, and town-dwellers are not as *civilisés* as courtiers) – it is, as we see, capable of very wide interpretation.

Who were these people? Not everyone of course. Turgot, for instance, in his *Tableau*, in the French text of his Sorbonne *Discours* and in his article on *Étymologie*, uses neither *civiliser* nor *civilisé*. Neither does Helvetius, in the *Esprit* of 1758; both are faithful to *policé*. The same is true of a great many men of this period. But Voltaire, for instance, early on joins *civilisé* to *policé*. We gave examples above taken from 1740. In the *Philosophie de l'Histoire*, *policé* occupies a very important place, but in ch. 9 (*De la Théocratie*) we find *civilisé* slipping on to his page. And with it there is a remark which betrays scruple: '*Parmi les peuples*', he writes '*qu'on appelle si improprement civilisés*' (among the peoples who are so improperly called *civilisés*).[49] Voltaire uses that same improper word, however, once or twice more in the *Philosophie de l'histoire*. '*On voit*', he notes for instance, '*que la morale est la même chez toutes les nations civilisées*' (we see that morality is the same throughout all nations which are *civilisées*). And in ch. 19 we read: '*Les Égyptiens ne purent être rassemblés en corps, civilisés, industrieux, puissants, que très longtemps après tous les peuples que je viens de passer en revue*' (the Egyptians could not have joined together, become *civilisés*, *policés*, industrious and powerful, until long after all the other peoples which I have considered).[50] It is an interesting gradation – formation of society (synoecism); refinement of moral conduct; establishment of natural laws; economic development; and finally mastery; Voltaire weighed his words and did not put them down at random. But he still uses two where twenty-five years later Volney,[51] taking up the ideas set forth in the *Philosophie de l'histoire* in a curious passage in his *Éclaircissements sur les État-Unis* only uses a single one, at a time when the substance of the word *civilisé* has assimilated all the substance of the word *policé*. And this dualism enables us to see clearly the scope provided by the language of the men of the time. They were tempted to include under *policé* all the ideas implied by *civilité* and *politesse*; but in spite of all, *policé* resisted; and then there was *police* lying behind it which was a considerable nuisance to the innovators. What about *civilisé*? They were tempted in fact to extend its meaning; but *policé* put up a struggle and showed itself to be still very robust. In order to overcome its resistance and express the new concept which was at that time taking shape in people's minds, in order to give to *civilisé* a new force and new areas of meaning, in order to make of it a new word and not just something that was a successor to *civil*, *poli* and even, partly, *policé*, it was necessary to create behind the participle and behind the verb the word '*civilisation*', a word form which was a bit pedantic perhaps but which did not surprise anybody, as its sonorous syllables had long been heard to echo beneath the vaults of the *Palais* and above all it did not have a compromising past. It was far enough from *civil* and *civilité* for people not to have to worry about those outmoded predecessors. It could, as a new word, refer to a new concept.

Civilisation was born at the right time. I mean to say at a time when the great effort of the *Encyclopédie* was coming to a conclusion, having commenced in 1751 and been twice interrupted in 1752 and 1757 through the rigours of the ruling power; resumed in 1765 as a result of Diderot's perseverance and daring, it finally ended in triumph in 1772. It was born after the *Essai sur les moeurs*, 1757, had flooded learned Europe with the 7,000 copies of its first edition and made an initial attempt to achieve a synthesis of the main forms of human, political, religious, social, literary and artistic forms and to integrate them into history. It was born when that philosophy founded on the fourfold basis of Bacon, Descartes, Newton and Locke which d'Alembert saluted in his *Discours préliminaire* as the final conquest, the coronation of modern times,[52] was beginning to bear its first fruits. Above all, it was born at a time when, emerging from the entire *Encyclopédie*, the great concept of rational and experimental science was beginning to make itself felt, constituting a whole in its methods and procedures whether it was concerned in the manner of Buffon, to put the Bible completely on one side and conquer nature, or in the footsteps of Montesquieu, to classify the infinite variety of human societies. Someone put this in words: 'Civilisation is inspired by a new philosophy of nature and of man.'[53] It was right to put it in that way, even if it was going a little ahead in time to add: 'Its philosophy of nature is evolution. Its philosophy of man is perfectibility.' In fact the fine work done by Henri Daudin on Lamarck and Cuvier showed this; evolution took more time than one might think to be conceived in its true sense and in its modern spirit.[54] But it is none the less true that 'the recent attitude of enlightened man to explored nature' had a powerful role to play in modifying the conceptions of thinkers at the end of the eighteenth century.[55] Lending their ear as they did to the suggestions and advice of science meant that they were moving along the path that led to the future, and putting the fanaticism of hope in place of the nostalgia for times gone by. We should fail to understand the birth and quick spread in our language of the word which conveyed the concept of civilization if we overlooked the tremendous revolution which took place in people's minds as a result, firstly, of the work and discoveries of Lavoisier, who, from 1775 onwards published the famous notes summed up in the *Traité élémentaire de chimie* of 1789, and, secondly, at a later date, all the research work and organizing work done from 1793 onwards at the Museum, 'that vital central point for all the sciences', as the *Décade philosophique*[56] put it when it first appeared expressing its pleasure at seeing it make, 'by presenting it with the facts, an important contribution to the true education of a free people'. Facts. The *Décade* was right and expressed the great aspiration of the men of the age. It reminds us of Fourcroy who in 1793 also produced the fifth edition of his *Éléments d'histoire naturelle et de chimie* (the first dating from 1780) and felt himself obliged to explain to his readers that he was having a very hard time of it to truly follow the extremely rapid revolution in chemistry from one edition to the next; 'All we are really doing', he explained, 'is to extract simple results from a large number of facts. We only accept strictly those things given us by experiment.'[57] It is the definition of experimental science in revolt against speculation, whether we consider the phlogiston overcome by Lavoisier or those 'cosmogenical romances' written by Buffon and bitterly denounced around 1792 by the young naturalists of the Museum.[58] A method of this sort was of course valid for the natural sciences but not only for them.

For the analysts of humanity and the analysts of nature had both very early on had a healthy respect for fact and it became more and more apparent in both as the eighteenth century came to its close. The former were no less eager than the second, and the attempt to base their work on facts had something heroic and moving about it. Were they concerned with the present? The eighteenth century was, as far as political and constitutional problems were concerned, the century of memoirs; in the economic and social sciences it was the century of the birth of statistics and figures; in technology it was the century of investigation. Every question whether theoretical or practical, concerning population, wages, supplies or prices, any questions concerning the initial efforts of the first 'scientific' farmers or the promoters of modern manufacturing processes, automatically brought forth written works in dozens – books, booklets, detailed surveys, and works by independent individuals, learned associations and royal officers. We only have to call to mind the provincial Academies, agricultural societies and inspectors of factories whose attempts to establish stocks of fact seem to us today so remarkable. And were Europeans concerned with the past, or rather with that enormous part of the contemporary world which seemed to go back to a remote age, when, at the end of the eighteenth century, they compared other continents with their own – here too there were abundant facts and they were not to be left on one side; is there any need to say that though the *Encyclopédie* was something more besides, it was first and foremost, and it set out to be, a compendium of all known facts around the year 1750,[59] a vast collection of documents taken straight from the work of the great scholars of the previous hundred years or from the written accounts of innumerable journeys that extended the intellectual horizon of civilized white men right to the shores of the Far West, America and, very soon, the Pacific? And when Voltaire expresses his aversion to hazardous attempts at systemization and shows his sharply focused, lively interest in the particular and the individual, what is he doing if not establishing and grouping firmly controlled facts?

Only such harvests are not to be gathered in a single day. About the middle of the eighteenth century and at the time when *civilisation* was born, the world was not yet known in its entirety, far from it – that is, the present world, and the past was even less well known. The science of the men who were most careful in gathering and criticizing historical or ethnological facts capable of leading to overall views of humanity and its development remained full of holes, gaps and obscurity. Apropos of such facts we too should say, thinking of ourselves and our own disciplines, what Henri Daudin formerly said when he wondered, in connection with a remark made by Lamarck and Cuvier, 'how a science of observation whose object is a very complex and highly diversified concrete reality, and which is still only at a very rudimentary stage in cataloguing and ordering that reality, can possibly manage to find its way along and achieve any real results'.[60] But both for ourselves and for him, I mean the historians and sociologists who were groping their way along in the second half of the eighteenth century and the naturalists whose methods he studies and one might say dissects, it is quite certain that 'facts could not be taken in by the intellect in their pure state or independently of all psychological contingencies'. It was on the other hand quite natural 'that verification of the preconceived idea should itself to a large extent be under the dependency of the preconceived idea'.[61] So should we be surprised if an absolute concept of a single, coherent, human civilization grew up and not a relative concept of highly particularized and sharply individualized ethnic or historical civilizations?

Here too we should bear in mind the conceptions of the naturalists of the age, the vitality and outward manifestations of that 'series' concept which they place in conjunction with the concept of a 'natural order' that found its justification within itself.[62] When Lamarck, around 1778, sought to obtain some idea of that 'natural order' he conceived of it as a gradual, steady progression. And when at the beginning of the nineteenth century, after a long excursion into the fields of physics and chemistry, he came to publishing his naturalist views, the main argument and guiding doctrine which he set forth above all others in his lectures and books was that of a single, graduated series of animal societies.[63] Of course we should not go too far here – but it would be doing violence to the true historical spirit to overlook connections of this nature. Do they not help us to understand how, at the top of the great ladder whose bottom rungs were occupied by savagery and whose middle rungs were occupied by barbarity, '*civilisation*' took its place quite naturally at the same point where '*police*' had reigned supreme before it?

So the word was born. And it spread. A word which was to survive, make its way and have enormous success. As soon as it appears we are only too pleased to clothe it with the rich mantle of ideas which the years were to weave for it. And our haste is somewhat laughable. Let us just look for texts and read them without preconception. For a long time, for a very long time, we will search and find nothing, I mean nothing that really justifies the creation of a new word. This new word comes and goes, rather at sea between *politesse*, *police* and *civilité*. Certain efforts to define it better and ascertain, in particular, its relations with '*police*' do not lead to very much,[64] and very often we have the clear impression that this neologism, even for those who used it, did not yet correspond to a definite need.

Of course, there was discussion on certain points. Or, more precisely, ideas were expressed which went different ways. How did '*civilisation*' operate? D'Holbach replied in 1773: 'A nation becomes civilized through experiment.' The idea is not to be derided. He develops it a little further on: 'Complete *civilisation* of peoples and the leaders who govern them and the desired reform of governments, morals and abuses can only be the work of centuries, and the result of the constant efforts of the human spirit and the repeated experiments of society.'[65] Opposed to this broad but somewhat confused doctrine are the theories of the economists. The physiocrats also had their doctrine; we may recall Baudeau's early text in 1767: 'Land ownership, which attaches man to the land, constitutes a very important step towards the most perfect form of civilization.' For Raynal commerce is what counts. In 1770 he writes: '*Les peuples qui ont poli tous les autres ont été commerçants*' (The people who have *poli* (polished) all others were merchants),[66] and here we can actually see that uncertainty of meaning which we noticed just now; for *poli* in Raynal's text means quite precisely *civilisé*, since he writes a little further on, this time using the newer word in place of the older one: '*Qu'est-ce qui a rassemblé, vêtu, civilisé ces peuples? C'est le commerce*' (What gathered these people together, clothed them and civilized them? It was trade).[67] It is a utilitarian theory; it was to be used by the Scots, Millar for example, for whom in the *Observations sur les commencements de la société* (translated version, 1773)[68] civilization was '*cette politesse des moeurs qui devient une suite naturelle de l'abondance et de la sécurité*', and Adam Smith was in the same way to bind wealth and civilization tightly together.[69] On the other hand Antoine-Yves Goguet, who, so it seems, did not know the word *civilisation*, seems to be making a direct answer to Raynal when he states in 1778 in his book which bore the title *De l'origine des lois, des arts et des sciences et de leurs progrès chez les anciens peuples*, '*La politesse ne s'est jamais introduite dans une contrée que par le moyen des lettres*' (*Politesse* never entered a region except through literature).[70] This is the doctrine of all those who were so numerous at that time and who thought, along with Buffon, that '*sur le tronc de l'arbre de la science s'est élevé le tronc de la puissance humaine*' (on the trunk of the tree of knowledge grew the trunk of human power), or who, along with Diderot, looked for the source of civilization in the progress achieved in human knowledge and looked upon it as a sort of ascent towards reason: '*Instruite une nation, c'est la civiliser; y éteindre les connaissances, c'est la ramener à l'état primitif de barbarie . . . L'ignorance est le partage de l'esclave et du sauvage*' (Instructing a nation is the same as civilizing it; stifling learning in it means leading it back to the primitive state of barbarity . . . Ignorance is the lot of the slave and the savage).[71] Later Condorcet in a famous passage in the *Vie de Voltaire* was to echo the author of the *Plan d'une université pour le gouvernement de Russie*: '*Ce n'est point la politique des princes, ce sont les lumières des peuples civilisés qui garantirent à jamais l'Europe des invasions; et plus la civilisations s'étendra sur la terre, plus on verra disparaître la guerre et les conquêtes, comme l'esclavage et la misère'* (Not the policies of princes but the enlightenment of civilized people will forever protect Europe against invasion; and the more civilization spreads across the earth, the more we shall see war and conquest disappear in the same way as slavery and want).[72] In practical form divergences do not go very far. At least they do not change the essential thing. For all these men, whatever their individual tendencies may have been, civilization remains first and foremost an idea. To a very large extent it is a moral idea. '*Nous demanderons*', Raynal asks, '*s'il peut y avoir de civilisation sans justice?*' (We shall ask whether there can be any civilization where there is no justice?).[73]

This is true even of the philosophers who, following Rousseau on to his own ground, applied themselves with varying degrees of conviction to the problem of value raised in 1750 by the Dijon *Discours*. The new word, so it seems, was just what was needed to help in discussing Rousseau's paradoxes. It served as a handy term to apply to the enemy against which he had risen up with such violence – in the name of the primitive virtues and the unspoiled holiness of the forests – but without using the word, a word he seems never to have known. And so there were very animated discussions which went on a long time, long after the death of Rousseau and right into the middle of the nineteenth century. At the end of the eighteenth century these discussions never led to any critical study of the very concept of civilization. People simply approved or disapproved of the thing – that ideal civilization, that perfect civilization which all the men of the age bore to varying degrees in their heart and mind like a sort of compulsion but not as a clear concept. And it was a thing which in any case no one yet wanted to limit or particularize in its universal scope. There was alive in men an idea which was not the subject of the least doubt, yet it was the absolute and single concept of a human civilization which was capable of winning over little by little every ethnic group and which had already won over from savagery all peoples who were *policés* including the most outstanding ones, even the Greeks, who, Goguet depicts for us 'in heroic times' as having neither morals nor principles and having no more terms with which to describe 'justice, probity and most of the moral virtues' than the savages of America.[74] People believed in a single series, a continuous chain linking peoples together; d'Holbach stated in the *Essai sur les préjugés*, 'that a chain of successive experiments leads the savage to the state in which we see him in a civilized society, where he concerns himself with the most sublime sciences and the most complicated branches of learning',[75] and this is not only countered by Raynal when he noted that 'all the peoples who are *policés* were savage and all savage peoples left to their natural impulses were destined *to become policés*',[76] but by Moheau as well when he wrote quite serenely: 'It should not surprise us that man in his brute and savage state was inclined to adore man in his civilized and perfected state.'[77]

However universal and moving it might be, a consensus of this sort did not lead very far. In order to get out of that vague optimism, what was needed above all was a sustained attempt to formulate all the component parts of a coherent and valid concept of civilization. But to do that it was necessary not only to break up the old single world and finally arrive at the relative concept of '*state of civilization*' then soon after that to the plural, '*civilisations*' which were more or less heterogeneous and autonomous, and conceived of as the attributes of so many distinct historical or ethnic groups. This stage was arrived at between 1780 and 1830, which are fairly broad dates, as a result of a series of progressive steps and, as d'Holbach would have said, as a result of experiments. The history we are dealing with here is not simple. How could it be when the very concept of civilization is, when all is said and done, a synthesis?

Let us take a jump ahead beyond the Revolution and the Empire. We come to Lyon in the year 1819. A book appears with a title which gives its date away, *Le Vieillard et le jeune homme*, written by Ballanche, full of all sorts of ideas, in his usual disorder, just re-edited with a commentary.[78] If we take the trouble to read the fifth of the Seven Conversations which the work consists of we twice come across a remarkable innovation, though it might well remain completely unnoticed to contemporary readers. '*L'esclavage*', Ballanche writes on p. 102 of the Mauduit edition, '*n'existe plus que dans les débris des civilisations anciennes*' (Slavery continues to exist only in the remains of ancient civilizations). And a little further on (p. 111) he shows religions in the Middle Ages gathering '*l'héritage de toutes les civilisations précédentes*' (the legacy of all previous civilizations). Was this the first time that '*les civilisations*' was substituted for '*la civilisation*' in a printed text by a French author, thus setting aside a fifty-year-old usage? I should refrain from saying that it was as I do not claim to have read everything that was written in France between 1800 and 1820 with the intention of tracking down the appearance of an 's' on the tail of a substantive. But I should be very surprised if any uses of '*civilisations*' were found much before that date and before the example which good fortune brought before me (not without some assistance). The importance of the fact needs no emphasis. Ballanche's plurals marked the end of a long patient search for information and the culmination of reasoned investigation.

We mentioned above the taste which the historians of the eighteenth century and, generally speaking, the promoters of the future social sciences, showed for fact on every occasion. This taste was as definite in them as it was in the naturalists, physicists and chemists who were their contemporaries. We only have to look at the *Encyclopédie*. We know how, at the end of the century, the great sailors, especially the travellers who went on voyages of discovery in the Pacific, and the many accounts which they published everywhere in French and in English, which very quickly moved from one language to the other, satisfied all the curiosity aroused by supplying new stocks of evidence on man, or rather on men, and on their manners, customs, ideas and institutions. All this was soon gathered, compiled and classified by workers who resumed the task of men like Démeunier and Goguet[79] and tried to make records as full and detailed as possible of the 'savage' peoples who were coming to light. 'I am a traveller and a sailor, that is to say a liar and a fool according to that class of lazy, arrogant writers who, in the darkness of their study philosophize till kingdom come on the world and its inhabitants and subject nature to their personal imagination.' That is how Bougainville sharply put it in the account of his *Voyage autour du monde en 1766, 1767, 1768 et 1769*, that same Bougainville who caused people to write and say so much about him.[80] But the indoor scientists whom he was laughing at, 'those dark speculators of the study room', were, little by little, in their turn, to have their faith in the firmness of the great unitary structures shaken as a result of 'the very great differences' which they were to notice, in the wake of sailors, 'in the various regions' where they were taken in descriptions of voyages.[81] The author of the *Voyage de La Pérouse*, Milet-Mureau, went on complaining twenty years later that the accounts written by explorers still allowed some to assert, 'by making a pretentious comparison between our customs and habits and those of the savages, the superiority of civilized man over other men'.[82] The fact that he takes to task all those who still held, even at that time, to the old prejudices (which a man like Démeunier long before had already attacked) at least shows that he himself was free of such prejudices and that all the facts and documents collected by La Pérouse and his fellows were beginning to inspire new thought. Taken simply by itself a work such as Volney's shows over and over again that the minds of men were at work. We shall come back to his overall conception of civilization. But when in the *Ruines* he speaks of the 'abortive civilization', of the Chinese, when in particular in the *Éclaircissements sur les États-Unis* he speaks of the 'civilization of the savages' I am prepared to admit that he is still giving the word civilization the meaning of a moral process, but all the same the expressions seem to have a new ring to them.[83] Some years later, this is truer still in the cause of Alexander von Humboldt. 'The Chaymas', he writes for instance in his *Voyage aux régions équinoxiales du nouveau continent* (the first folio edition of which dates from 1814), 'have considerable difficulty in grasping anything to do with numerical relationships . . . Mr Marsden observed the same thing among the Malays of Sumatra, *although they had had more than five centuries of civilization.*'[84] Further on he speaks of Mungo Park, 'that enterprising man who on his own penetrated to the centre of Africa to discover there in the midst of barbarity the traces of an ancient civilization'. Or, in connection with his *Vue des Cordillères et monuments des peuples indigènes du nouveau continent*: 'This work', he says, 'is intended to throw light on the ancient civilization of the Americans through studying their architectural monuments, their hieroglyphics, their religious cults and their astrological fancies.'[85]

In fact here we are not far from the concept of '*civilisations*' in the plural, both ethnic and historical dividing the huge empire of '*civilisation*' into autonomous provinces. We should note that in the wake of geographers and the precursors of modern sociology the linguists in their turn accepted this new concept gladly. It is well known that Alexander von Humboldt owed much to his brother, whom he often quotes, referring readily to his ideas (which we shall return to) on civilization, culture and *Bildung*. Probably as a result of his brother's work, in the *Cosmos* he speaks of Sanskrit civilization as being conveyed to us by language.[86] In France it was in the *Essai sur le Pali* by Burnouf and Lassen that I found (dating from 1826) a new example of the word *civilisation* used in the plural. This language, so the authors state, 'tightens the powerful link which, in the view of the philosopher, joins together in a sort of unity peoples who belong to such diverse civilizations as the heavy and coarse mountain-dweller of Arakan and the more "*policé*" inhabitant of Siam. The link here is the religion of Buddha.' We should have a look at some of Burnouf's subsequent works; in them all we shall find everywhere quite modern usage of the word '*civilisation*', whether he is talking about the 'origin of Indian civilization' or the originality of the *Véda* in which 'nothing is borrowed from any previous civilization or from foreign peoples.'[87]

However scattered these texts may be they do suffice to show the role played by travel, the exegetists of travel and the linguists of the end of the eighteenth and the beginning of the nineteenth centuries in establishing what Nicefore calls 'the ethnographical conception of civilization'. Is it necessary to add that the evolution of their ideas might have or must have been helped along by a no less swift and decisive parallel evolution which was taking place at the time in the natural sciences?

Luckily we have two texts by one and the same author, precisely dated (one is from 1794 and the other from 1804) which enable us to gauge with rigorous precision the transformation that took place, between these two strictly defined time-limits, in the most fundamental conceptions of scientists. And although I have quoted them already elsewhere,[88] I ask you to bear with me if I recall at least the essential passages. In the first, which appears at the head of volume v of *Éléments d'histoire naturelle et de chimie*,[89] Fourcroy when speaking rather contemptuously of the classifications founded for convenience's sake on 'the differences of form which animals show from one to another', at once observes 'that such sort of classifications do not exist in nature and that all the individuals created by nature form one uninterrupted and unbroken chain'. The argument is well known, it is the one which all the scientists of the age set forth here, there and everywhere, whereas historians and philosophers for their part sing the monotonous epic of civilization making steady progress from savage peoples to '*peuples policés* and from primeval man to the contemporary of Diderot and Rousseau. In the year XII, 1804, Fourcroy wrote the introduction to Levrault's *Dictionnaire des sciences naturelles*. And this time, exactly ten years later, he wrote:

> Famous naturalists (Cuvier and his disciples) deny that it is possible to form this chain (the uninterrupted and unbroken chain of living creatures) and maintain that there is no such series in nature; that nature has formed simply groups which are separate from one another; or rather that there are thousands of independent chains which are continuous in themselves in their own series but which do not join up with one another at all or which cannot possibly be brought together.

Quite clearly, there is an abyss between the two statements. It was a revolution which started in the *Muséum*, led by Cuvier and which, in the space of a few years gave the most level-headed men conclusions which were radically opposed to the old ones. It represented, for natural scientists, the beginning of the long specialization process and the great relativist development of the '*universelles*' ideas of the eighteenth century, which was to take place, in parallel fashion, in the fields of history, ethnography and linguistics.

A historian could hardly fail to observe the extent to which political events or, in a word, the Revolution acted in support of this evolution. We noted above that the word *civilisation* triumphed and won a place for itself during the years of torment and hope experienced by France, and along with France, by the whole of Europe from 1789 onwards. It was not just a matter of chance. The Revolutionary movement was necessarily a movement of optimism entirely orientated towards the future. Behind this optimism there was, supporting it and justifying it, a certain philosophy – the philosophy of progress and of the infinite perfectibility of human beings and the creatures that depended upon them – each stage along this path marking some new piece of progress as it was completed. We should not dismiss as insignificant or meaningless Barère's statement when he writes: 'For the philosopher and for the moralist the principle that lies behind the Revolution is progress in human enlightenment and the need for a better civilization.'[90] This is what lies behind all the heated discussion and violent refutation in the period of Rousseau's arguments negating progress and pronouncing anathema on civilization.[91]

But little by little the Revolution evolved and produced its effects. It founded a new order – but only on the ruins of the ancient order; and an enterprise of that sort cannot fail to produce a marked state of anxiety and instability in a good many men. What the initial consequences were, on the one hand for letters, and on the other hand for those travellers who had no choice but to travel – '*émigrés*' – we can find out by turning to a book by Fernand Baldensperger.[92] And we, for our part, find it very hard to overlook the effects of such travel whether forced or otherwise on the thought of the men of the age. It at least prepared them for a better understanding and better assimilation of the experiences of all those sailors and discoverers of unknown societies and all those naturalists too, who were the faithful companions of the ethnographers, who drew their contemporaries' attention to the rich variety of human manners and institutions.[93] Should we perhaps take note of the fine text by

Talleyrand in his first memorandum to the Institute on 15 *Germinal* in the year V, concerning his journey to America: 'The traveller passes successively through all the stages of civilization and industry going right back to the log cabin made of newly felled trees. A journey of that kind is a sort of practical and living analysis of the origin of peoples and states . . . One seems to be travelling backwards through the history of the progress of the human spirit.' But there are other texts as well.

If we open the conversations between *Le Vieillard et le jeune homme* by Ballanche, which have already provided us with a valuable text, we will find certain lines at the very beginning which are highly illuminating on this point.[94]

> 'Looking around you', [the wise Nestor said to his catechumen] 'You have seen ancient society in its death agonies. You say all the time: "What will become of the human race?" I see civilization moving every day further and further, deeper and deeper into an abyss in which I perceive nothing but ruin. And then you say, "History teaches me that societies which became *policées* perished, and that empires ceased to exist, that dark eclipses for centuries covered the whole of humanity. And at the present time I observe similarities which make me fear the worst . . ."'

Here let us leave the inflated, whining prose of Ballanche; we shall not quote any more of it. The men who lived through the Revolution and the Empire learned one thing which their predecessors had not known when they brought the word *civilisation* into circulation about the year 1770. They learned that civilization could die. And they did not learn this simply from books.[95]

Is that all? Above we referred to a state of anxiety and instability; and we mentioned to support our argument the large numbers of *émigrés*, refugees and travellers of every type and every situation. But they were all aristocrats and isolated individuals. In fact it was the 'nation', as people were beginning to call it, the whole nation which felt far more profoundly the effects of a crisis which caused 'vague unrest' and 'doubt and uncertainty' of course, and something else besides – very precise economic disorders and social upheavals. And the outcome was a very strange thing – Rousseau's pessimistic theory, which the Revolution had, when intoxicated with itself, seemed to annihilate by its very success, was suddenly revived by that same Revolution as a result of the disorders which it had itself engendered, the thought to which it had given birth and the situations which it had created or helped to create – and we find other men, once the great crisis was over, taking up Rousseau's theory on their own account, of course with a quite different emphasis. 'Great men of all the ages, Newton and Leibniz, Voltaire and Rousseau do you know what you are great in? You are great in blindness . . . for having thought that civilization was the social destiny of the human race . . .' Who is this belated orator lending his rather superfluous assistance to Rousseau? The article bears the title 'Harmonie universelle'; it appeared in the *Bulletin de Lyon* on 11 *Frimaire* in the year XII, and its author was a Besançon shop assistant by the name of Charles Fourier.[96]

> All you learned men [he goes on] behold your towns peopled by beggars, your citizens struggling against hunger, your battlefields and all your social infamies. Do you think, when you have seen that, that civilization is the destiny of the human race, or that J.-J. Rousseau was right when he said of civilized men, 'They are not men'. There has been some upheaval the cause of which you cannot 'penetrate'.

Thus the father of societarian Socialism was writing his preludes whereas Mme de Staël felt the need to defend the system which upheld human perfectibility 'which had', she said, 'been the system of all enlightened philosophers for the past fifty years'.[97] In fact something had changed in the minds of men. And, with the combined efforts of the scientists, travellers, linguists and all those whom we have to call, for want of a more precise name, the philosophers, the concept of civilization which had been so simple when it had first appeared, had taken on a good many new features and shown some quite unexpected facets.

A more precise definition then became necessary. It was not sought by one party alone. In the Restoration, which was in essence a period of reconstruction and reconstitution, theories of civilization which varied in precision and scope sprang up on all sides. We need only mention a few names and works. In 1827 an old work, *Idées sur la philosophie de l'histoire de l'humanité*,[98] appeared in the bookshops translated and equipped with an introduction written by Edgar Quinet. In the same year the *Principes de la philosophie de l'histoire* were published in Paris, being a translation of G.-B. Vico's *Scienza nuova*, preceded by an introduction on the author's system of thought and life written by Jules Michelet.[99] In 1833 Jouffroy gathered together in his *Mélanges philosophiques* a large number of articles from the years 1826 and 1827 (especially two lectures from a course on the *Philosophie de l'histoire* delivered in 1826)[100] which dealt partially or directly with civilization.[101] But there is one man in particular who puts his finger, one might say, on the very concept of civilization and its historical interpretation and it is François Guizot, who, in his 'Tableau philosophique et littéraire de l'an 1807', which appeared in the *Archives littéraires de l'Europe* in 1808 (vol. xviii), had already written:[102] 'The history of men should only be looked upon as a collection of material gathered together for the great history of the civilization of the human race.' We know what the subject of his lectures was when he took his chair again at the Sorbonne in 1828; he dealt successively in 1828 with *La Civilisation en Europe* and in 1829 with *La Civilisation en France*;[103] undertaking a methodical and one might say systematic analysis of the very concept of civilization he provided his contemporaries not only with a remarkable survey of existing ideas, but also with a perfect example of one of those great, typically French constructions in which, with great mastery (and a few expert touches), he presents us with a synthesis of the most diverse points of view and (naturally not without certain rather daring simplifications) a way of unravelling, clarifying and rendering attractive and appealing the darkest obscurities and the most inextricable complexities.

Civilization, Guizot started by saying, is a fact, 'a fact like any other' and capable, 'like any other of being studied, described and explained'.[104] It is a somewhat enigmatic statement but it is explained straightaway by a historian's reflection: 'For some time there has been a lot of talk, quite rightly of the need to enclose history within facts.' And immediately one thinks of the remark made by Jouffroy, in his article in the *Globe* of 1827 on 'Bossuet, Vico, Herder': 'What stands out in Bossuet, Vico and Herder, is contempt for history – facts give way under their feet like the grass.'[105] So Guizot's rather surprising concern (and one which Gobineau was later to reproach him for in lively but rather artificial fashion) is easily understood. He wants to be seen as a historian and does not want to be called an ideologist simply because he intends to deal with general and not with particular facts. But the 'fact' which, 'like any other', the general fact, 'hidden, complex and very difficult to describe and explain, but there none the less', which belongs to that category 'of historical facts which cannot be excluded from history without its being mutilated', is known by Guizot, as he says a little further on, to be 'a sort of ocean which is the whole wealth of a people and which contains all the elements in the life of a people and all the forces that operate in its life'.[106] It is strange to note that he at once adds that even though facts 'which really speaking cannot be called social facts but which are individual facts which seem to concern the human spirit rather than public life, such as religious beliefs and philosophical ideas, the sciences, letters and the arts', can and should be looked upon 'from the point of view of civilization'. It is a fine text for anyone wishing to assess the conquest of sociology with any precision and judge the differences in tone which an interval of a hundred years can make in certain words looked upon as clear and explicit.

From these prolegomena at least we can draw two conclusions. One is that Guizot chose the nation or rather, as he puts it, the people as the framework of his studies. True, he does talk of European civilization. But what is Europe other than a people to the power two? And does not Guizot study European civilization via France,[107] that superlative creator and propagandist? Thus he adopts Jouffroy's point of view and speaks of 'each' people, 'each' civilization, while it is quite clearly understood that there are 'families of peoples' in existence;[108] and the whole is under the shade of 'that tree of civilization which must, one day, cover the whole earth with its foliage'.[109] This is the solution proposed by Guizot to the problem of establishing 'whether there is such a thing as one universal civilization of the human race, one common human destiny, and whether the peoples have handed something down to each other from century to century that has not been lost', and, we should add, whether there is such a thing as 'general progress'. Guizot replied, 'For my part I am convinced that there is such a thing as the general destiny of humanity, and the transmission of humanity's assets and, consequently, one universal history of civilization which needs to be recorded and written about.'[110] Further on, 'The idea of progress and development seems to me to be the fundamental idea contained in the word civilization.'[111] So we see a delicate question solved by means of a skilful synthesis. There are such things as civilizations. And they need to be studied, analysed and dissected, in themselves and on their own. But above these there is indeed such a thing as civilization with its continuous movement onwards, though perhaps not in a straight line. Civilization then, and progress. But progress of what, exactly?

Guizot said on this point that civilization was basically the product of man and a certain development in the social condition of man and a certain development in his intellectual condition. These are rather vague terms, and he endeavoured to give them a more precise definition. On the one hand we have the development of the general external condition of man, and on the other hand the development of the internal and personal nature of man, in a word, we have the perfecting of society and the perfecting of humanity. Guizot in fact insists that these two factors are not merely added to one another and placed in juxtaposition, but that both elements, social and intellectual, occur simultaneously, are intimately and swiftly bound together, and act upon one another reciprocally in a process which is indispensable to the perfection of civilization. If the one shows too much advance on the other, there is unrest and anxiety. 'If major social improvements and major progress in the material well-being of man manifest themselves in a people without going together with some great movement of intellectual development and some similar progress in the minds of men, then the social improvements seem to be precarious, inexplicable and practically unwarranted.' Will it last and spread its influence? 'Ideas alone are able to make light of distances, traverse seas and make themselves everywhere understood and accepted'; and in any case 'social well-being remains somewhat subordinate in character as long as it has not borne any fruit other than well-being itself'; it is a curious statement to find on the lips of a man who some years later was to be denounced by his opponents as the cynical high priest of wealth.[112] Conversely, if some major development of the intellect breaks out somewhere and no social progress appears to go with it then the result is surprise and uneasiness. 'It is as if a beautiful tree were bearing no fruit ... ideas are held in a sort of contempt ... when they do not lay hold of the external world.'

We know the course of Guizot's argument after that. The two main elements of civilization are, then, intellectual development and social development and they are intimately linked together. Perfect civilization is achieved where the two elements join together and take effect simultaneously. So a rapid review of all the various European civilizations was sufficient to show him in England a civilization almost exclusively orientated towards social perfection but whose representatives proved to be lacking in the talent required 'to light those great intellectual torches which illuminate whole eras.' Conversely, German civilization was powerful in its spirit but feeble in its organization and in its attainment of social perfection. Was it not true to say that ideas and facts, intellectual order and material order were almost entirely separate in that same Germany where the human spirit had for so long prospered to a far greater degree than the human condition? On the other hand, there was a country, the only one, able to pursue the harmonious development of ideas and facts, of the intellectual and the material order – that country was of course France, the France in which man had never lacked individual greatness, and where individual greatness had never failed to bring consequences that contributed to the public weal.[113]

Here too, the synthesis was skilfully engineered. Difficulties vanished without a trace. The concept of material well-being and the efficient organization of social relations, the concept 'of a more equitable distribution among individuals of the power and well-being thus produced' by human groups – the very things which Fourier, as early as 1807, had blamed civilization for neglecting, were included by Guizot among the various elements which any civilization worthy of the name should display to any observer. And, putting an end to an old debate he showed that '*police*' and '*civilité*' conspired together to produce such civilization. More precisely, we might say that his breadth of view in making room within his attractive and admirably proportioned construction not only for the means of power and well-being in human societies and for the means of developing and personally and morally enriching man and all his faculties, feelings and ideas, but also for letters, the sciences and the arts, those 'glorified images of human nature',[114] his particular brand of tolerant comprehension, was entirely apposite in preventing the completion in France of a serious divorce, the very divorce which did occur in Germany in that period and which certain individuals may well have had in mind in France – I mean the divorce between '*culture*' and '*civilisation*'.

No work has been done on the concept of culture in France. I would say 'of course not' if a certain brand of off-hand irony were appropriate when observing such monstrous gaps in our knowledge. But however little I may know about the history of the concept of culture I can at least say that it does exist, that it would be well worth while retracing it and that it is a subject of considerable importance.

Let us stick to the essential points. It is not for me to research into the history of ideas in Germany, to discover the date when the word *Kultur*[115] first appeared and the circumstances in which it appeared. Or to raise the question of origins. I note simply that in our *Dictionnaire de l'Académie* in the 1762 edition *culture* in French is said to be used in the figurative sense, 'of the cultivation of the arts and the mind' and two examples are given: '*la culture des arts est fort importante; travailler à la culture de l'esprit'* (*'culture'* of the arts is very important; to work on the '*culture*' of the mind). It is a rather flimsy definition. It will probably get fuller as time goes on. In the 1835 edition of the same *Dictionnaire*, we read: '*se dit figurément de l'application qu'en met à perfectionner les sciences, les arts, à développer les facultés de l'esprit* (is used in the figurative sense to refer to the applications with which one perfects the sciences and the arts and develops the faculties of the mind). True, this is a paraphrase rather than a meaningful explanation; but even put in this way the concept is a long way off the rich definition given on the other side of the Rhine by Adelung's dictionary in the 1793 edition of the word *Kultur*: ennoblement, refinement of all the spiritual and moral powers of a man or a people. I would recall as well that Herder, Quinet's Herder, attributed to the same word a whole string of very rich meanings including the following: aptitude for domesticating animals; clearance and occupation of the soil; development of the sciences, the arts and commerce; finally '*police*'. We often come across ideas of this sort expressed in our own language. But I would note in passing, we should not be too hasty in thinking that such concepts were borrowed and it is striking that in France such concepts are always classified under the heading civilization.[116] Thus, for Mme de Staël, '*la multitude et l'étendue des forêts indiquent une civilisation encore nouvelle*' (the vast number and extent of the forests point to a *civilisation* which is still new); culture in this sentence would indeed have had a puzzling effect.[117] A word once more enables us to observe that the ideas of Herder are more or less identical with those of Kant, who associated the progress of *culture* with that of reason and saw universal peace as the ultimate effect of both.[118]

But there is no doubt that these ideas were known, at least in bits and pieces, in France. Without doing any lengthy research we only need to think of that germanized Frenchman, Charles de Villiers who developed such a strong passion for the German thought of his age. The ideas of Kant did not go unnoticed by him. The only evidence needed is the little octavo booklet of forty pages which made the *Idée de ce que pourrait être une histoire universelle dans les vues d'un citoyen de monde* accessible to French readers; Kant's essay had appeared for the first time, unless I am mistaken, in 1784 in the *Berlinische Monatschrift*; the translation bore the date 1796. In it there was a lot of talk about '*l'état de culture*' (state of culture) which 'is nothing other than the development of the social worth of man';[119] and the translator, taking the floor on his own account, explains to his readers (p. 39) that they had already emerged step by step from the 'savage' state, from that of complete ignorance and 'barbarity' and had entered the period of 'culture'; the era of 'morality' still remained before them. Elsewhere in his *Essai sur l'esprit et l'influence de la Réforme de Luther* (1804) and in his *Coup d'oeil sur l'état actuel de la littérature ancienne et de l'histoire en Allemagne* (1809), Charles de Villiers drew the attention of Frenchmen to the growth of a cultural history, *Histoire de la culture*, *Kulturgeschichte*, which the Germans created by presenting 'the effects of political history, literary history and the history of religions in their relations with civilization, industry, well-being, morality and the character and way of life of men' and which, as he put it, brought forth in them 'profound and remarkable writings'.[120] All that was still fairly vague, so it seems, and rather confused. In any case there does not appear to be any clear opposition between *culture* and *civilisation*.

We do not find such an opposition, formulated in any systematic way by Alexander von Humboldt either. He often uses the word *Kultur* in his writing, together with *Zivilisation*, and without bothering, so it seems, to define these terms in relation to one another.[121] But he does like to refer, on the other hand, to his brother Wilhelm, the linguist[122] – and he for his part, had very clear ideas on the matter which he was able to formulate. In his famous study on the *kawi* language,[123] he explains them at length. He shows how by means of a very clever but rather artificial gradation, the curve of progress rose from man who was gentle and humanized in his behaviour to man who was learned, artistic and lettered, finally reaching Olympian (I am tempted to say, Goethian) serenity, as the man who was completely formed. Those were the steps which constituted *Zivilisation*, *Kultur* and *Bildung*. For Wilhelm von Humboldt civilization, when all is said and done, annexed the domain of '*police*' in its ancient form – security, order, established peace and gentleness in the field of social relations. But gentle people and people with good *police* are not necessarily cultured in the intellectual sense; certain savages may have the most excellent private manners and yet be still totally unaware of anything pertaining to the cultivation of the mind. And the reverse is true. Hence the independence of the two spheres and the distinction between the two concepts.

Did these ideas make much headway in France? We should simply note that they were capable of strengthening or supporting a certain intellectual attitude of which an example is given us by Volney very early on, an excellent example. Intent on refuting Rousseau's ideas on the perversity engendered in man by the development of letters, the sciences and the arts – like so many of his contemporaries, as we have already said – he in fact proposed a radical method intended to do away with civilization altogether, by taking drastic action to clear the ground if necessary.[124] Rousseau could have, so he said, and should have, realized and stated that the fine arts, poetry, painting and architecture were not 'Integral parts of civilization and sure indications of the well-being and prosperity of peoples'. There had been plenty of examples, 'taken from Italy and Greece', which proved incontestably 'that they could blossom in countries which were subject to military despotism or fanatical democracy, both of which were equally *sauvage* in nature'. True, they were like decorative plants; 'to cause them to blossom it was enough for a temporarily strong government of any kind whatsoever to encourage and reward them'; but to over-cultivate them was dangerous: 'the fine arts, encouraged by the tribute paid by the people to the detriment of the more practical basic arts, can very often become a way of misusing public funds and consequently have a subversive effect on the social state of men and on *civilisation*.' Rousseau, revised, corrected and rectified by Volney, thus becomes something fairly puerile, when all is said and done. Guizot, in his broad synthesis, had the distinct virtue of maintaining among the essential elements in the concept of civilization 'the development of the intellect'.

It was a virtue that was not always recognized. When in 1853 Gobineau, in his book *De l'Inégalité des races humaines*, attempted in his turn to define the word *civilisation*,[125] he began by attacking Guizot with some vigour. Guizot had defined *civilisation* as *un fait* (a fact). 'No', said Gobineau, 'It is a series, a chain of facts.' Guizot was not unaware of this, and he says so; the truth was that Gobineau had read him rather quickly. But what he blames the author of *l'Histoire générale de la civilisation en Europe* for above all was that he had not ruled out the concept of 'governmental forms'. On examining Guizot's ideas one quickly saw, as Gobineau asserted, that before a people could claim that it was civilized it had to 'enjoy institutions which temper power and freedom at one and the same time, and through which material development and moral progress are precisely co-ordinated, so that government and religion are confined within clearly defined limits.' In short, he concluded with some malice, it was easy to see that according to Guizot, 'the English nation was the only truly civilized one'. He was cocking a snook and would in fact have done far better not to take up so many pages with his quibbles. Gobineau's position was in fact a rather curious one. He reproached Guizot for having continued to include '*police*' as one of the fundamental elements in the concept of civilization. One feels sorry for the concept and sorry for Guizot. Some called upon him to throw overboard literature, science and the arts, in fact everything that constituted *culture*; others wanted him to jettison political, religious and social institutions. He did neither and, in his way, he was not wrong.

But he still had certain misgivings. He expressed them in his *Histoire générale de la civilisation en France* in a remarkable passage.[126] Formerly he points out, 'in the sciences which are concerned with the material world', facts were badly studied and little regard was had for them; 'people simply went where their hypotheses led them and followed a risky path without any other guide than their own deductions'. Nevertheless, in politics and in the real world, 'facts were omnipotent and were held to be legitimate more or less by their very nature; it would have been out of place to expect an idea, in the name of mere truth, to play any part in the affairs of this life.' But over the previous century (which brought Guizot's reader to the beginning of the reign of Louis XV), a reversal had taken place. 'On the one hand facts have never played such an important part in science; on the other hand ideas had never played such an important part in physical reality.' This was so true that the opponents of the civilization of the time were always complaining about it. They spoke out against what they thought of as the sterility, pettiness and triviality of a scientific spirit which 'debases ideas, freezes the imagination, removes all that is great from the intelligence, particularly its freedom, and shrivels and materializes it'. On the other hand, in politics and in government of societies they saw nothing but fanciful notions and ambitious theories – attempting the same feat as Icarus would only bring a fate similar to the one he suffered. Hollow complaints, Guizot said. That was how things should be. Man, faced with the world which he neither created nor invented, is first a spectator and then an actor. The world is a fact and man studies it as such; he exercises his mind on facts; and when he discovers the general laws which govern the development and life of the world, even those laws are simply facts which he observes. And then the knowledge of external facts develops in us ideas which dominate these facts. 'We are called upon to reform, perfect and regulate all that is. We feel able to act upon the world and to extend throughout it the glorious empire of reason.' That is the mission of man – as a spectator he is subject to facts; as an actor he remains master in imposing upon them a more regular and a purer form.

It is a remarkable passage. Of course there had been a conflict. Between two attitudes, two methods and two sorts of preoccupations. There had been a conflict between the spirit of research and enquiry, the positive scientific method founded on the study and compilation of facts from purely disinterested motives – and the spirit, we might say, of intuition and hope and of the imagination which precedes and anticipates facts, the spirit of social improvement and pragmatic progress. And it is all very well to want, as Guizot did, to settle the quarrel on paper and to place intellectual progress and social perfection in harmony with one another. But how were things in practice? Both were very powerful gods, and how could one be subordinate to the other or – a rather naïve notion – how could they be made to exist side by side?

In fact, what had taken place when Guizot wrote these words and when he was giving his lectures in 1828 and 1829? In the first instance experimental scientific methods had not penetrated very far into those branches of learning which from then on were to be called the moral sciences. And why not? Rather, what complex combination of heterogeneous factors was responsible for the situation? To show this would require an enormous amount of labour. And in order to do so we should have to give our attention to the problem of the origins, causes and spirit of Romanticism, and that is a problem which is nowhere near being solved with any degree of unanimity.

And there was another thing. Civilization did not appear to Guizot's contemporaries simply as an object of study. It was a reality in which they were living. For better or for worse? Many would reply for worse. Now, from the standpoint which we have taken up in this study, this fact is very important. For the complaints of the 'opponents of civilization', as Guizot calls them, the complaints which are taken up and formulated endlessly by every school of social reform, the same complaints which were to inspire something more substantial than books and essays, may in fact have been preparing the ground for future, scientific criticism of any concept of civilization that implied a value judgment, making such criticism easier and more desirable in advance. In other words we may ask the question whether all these complaints were not conspiring to bring about that dissociation which we support and which was finally completed over the last fifty years of the nineteenth century, the dissociation of the two concepts, the scientific one and the pragmatic one, of civilization; the one finally leading to the view that any group of human beings, whatever its means of material and intellectual action on the universe may be, possesses its own form of civilization; the other, even so, maintaining the old concept of a superior civilization carried along and transported by the white peoples of Western Europe and Eastern America and taking shape in facts as a sort of idea.

For our part we do not need to follow the divergent trails of these two concepts throughout the nineteenth and twentieth centuries. We are sketching the history of a word. We have taken our sketch to the point where *civilisations* appears in current use alongside *civilisation*. Our task has been completed. It was simply a preface. We should simply note that the practical, radical and, in itself incontestable view which asserts the existence of each individual people and each individual civilization does not prevent the old concept of a general human civilization remaining alive in people's minds. How can we make the two concepts agree? How are we to conceive of their relation with one another? It is not my job to do that. My job was simply to show how the terms of the problem emerged little by little and made themselves clear for us in our very language throughout a century and a half of research, meditation and history.

Notes

1 Let it be said in parenthesis that the fact that no teacher of history has ever suggested and no young historian has ever himself conceived the idea of undertaking a detailed study of the history of these words or of writing a doctor's thesis on such a subject, well illustrates a lack not of material but of spiritual organization – which the study of modern history still suffers from. Studies of this sort have been done on ancient history and have proved to be extremely valuable and instructive as we know. Of course they would not be easy to write. We should need for that purpose historians with a very solid philosophical background – *aves rarae*. But there are some. And if there are not, then perhaps we should think about producing some.

2 A. Niceforo, *Les indices numériques de la civilisation et du progrès*, Paris, 1921.

3 Texts quoted by Albert Counson, *Qu'est-ce que la civilisation?* (Published by the *Académie de langue et littérature française*, Brussels, 1923.) By the same author *La civilisation, action de la science, sur la loi*, Paris, Alcan, 1929, pp. 187 and 188, footnote.

4 Counson, *op. cit.*, p. 11.

5 As M. Schelle has clearly shown Dupont de Nemours was always doing it; he took very great liberties with Turgot's texts.

6 But it is included in vol. i, p. 214, of the *Oeuvres de Turgot* (Paris, Alcan, 1913), in a summary at the beginning of the *Tableau philosophique des progrés successifs de l'esprit humain*; the summary is by M. Schelle.

7 They will be found assembled in vol. i of the *Oeuvres de Turgot*, ed. Schelle.

8 Book VI, ch. 2, p. 404–5 of vol. iii of the 12mo ed.

9 Cf. *Système social*, London, 1773, vol. i, ch. 16, p. 204; *Histoire de l'électricité*, Paris, 1771.

10 Cf. vol. i, p. 210, ch. 16: 'Complete civilization of peoples and the leaders who govern them can only be the work of the centuries.' In the same work, *civiliser, civilisé* are used currently; similarly, in the *Système de la nature*, 1770, in which I could not find *civilisation*.

11 February 1767, p. 82. Quoted by Weulersse, *Les Physiocrates*, ii, p. 139.

12 Ch. 6, art. 6 (*Coll. des économistes*, p. 817): 'in the present state of civilization in Europe'.

13 Cf. the Geneva edition, 1781, vol. x, Book XIX, p. 27: 'The liberation or, what amounts to the same thing under a different name, the civilization of a state is a long and difficult process . . . The civilization of States has rather been a product of circumstances than of the wisdom of sovereigns.' *Ibid.*, p. 28, on Russia: 'Is the climate of this region really favourable to civilization?' and p. 29: 'We shall ask the question whether there can be any civilization without justice?' Cf. also, vol. i, p. 60: 'A mysterious secret which held back . . . the progress of civilization'.

14 *Oeuvres*, ed. Tourneux, vol. ii, p. 431: 'I think also that there is a purpose in civilization, a purpose which is more in conformity with the happiness of man in general.'

15 He quite naturally and frequently uses *civilisé* and *civiliser*. Introduction, p. x: 'What are civilized men?'; vol. ii, ch. 10, p. 127: 'Do you applaud the fact that Czar Peter began to civilize the Hyperborean regions?'

16 In the *Avertissement*, cf. Van Gennep, *Religions, moeurs et légendes*, 3rd series, Paris, 1911, p. 21 *et seq.*

17 Numerous texts. Some examples: 1787, Condorcet, *Vie de Voltaire*: 'The more civilization spreads throughout the earth, the more we shall see war and conquests disappear.' 1791, Boissel, *Le Catéchisme du genre humain*, 2nd edition, according to Jaurès, *Histoire socialiste, la Convention*, vol. ii, p. 151 *et seq.* 1793, Billaud-Varennes, *Éléments de républicanisme*, according to Jaurès, *ibid.*, vol. ii, p. 1503 and p. 1506. 1795, Condorcet, *Esquisse d'un tableau historique des progrès de l'esprit humain*, p. 5: 'The first state of civilization in which the human species has been observed'; p. 11: 'It is between that degree of civilization and the one we can still observe in savage people'; p. 28: 'All the epochs of civilization'; p. 38: 'Peoples who have reached a high degree of civilization', etc. 1796, *Voyages de C. P. Thumberg au Japon, traduits per L. Laigles et revue per J.-B. Lamarck*, 4 vols, vol. i, Paris, year IV (1796). *Préface* by the editor: 'It [the Japanese nation] has retained a degree of freedom acceptable in its state of civilization.' Finally, the word had come into such current usage that on the 12 of Messidor in the year IV (30 June 1798), on board the *Orient*, on the eve of the landings in Egypt, Bonaparte, in his proclamation wrote: 'Soldiers, you are going to carry out a conquest the effects of which are incalculable for civilization and the commerce of the world.' We have tried to take examples from all the different categories of writings of the age.

18 Littré thus makes a serious mistake when in his *Dictionnaire*, under the article on civilization (which is in fact a very indifferent one), he asserts 'that the word only appears in the *Dictionnaire de l'Académie* from the 1835 edition onwards and has only been used to any extent by modern writers when public thoughts began to centre on the process of history'.

19 *Dictionnaire universal français et latin, nouvelle édition, corrigée, avec les additions*, Nancy, 1740. The 1762 edition of the *Dictionnaire de l'Académie* had added a large number of words which did not appear in the 1740 edition (5,217 according to Gohin) and showed a considerable extension of the concept of the dictionary. It is all the more noteworthy that *civilisation* did not appear in it. The 1798 edition contained 1,887 new words and especially testified to a new orientation: it does honour to the philosophical spirit of all the progress made in language; it is not limited simply to recording usage; it judges usage. The 1798 definition is however very simple if not poor: 'Civilization, action of civilizing or state of that which is civilized.' All the dictionaries take it up until we read in the *Dictionnaire général de la langue française du commencement du XVIIe siècle à nos jours*, Hatzfeld, Darmesteter and Thomas, Paris, undated (1890): 'By extension, neologism: progress of humanity in the moral, intellectual and social spheres, etc.'

20 J. A. H. Murray, *A New English Dictionary*, vol. ii, Oxford, Clarendon Press, 1893, verso *Civilization*: 1772. Boswell, *The Life of Samuel Johnson*, xxv.

21 The first English edition of *The history of the reign of the Emperor Charles V* dates from 1769.

22 *Préface*, p. xiv: '*L'influence des progrès de la civilisation et du gouvernement*'. Section II of ch. 4, p. 304, bears the title: '*Des changements produits dans le gouvernement d'un peuple per ses progrès dans la civilisation*';

similarly section II of ch. 5, p. 347, bears the title '*Des effets ordinaires de la richesse et de la civilisation relativement au traitement des serviteurs*'.

23 Ed. Tourneux, vol. x, Paris, 1879, p. 317, November 1773: 'The successive progress of civilization . . . the first progress of civilization.'

24 Vol. ii, p. 164.

25 The translation is based on the fourth edition. Cf. vol. i, ch. 3, p. 40: '*Les nations qui . . . semblent être arrivées les premières à la civilisation furent celles à qui la nature avait donné pour patrie les côtes de la Méditerranée*'.

26 At least in the cultural sense for, in English as in French, civilization is an ancient word in the legal sense (that given in the Trévoux Dictionary). Murray gives some examples for the beginning of the eighteenth century (Harris; Chambers, *Cyclopaedia*, etc.).

27 *Essais*, Book I, ch. 25, '*Du Pédantisme*'.

28 *Oeuvres de Descartes*, ed. Adam, vol. vi, *Discours de la Méthode*, part 2, p. 12: 'Thus I imagined that those peoples who formerly were semi-savages and civilized themselves only gradually producing their laws only when they were forced to as a result of the disorders caused by crime and conflict, could not be as well *policez* as those who had observed constitutions created by prudent legislations right from the start of their group life.' A little further on there is another text which defines the barbarian and savage as being without reason: 'Having recognized that all these peoples which have sentiments very much opposed to our own are not simply because of that, barbarians or savages, but that many of them make use of their reason as much or more than we do.' These texts were pointed out to me by M. Henri Berr.

29 Especially since precisely in the eighteenth century verbs in '*iser*' appeared in great numbers, M. Frey has made a great list of them for the revolutionary period in his book, already referred to, on the *Transformations du vocabulaire français a l'époque de la Révolution*, p. 21 (*centraliser, fanatiser, fédéraliser, municipaliser, naturaliser, utiliser*, etc.). But M. Gohin had already given for the preceding period another list of similar verbs attributed to the Encyclopedists: among them we find *barbariser*.

30 *Oeuvres de Voltaire*, ed. Beuchot, vol. xv, pp. 253, 256.

31 *Contrat social*, ch. 8 of Book II.

32 The word does not appear either, according to the check I made, in the Dijon *Discours* of 1750 (*Si le rétablissement des sciences et des arts a contribué à épurer les moeurs*). In it Rousseau only uses *police* and *policé*, just like Turgot in the same period in the *Tableau philosophique des progrès successifs de l'esprit humain* (1750), or Duclos in the *Considérations sur les moeurs de ce siècle* (1751), or a good many more of their contemporaries.

33 *Dictionnaire de l'ancienne langue française*, Paris, 1881. Nicolas Oresme's *Éthiques* are also referred to in the article on '*Civilité*, by Hatzfeld, Darmesteter and Thomas in their *Dictionnaire général*.

34 *Civiliser* is defined by the same 'Furetière': to make *civil*, and *poli*, amenable and courteous, e.g. 'The preaching of the gospel has *civilisé* the most savage barbarian peoples.' Or, 'Peasants are not *civilisés* in the same way as townsfolk, and townsfolk are not *civilisés* in the same way as courtiers.'

35 '*Courtois* and *affable*', F. de Callières says (*Du bon et du mauvais usage dans les manières de s'exprimer*, Paris, 1693), 'are hardly used any longer by those who move in society and the words *civil* and *honnête* have taken their place.' Bossuet points to the fact that *civilité* has lost all its political meaning, in a passage in the *Discours sur l'histoire universelle*, part III, ch. 5, in which he sets the way in which it was used by the ancients against that of the moderns:

> The word '*civilité*' did not only signify for the Greeks the gentleness and mutual deference which makes men sociable; a man who was *civil* was nothing more than a good citizen, who always looks upon himself as a member of the State, who allows himself to be governed by the laws and conspires with them to bring about the public weal, without engaging in any act that may be harmful to any other person.

Tuscan usage of the word retained for *civilità* a little more of the legal meaning, which in France was only retained by the word *civil*, if we are to go by the *Vocabolario degli Accademici della Crusca*; in the meaning of '*costume e maniera di viver civile* (Lat. *civilitas*)', it added that of 'citizenship'.

36 The edition revised by Beauzée. The first edition of Girard's work dates from 1718 (*La justesse de la langue françoise, ou les sinonimes*); the second, from 1736 (*Les Synonymes français*); the third, revised by Beauzée dates from 1769; re-ed. in 1780.

37 *Op. cit.*, vol. ii, § 112, p. 159.

38 *Op. cit.*, Book XIX, ch. 16. He is referring to the Chinese who, desirous 'of helping their people to live peaceful lives', have 'extended the rules of *civilité* as widely as possible'.

39 *Contrat social*, iii, ch. 8: 'The places where the labour of men produces only that which is necessary should be inhabited by barbarous peoples: any *politie* would be impossible there.' Cf. *ibid.*, iv, ch. 7: 'The result of this dual form of power has been perpetual conflict in jurisdiction which has made any good *politie* in Christian States impossible.' Godefroy gives as the medieval forms of the word, *policie, pollicie, politie* and records the shortlived substantive, *policien*, meaning a citizen, as used by Amyot.

40 (*Odyssey*, IX).

41 *Op. cit.*, vol. i, p. 2. Sixty years later, Fr.-Jean de Chastellux, in his book *De la félicité publique ou Considérations sur le sort des hommes dans les différentes époques de l'histoire*, vol. i, Amsterdam, 1772, notes that 'still today, *Police* can be used to refer to the government of men' (ch. 5, p. 59).

42 La Bret's definition, which is also a professional definition, was not yet limited to a town situation. 'I call *police*', he wrote (iv, ch. 15), 'the laws and decrees which have always been published in well-ordered States to control commerce in food stuffs, to curb abuses and monopolies in commerce and in the arts, to prevent the corruption of morals, to curb wanton luxury and to banish unlawful sports from the town.'

43 *Oeuvres complètes*, ed. 1806, vol. i, p. 70. Duclos further states: 'Among barbarians, the laws should shape morals; among peoples who are *policés*, morals should perfect the laws and sometimes supplement them.'

44 *Considérations*, ch. 12 (*Oeuvres*, 1806, i, p. 216).

45 Voltaire, *Oeuvres*, ed. Beuchot, vol. xv, pp. 16, 21, 26.

46 *Oeuvres de Turgot*, ed. Schelle, vol. i, p. 241 *et seq.*

47 Letter dated 15 June 1680. It is strange to note that people spoke of 'being far from *politesse*, and returning to *politesse*', just as we say: 'returning to civilization'.

48 *Oeuvres de Turgot*, ed. Schelle, vol, i, p. 222.

49 Ed. Beuchot, vol. xv, p. 41.

50 For these last two quotations, cf. Beuchot, ed., vol. xv, pp. 83 and 91.

51 Volney, *Éclaircissements sur les États-Unis* (*Oeuvres complètes*, Paris, F. Didot, 1868, p. 718):

> By *civilisation* we should understand an assembly of the men in a town, that is to say in an enclosure of dwellings equipped with a common defence system to protect themselves from pillage from outside and disorder within . . . the assembly implied the concepts of voluntary consent by the members, maintenance of their natural right to security, personal freedom and property . . . thus *civilisation* is nothing other than a social condition for the preservation and protection of persons and property etc.

The whole passage, which is an important one, is a criticism of Rousseau.

52 See the second part of the *Discours sur l'Encyclopédie* as a reasoned dictionary of the sciences and the arts: 'These are the principal masterminds which the human spirit should look upon as its masters', d'Alembert concludes.

53 Counson, *Discours, op. cit.*

54 *Cuvier et Lamarck*, 'Les classes zoologiques et l'idée de série animale (1790–1830)', Paris, Alcan, 1926, *passim* and particularly vol. ii, ch. 10, vol. v and 'Conclusions', p. 254 *et seq.* See also Lucien Febvre, 'Un chapitre d'histoire de l'esprit humain: les sciences naturelles de Linné à Lamarck et à Georges Cuvier', *Revue de Synthèse historique*, vol. xliii, 1927.

55 Counson, *Discours, op. cit.*

56 Vol. i, year II, 1794, pp. 519–21; cf. H. Daudin, *op. cit.*, vol. i, p. 25, n. 4 and generally, the whole of § II of ch. 1 of Paris one: *le Muséum*.

57 *Op. cit.*, Paris, Cuchet, 1793, vol. i, *Avertissement*, p. ix.

58 Millin in particular. Cf. H. Daudin, *op. cit.*, vol. i, p. 9 and n. 1. The about-turn was in fact a very rapid one as far as Buffon was concerned. Cf. *ibid.*, p. 38, n. 3.

59 On all this refer to the work done by René Hubert, *Les sciences sociales dans l'Encyclopédie*, Lille, 1923, in particular the first part, p. 23 *et seq.*, and 'Conclusions', p. 361 *et seq.*

60 *Op. cit.*, 'Conclusions', *L'idée scientifique et le fait*, p. 265.

61 *Ibid.*, pp. 269–70.

62 On its origins and developments throughout the eighteenth century, cf. the first of the three

volumes by H. Daudin: *De Linné à Lamarck: méthodes de la classification et idée série en botanique et en zoologie (1740–1790)*, Paris, Alcan, 1926.

63 Daudin, *Cuvier et Lamarck*, ii, pp. 110–11.

64 See in Fr.-J. de Chastellux, *De la félicité publique ou Considérations sur le sort des hommes dans les différentes époques de l'histoire*, his attempt to set all that was particular in political constitutions in *police* against all that was universal in 'the greatest possible happiness' – a concept which is obviously confused in his mind if not in his vocabulary (the author does not know the neologism) with that of *civilisation*. (Cf. in particular *op. cit.*, vol, i, p. xiii: 'All nations cannot have the same government. All the towns and all the classes of citizens in one and the same customs. But all may generally lay claim to the greatest possible happiness.')

65 *Système social*, London, 1773, vol. i, ch. 14, p. 171.

66 *Histoire philosophique et politique des éstablissements et du commerce des Européens dans les deux Indes, 1770*; ed. Geneva, 1781, vol. i, p. 4.

67 *Ibid.*, p. 4.

68 According to the 2nd ed., Amsterdam, 1773; *Préface*, p. xviii. Section II of ch. 5 of the book is called 'Des effects ordinaires de la richesse et de la civilisation relativement au traitement des serviteurs' (p. 347).

69 *Recherches sur . . . la richesse des nations*, translated from the 4th ed. by Roucher, annotated by Condorcet, vol. i, Paris, 1790, p. 3. (Introduction): '*Chez les nations riches et civilisées au contraire, etc.*'

70 Vol. iv, Book VI, p. 393.

71 *Oeuvres*, ed. Assezat, vol. iii, p. 429 (*Plan d'une université pour le gouvernement de Russie*, about 1776?, published for the first time in 1875).

72 The idea that peace and generally speaking the civilization for which it seemed to be the main precondition does not depend on sovereigns or on their power is often expounded throughout the course of these years. See e.g. Raynal, *Histoire philosophique*, ed. Geneva, 1781, vol. x, p. 31: 'Though soldiers may defend the provinces they do not civilize them.'

73 *Histoire philosophique*, vol. x, p. 29. See also *ibid.*, p. 28: 'Is it possible that barbarian peoples can become civilized without developing morals?'

74 *De l'origine des loix*, Paris, 1778, vol. iv, Book VI, p. 392.

75 *Essai sur les préjugés* (1770), ch. II, p. 273.

76 *Histoire philosophique*, vol. x, Book XIX, p. 15.

77 *Recherches et considérations sur la population de la France*, Paris, 1778, p. 5.

78 Ballanche, *Le Vieillard et le jeune homme*, New edition, with introduction and notes by Roger Mauduit, Paris, Alcan, 1928. See our account in the *Revue critique*, 1929.

79 Démeunier's book, *L'esprit des usages et des coutumes des différents peuples, ou Observations tirées des voyages et des histoires*, was published in 1776. It was translated into German in 1783 (*Ueber Sitten und Gebräuche der Voelker*) by M. Hismann, Nuremberg. Cf. Van Gennep, *Religions, moeurs et légendes*, Paris, *Mercure de France*, 3rd series, 1911, p. 21 *et seq*. The Avertissement is quite clear: 'Although there have been so many books on man, there has been no attempt to bring the morals, customs, habits and laws of the various people together. The intention is to repair this omission.' But he added: 'We have endeavoured to follow the progress of *civilisation*.'

80 New edition, enlarged, Part I, Neuchâtel, 1772, *Discours préliminaire*, p. 26.

81 Letter from M. Commerson to M. de la Lande, from the *Isle de Bourbon*, 18 April 1771, following the *Voyage* by Bougainville, p. 162.

82 *Voyage de La Pérouse autour de monde*, Paris, Plassan, 1798, vol. i, p. xxix.

83 Cf. for the quotations, *Oeuvres complètes*, F. Didot, 1868, p. 31 (Ruines, ch. 14); p. 717 (*Éclaircissements*). Together with these texts we should take an extract from the *Discours sur l'étude de la statistique* by Peuchet (at the beginning of *Statistique élémentaire de la France*, Paris, Gilbert, 1805); he mentions the peoples of Africa 'always at war with the neighbouring peoples, so that their civilization makes but slow progress'.

84 I quote the *Voyage* from the 8vo edition, Paris, 3 vols, 1816–17. Cf. on the Malays, vol. iii (1817), p. 301; on Mungo Park, p. 50.

85 *Voyage*, vol. i, 1816, p. 38. Previously, p. 35, Humboldt analyses his *Essai politique sur le royaume de la Nouvelle Espagne* which, he says, provides consideration concerning 'the population, the morals of the inhabitants, their ancient civilization and the political division of the country', and in which he examines 'the quantity of colonial foodstuffs needed by Europe in its present state of civilization'.

86 *Cosmos, essai d'une description physique du monde*, translated by Faye, Paris, Gide, 1847, vol. i, *Considérations*, p. 15.

87 The *Essai sur le Pali* appeared in Paris in 1826. (Cf. p. 2.) Cf. also the opening address at the Collège de France by E. Burnouf, 'De la langue et de la littérature sanscrites'; it appeared in the *Revue des deux mondes* of 1 February 1833 (see in particular p. 12 of the special edition). See also by the same author, the *Essai sur le Véda*, Paris, 1863, pp. 20, 32, etc. These are only samples.

88 L. Febvre, 'Un chapitre d'histoire de l'esprit humain', *Revue de Synthèse historique*, vol. xliii, 1927, pp. 42–3.

89 5th ed., Paris, Cuchet, year II, 5.

90 *Réponse d'un républicain français au libelle de sir François d'Yvernois*, text quoted by Counson, *Discours, op. cit.*, p. 8, n. 1.

91 We find them not only in books intended for an educated public; cf. in the *Éclaircissements sur les États-Unis* by Volney, *Oeuvres*, p. 718 *et seq.*, his long, interesting discussion intended to show that if there are vice-ridden and depraved peoples, 'the reason was not that formation into a society brought out vicious tendencies, but that they were transferred there from a savage state, which is the origin of every nation and every form of government' – and that, moreover, one could reject the argument that fine arts and literature were 'integral parts of civilization' and 'sure tokens of the happiness and prosperity of peoples'. Little propaganda booklets were also full of such points (cf. the *Catéchisme du genre humain* by Boissel, 2nd ed., 1791); Boissel's argument is in fact a curious one in so far as he counters Rousseau who bases himself 'on consideration of the original foundations of civil society whose disastrous faults made him prefer an uncivilized way of life' [!], with the law and those principles which should today (1791) serve as a basis and as a foundation for civilization, but of which Rousseau was of course unaware.

92 *Le mouvement des idées dans l'émigration française*, vols. i and ii, Paris, 1924.

93 American and French thought or more generally European thought from 1718 to about 1850 would make the subject of a fine book. A history book, I mean, and a philosophical book. Sociology would find out a lot about its origins in such a work. We are a little bit too hypnotized by the literary example of Chateaubriand; there is much that is more worthy of study and analysis than the *Natchez*; we should be surprised I think at the mass of ideas, reflections and forecasts which an attentive look at the civilization of the United States aroused in alert minds, from Volney (to mention just one) to Alexander von Humboldt, and Michel Chevalier, *Lettres sur l'Amérique du Nord* (1834–5) or Tocqueville, *la Démocratie en Amérique* (1835). There would of course be counter-evidence. We need hardly mention Ballanche, whose *Palingénésie* took no more account of America than Bossuet's *Histoire universelle* – it is well known that Auguste Comte, justifying Bossuet for having 'limited his historical view to the sole examination of a homogeneous and continuous series which can none the less be fairly called universal', was setting on one side what he called 'the various other centres of independent civilization whose evolution has, for various reasons, been blocked until now and kept in an imperfect state'; and by this he was referring not only to America but to India, China, etc. It is true that he added (somewhat platonically): 'unless a comparative examination of such accessory series is able to throw some light on the main subject' (*Cours de philosophie positive*, vol. v, containing the historical part of social philosophy, 1841, p. 3 *et seq.*).

94 p. 48 *et seq.* (*premier entretien*). The text dates from 1819. Two years later Saint-Simon's *Système industriel* appeared with its address to the king: 'Sire, events are aggravating more and more the crisis in society not only in France but in the whole great nation made up of the various western peoples of Europe.'

95 Much later, J. A. de Gobineau was to write in Book I, ch. 1 of the *Essai sur l'inégalité des races humaines* (1853): 'The fall of civilizations is the most striking and at the same time the most difficult to understand of all the phenomena of history.'

96 Cf. Hubert Bougin, *Charles Fourier*, p. 70. It appears that previous to Fourier's protests and his theory of civilization, seen as a system of free competition and deceitful anarchy, there had been a sort of Spartan-like condemnation issuing on all sides from a number of very dissimilar spirits: cf. texts such as this one which is by Billaur-Varennes (*Éléments de républicanisme*, 1793, quoted by Jaurès, *Histoire socialiste: la Convention*, ii, p. 1503 of the original edition): 'Who does not know that as civilization plunges us all like Tantalus into a river of sensations, the enjoyments of the imagination and the heart make the purely animal enjoyments quite secondary'. Cf. also a text by Chamfort, *Maximes et Pensées* (before 1794): 'Civilization is like cooking. When you see light, healthy and

well-prepared food on the table you are very pleased to realize that cooking has become an art; but when we see juices, jellies and *pâtés* with truffles we curse the cooks and their art for producing such wretched results.' We can conclude, by the way, Chamfort did not have Brillat-Savarin's stomach.

97 *De la littérature considérée dans ses rapports avec les institutions sociales* (*Oeuvres complètes*, vol. iv, p. 12). We should note a little further on (p. 16) the remark which reveals a very different attitude from that of Auguste Comte's which we mentioned above: 'Every time a new nation such as America, Russia, etc., makes progress towards civilization the human species is becoming more perfect.'

98 Strasbourg, Levrault, 3 vols, reprinted in 1834. On the fortunes of the book, cf. Tronchon's doctoral thesis (Sorbonne), *La fortune intellectuelle de Herder en France*, Paris, 1920.

99 Paris, Renouard, 1827.

> The other sciences [Michelet said in his Discours (p. xiv)] are concerned with directing man and perfecting him. But none has yet attempted to find out the principles of civilization on which they are based. Any branch of science which revealed these principles would be putting us in a position to measure the progress of peoples and their decay, and we should be able to calculate the ages in the lives of nations. Then we should know the means by which any society could raise itself or return to the highest degree of civilization of which it is capable; then theory and practice would be in harmony.

100 Published under the title 'De l'état actuel de l'humanité' (*Mélanges philosophiques*, p. 101); in the same series which appeared in Paris, Paulin, we should also point out in particular, p. 83, an article from the *Globe* (11 May 1827) and bearing the title 'Bossuet, Vico, Herder'.

101 Between 1832 and 1834 a *Revue sociale* was even seen to appear. *Journal de la civilisation et de son progrès. Organe de la Société de civilisation* (6 numbers, 1832–4, pointed out by Tronchon, *La fortune intellectuelle d'Herder en France, bibliographie critique* (*thèse complémentaire*), Paris, Rieder, 1920, p. 28, no. 265).

102 Tronchon, *op. cit.*, p. 431.

103 The two courses became two books: *Cours d'histoire moderne, Histoire générale de la civilisation en Europe*, Paris, Pinchon and Didier, 1828, and *Histoire de la civilisation en France*, Pinchon and Didier, 1829. These works have often been reprinted.

104 *Civilisation en Europe*, p. 6.

105 *Mélanges philosophiques*, Paris, 1833, p. 88.

106 *Civilisation en Europe*, p. 9.

107 *Ibid.*, p. 5: 'There is hardly any great idea or any great principle of civilization which has not first passed through France before being diffused everywhere.'

108 'For instance although the civilization of Russia is a far cry from that of France or of England it is easy to see that the Russians are engaged in the same system of civilization as the French and the English . . . They are the younger children of one and the same family, the less clever pupils in one and the same school of civilization.' ('De l'état actuel de l'humanité, *Mélanges*, 1826, p. 101.)

109 'Du rôle de la Grèce dans le développement de l'humanité', *Mélanges*, 1827, p. 93.

110 *Civilisation en Europe*, p. 7.

111 *Ibid.*, p. 15.

112 All these texts are from *La Civilisation en France*.

113 Guizot thus takes up and particularizes, quoting the peoples to which he refers, the general and impersonal argument contained in *La Civilisation en Europe* (pp. 12–13).

114 *Civilisation en Europe*, p. 18.

115 Cf. the information given by M. Tonnelat.

116 Cf. Buffon, *Époques de la nature*, p. 101: 'The first characteristic of man beginning to civilize himself is the control he develops over animals.'

117 This is an effect we should watch out for. When for instance we read in Condorcet's *Vie de Voltaire* 'that when one extends the space within which *culture* flourishes, commerce is secure and industry thrives, one is unfailingly increasing the total amount of enjoyment and resources available to all men', we might in the first instance think that the word *culture* is being used with the German sense of *Kultur* and fail to realize that it simply means agriculture.

118 This was Condorcet's idea, in his *Vie de Voltaire* (1787): 'The more civilization spreads throughout the earth the more we shall see war and conquest disappear together with slavery and want.'

119 *Op. cit.*, pp. 13, 23, 25, etc.
120 *Coup d'oeil*, p. 118, note. On Ch. de Villiers, see L. Wittmer, *Charles de Villiers, 1765–1815*, Geneva-Paris, 1908 (Geneva thesis), and Tronchon, *Fortune intellectuelle de Herder en France, passim.*
121 See *Voyage aux régions équinoxiales*, ed. 8vo, 1816–17, vol. iii, p. 287: 'Intellectual *culture* is the thing that contributes most to the diversifying of human characteristics.' *Ibid.*, p. 264: 'I hesitate to use the word *sauvage* because it suggests that there is between the Indian who has been *réduit* (reduced) and is living in a mission, and the free or independent Indian, a difference in *culture* which is often belied by the observed facts.' *Ibid.*, p. 260: 'The barbarity which reigns in these regions is perhaps less due to an actual lack of any *civilisation* than to the effect of a long decline . . . Most of the tribes which we describe as savage are probably the descendants of nations that were formerly more advanced in their *culture*.'
122 Cf. in the *Cosmos*, translated by Faye, vol. i, Paris, 1847, p. 430 and note.
123 Wilhelm von Humboldt, *Ueber die Dawi-Sprache auf der Insel Java.* Cf. *Einleitung* at the beginning of vol. i, Berlin.
124 *Oeuvres complètes*, ed. Didot, 1868, p. 718 *et seq.* (*Éclaircissements sur les États-Unis*).
125 Book I, ch. 8: Definition of the word *civilisation.*
126 *Op. cit.*, original ed., pp. 29–32.

13

CIVILIZATION AND CULTURE – A SYNTHESIS

"Fundamentals of Culture-Sociology: Social Process, Civilizational Process and Culture-Movement" (1921)

Alfred Weber (1868–1958)

Alfred Weber was an important contributor to the debate about civilization and culture in the first part of the twentieth century, particularly in Germany.

The importance of this essay is the way in which Alfred Weber draws on Dilthey's attempt to construct a sociology of culture, as well as Tönnies's image of *Gesellschaft* where the concept of civilization is transposed into that of society. Alfred Weber works further with these two currents to develop distinctions between social processes, which refer to the material world, civilizational processes, which refer to the world of high culture, and culture movement, which refers to cultural innovation. In this essay, Alfred Weber draws on both notions of culture and civilization, and moves them to a higher level of abstraction and generalizability beyond the concerns with identity so prevalent, for example, in the essay by Thomas Mann. Alfred Weber was also to draw on the image of civilization as a means for national reflexivity in a later essay at the end of the Second World War entitled *Farewell to European History or The Conquest of Nihilism* (1945).

I

It seems expedient for all culture-sociology to distinguish between three different spheres of historical events, namely: social process, civilizational process, and culture-movement.

It is the nature of political as well as economic and social history to examine the destiny of great historical organisms, those great geographic, cultural, and dramatic units of mankind, to examine them with the purpose of clarifying their peculiar destinies by establishing the concrete facts essential to the total process. These disciplines regard the Chinese, Hindu, West-Asiatic-Egyptian, Classical, Arabian, Germano-Roman, and other historical spheres each as a partly "corporeal unit" containing a course of events that gives it temporal and spatial identity; and for the collective destiny of each they assume the task of collecting the principal data. Accordingly they seek to base their version and, in part, their explanation of the major historical events, the portraits of great men and the fate of the masses, upon the body economic, the structural development of political patterns, the social metamorphoses, and upon other corporeal formations and transformations. Their task is concrete historical morphology.[1] The introduction of so-called mental factors and currents does not disturb their essential preoccupation with corporeal destiny. At the same time the histories of art, literature, music, religion, philosophy, and science, in a word, all the parts of culture history which are today separate disciplines (cultural history does not exist as a unified discipline)[2] operate in a profoundly different manner and fairly independently of one another.

For them, corporeal formations of history do not exist as essential objects of examination or data of development. The interpretation of the great cultural emanations and movements with which they are concerned, the mental currents and systems of thought which they seek to expound in principle and bring home to us, proceeds (insofar as they consider it incorrect to restrict themselves to the mere portrayal of form and content) from the disclosure of coherences – coherences, generally speaking, between "problems" to be solved in the cultural field on the one hand (problems in history of philosophy, etc.) and, on the other hand, chiefly the working methods of the various fields, their development and expressive value (development of painting and plastic technique, laws of harmony in music, laws of language development, of literary styles and forms of expression, etc.). The result is a substantiation of a sequence and rhythm of events usually left open for more methodical investigation, substantiation of a conflict of "mental currents," styles, forms, and sundry – always a substantiation of an even progression which, according to its nature, seems to lie either technically or intrinsically within the principles of the cultural field proper. These disciplines, according to the principles of their operation, view cultural history largely as an autonomous historic sphere whose movement and development they seek to explain from within.[3] The political historian thereupon assumes the right to weave somehow the products of all these cultural-historical disciplines into his view of historical events; to place the "mental currents and facts" illuminated by the other disciplines into the setting of "corporeal" events which he in his turn illuminates; to assemble his versions of the destiny of the great historical organisms (*Geschichtskörper*) into a general view, and when he has combined all these general views, to write universal history.

For reasons pertaining not only to the history of science but also necessarily to working technique and methods, it is really a fairly motley, incoherent, at best, a loosely and superficially matched collection of building stones that confronts the sociologist when, in his turn, he finally undertakes to view things uniformly. For example, let him but try to comprehend as a whole any part of historical fact, like cultural process; let him try to comprehend the necessity by which it grows out of the general movement of history and undertake to establish its typical and lawful connection with this general movement. The same is true if, as sociologist, he tries logically to bind the cultural emanations of the Occident – their essential import – the recurrence or non-recurrence of their typical forms and aspects to the larger collective destiny of the Occident. If he tries to place these emanations in distinct and intelligible relationship with the factual sequences (corporeal sequences) which the various historical disciplines unearth and which mark history's general course, he is confronted at the outset, as we have said, by event-series, factually discrete and, in the general version of history, only superficially connected. Should he wish to connect these series, the difference in objective between himself and the various special disciplines will force him to organize his material accordingly. For his purpose he must attempt a conceptual regrouping of the synthesis. Thus, whatever facts the political, economic and social historians have established concerning the external form of history will necessarily fall into a new perspective. And there will be disclosed to him a great unified social process which, despite the widest variations in the different collective destinies, will reveal typical forms and stages of development. The major events (wars, revolutions, reformations, and the like) will in some typical fashion become incorporated in these forms and stages, and great men will arise not accidentally but necessarily in certain places. Furthermore, he will find that this social process is influenced by the mental sphere, that is, by those facts and processes presented by the cultural disciplines. When he now examines its kernel, he will see it as the form which gives some necessary pattern to the totality of natural human forces of impulse and will (operating as "population" in the various communal destinies), a pattern limited, of course, by certain natural (geographic, climatic, and other) conditions. The impressed pattern, or patterns, will undergo developmental alteration, will oppose and replace one another and in their struggle produce the great *peripeteiai*, the secular historic events. At the same time he will notice how this process in the larger collective destinies, which he likewise views as corporeally closed systems, arises from primitive relationships, residues of gentilic forms, in which they first appear on the historical stage, and passes through similar forms everywhere though, to be sure, in totally different groupings. He will observe how it seems to lead over spaces of social movement to different final outlets, to a lasting paralysis of form, to senile decay, or to a world expansion of forces, passing through like phases to various outlets which empty into the universal stream of human history. He will see the Chinese and Hindu historical cycles – once their natural conditions and direction of development are given – pursue a necessary social course through the millennia and finally yield to that senile torpor in which they remained through the centuries, and in which they still remain today, washed by the tide of Occidental world-expansion. Likewise, by considering the natural conditions of existence (chiefly the systems of canals and irrigation), he will distinctly recognize the type and direction of social development in the West-Asiatic and Egyptian culture-cycle, whose early millennia BC he can today reinvestigate by means of unearthed documents. And in terms of these natural conditions of development will he understand the senile torpor in which both were caught during the last millennium BC by that new wave of development, the Classical-Mediterranean cycle. He will observe how the conditions of existence, notably the sea, its commerce and "freedom" similarly propel the latter through a given social development – social development in the widest sense, comprising, as suggested, the total corporeal event of the historic cycle – and he will follow its lead to a type of world-expansion wherein must ensue the senile decay of the forms and corporeal identity of the cycle. The historic lapse of the late Classical period in the time of the Caesars is exactly this kind of senile decay. And likewise with reference to the conditions which ushered it in, he will observe the Occidental cycle which followed the Classical and, after the migration of races, carried the scene of history northward; he will observe how it passes through an entirely different yet equally necessary development, one that retains its corporeal identity through many revolutionary stages and convulsions to reach the greatest world-expansion known, embracing the entire globe. And now its inherent forms seem to be dissolving, and the cycle itself is probably passing over into something new: utter decline or the emergence of another historical organism.

In brief, the concrete event-process of the various great historical organisms, their more or less corporeal destiny which the political, economic, and social historians present, will always be viewed by the sociologist as a social evolution, specific but nevertheless fundamentally determined by natural necessity, which undergoes regroupings and realignments of general forms, runs through a predetermined number of stages and reaches a predetermined result. In this evolution the universally given social forces always assume specificity, universally given social forms present a definite and specific character and urgency, universally given processes occur in different groupings and with different results – all of which means that a general social principle of development functions in different guise. The major events and upheavals substantiated by the historian thus become landmarks indicating stages of development, or the expression of the vicissitudes bound up with evolutions, and the great men seem to rise as shield-bearers and exponents of new periods.

This is the way the sociologist transforms the concretely individuated material supplied by the historian, the "corporeal" development of the different historic cycles, into a new conceptual form adequate for his mode of thinking – the way he transforms the mass of historic events pertaining to these cycles into his view of that sphere, which I intend to call the "social process."

II

In this process, primarily moved, in his view, by the natural impulse and will of mankind and primarily determined in form and direction by the natural conditions peculiar to each historical organism, he will recognize secondary factors which the other group of historians substantiate: ideas, "mental currents," artistic views, religious convictions, etc. He must at first be indifferent to their closer dynamic relation to the stages, vicissitudes, social formation, and all else pertaining to "corporeal" development, their causal influence on this development, or the *prius* and *post* of the form and content of the "mental" and "corporeal" spheres.[4] What he does see is a mental-cultural sphere existing as a totality in each historical organism along with the "corporeal." And no matter what he may think of their mutual interaction, he notes in this mental-cultural entity, just as in the social process, certain regularities whose connection with the corporeal social process is still obscure. He discerns in it a surge and a decline; he sees parallels between the destinies of the "cultures" of the various historical organisms, a somehow predetermined appearance of successive developmental stages, a characteristically recurring rhythm of productivity, an emergence, variegated yet exhibiting certain regularities, of the different cultural expressions (religion, philosophy, art, and within art: music, epic, lyric, drama, painting, etc.) and modes (classic, romantic, etc.), a characteristic recurrence of great religious movements and related currents of ideas under similar conditions, in the social process of the various "organisms." In short, he notes a mental-cultural development in the various historical organisms that is related in some fashion, or at least is somehow parallel to their social process. He is compelled as a sociologist to view this mental-cultural development also as a unit, a second sphere of historic events. For this purpose he has to order the disconnected facts presented to him by the different branches of knowledge into a whole historical movement which he sets as a total process occurring in the various historical organisms side by side with their social process. He is thereby tempted – in fact, he now feels it his duty – to clarify the actual dynamic relationships between these spheres in the various historical organisms.

But the attempt to fulfill this duty, to scrutinize the mental-cultural sphere, has a peculiar consequence. He notes that between the social process and the truly cultural parts of this mental-cultural sphere with its various aspects and expressions in religion, art, etc., a third element is interposed, a mental intermediary realm that is related far more vitally and distinctly to the shape and course of the social process than the truly *a postiori* cultural phenomena (the emergence of religions, systems of thought, art-periods, etc.) – an intellectual cosmos, in fact, which supplies the social process with the technical means for its forms and structures and likewise appears to be one of the grounds of culture-phenomenology. More accurately expressed: he discovers that the mental-cultural process of the various historical organisms, viewed tentatively by him as a unity, is really in its essence, in its developmental phenomena, and in its relations to the social process no unity at all, but a duality, and that it carries within itself two entirely different spheres of human historical development.

What is revealed upon closer scrutiny is that in every great historical organism this "mental-cultural" process contains a threefold entity: first, purely mental and innermost, the development of a popular consciousness which proves to be the kernel of the purely mental process of growth and decline in the historical and cultural organisms once these are viewed from the mental-cultural angle. In all the great historic cycles within the range of his observation, including the Chinese, Hindu, Classical, and Occidental, the sociologist can observe that the development of consciousness proceeds typically toward the clarification of existence. Beginning with primitive stages when the forms, in which the world and one's own ego are seen, resemble those of the modern primitive and half-civilized peoples, he will watch consciousness in its development advance to deeper and deeper reflection about existence and discard the totemistic and then the mythical notions, or at any rate, give them a reflectively determined, less naive place in existence; he will watch it advance from a purely empirical attitude toward world and ego to a more or less scientific or, at least, an intellectual attitude – i.e., determined in some way by intellectual abstractions. He will see how these abstractions are further developed, how at a certain stage every historical organism harbors some rationalized world-view that can be still further elaborated and changed, a world-view into which not only external experience, "the world," but also the personal ego, its emotions, its drives, and its immediate perceptions are woven by a process of systematized, intellectual reflection and given definite though varied forms.

The sociologist discovers that this process, occurring in all the historical organisms under his observation, is intimately bound up with a second and third process within the same unity. The second is an increasing mental domination over nature that presents, parallel to the intellectualization of world and ego, an intellectual structure of utilitarian science, experience, and wisdom, a process which, like the first, tends towards intellectual systematization. Moreover, it remains a self-contained process, retaining its identity through any number of changes in the various historical organisms.

Finally, the third mental process is none other than the actualization and concretion of this second intellectual cosmos; the objectification of this system of practical knowledge through the cultivation of an apparatus of tools and methods, principles of organization, etc., which give concrete structure to existence.

At this point the whole mental sphere, projected in both the above named senses and propelled from within by the development of rational consciousness, impinges upon the social process, influencing it through this technical apparatus. He now sees one distinct and self-contained rationalization-process with only different aspects of expression pervading all the great historical organisms, codetermining their forms and its emanations affecting the inner existence as well as the observational and practical technique of the outer. This rationalization-process has its own laws of development, necessities of growth and conditions of stagnation. Manifestly, it is an essentially different entity from the emergence of religions, systems of thought, works of art, and cultures. It is a unique and vast sphere of development related to the social process quite differently from these. Once seen as a unity, it breaks up the previously assumed unity of the mental-cultural sphere into a "duality." This process of intellectualization and rationalization which pervades the historical organisms, the intellectual cosmos everywhere set up by this process, its unity which is reflected in its three expressions (inner intellectual enlightenment, bodies of intellectual knowledge and intellectualized external apparatus), its operations, forms and structures – all these were on the whole not marked by previous historical and sociological thought as a vast and distinct sphere of historical events which should be separated conceptually both from the sphere of social process and from culture-movement proper and investigated as a unity of functions and specific sequences.[5] I propose to call it the civilizational process and to demarcate sharply and fundamentally both the process and its sphere from social process and culture-movement. The latter is also grounded in the social process of the great historical organisms but is related to it quite differently from the civilizational process. As we shall see, it is governed by entirely different laws of development, is of an entirely different nature and has an entirely different place in the course of history. I propose, for the purposes of the culture-sociological approach – perhaps for the sociological approach in general – to resolve the process of history so that the "corporeal" element in its development (that which we have named social process, the realm of originally natural impulse and will and their patterns) can be posited separately and considered, first, as being influenced by the civilizational process, man's sphere of rationalization. Then one can ask how the culture-movement proper is related to both and to their interaction, whether it grows in some recognizable fashion out of the interplay of their forms and structures, whether and to what extent it proceeds independently of them, and how much it reacts upon both. I am proposing this kind of trichotomy because this is the way to attain a unified sociological view of the course of history and, especially (as I believe and intend to prove), a sociological analysis of its culture phenomenology.

III

The civilizational process and culture-movement are, as we have said, intrinsically different; they have divergent forms and laws of development and appear before us in the general course of history as mutually exclusive phenomenologies. The civilizational process with its various composite parts: its picture of world and ego, formed by the intellect (macrocosmos and microcosmos); its world of pragmatic knowledge; and its intellectually formed equipment for mastering existence may reach entirely different levels in the different historical organisms. It may variously express its world-view, but in every historical organism it always builds, little by little, a cosmos of knowledge whose three indicated parts are merely aspects of the same thing and which, once launched in a certain direction, proceeds by a logic as strict as that of the inherent causal laws underlying the construction of a building. Whatever emerges is a whole and its parts are not "created" but "discovered" (given the direction of the intellectual movement); they are already there before they are found, that is to say – from the point of view of development – pre-existent. It is as if these parts were merely drawn into the realm of human consciousness, into the illumined sphere of being with which man surrounds himself. This applied to the entire world of practical knowledge in the natural sciences, to every separate "discovery" of natural science, to every theory of knowledge and epistemological insight. But it also applies to the entire technical apparatus: tools, machines, and methodical principles of work and organization. The propositions of Euclidean geometry are "present" prior to "discovery," else they would be undiscoverable; and the same is true of the Copernican formulas for planetary motion and Kant's a prioris to the extent that all these are "correctly" discovered and formulated – and likewise the steam engine, telephone, telegraph, axe, shovel, paper money, division of labor and the whole body of technical means, methods, and principals concerned with the mastery of life and nature. Such are the "objects" of our pragmatic cosmos, those we already possess or shall acquire in the future; all of them are in essence there, i.e., they are "pre-existent" before we have had the chance to attract them into the conscious sphere and put them to use. The total civilizational process that actualizes this whole cosmos and supplies us with all its "objects," including the discoveries of a purely mental nature, merely discloses a world universally "prior" for all mankind and renders it progressively accessible. In this world every part is valid for all mankind. This is proved – I shall soon touch upon apparent deviations – by the fact that the mental and physical concretions of this realm, whenever they are discovered in some historical organism, no matter where, and become a part of conscious life, spread as a matter of course throughout the world as if by natural movement. And they penetrate other historical organisms, to the extent that their social processes are sufficiently developed to receive them and their mental development high enough to "see" them – provided, of course, that intercommunication makes this penetration at all possible. The universality of technical discoveries is well known. But this universality is not restricted to the "technical" cosmos of civilization whose material and mental objects, whose methods and means, from the knowledge of working metals and the use of fire to modern ways of communication and production, have always spread with something akin to the speed of lightning, both in periods of universal communication or isolation. It holds good as well for the realm of intellect, although here the insights in mathematics, astronomy, the natural sciences, etc., may spread at times more slowly, since their reception depends on the level of consciousness attained in the different historical organisms and since many of their practical products, as for instance chronology or accounting, may find no place in the social organization. But this does not prevent them from finally penetrating everywhere in the same measure. And the same universality, with certain modifications in the form and manner of expansion, soon to be discussed in further detail, holds good for the disclosure of new parts of the intellectually shaped view of world and ego, the intellectual results of enlightenment, the clarification of the partly inner aspect of the pre-existent civilizational cosmos. The phenomenology of actualization and development of the civilizational cosmos, both in its practical and theoretical aspect, implies, when viewed as a unified historic picture, that the great historical organisms build entirely upon one another in the development of their civilizations and operate as if by agreement in the direction of ultimate unity – this despite wide divergence in their social and cultural development. Indeed, so viewed, the general course of history is really the process of elaborating the unified and universal civilizational cosmos, and mankind, as such, takes control in the halts, gaps, and breaks inherent in the destiny of the different historical organisms. The old West-Asiatic-Egyptian, Classical, Arabian, the modern Occidental, and (less strictly) the Chinese and Hindu cycles, no matter how acutely they deviate in their historic course, social development and culture-movement, all are in this view only links, auxiliary factors in the continuous, logical elaboration of the civilizational cosmos which today is common to all mankind.

The technical parts of this civilizational cosmos first appear in their rational form in the organization of instruments and labor by the Egyptians and Babylonians as far back as 3000–4000 BC. Having evolved in correlation with the historical cycles of India and China (the details of which are not known), this technique became not only the foundation of the whole civilized technical apparatus of the Classical and Arabian historical organisms, but through those of the Occident as well. The latter, taking the lead in technical invention since the 14th century, produced from the 18th century onward the modern apparatus of world-civilization on the world-wide basis previously established.

In like fashion, the mental parts of this world-wide civilizational cosmos, mathematics, astronomy and natural science, apparently had their intellectual inception in the enormous depths of the first and second historical organisms on the Euphrates and the Nile. They are then brought into sharper relief by the Classical, the Arabian and the Chinese organisms, are taken over by the Occident during the period of expansion after the 16th century and carried through the famous "Era of Discovery" to the present universally prevalent conception of the world based on mathematics and the natural sciences, a conception which is valid for all mankind and universally accepted.

The "realm of intellect" which, despite its present diverse forms, by its content is common civilizational possession of mankind, the intellectual notion of world and ego belonging to a single sphere, first seems to have received conscious impulse in the Brahmanic wisdom of the Hindu cycle. It then becomes a subject in the Classical and Arabic as well as the Chinese historical spheres, and finally, in the Occidental philosophy of the 18th century (Kant), it receives formal principles which seem to show the limitations of knowledge and at the same time bring together the different forms of enlightenment of the various historical spheres, and, insofar as they possess intellectual content, generalize them.

In this gradual emergence of the pre-existent mental and material civilizational cosmos from the darkness into the light of man's collective consciousness, sketched here only in an amateurish and inadequate manner, it is of small moment – nay, it is no more than a "misfortune of a day" – if certain gained knowledge or insights get temporarily lost through historic contingencies, chiefly through the way history has of telescoping the series of historical organisms that become the carriers of enlightenment. Take, for example, the knowledge of the Copernican world-view which, after its discovery during Graeco-Roman antiquity, slumbered in the lap of history until its independent rediscovery by the Occident after the 16th century. It is likewise irrelevant to the nature of the whole process that in the projection of the "technical cosmos" certain technical means of civilization, "accidentally" discovered somewhere, perhaps remain at first unused until their rediscovery somewhere else, when they suddenly receive enormous significance and a universal, practical application. Thus, although the early Chinese discovery of the mechanical clock or the engine was not followed by social application, their rediscovery in the Occident ushered in the great technical revolution of modern times. These are not changes in the nature of development but the "jests" and curling arabesques that result from the lodgment of the process in the social and cultural movements.

And lastly, it is irrelevant to the essence of the civilizational process as a gradual emergence of a mental type of unity if the development of consciousness underlying it receives a severe set-back in the early "history" of the various historical organisms and if somewhere it has to begin anew from a relatively primitive state. Note the development of the Classical consciousness, succeeding the West-Asiatic-Egyptian. (The migrating and invading Greeks were obviously barbaric compared to the Creto-Mycenaean offshoot of the West-Asiatic-Egyptian cycle which they met.) Note the development of the Arabian consciousness succeeding the Classical and that of the Occidental cycle succeeding both. This merely implies that where there is an influx of new peoples into the general civilizational cosmos of mankind, the "subjective" civilization or "civilized quality" of the new populations must always re-ascend the stages that have already been disclosed and traversed by others within the general objective and subjective civilizational cosmos. Here, by the way, the climbing and reaching for old subjective heights of civilization is always considerably facilitated by the fact that the most essential objective elements of civilization are taken over by each new historical organism and also those which are of supreme importance for the acceleration of the subjective process of civilization, the subjective intellectual enlightenment and the conscious mastery of existence. When, for example, the Classical historical organism took over from the West-Asiatic and Egyptian not only the technical apparatus and the principles and forms of division of labor but also coined money, mathematics, and astronomy, it thereby took over the crucial elements of "objective" civilization which made possible directly a measurable intellectual mastery of existence and enormously facilitated the rationalistic domination of "inner" and "outer" things. They were certainly definite contributory factors in the rapid enlightenment and civilizational development of the "Greek barbarians" that lasted a few centuries after their incursion through the Doric migrations. These civilizational elements also influenced, in the matter of content, the remarkable early rational formulation of their view of world and ego. But this is only in passing. The same thing can be said, for example, of the transmission of the Classical money-accounting to the Occidental cycle after the migrations of the peoples, its effect in terms of development of consciousness and civilization upon this historical organism which had sunk back into a vast ignorance and expressed itself only in primitive social forms. We find a general money-accounting and, at the same time, the beginnings of "a calculating spirit" in the Graeco-Roman historical organism – as is evident from the *leges barbarorum* – long before the essential importance of a constructed money-exchange economy came to light.

There is no doubt that "subjective civilization" is set back for centuries whenever there emerges a new historical organism, and whenever the new historical process shifts its center of gravity into a new geographical setting in which the historical organism must then grow and go through its social and cultural development. Subjectively, a type of antiquity must always recur, then a middle age, and a modern time. Consequently, the subjective civilizational process of all mankind presents a picture of constantly recurring darkness in certain of the "areas" where men are historically rooted, until gradually the earlier enlightenment reappears and is then surpassed. Unquestionably, however, the preservation of objective civilizational elements and subjective enlightenment in the other undisturbed historical "areas" creates the means whereby the losses of single parts can be speedily recovered and the general enlightenment reintroduced. This general enlightenment is the logically causal, though unevenly graded, disclosure of a new unity valid for all mankind, mankind's universal civilizational cosmos, objectively and subjectively pre-existent.

Which aspect of the enlightenment-process will predominate depends on the specific internal arrangement (I shall not as yet use a more specific or fundamental term) of the various great historical organisms, and (as is recently contended) perhaps also on the spiritual equipment of their populations, shortly to be discussed. The old West-Asiatic-Egyptian organism was led by its arrangement toward practice and technique. On the "theoretical" side it cultivated only the purely quantitative parts that were indispensable for the immediate mastery of existence (astronomy, time-reckoning, accounting, etc.). On the other hand, the Classical organism, prevented, as it were, by its specific arrangement from "seeing" the technical parts of the civilizational cosmos, simply passed them by without special interest. (Except for the arch, no technical invention of Antiquity is worthy of mention.) Its field of attention was restricted to the intellectual and theoretical front, and hence it laid the foundations for mathematics, the natural sciences, philosophy, and all the other disciplines which we now call "sciences." At the same time, the Hindu historical organism with its remarkably appropriate arrangement, wrapped as it was in religious contemplation, chose for its single, and indeed, highly successful objective the philosophical illumination and penetration of the inmost cognition-fields of world and ego, virtually ignoring everything else. Because of specific arrangement and specific means of expression, it is quite reasonable that every historical organism should clothe its insights, especially the most philosophical ones, in forms that do not always immediately reveal their universality and impede their general expansion and application. This is particularly true when the insights, mixed with extra-civilizational elements, appear in religious and metaphysical systems of thought, as illustrated by the "epistemological" inferences of the Brahmans. Further, it should be stressed that every historical organism has a repertory of ideas and concepts, consciously or unconsciously operative (which always contains a definite system of mathematics, i.e., a definite structure of temporal and spatial ideas), and that the quality of these ideas and concepts can set quite various limits to enlightenment: without the idea of "function," which appeared first in the Occidental cycle, not only all higher mathematics, but the whole of modern Occidental knowledge could not have been built up. The same relation exists between the Euclidean idea of three-dimensional space and the whole knowledge of Antiquity, and between the Hindu idea that material being is mere "appearance," and all Hindu philosophy. But it was a distinct misapprehension to claim or, at least, to suggest the deduction that the "insights" (in our terminology, the disclosed parts of the intellectual civilizational cosmos) are therefore mere "symbols of the soul" of the various historical organisms, valid only for them, and that there existed, for example, an Occidental-Faustian, Arabian-Magian, or Classical-Apollonian mathematics whose truth and application were correspondingly limited to these organisms. The development of Euclidean geometry may have been a result of the "Apollonian soul" of Hellenism – we shall not dispute the fact here – and, at first, may have been expressed in purely Hellenic form. But its content of truth and knowledge is, in the human sense, eternal, i.e., universally valid and necessary for all mankind. The same is true of the cognitive content of the Faustian infinitesimal calculus and all its consequences, or of the Kantian a prioris or of the Hindu opposition of "Appearance and Reality." It follows that whatever Kant in his test of the formal premises of knowledge excluded from the sphere of pure empirical knowledge and labelled metaphysics must once and for all be excluded from the temples of universal "knowledge," from the temple of civilizational knowledge and therewith from the enlightenment of the universal pre-existent civilizational cosmos, its theory and its practice – not, however, from the temple of "truth" in general. For these metaphysically or religiously conditioned parts of the "mental realm of knowledge" we shall meet again in the realm of culture and culture-movement. As will appear, they possess in this realm – no matter how slight their civilizational (universally valid and necessary) content – a wealth of cultural and, yes, spiritual truth which determines the content and essence of the cultural emanations. But of this later.

Let us now summarize: The phenomenology and apparent form of the *civilization process* consist in the logically causal mode of development, the unevenly graded, accumulative clarification of something pre-existent and latent in all mankind, and in the disclosure of this as universally valid and necessary. And the civilizational cosmos is an intellectually formed cosmos of universally valid and necessary things which cohere internally and, considered in their practical aspect, are equally and universally useful (i.e., empirically true) for human ends, and considered in their theoretic aspect, are equally inevitable (i.e., theoretically true) and in the illumination of world and ego, intuitively evident (i.e., true a priori).

This cosmos is the epitome of mankind's increasing enlightenment. Its disclosure proceeds by the laws of logical causality. At every step in the disclosure the concepts, true or untrue, are applicable. And its disclosed and illumined objects bear the stamp of universal validity and necessity, and spread throughout the trafficked world for the very reason that they are pre-existent for all mankind.

IV

Exactly the opposite applies to the culture-movement and everything that originates or moves within its sphere. This sphere produces no cosmos of universally valid and necessary things. Rather, everything that is born here remains by its very nature confined and internally bound to its own historical organism. There is produced not an objective cosmos, but a spiritually tempered aggregation of symbols. The following are types of independent symbolic worlds, with runic characters of their own and an ultimately untransferable content: The Chinese, the Hindu, the Egyptian, the Babylonian, the Classical, the Arabian, and the Occidental. They are all different cultural worlds with differences in all that is truly cultural in them. It is impossible to separate Greek culture from its historical organism, to approximate, transplant, or duplicate its content – despite the often repeated attempts to do so with its plastic arts, its drama, and its systems of philosophy. Every renaissance – and there have been many attempted renaissances of Greek culture, from the Augustan in Rome and the Graeco-Buddhistic in the Gandhara region to the Italian, the Empire renaissances and others – every renaissance leads to something radically different from a revival of cultural Hellenism even though certain external forms are always taken over, and content for a similar spiritual redemption is often sought. The content of spiritual redemption as well as the forms of redemption crystallized in works of art and ideas, in other words, the whole new culture is always quite different from the Hellenic; and the alleged renaissance is really a new and distinct creation. The same holds true for the appropriation and dissemination of the purely religious redemption. In the spread of "world-religions" one apparently meets – but only apparently – something similar to the spread of the content of civilizational knowledge, namely, their release from confinement within their native historical organisms and universalization of at least their most important parts for all of mankind. The mental and spiritual universalization of the world-religions, Christianity, Mohammedanism, Buddhism, is an illusion, even granting the limits within which it occurred. Viewed more clearly, it may be nothing more than the result of the military expansion of their native historical organisms. For example, the spread of Mohammedanism is almost concomitant with the final expansion of the "Mongoloidized" Arabian historical organism. Or this universalization can be illustrated by the spread of Buddhism to eastern Asia, resulting in a "transvaluational" renaissance of Buddhism in a different historical organism, i.e., essentially one of those "new creations" we have already seen in art. In the case of the "renaissance" of Buddhism there is not even retained a similarly directed spiritual yearning for redemption. For the "Mahayana" that supplied the raw material for East Asian Buddhism and in this Buddhism received its further development is really an entirely different religion of subjectively beatific instead of cosmologic content, something essentially alien to the true Hindu Buddhism still extant in Ceylon. It applies the intuitive forms of true Buddhism but manifests in all its various guises a different spiritual content.

Or finally, in this apparent universalization, the powerful expansion of the historical organism and the newly creative transfer of values may combine, as in the case of Christianity and its universal expansion. Born as a spiritual old-age phenomenon of Classical antiquity, Christianity was reborn into something completely different in the Germano-Roman historical cycle at the time of its inner acceptance by the modern world, which did not begin until the year 1000. Since then it has changed not only in its dogma but in its very nature from Oriental Christianity. The latter's spread into Russia also led to a whole series of new creations. And here as in Russia renaissances (called "reformations") have occurred which in the different historical organisms always led to new creeds (Troeltsch quite correctly expresses the opinion that we should call them new religions), to the formation of new sects of quite varied content and apparently quite varied forms of expression. Christianity spread its various forms over the earth at first within the limits of the expanding Occidental organism, and then, since the 18th century, beyond these limits. But even this alleged "universal religion," and notably this, is today a conglomeration of many different religions which coexist with, and succeed, one another. Each is of equal spiritual truth for its native historical organism; each may express equally well the spiritual situation current in its proper organism. But each in its essence, content, and mode of expansion is actually confined to its own organism.

Moreover, the religious and spiritual expression of culture usually arrays itself in "categories of intuition." It presents itself as "revelation," as "insight," as "certain (immediately intuited) conviction of something unseen" and "knowledge of the invisible" to usurp universal validity and necessity, to evangelize, to convert, and especially, in the case of Christianity, to persecute and burn all those of different faith. But all this merely points to the underlying fact that essentially different expressions of spirit will conflict, bound as they are to spiritual adjustments in the different historical organisms.

What is true of religion is ultimately true of the metaphysical ideas of all philosophical systems, ideas which are always purely and simply a cultural expression of a particular historical organism. It is utterly impossible to convey to the Occidental or any other organism the intrinsic content of Hindu metaphysics, its belief in metempsychosis and its longing for release from individual existence. If we attempt this, we arrive at Schopenhauerianism or theosophy which, although they may externally apply the same or similar forms of concepts or ideas, completely alter their original content. Likewise, it will never be possible to universalize Greek Platonism. It has undergone numerous renaissances in the form of Neo-Platonism, Renaissance Platonism, German Idealism, etc., each of which represents a completely new creation in essence and content.

All cultural emanations in religions, systems of thought and art creations are in complete antithesis to all civilizational expressions; they are confined, so far as their truth-content is concerned, to the time and locality of their native historical organism. Their transfer to other times and other historical organisms is always a mere transfer of their expression and spiritual redemption-values, a transfer of value leading to the so-called "expansion." This has no connection, however, with the logically causal expansion of the illumined parts of the universal civilizational cosmos.

Thus, all cultural emanations are always "creations." They bear the salient traits of all creations, the characteristics of "exclusiveness" and "uniqueness" as opposed to the things disclosed by the civilizational process which always have the characteristic of "discovery" and thereby of universal validity and necessity, the characteristic of having been implicit before disclosure.

Correspondingly, the phenomenology of culture-movement, the type of development in the sphere of culture, differs radically from that of civilization. In the latter, as we have seen, there is a development, broken, of course, and subject to historical contingency but nevertheless occurring by gradations, a unified process of enlightenment covering the whole history of humanity and leading to a definite goal: the total illumination of the pre-existent. In the sphere of culture, on the other hand, we have a bud of productivity cropping out here and there in an apparently inexplicable manner, something suddenly great and unique – an incomparable creation related by no underlying necessity to other things. And if we attempt to observe and establish certain regularities and relations, we arrive not at "gradations of development" but disconnected periods of productivity and unproductivity, periods of decay and stagnation, sudden reversals, conflicting currents – not stages, but expressions of new spiritual situations, an uneasy sea, by turns tempestuous and placid, stirred by this or that "spiritual" wind but having no "constant flow," no destination. So far as we can tell, the term "development" can only apply to the technical means for the expression and elaboration of culture, to the somehow coherent sequence of naturalistic, classical, romantic, and baroque types of expression in the various disparate periods of productivity, to the alternation, somehow conditioned, by more emotional and more rationalized cultural expressions (religions, works of art, etc.), and to the superseding of mythically veiled expressions by unmythical ones at the ageing of the various historical organisms. In short, the term "development" can apply not to the content but to the surface movements which, we must remember, operate independently within each historical organism as if in a separate world.

In the culture-movement of the various historical organisms we are confronted with totally different "worlds" in the making, worlds which come and go along with their respective historical organisms, which are unique and exclusive throughout, and hence are fundamentally different from the uniform cosmos produced by the civilizational process.

Whereas we can apply "intellectual" concepts, modern scientific concepts, to the objects of the universally valid and necessary civilizational process and thereby construct a conscious picture of this process and its consequences, the objects of culture-movement and the various exclusive and unique cultural worlds can only be approached by means of "historical concepts," concepts and ideas dealing in "unique essences." And for the sociological examination of the worlds and movements of culture, it can, therefore, only be a matter of elaborating types, i.e., the comparative presentation of a recurring phenomenology of the surface appearance and an attempt to discover some intelligible connection between this phenomenology, with its unique content, and the general processes of civilization and society in the various historical organisms. Roughly, this is the task of culture-sociology.

V

We can now approach the inner nature of "culture" as opposed to "civilization," their dynamic interrelation and the relation of both to the social process – i.e., we can now approach the central question of culture-sociology.

No matter how we explain the origin of the civilizational element in mankind's historic process, or its slow and gradual disclosure, it is certain that this cosmos is man's most essential resource in the struggle for existence, a mental as well as a material resource. Man dominates nature by intellectualizing the stuff of experience. Through the resulting emergence of the pre-existent civilizational cosmos, he really introduces between nature and himself an intermediate realm composed of information, insights, and ways and means of subduing nature, efficiently organizing his own existence, and revealing and expanding his own natural possibilities. Indeed, this civilizational cosmos is nothing more than this expedient and useful mid-region, and the range of its universal validities and necessities extends just as far as these expediencies and utilities have any meaning. The civilizational cosmos appears as the crystallization of a world of concepts and ideas, as the cultivation of a philosophy of nature, world, and ego, the purpose of which seems to be first intellectual and then practical mastery of nature, world and ego by subjecting them to the light of the intellect.[6] It is the "picture" of nature, world, and ego adapted to the struggle for existence, even if not produced by it. And the innermost structure and formal elements of this picture, its a prioristic intuitive forms, its categories, and its synthetic mathematical judgments a priori all appear as the instrument, somehow developed in the human mind, for the slow creation of this cosmos of control. Since the fundamentals of the struggle for existence are everywhere alike for all mankind, it seems evident that these categories of intuition, the inner mental instrument in the struggle is also alike for all, and that the "picture" of the civilizational cosmos disclosed by this instrument must be common to all, i.e., possess universal validity and necessity. Immediately its singular pre-existence ceases to be miraculous: it is the consequence of the basic categories of intuition developed everywhere in the same way. The civilization cosmos is nothing but a "world-picture" slowly constructed and illumined on the basis of these categories, the aspect of nature "fabricated" by them. This view of nature is eminently suited to the purpose of dominating nature and existence in general and creating the "external realm of domination," i.e., the civilizational apparatus, because it grew out of categories which in turn appear to have arisen for just this purpose.

This is the true character of the civilizational cosmos, which therefore represents the great illumined realm of purposeful and useful forms and which, in its moulding of existence, is guided entirely by the point of view of purposefulness and utility.

The cultural moulding of existence has, however, nothing to do with purposefulness and utility. Whatever in religions and systems of ideas influences existence; whatever is mirrored in works of art and "forms" (*Gestalten*) springs from a sphere of quite different categories and intuitions, from the province of the soul. The spiritual elaboration and moulding of the stuff of existence is opposed to civilizational, i.e., intellectual, elaboration. The 19th century is greatly to blame for smothering, as it were, the function of the soul, the spiritual sphere of mankind, as the ultimate and most profound medium for contemplating and intuiting the historical process. It has blinded historical philosophy and all sociological speculation as well to this most intrinsic sphere of being which sees or ought to see all existence as the expression, the form, incarnation, reflection, facsimile, or symbol of a "soul-like essence." The 19th century has done this through the notion of "spirit," chiefly the Hegelian "objective spirit." This notion of objective spirit bound up the intellectual elements (mastery of existence) with the elements of spiritual expression, thus actually identifying intellect and soul,[7] and hopelessly confusing civilization and culture. Culture, however, is simply the soul's will and expression; therefore the will and expression of an "essence" lying behind all intellectual mastery of existence, of a soul which, in its desiring and striving for expression, does not concern itself with purposefulness and utility but only with the penetration and moulding of the life-substance. This soul exhibits a sort of likeness of itself, and through this likeness, through the imposition of form, at least external form, upon the life-substance, facilitates its own redemption. All culture is just this striving for redemption by the soul of the various historical organisms. It is the soul's attempt to achieve the expression, form, structure, and image of its own being – either to mould the given stuff of existence or, if this is impossible, to escape to a transcendental milieu for its transfiguration and redemption.

This means that if the social process is the "corporeal" in the development of the different historical organisms, then the civilizational process supplies it with the technical means to build up this or that purposeful or useful form of existence. But all this is still merely raw material which the culture-movement must spiritually elaborate and transform into an expression of the character of the living soul. Thence follows the concept of culture as the form of spiritual expression and redemption, imposed at any time upon the given mental and material stuff of existence. We thus get a clue to the reciprocal dynamic interrelationship of social process, civilizational process, and culture-movement and to the rhythm of cultural productivity in the various historical organisms.

VI

The social processes of the various historical organisms, i.e., the corporeal historical process, viewed sociologically, along with the affinities and conflicts of indigenous natural-human forces, passes through various stages It passes from simple to complex forms of life-aggregates; it undergoes complete social regroupings, broadening and narrowing of horizons, paralysis and dissolutions of its social forms. It undergoes a certain amount of resifting of the stuff of experience (all this considered from the viewpoint of the indwelling soul as experience and plastic material) and passes through complete regroupings of the life-elements which present existence as a new experiential entity; and on the other hand, it also passes through longer or shorter periods of paralysis, periods of "aggregative lethargy," of pure repetition of experience, which for generations or even millennia offer the soul the same experiential and moulding material. Besides, through the presentation of new technical methods for moulding existence and new knowledge and horizons, the civilizational process is the most essential factor in urging the corporeal structure of society from simple to complex forms, in allowing for the further development and displacement of the corporeal life-aggregate, and in bringing about, by discoveries and inventions, drastic changes, great reconstructions and complete reorganizations. Furthermore, by persisting in some historical organism, it can contribute to its corporeal paralysis and further its senile dissolution. It creates, therefore, new external life-aggregates in conjunction with the natural forces of the social process.

It can also create, however, a purely mental regrouping of life-elements without this sort of transformation of the external life-aggregate merely by bringing forth a purely mental enlightenment or penetrating with such an enlightenment from without into some historical organism. And it does this purely by means of a new mental organization of the elements of existence quite independently of corporeal transformation – yet often with as great effect as any induced by such corporeal change. If hitherto the world was seen as a plate-like disk, over which the "canopy of heaven" arched like a foreshortened bell, and now the Copernican view of the universe with its infinite perspective suddenly springs up instead and is universally accepted, a regrouping, a mental revolution and re-ordering of all life-elements, is initiated – an effect just as great or, for the "soul," even greater than any similar effect of a corporeal transformation. The same sort of thing must follow when the external world is suddenly seen to be no longer independent of our ego and its forms and conditions, to be no longer a purely material being, but as a "product" of the psycho-physical receptibilities of our ego and its a prioristic forms of intuition (Kant). All experiential facts thus acquire an altered meaning for the soul, and a new position and meaning in relation to each other. Existence enters into a new "aggregation" for the soul without assuming a new external aggregation. Though usually less striking and far-reaching, the same holds true in greater or lesser degree for all other instances drawn from the mental aspect of the civilizational cosmos.

Now the "soul" in each historical organism attempts to adapt to its own nature the stuff of existence – which becomes, as we have seen, the stuff of experience – and to make it the expression of its inner being. In this way it creates "culture." It makes no difference, therefore, whether it does this through the transformation of its corporeal nature or through a new mental picture of existence. In either case it enters a new being through this "re-aggregation of all its life-elements," a new world with new stuff to be moulded. In every such situation its task begins anew, and here originates the drive and the necessity of "cultural productivity." This drive is simply the attempt to give this new existence, this new disposition of life-stuff, a spiritual mould.

It follows that periods of cultural productivity always come as the result of re-aggregations of the life-elements. Conversely, when this "new existence" is spiritually formed or expressed, there follows necessarily a cultural stagnation – perhaps relieved for a time by stilted reiterations of things already expressed – but finally utter quiescence. From the standpoint of the "collective soul" of the historical organism (scientifically expressed: its total spiritual constitution at any instant), this means that through the re-aggregation there emerges a new "life-feeling," a new way of responding to life as a whole, which strives toward new expression and spiritual re-orientation – a totally new outlook upon social and mental facts. New "ages" and cultural eras arise with new sensibilities. From the standpoint of the "productive minds" of the different historical organisms, it means that these minds organize the new sensibility and project it upon the objective world. They absorb the re-aggregated life-stuff as experience, bind it to their spiritual centre, transmute it in the crucible of their new life-feeling and produce in a "synthesis of world and personality" this new birth, their "creation." They either do this simply to produce a purposeless replica of the newly-felt world and its spiritually formed content in definite form – thus making a work of art – or with the purpose of spiritually transforming the natural, social, and civilizational form of existence, to make it the expression of the new life-feeling and its content, to re-found and re-mould it in "ideal" form. Or, thirdly, if this is impossible, if reality which faces them is such that the ideal forms are inapplicable to it and become valueless in this sense, they attempt to "salvage" these forms by placing them beyond reality, i.e., by giving them transcendental existence. In this way there arise, besides works of art, systems of ideas and religions which contain this duality of ideal and real. And the great artists, prophets, and revealers of the new life-feeling arise who embody this variegated projection, who "crown" the ages and periods of culture and who usher them in and out.

Thus, from a merely preliminary examination the following facts already become superficially comprehensible in their sociological aspect and significance: the rhythm of culture-movements, the alternation of their periods of productivity and inertia, the advent of their "ages," the conflict of their cultural trends (which is always an expression of conflict between some new life-feeling and some older feeling), the rise of great men (who, in this view, must generally appear at turning points of development) and the inevitable flocking of lesser productive minds at the appearance of a greater (the lesser seeking expression and pointing to the greater as "harbingers" or "allies"). The sociological type of the culture-movement, its articulation in ever new and disparate periods of productivity, the conflicting trends of culture and the position within these of great men somewhat like standard-bearers, the corona-like character of great cultural emanations possessing eternal content and always characterized by complete exclusiveness and uniqueness, emanations which the movement of culture places in such sharp polar opposition to the development of civilization – all this becomes comprehensible. At the same time, as intimated, the general direction and form of expression already have become more or less clear: the fact that the great cultural emanations can at one time signify abnegation (as do many great religions, early Christianity and Buddhism, for example, which despair of ever extending the spiritual emanation to life as a whole); that at another time they believe themselves able to transform this unaggregated existence by means of secular idealism (Mohammedanism, Lutheranism, German Idealism); whereas at a third time they are able to accept life joyfully as it is and in an affirmative spirit give it simple, definite, intensified expression (Periclean Antiquity, the late Renaissance, for example).

It will be the task of sociological research to disclose these modes of fragmentary or complete life-feeling and their urge for expression in different forms and conditions, to connect them with mentally or corporeally created re-aggregations of the life-elements, and in this way to explain – or more cautiously expressed – to interpret not only the great periods of cultural productivity, their repetition, their essential nature, and the place of great men within them, but also the emergence of the different phases of culture, the succession and alternation of their formal principles.

Since we are now concerned with the principles of culture-dynamics, there is still this to be said: each period of culture that follows from some new life-feeling, since it seeks to shape the stuff of existence and its social and civilizational aggregate and to lend it its own spiritual aspect, naturally reacts upon this corporeal and civilizational aggregate. It creates principles of structure which are conserved and propagated in religions by the Church, and in systems of ideas by mind and the idea. It creates in works of art objective images of eternity, and in great men personified "prototypes" of the life-patterns. Through social and mental channels it impels all these into all the pores of the social and individual structure and over the whole corporeal and mental habitus of the historical sphere in which it arose. In this way it permeates down with its principles of structure into the social and civilizational substratum of historical development and there saturates it. This is exactly its task and purpose as the spiritual mode of expression of the new life-aggregate. It thus influences in most thorough fashion the course of social development and the civilizational process in every historical organism. Its final development from the natural forces of impulse, will, and intellect is therefore complex – indeed, it is almost always in conflict with cultural formations of the previous aggregate, formations resulting from the very saturation mentioned. (We can recall as historical instance the self-assertion of the early capitalistic aggregate, which was a gigantic naturalism of will in conflict with the psychoculturally determined medieval life.) At a definite stage culturally acquired structure and rigidity can, in fact, bring the process of re-aggregation to a standstill by the founding of rituals and the chaining of all natural forces (India's religiously fixed caste-system). By means of such ideas bound together by ritual it can congeal the civilizational process. Thus cultural formation becomes relatively an essential element in the concrete structure of society and civilization. But this does not alter the fact that these processes are original and self-moved. They are self-moved in the degree that the one (social process) is propelled, within the limits of natural conditions, by natural forces of impulse and will, and in the degree that the other (civilizational process) is propelled by intellectual forces directed toward the mastery of existence. Nor does it alter the fact that each new aggregate thus formed is the source of new tasks and problems for the culture-movement and its inmost centre, the soul. Only then does the concrete solution of these problems create the forms and rigidities in which the historical organisms are from time to time arrested and from which their natural and intellectual forces continually try to liberate them. The result is the creation of ever new spiritual situations, a new soil for cultural productivity. Social process, civilizational process and culture-movement hang together in this correlative, reciprocal, dynamic fashion. But the concrete character of this interrelationship must be elucidated for each historical organism and for each historical instant by further monographic study, though in principle it must always follow the schema developed here.

Then we have historical organisms and periods in which the movement of culture – for reasons yet to be disclosed by more detailed monography – reacts less powerfully upon the "natural" structure of the whole historical organism or upon certain distinct formations than at other times; periods in which the movement of culture allows the natural structures to develop more or less according to their own laws and gives expression to the envisioned life only in inspirational form. Such a period is Classic Periclean Antiquity where economy, family, state (to a certain degree) and "knowledge" also could exist and develop according to their own natural laws, and only the state as polis was given a religious foundation. Works of art and ideas united this life to final spiritual judgments and thus gave it expression. The Western Asiatic and Egyptian Antiquities represent an entirely opposite type. Here the state and knowledge, at least, are completely enclosed by religious forms brought to a stability and a cultural ritualization which gave support and strength to the outcome of this peculiar social structure, namely, bureaucracy. The same may be said of the Hindu or Chinese historical spheres, though in quite different fashion and on quite different social grounds. From time to time the medieval feudal aggregate manifested similar tendencies to become rigid under the influence of the Church. The principal characteristic of the Renaissance was that the natural-social and rationalistic-civilizational forces burst these bonds, set the process of society and civilization free once more and gave the state, economy, and know-ledge a natural "structure" by "un-deifying" them so that – in real, though remote and exaggerated resemblance to Antiquity – "culture" could ally itself once more to the natural life. The main point at issue is this: the various social forms, state, class, family, etc., as well as the spheres of civilization and their parts, can attain different degrees of "cultural satur-ation" in the various historical organisms and in various periods, and can therefore vary widely in the degree to which they are bound in definite form. This is always a function of the correlation of the three spheres, the interconnections of which have still to be examined more closely.

Perhaps it would be pertinent to our present position and its application to make our-selves clear on the following: the spiritual elaboration of the "modern" life-aggregate (the aggregate beginning in the early capitalistic period and emerging out of the Renaissance) has its first real origins in the idealistic period of the 18th century. In this period, the prime necessity was that of giving new spiritual and cultural form to the new civilizational and natural forces which the "modern" organization of life brought to the surface. But this was not accomplished. The tremendous power of the natural social and civilizational forces, released since the Renaissance and to which the period was subjected from the first, scat-tered all plans to dominate it and introduced the 19th century with all its revolutionary changes. But all the cultural postulates we possess today to cope with the natural forces and tendencies of our life, all that we possess to cope with the provinces of economy, state, society, and family is in reality still drawn from the spiritual and mental arsenal of that earlier attempt at supremacy. We have not yet created a new ideology with which to confront our modern life-aggregate. Socialism in all its modern interpretations is really the postulate of a new cultural form of economy and society directed by that early life-feeling against capitalist forces, a postulate laden with all the frailties and anachronisms of that former spiritual and mental attitude. The modern theory of the state is in the same quandary, and no other has as yet been thought out to cope with the actual new life-aggregate that since has taken place and to master it culturally. The new "theory of the family," the center of so much conflict today, is having the same difficulties in its sphere. And so on to the idea of "nation" and of "humanity," these last-to-be-conceived and highest organizations of mankind which we still try to grasp and conceptually order in terms of the tentative schema of the 18th century.

The battle between the modern soul and the modern life-aggregate continues even today. It is wages with the old, half-blunted weapons of this earlier time with no hope as yet of a new spiritual grasp of life as a whole that would put newer and more effective weapons into our hands. Therefore our battle is harder and more desperate than ever. The approach to the problem has gradually been forced to lower levels until today the essential objects at issue rest in the ultra-simple social groundwork, in the natural foundations of existence. In the event of a complete upheaval – if it arises out of the nature of the life-aggregate – these foundations can easily become the real and primary objects of spiritual exertion, an exertion which must direct itself downward to achieve a radically new orientation at the very roots of existence.

This much, however, can be said in general conclusion: that culture-movement has widely varying degrees of success in drawing the social and civilizational products into its path, depending on the time and the historical organism. Moreover, its desire to do so varies just as widely in different times and periods; for the life-feeling of the soul, which is confronted by a definite life-aggregate and grows out of it, is only capable of this effect within the limits of its own strength. It sees varying degrees of possibility, and in "happier times" necessity, of a complete organization of the stuff of experience. All this will be the object of a closer study of culture-sociology. Here we are concerned only with clearing up the fundamental nature of the concepts, culture, culture-movement, civilizational and social processes and their reciprocal dynamic relations, in so far as it is possible briefly to do so.

VII

From this point of view we can take a position with respect to the two ways in which culture-movement has generally been considered by historical philosophy and sociology, namely, the "evolutionary" approach and the approach lately called "morphological."

The evolutionary, historico-philosophical approach to culture-movement has its origin in the confusion of the intellectual and spiritual spheres under the collective concept of "mind" and consequently in the confusion of civilizational process and culture-movement under the collective idea of "mental development," a confusion for which the 18th century paved the way and which German Idealism brought to its climax. As a consequence the civilizational process and culture-movement are so entangled that the regularities of civilizational development, first in the guise of "mental development," and then of general "development," have been paraded as the intuitive form for the historico-philosophical study of the total process of human history. Condorcet regards all history as the gradual process of man's perfection, the real import of which is really "enlightenment," i.e., in our own parlance, entirely and exclusively the product of a portion of the civilizational cosmos. Kant, Fichte and Hegel, despite the difference in their sociological constructions, regard in common the import of history as the illumination of consciousness (another aspect of the civilizational process) with the goal of revealing the "consciousness of freedom," which will supply the conditions for the realm of reason. It is immaterial whether this illumination of consciousness is revealed in more rational form (attraction and repulsion, solidarity and individualistic forces, the outcome of which ultimately leads to the realm of reason – Kant), whether it receives a Biblical-Protestant cloak as in Fichte (stage of innocence, of growing and complete sinfulness, of liberation, and finally of the supremacy of reason) or whether it assumes the grand Hegelian form of evolution of the world spirit which utilizes the drives and passions of mankind and his struggle for the light and for national order, so that through thesis, antithesis, and synthesis – unfolding in a logical process of self-development – the realm of "reason" finally arrives incarnate in the state. It is clear that the development takes place in each case according to logical and intellectual principles. And the finally disclosed realm of reason into which the individual must assimilate himself in all "freedom of consciousness" is at bottom none other than our disclosed and illumined civilizational cosmos which is made to absorb everything else – art, religion, ideas, etc., and all cultural emanations as elements of its "rational" progress, engulfing them all in its final, logical form. The newly discovered psychological aspect of the civilizational process obscures the true nature of culture, and under the concepts "realization of reason" and "spontaneous evolution of spirit" the totality of historical facts is drawn into the province of civilization. Marx is guilty of the same general type of confusion. What he sees is simply another side, the material and technical side of the unfolding of the civilizational cosmos. He permits it to pass as the final principle of historical development of which all social processes are mere expressions and all cultural movements mere reflections. The positivists, from their gifted founders, St. Simon and Comte, to the modern pragmatists, perceive the line of mental and scientific development, see the ever more rapid removal of mythical veils from the world-view, the constantly growing influence of intellect and science on the structure of being and society (industrial system in St. Simon) and finally allow everything, including culture, which naturally they do not recognize as being of different nature, to vanish in their civilizational and positivistic form of world and being – which again is equivalent to the revealed cosmos of civilization. Therefore, as far as the general approach is concerned, it is immaterial if they then attempt to give this rationalized and pan-organized civilizational cosmos (disclosed as the final goal of culture) some religious significance appropriated from cultural values (like St. Simon's *Nouveau Christianisme*). Later sociologists, like Spencer, who are under the spell of the positivistic civilizational attitude, organized the resulting view of the historical totality not according to the developmental facts of an objective spirit, the technical means of production, or the scientific mastery of existence, but according to the reflection of all these things back on the development of consciousness itself. Thus the militant, myth-making, and religious man of the early stages is succeeded by the rationalized, mercantile, and compassionate man as a necessary product of development. We might also view the effect of the development on the conscious attitude of the individual towards the collectivity. The early periods of corporative unity are succeeded by a period of individualism and perhaps finally by a period of so-called subjectivism which has never been clearly described (Lamprecht). In all cases it is simply the progress of civilization and its effects that are being viewed and investigated. Everything else is merely part, consequence, or reflection. Everywhere the disclosure of some aspect of the pre-existent civilizational cosmos and its effects are viewed as the import and goal of world history. For these persons the civilizational cosmos in its ultimately emerged phase is something definitive, the final goal toward which we must strive. And hence, it always happens that evolutionary civilizational sociologists and historical philosophers, even the most gifted among them, nay, particularly those, all offer eschatologies, predictions, constructs of a final stage of humanity; a final stage which is in all cases simply the last stage in the unfolding of the civilizational cosmos. As is well known, Hegal and Fichte considered their age as the dawning of practical reason, as the last age of men – a slight error, as we know. Marxism with its predictions of socialism as the rational realm of the future that would finally emerge in a logical and dialectical manner through a social process viewed as purely civilizational is just such another fragmentary civilizational eschatology, an attempt, for the purpose of social and political agitation, to throw premature epigrammatic light on the future civilizational cosmos and its forms.

It is not strange in the least that all these various theories of history and philosophies of culture, as different as they may be in their self-proclaimed principles, idealistic, materialistic, positivistic, psychological, etc., are nevertheless so basically connected that on closer scrutiny one unexpectedly merges into the other; in fact, one is nothing but the obverse of the other. One instance of this is the affinity, nay, more, the far-reaching sociological identity between Hegelianism and Marxism. This has been convincingly shown by Plenge to apply not merely formally but intrinsically to these two historical philosophers who confronted each other so inimically in their outward demeanor (evolution of spirit versus evolution of matter), while at bottom both asserted the necessary and universally valid evolution of a rational, world-wide, social organization in which the individual's only freedom lay in conscious "adaption." Let this pervasive identity be taken as the whole crux of all these theories of development and culture. For they are all merely different illustrations of the general rational principles that form and develop the inner and outer aspects of human existence, and these principles are allowed to obscure everything else.

All these authors stand, as it were, sociologically prior to the "primal sin" of basic insight. They do not see that rational organization, rational self-coordination, rational illumination of existence, or any other rationalization – even if we impute to them the emanations of world reason or relate them to the development of principles of freedom or to trends toward equality – never have anything fundamentally in common either with culture or with the inner, essential, structure of a historical organism. Moreover, they are not aware of the distinction between the civilizational trends of development in the historical organisms and the unfolding of culture. Otherwise they would perceive that all these phenomena of rationalization are only means and not the essence of the structure of existence. They would not be able to see any goals or ultimate ideas of human development in these facts, but rather the developmental universalities and necessities under whose widening supremacy the spiritual in the historical process is drawn, the spiritual whose task is the unending and ever harder struggle to conquer the natural existence in which universalities and necessities themselves have been among the creative factors. Of course, the eschatological, civilizational paradise of organization, which they all see, would then be deprived of divine attribute, and mankind of its universal "goal of culture." But they would have profited in a profound and ultimate sense on the question of culture proper.

VIII

The "morphological" approach to history and culture is the direct antithesis. It seeks to understand the "soul" as it maturates, awakens, runs its course and declines in the various great historical organisms, and as it gives forth cultural emanations as symbols of its exist-ence and destiny. The religions, systems of ideas, and art-forms are the utterly unique, incomparable expressions of the soul of the various historical organisms in their different stages of growth and decline, expressions that strive toward no universal human goal but have simply acquired a certain "form." History itself is not an inherently unified coherent process, but the province of morphological emergence, of the origin, growth and disap-pearance of some great organism from an environmental matrix. Each historical organism has its law, its own being, and its own peculiar soul that strives for expression. They all have "homologous" stages of development and "homologous" drives for expression to the extent that they are all young at some time, that they grow, flourish and grow old; and to the extent that they all seek to reflect the whole of their spiritual import in their manifest forms. But each single manifestation, civilizational as well as cultural, is as unique, exclusive and incomparable as the soul itself, a pure expression of its essence. Thus we have not only a Western-Faustian, an Ancient-Apollonian, a Magian-Arabian art, religion and metaphysics, but a science and mathematics as well, a distinct, untransferable system of knowledge – in our parlance, an inherently untransferable civilizational cosmos peculiar to each historical organism and neither universally valid nor necessary. All parts of the civilizational cosmos are viewed in general not as civilizational but as "cultural," i.e., as spiritual forms of expres-sion. Civilization and culture are thus once again fused as with the evolutionists, but this time with the opposite dominance. Culture and civilization are distinguished only to the extent that civilizational formation is viewed and defined as the conscious, rational "cosmo-politan" end-product of the historical process of each great organism, whereas culture, at a definite "homologous" stage of decline, yields to civilization, producing the so-called "rational senility." Thus the essence of the civilizational is seen and recognized to a certain extent as a rational organization of life and as conscious enlightenment. But the civiliza-tional process proper is not recognized as a unified process bound up with the destiny of mankind, a process present from the very beginning of all historical development and continuously operative through all the stages of each historical organism. Undoubtedly the increasing significance of civilizational organization which follows enlightenment is evident. This enlightenment, however, is not placed in its proper context, namely, in the general human enlightenment begun or already attained by a process of continual repetition and advance in other historical organisms; nor is the objective civilizational cosmos of this enlightenment presented, as it should be, as a clearly evident and undeniable whole, hardly fragmentary even in earlier times of less universal interralationship. Furthermore, those historical facts which actually follow their own laws, i.e., the realities and formal expressions of the social process in the various historical organisms, are interpreted arbitrarily as sym-bols of the will for spiritual expression, to the exclusion of true causes. In short, not only the civilizational but the social process as well is drawn into the "morphologically" viewed movement of culture for the sake of grasping the temporarily independent process of growth and decline and final destiny of the various great historical organisms. This presents a picture which has many comic aspects. For instance, it is droll to predict the decline of Occidental culture, giving it a hundred years' grace up to such and such a homologous stage. And this at a moment when this Occidental culture is caught up in a gigantic process of transformation through its involvement in the general destiny of mankind (the World War!), a process which is drawing culture toward an absolutely unpredictable destination. Whether it is moving toward disintegration of its historical organism and its "soul," whether toward metamorphosis or transposition into another emergent organism, or toward a complete, and perhaps very rapid "physical" decline, no one can know. The fallacy in this approach also follows from the characteristic inability to separate social process, civilizational process, and culture-movement, and from the attempt to understand and define the destiny of the various historical organisms solely in terms of some kind of spirituality without seeing the realities of the social and civilizational processes and their specific laws.

IX

Nevertheless, there can be no doubt that our own conception of culture is akin to the morphological view. For us, too, all cultural emanations are merely unique symbols, pointing to no general goal of development – mutually incomparable and exclusive expressions of the soul of the existing historical organisms. In any case they are symbols which receive their structure and content essentially from the extant aggregated life-substance, from the social and civilizational corporeality in which this soul appears in the various historical organisms and which the soul, through this cultural symbolization and externalization, attempts to remake after its own image. The material of society and civilization surrounds the soul of the various historical organisms with a stuff in itself alien to the soul, a material layer to which at each historical moment the soul seeks to lend its own "countenance," or, failing in this, to withdraw in abnegation (the great renunciatory religions). Or if one prefers another metaphor, a substance, a life-stuff obtrudes itself upon the soul according to its own inevitable laws and demands that the soul inspire it and inform it with culture. This is the cultural task of each period and the essence of its culture-movement, which, to repeat, is still therefore mainly dependent on other factors than the "spontaneous development" of the soul of each historical organism. Even in this view there is room for a spontaneous development of the soul, a growth, a bloom, and a decline. All this, however, cannot be considered as self-sufficient and independent of causality. It is conditioned by the conscious civilizational illumination of the life-substance of the different peoples; it is conditioned by the successive illumination of these peoples as they come within the range of the subjective aspect of the civilizational process. The early period of darkness and unenlightenment varies greatly in the different historical organisms both in type and duration, depending on the time, manner and place of their entrance into this civilizational cosmos. The period of awakening presents itself under widely varying conditions, in widely varying settings of psychic and physical objects already "given" by the civilizational cosmos. And from this varying point of departure it leads the various historical organisms in extremely diverse ways to high points of conscious, productive, spiritual domination of existence and to periods of decline which are never identical and cannot be predetermined. Further, just as the whole process of conscious, spiritual development is conditioned by the time, place and manner of inclusion within the general civilizational cosmos and is thereby conditioned in tempo and in the emergence of its initial and middle stages, so is it likewise conditioned in its further development (as our culture-sociological investigation of the various historical organisms will show) by the widely varying course and structure of the social process. This latter condition may take several forms: completely unconscious or half-conscious strata may be at first retarded in the historical organism but, as history progresses, ascend and thus advance enlightenment once more (as in the Occident the successively ascending strata of clerics, knights, burghers, workers, etc.); or there may occur a simultaneous general enlightenment of a people, viewed socially, as in Classical Antiquity (a development in one stage!), or a fixed social and mental organization of superimposed strata may result from the dynamics of the social, civilizational and cultural process, as in India, etc.

In our view, therefore, the process of spiritual enlightenment, growth and decline of the cultural organism, together with all its cultural expressions and potentialities, is embedded like everything else in the mutual dynamics of the processes of society, civilization and culture. It therefore has entirely different points of departure in the different historical organisms. (The Arabian historical cycle began at a stage of consciousness entirely different from the Classical because of its different position in the civilizational cosmos, and it never knew a real mythology.) The process also has quite varied potentialities of development (single stage, multiple-stage, etc.). And by means of the varied interconnections of the historical organisms, it flows into the total process of history (remaining in more or less complete isolation, as in China or India, or interpenetrating and perhaps achieving world-wide expansion as in Classical Antiquity, Arabia, and the modern Occident) and then passes into completely various final states not amenable to schematization. All this, the phases and expression of cultural "movement" as well as the "destiny" of culture, is to be explained through a treatment of facts that must never lose sight of the total course of human histor-ical development, a treatment that must operate, as has already been explained, on three planes and subject its material to careful threefold division:

First, one thing must be accepted simply with no attempt to analyze or explain it – namely, the specific quality of the soul that "dwells" in the various historical organisms and constantly struggles for expression within the compass of their general destiny. This specific quality of the soul is to be comprehended exclusively through empathy. For anyone who understands this empathy, it is possible to grasp the spiritual factor in every cultural object-ification, conceive it in its essence, interpret and lay it bare as the specific "core" of the culture in question. But the sociologist, at least with respect to the aims pursued in these pages, must leave this untouched. Its interpretation and presentation must be left in more delicate hands – as well as the interpretation and presentation of the inmost meaning of great cultural objectifications in general.

The next thing he has to consider is the direct antithesis, namely, the "surface-movement" which this nucleus produces in its struggle with the outer life-stuff. In this surface-movement he must establish the typical and the recurrent; he must establish the succession of eman-ations, the casting off of certain aspects and forms of expression, the typical periodicity, the manner and kind of impact – thus disclosing the "rhythm of culture-movement"; and he must do this, of course, as far as possible in all historical and cultural organisms that lend themselves to analysis. In this analysis he must ask to what extent the established typicality is bound up with the corporeal and the intellectual-civilizational (the processes of society and civilization) that environ the spiritual "nucleus," i.e., to what extent this typicality follows from the situations, modes of life-aggregate, in which these place the soul-nucleus. In this connection he must present inductively a general formal study of types of culture-movement, clarifying sociologically the surface-movement of cultural development. Such a study takes its place side by side with the dynamics of the different spheres, as we have propounded them.

Then, thirdly, he can attempt to go deeper and inquire into the special destiny of the spiritual "nucleus" of this movement. He can trace the development of the spiritual "nucleus" of the various historical organisms within the processes of society and civilization. He can examine the intrinsic "maneuvers" by which the nucleus "struggles" with the fate imposed upon it by the processes of society and civilization. He can perhaps explain how the advent of great men follows from this struggle and these "maneuvers," how the great "eras" and cultural trends and counter-trends result, and how the great material lines of cultural history grow distinct. Perhaps! He should at least make the attempt. He would thus introduce a content, a sociologically clarified material, into the superficial types of formal sociology and at the same time create a bridge to the intrinsic interpretation and understanding of the essence of the great cultural objectifications and phenomena, which, however (as we have said), it is not his task to interpret in the most profound sense. But to understand them adequately he can build an environment after his own fashion, a sociological rigging and shell, as it were, in which the golden globes of cultural history lie. In this way, perhaps, they can be seen to greater advantage and their essence more easily grasped than through mere "empathy" in "empty space." In this last attempt he will have almost overstepped the bounds of the pure sociological approach. But if he gets this far, he will make his contribution to our ultimate goal in the intuitional understanding of cultures: their spiritual renaissance in ourselves.

Notes

1 It should be noted that this concept did not originate with Spengler but that it lies implicitly or explicitly at the bottom of all the more recent historiography. Likewise, the "adolescence" and "maturity" of historical organisms have long been ingredients in this point of view.

2 Despite the brilliant personal contribution of Jacob Burckhardt and others.

3 We are not overlooking such comprehensive treatments as those of Max Weber and Troeltsch in the history of religion, nor the partly "impromptu" attempts to be found in the numerous recent treatises on the different cultural fields.

4 Clearly, we are now dealing with marginal questions of the materialistic interpretation of history. This school's inquiry into "interest" does not lead to the clarification of the final categories of cognition.

5 Despite the many points in common between the above and the deductions of Max Weber in his essays on the sociology of religion, the latter derive from a somewhat different point of view which unfortunately does not permit of analysis here.

6 Here the etiology and the epistemology of the Bergsonian intuitions are neither accepted nor rejected within their philosophic scope.

7 Hegel's protest against the overvaluation of the understanding does not decrease his own implication in this view through his concept of the supreme reason.

14

CITIES OF CULTURE, CITIES OF CIVILIZATION

'The Problem of Cultural Differences' (1931)

Robert E. Park (1864–1944)

The Chicago School in America provided an integrated institutional setting for a collective intellectual enterprise similar to the Durkheimian one in Paris. This was particularly so during its most creative period from 1915 to 1935. Robert E. Park, along with William Thomas who published *The Polish Peasant in Europe and America* (1918/1920), constituted the centre of gravity for the Chicago School, whose other members included Ernest Burgess, William F. Ogburn, and Louis Wirth, who published his study *The Ghetto* in 1928. The unity of focus was achieved not so much through concerns with sociological method, as through attempting to understand the nature of contemporary American civilization. If Jefferson's American civilization was centered on a 'home-grown' democratic republic of towns, then the Chicago School's was centered on the immigrant city. Chicago, itself, was representative of the contemporary city-type of a New World immigrant society. It was at once industrial, cosmopolitan, divided, and it was this multi-faceted phenomenon to which Park and Burgess, in particular, turned their attention in two works, 'The City: Suggestions for the investigation of human behavior in the city environment' (Park, 1915), and *The City* (Park and Burgess, 1925).

Chicago, as ethnic and racial 'melting-pot', ensured that the problem of culture was also explored. It was explored, moreover, from the vantage point of cultural diffusion. For Parke, the specificity of a culture is denoted by the congruence and integration of diffuse elements. None the less, Parke's theorization of culture, which stands in a line that runs from Herder to Boas, also draws on the German distinction between *Kultur*, which refers to ends and values, and *Zivilisation*, which refers to the means and techniques required for material life. He thus articulates many of the suppositions present in Alfred Weber's essay prior to the reception of this version of culture in American sociology.

Culture, which is a character we ordinarily attribute to communities and peoples, is a term not unlike personality, which is a character we attribute to individuals. Personality has sometimes been described as the individual and subjective aspect of culture. In that sense we may say that culture consists of those habits in individuals that have become customary, conventionalized, and accepted in the community.

Culture includes, therefore, not merely all that Sumner has described as the folkways but it includes, also, art, science, philosophy and formal law, all the technical and rational devices, in fact, by which men have at all times sought to control not only their environment but themselves. It is because what is customary in the community becomes habit in succeeding generations that the fund of tradition which we call culture persists and accumulates. Once habits formed by individuals have become conventionalized, sanctioned, and transmitted they become a communal possession.

It is the community that conserves and transmits them. It is characteristic of culture that it is at once diffused and transmitted, and by the diffusion and transmission of its folkways society at once extends and gives permanence and consistency to the influences that it exerts upon the individuals who compose it.

"Society exists," as Dewey expresses it, "through a process of transmission, quite as much as biological life. This transmission occurs by means of communication of habits of doing, thinking, feeling from the older to the younger. Without this communication of ideals, hopes, expectations, standards, opinions from those members of society who are passing out of the group life to those who are coming into it, social life could not survive."[1]

Every individual is the inheritor of a double inheritance, physical and moral, racial and cultural. It is, however, by association, by education and, fundamentally, by communication, that these individuals come into possession and become the bearers of their cultural heritage.

All this indicates what culture is. It is not an artifact merely, nor something that can be bought, sold, and "distributed." It is not even something that can be collected, classified, and exhibited in anthropological museums or in art galleries. The exchange of economic goods and the distribution of foreign commodities unquestionably does modify and eventually transform indigenous cultures. But cultural traits cannot be exported or transported. They can be transmitted and diffused. A cultural trait is transmitted from one generation to another, or diffused from one culture to another, when it has been incorporated into the traditional culture complex and thus become an integral part of the customary and accepted practice of the community in which it has been "diffused."

Transmission and diffusion inevitably involve, as Malinowski has insisted, some modification in the character of the traits diffused and some accommodation and adaptation of the culture into which diffusion takes place. "Just because no idea and no object can exist in isolation from its cultural context, it is impossible to sever mechanically an item from one culture and place it in another. The process is always one of adaptation in which the receiving culture has to re-evolve the idea, custom or institution which it adopts. . . . Diffusion, invention, are always mixed, always inseparable."[2]

It is because the transmission and diffusion of cultures involve some re-discovery and re-evolution of the ideas, customs, or institutions transmitted that one may say that culture exists in and through transmission and diffusion, in the same sense that society may be said to exist in and through communication.

A society may be described as a group of individuals who are capable of some sort of concert and collective action. This usually implies the possession of institutions by means of which collective action can be maintained and controlled. The diffusion of culture makes it possible to act collectively over a wider area and to maintain some sort of concert among, and control over, a larger number of individuals. The transmission of a cultural tradition, on the other hand, tends to make that action more consistent and more intelligent.

Culture, as the anthropologists conceive it, is a constellation of individual elements and of complexes of elements or traits. A cultural trait is, theoretically at least, a unit of cultural description and analysis. In practice it is any increment or item of any existing culture that is capable of independent diffusion or modification.

"A trait," said Wissler, "grows out of an idea or an invention, as the case may be, but does not rise to the level of a cultural trait until a standardized procedure is established in the group. A single individual may have started it, may have practiced it for a long time, but until a number of his fellows adopt it and pass it on to the rising generation, it is not a trait for culture."[3]

As a matter of fact, under the influence of cultural contact, migration and conquest, cultural complexes break up into smaller units and are transmitted and diffused independently of the cultural context in which they had, presumably, their origin. One of the first and most perplexing problems of cultural anthropology and sociology is to discover the conditions and the processes by which cultural traits have been diffused and modified. In regard to the exact nature of this process of diffusion there is a growing diversity of opinion, but there is, at the same time, an increasing appreciation of its complexity and its importance.

Cultural diffusion inevitably involves, as I have suggested, a breaking up of cultures and cultural complexes. Cultural traits are not taken over wholesale from one culture to another. What ordinarily happens when people of widely divergent cultures come into contact and conflict is that certain elements of the invading or borrowed cultures are assimilated first, while others are incorporated in the complex of the invaded culture only after a considerable period of time, if at all.

Diffusion of cultures takes place, in some instances, in a manner analogous to that in which, in a plant community, an existing "formation" is broken up by the invasion of alien species. In this case the plant formation corresponds to the cultural complex This plant formation, like the cultural complex, "is a highly complex structure in which the interruption of one function tends to throw the whole into confusion."

Diffusion does not always take place by a process that can be described as invasion nor by the imposition of one culture upon another. It sometimes takes place by what Wissler describes as "spontaneous borrowing." Individuals and peoples borrow from the cultures of their neighbors, particularly from the peoples with whom they are in competition and conflict, and more particularly from the people by which they have been subjugated and reduced to a status of conscious inferiority.

Anthropologists have generally sought to preserve, as far as possible, the native cultures of the peoples with whom they have become acquainted, and in order to do this they have sought to protect these peoples from the corroding and destructive effects of contact with traders and missionaries. They have not always reckoned, however, with the human nature of the natives themselves. Wissler quotes from the experience of a correspondent, writing from Africa, who has discovered "that if you tell a native to do a thing in as native a manner as possible, he will do it in his best possible imitation of a European way. If you try to persuade him to wear suitable indigenous clothing rather than follow the most unsuitable castoffs of Europeans, or if you try to persuade him to develop his own educational system, he at once becomes suspicious and angry; to him all that is European represents civilization and if you want him to follow his own customs then you must try to keep civilization from him and to keep him a serf race! The greatest enemy of the whole experiment is the native himself."[4]

It is evident, however, that in what seems like similar circumstances not all natives behave in precisely the same way. Maurice Evans, observing the native rickshaw men in Natal, South Africa, is impressed by their "barbaric splendor and mighty physique," but he is amazed that living, as they do, in the midst of the strange intriguing sights of a European civilization, with its imposing structures, complicated machinery, and its stimulating bustle and movement, the native, the *Abantu*, is quite unimpressed and seemingly untouched by the wonders of the white man's world. He neither understands nor cares to understand what it is all about, and presently, when the desire comes upon him to see his home again, no wage offered him, no sense of gratitude or of loyalty, nothing will keep him away longer "from the kraal by the rushing Umbagi, from the girls and the cattle."[5]

What one cultural group borrows from another is determined first and last by the use it can make of what is borrowed. Cultures diffuse in much the same way that news travels, but not so rapidly. What is interesting and disturbing travels most rapidly and most widely, and other things being equal, it reaches the people most concerned first. One of the marvels of the modern world is the rapidity with which knowledge of world events reaches peoples in the most remote corners of the earth. On the other hand, it is shocking to discover how ignorant people in different parts of the world are likely to be of events which do not immediately concern them, or of events the import of which they do not fully understand. In the modern world, which the telegraph and the radio have converted, as has so often been said, into one vast whispering gallery, the only obstacle to the circulation of intelligence seems to be the inability of the purveyors of news to make the reports of events not merely accurate but interesting and intelligible.

To recognize that culture is transmitted and diffused rather than transported and distributed, is to recognize that cultural traits have their roots and their sources in the instincts and habits of human beings. It is this that gives them that dynamic character by which they interact and modify one another. They are not merely diffused, but in the process of diffusion they are transformed, recreated.

This is no doubt what Teggart had in mind when he wrote: "It should be observed that the word 'culture' is frequently used to designate the sum-total of the acquisitions of any human group, in language, in rites, customs, practices, material objects, in ideas. Strictly speaking, however, 'culture' signifies the work of cultivation; it means the *activity* through which the products which we assemble in ethnological museums, and which we describe in books, have been brought into existence."[6]

It is in this sense that we must conceive the folkways as Sumner describes them. They are cultural traits from the point of view of action. They are ways of doing things, action patterns, habits arising in the individual, conventionalized and transmitted by society as part of the cultural heritage.

"Arts and crafts, language, science, political organization and institutions are merely the extension of structures and of functions of which the habits of the individuals and the customs of the group are the most elementary expression."[7]

Cultural traits seem to spring up spontaneously and, in certain historic periods, burst forth in great diffusion, manifesting themselves in changing fashions and innovations and inventions of all sorts. Among these there is, naturally, a struggle for existence; and of the multitude of novel ideas and devices that appear, relatively few survive and are permanently incorporated in existing cultures. There is, furthermore, as Sumner has noted, "a strain toward consistency" in the folkways and among the different traits which constitute any particular culture. Traits which were at first antagonistic, by modification and selection, achieve a stable equilibrium in which competition and conflict disappear and the different traits seem to cooperate and mutually support one another against the invasion of any foreign elements. The effect of this cooperation is to still further stabilize the existing equilibrium and prevent cultural change. This is what we have had, apparently, in China, and what we may expect in any civilization that has achieved any degree of antiquity.

It is this congruence and integration of the elements that constitute a particular culture, also, that gives it that harmonious and individual character which makes it possible to compare the civilization of one period and the culture of one people with that of others.

"The two great cultural divisions of the human race," says Sumner, "are the oriental and the occidental. Each is consistent throughout; each has its own philosophy and spirit; they are separated from top to bottom by different mores, different standpoints, different ways, and different notions of what societal arrangements are advantageous. In their contrast they keep before our minds the possible range of divergence in the solution of the great problems of human life, and in the views of earthly existence by which life policy may be controlled. If two planets were joined in one, their inhabitants could not differ more widely as to what things are best worth seeking, or what ways are most expedient for well living."[8]

Wissler thinks that the dominant characteristics of American culture – those traits, namely, that one would meet, if one should look for them in every American village, may be reduced to three general categories: mechanical invention, mass education, and universal suffrage.

These are indeed universal characteristics of American life. A little reflection will suggest that there is a more intimate connection between them than is likely to appear at first glance. In fact, these connections are so close and so real that it is difficult to conceive any one of them existing in the absence of the others. These three characteristics, mechanical invention, mass education, and universal suffrage, include not merely a multitude of individual traits but they represent, as Mr. Wissler puts it, "a core of ideas and beliefs actuating the [American] people and in large measure, controlling their career." They give to American life, in short, that consistency and unity which impresses the stranger but which is not always manifest to Americans themselves.

An analysis of culture will almost certainly reveal the fact that every single trait presupposes the existence of most others. This is more particularly the case in those societies in which the constituent traits have achieved a relatively permanent and stable equilibrium, as is notably the case with China and the Orient as compared with America and the Occident.

One of the notorious differences between the Orient and the Occident concerns the attitudes prevalent in these two grand divisions of culture in the world in respect to change. The soul of the East, we have been told, is repose. By the same token, the genius of the West is action. The unchanging East is the antipodes of the mobile West.

As a matter of fact, most of the ideas, beliefs, and practices peculiarly characteristic of the Occident are associated with the fact of change. The Western outlook on life is prospective rather than retrospective. Its mood is one of anticipation rather than of reflection. The Western attitude towards change is embodied in the concept of progress. Progress, says J. B. Bury, is "the animating and controlling idea of Western civilization."

The control that this conception exercises, however, is not that of an ideal, like the notion of democracy. It is that of an article of faith, like the belief in Providence or in Fate. In fact, Progress has superseded Providence as a dogma of popular religion in the modern world, just as Providence has replaced Fate or Destiny in the ancient.[9]

There are, however, dissenters who do not accept the dogmas of the popular religion. Among the most eminent of these is Dean Inge, who speaks of progress as a modern superstition which has only established itself as a popular belief during the last one hundred and fifty years. Among its prophets is Herbert Spencer, who asserts the perfectability of man, as Dean Inge says, "with an assurance which makes us gasp."[10]

Not only do the East and West differ in their traditional attitudes toward the fact of change, but they have differed in the past, and probably differ still, in the extent of change which is actually taking place in their different worlds.

Recently Rudolph Heberle published a survey of American contemporary life in which he sought to estimate, on the basis of statistical studies, the extent of the population movement of the United States, and to indicate its consequences as reflected in the structure of American society and in the personal characteristics of the American people.

To a European observer, the outstanding characteristic of American life, as compared with that of Europe, is the extraordinary mobility and restlessness of the American population.[11] This mobility, so strikingly exhibited in America, is characteristic of the modern world. It is peculiarly characteristic, however, of the Occident as compared with the Orient.

Migration and movement are not always, perhaps, original causes of social change, but they are at least incidental to it. When the existing economic and social order is disturbed, migration and population movements take place in an effort to achieve a new equilibrium.

It is, no doubt, the machine and the progressive application of machine methods – i.e., routinization, standardization, coordination and, in general, what is called rationalization – to the collective activities of an ever-expanding world economy that is responsible for the speed and tempo of modern life. But this has been accomplished and accompanied by an increasing mobility of the population involved. Thus, one of the indices, if not the causes, of cultural change is the increased use in recent years of new means of locomotion and of communication.

So far as mobility is a measure of social change, present indications are that – in spite of all that has taken place in the Orient in recent years, – the pace and tempo of the Occident, and particularly of the United States, is now, as it has been in the past, more rapid than that of the rest of the world. In a recent issue of the *American Journal of Sociology*, statistics showing the increased use in the United States, during the year 1930, of the automobile, the aeroplane, the radio, the telephone; the increased attendance of motion pictures and circulation of newspapers have been summarized. The authors of this report, Malcolm M. Willey and Stuart A. Rice, in summing up the results of their inquiry, say that while it is impossible to follow "the ramification of the most obvious changes in American life" summarized in the data presented, they are nevertheless led to "marvel at the way in which American life and the habits of the individual citizens are being transformed."[12]

One may, perhaps, discount the conclusions which are likely to be drawn from the statistics of mobility in the United States, since Americans, who have long been habituated to social changes of every sort, have become, like the Gypsies, more or less immune to their consequences.

Cities have always been the centers of social change because they have been the points at which people came together to exchange their products and to get the news. Modern life is characteristically urban, but modern cities are notoriously the products of the steamship, the locomotive, the automobile. Modern life is, by the same token, the product of the telegraph, the telephone, and the newspaper, particularly since communication has, in the long run, the same social consequences as locomotion. Both tend to break up what Bagehot calls the "cake of custom," to release the individual from the routine of tradition, and to stimulate him to undertake new enterprises.

Differences in customs, manners, philosophy, and in general, the style of life, between a society that is mobile and one that is relatively immobile are likely to be, in the long run, very great. In an immobile society, habits are inevitably fixed. All the activities of life tend to be controlled by custom and to conform to the normal expectation of the community. In an immobile society, personal and social relations tend to assume a formal and ceremonial character. Social status is fixed by tradition; social distances are maintained by social ritual and etiquette. The individual is born into an established tradition, his place and function are defined by ancestral custom. Subordinated in most of his activities to the traditional interests of the group, he tends to lose his individual initiative and spontaneity of action. It is, with a society as with an individual: as they grow older, security seems more desirable than adventure.

On the other hand, in a mobile society, such as exists in America, particularly on the frontier and in the cities, where changes of fortune are likely to be sudden and dramatic, where every individual is more or less on his own, the influence of tradition is inevitably minimized. Personal relations are easily established but quickly dissolved. Social forms are flexible and in no sense fixed. Fashion and public opinion take the place of custom as a means and method of social control. The individual is emancipated, and society is atomized.

Under these circumstances the character of law and legislation changes. Statutory regulations take the place of general consensus, and of that form of common sense known as the common law. Law, no longer supported by a body of mores common to a whole community, assumes the character of a traffic regulation. There is nothing sacred about social regulations whose authority rests upon a changing public opinion rather than upon a venerable tradition.

What I have described as the atomization of society eventually affects the individual's sense of inner security, upon which the control and direction of his personal life finally rests. This sense of insecurity is reflected in art, in literature, and in a general lack of religious conviction. As Walter Lippmann has put it, "surveying the flux of events and the giddiness of his own soul, he comes to feel that Aristophanes must have been thinking of him when he declared that 'Whirl is King, having driven out Zeus.'" [13]

These divergencies in the character of civilization, which rest, the one upon a mobile, and the other upon an immobile population, have by no means escaped the observation of students of society and civilization. Ferdinand J. Tönnies, in his volume, *Gemeinschaft und Gesellschaft*, has made a classic statement of the characteristic traits of what one may, perhaps, describe as the sacred and secular societies. [14]

What characterizes a sacred society is not so much antiquity as immobility. The sacred society is typically a small, isolated community and more particularly the primary group – i.e., the family, the clan, or the religious sect, – a society, in short, where everything is known and every one is bound to every one else by obligations that are at once personal and sacred.

The thing that characterizes secular society, on the other hand, is its mobility. It is composed of people who come together because they are useful to one another; because they have interests, permanent or temporary, that make association profitable; or merely because they are curious one about another, and about the world in which these others live. The inevitable focus of such a society is the market place, where people come together, not because they are alike, but because they are different, not for collective action, but for trade; for exchange of goods, of services and of ideas. The ideal type of such a secular society is the bourse, the money market, or the gaming table, where nothing is sacred, and where men are moved to action neither by piety nor by duty but by an intense and undivided interest in the gains and losses that their decisions are likely to entail.

In a sacred society the typical virtue is that of piety, filial piety, and respect for tradition. Under the influence of the sentiment of piety, one does what is right, proper, and expected. In a secular society, on the contrary, the typical virtue is efficiency, and the thing one seeks to achieve is not conformity, but success.

It is evident that these two types of association, *Gemeinschaft und Gesellschaft*, societies sacred and secular, can, and do, exist in the same community. The history of the Jews proves that it is possible to maintain a vigorous family life and, indeed, a form of tribal culture, with an extraordinary degree of mobility and a lively interest in, and aptitude for, trade.

On the other hand, one cannot escape the conclusion that mobility tends, not merely to undermine the existing social order, but to progressively complicate social relations, and by so doing, release and emancipate the social units of which society is composed.[15]

What has been said suggests the significance of the statement that Chinese and Oriental civilization generally are based on the family. There they have had their origin, and from that source they have derived those controlling ideas that constitute their philosophy of life – the ideas that maintain the unity of their diversified but closely integrated cultures.

On the other hand, Occidental, and particularly modern and American, culture may be said to have had their origin and to have found their controlling ideas in the market place, where men come together to barter and trade, and by the exchange of commodities and services in order to improve – each for himself, and according to his own individual conception of values – his condition in life.

One of the characteristic traits of Occidental, as contrasted with Oriental, civilization is that marriage is the proper termination of courtship and romance. Romantic love as a phenomenon is not unknown in other parts of the world, but it is only in Western Europe, and particularly in America, that it has come to be regarded as a sufficient ground for marriage or for divorce.

Men and women have always been disposed to fall in love, but not until very recent times have they assumed that a romance was a safe or proper basis upon which to establish a family. There is probably no institution, outside of the Protestant Church, where the individualism of the West, as compared with the communism of the East, has found a more decisive or more characteristic expression.

Romantic love, like progress, is a conception which has exercised a controlling influence upon the life and institutions of Western peoples. Only recently has this notion invaded the Orient. It has come in with the American cinema and with the "social dance." With the acceptance of the dogma which asserts that a man is entitled to choose his own wife, and the woman is entitled to choose her own husband, the ancient and inherited type of family, one of the foundation pillars on which Oriental society is based, has begun to crumble. But then, everything in our modern world, under the pressure of changing conditions, has begun to crumble. This is even true, as one gathers from Oswald Spengler's *The Decline of the West*, of the Western world's conviction of its own superiority; the one indomitable idea on which its faith in its future is finally based, has also begun to crack.

Notes

1 John Dewey, *Education and Democracy*, New York, 1916, pp. 1–11.
2 Elliott G. Smith, B. Malinowski, Herbert J. Spindon, A. Goldenweiser, *Culture, The Diffusion Controversy*. New York, 1927, p. 106.
3 Clark Wissler, *An Introduction to Social Anthropology*, New York, 1929, p. 358.
4 Clark Wissler, *op. cit.*, p. 360.
5 Maurice Evans, *Black and White in Southeast Africa*, London and New York, 1911, p. 3.
6 Frederick J. Teggart, *Theory of History*, New Haven, 1925, pp. 189–190.
7 Stuart A. Rice, *Methods in Social Science, A Case Book*, Chicago, 1931, pp. 150–156.
8 William Graham Sumner, *Folkways*. New York, 1906, p. 6.
9 J. B. Bury, *The Idea of Progress*, London, 1921, p. 1.
10 William Ralph Inge, *Outspoken Essays* (Second Series), London, 1923, p. 163.
11 Rudolph Heberle, *Mobilität der Bevölkerung in den Vereinigten Staaten*, Jena, 1929.
12 Malcolm M. Willey and Stuart A. Rice, "Communication," *American Journal of Sociology*, Vol. 36, No. 6, May, 1931.
13 Walter Lippmann, *A Preface to Morals*, New York, 1920, p. 4. See also *The Melody of Chaos*, by Houston Peterson, New York, 1931.
14 Ferdinand J. Tönnies, *Gemeinschaft und Gesellschaft*, Leipzig, 1897. See also Durkheim, Emile, *La Division du Travail Social*, Paris, 1902.
15 See Frederick J. Teggart, *Theory of History*, Chapter XV, "The Methods of Hume and Turgot," where he reviews the theories of those writers, including Waitz and Bagehot, who have sought to explain progress as an incident of the migration and movement of peoples.

15

CIVILIZATION, CULTURE, IDENTITY

'"Civilisation" and "Culture": Nationalism and Nation-State Formation': an extract from *The Germans* (1989)

Norbert Elias (1897–1990)

If one of the themes of *Classical Readings in Culture and Civilization* is the relation between nation-building and the concepts of civilization and culture (see for example the essays by Jefferson, Mann and Febvre above), then this aspect comes to the fore in this essay by Norbert Elias, 'Nationalism and Nation-State Formation'. This extract, taken from the more recently published *The Germans*, builds on the foundations already laid in his *The Civilizing Process*, which was completed in Britain after Elias had left Germany in 1933, and published in German in 1939. The first volume concentrated on the relation between the image of civilization and transformations in conduct, while the second presents an empirically grounded model of the formation of states in Europe since the Middle Ages, and shows how changing power ratios and the monopolization of violence within society are connected to the 'curbing of affects' and changing patterns of both manners and people's habitus in the civilizing process proper.

Elias argues that the images of 'civilization' and 'culture' emerge in the context of the formation and transformation of elites, who define themselves against other elite groups, or against other social groups altogether. This is particularly clear in the development of the German nation-state and German nationalism, in which 'civilization' came to be associated with other countries' values – especially those of France – while 'culture' became the badge of distinctively German values.

The dual figuration of the nation-state: 'culture' and 'civilisation'

Studying the long-term development of the words 'culture' and 'civilisation' leads to a number of relatively unexpected discoveries.[1] one is that in the eighteenth century both terms to a large extent referred to *processes*, while in the twentieth century they represent something almost entirely static. This declining sense of the dynamics of social processes is by no means confined to the changing meanings the concepts 'culture' and 'civilisation'. The increasing tendency to conceptualise processes as if they were unchanging objects represents a more widespread pattern of conceptual development running conversely to that of society at large, the development and dynamics of which have noticeably quickened from the eighteenth to the twentieth centuries.[2]

The paradox was not confined to Germany, but the way it developed in Germany can serve as an illustration. It also suggests an explanation.

That the term 'culture' once referred to a process of cultivation to the transformation of nature by human beings is almost forgotten today – in Germany as elsewhere. Even when it was gradually adopted by the rising German middle-class elites of the eighteenth century as an expression of their self-image and their ideals, it represented their image of themselves as they saw it, namely within the wider context of the development of humanity. The vision of this development of the German middle-class intelligentsia was very similar to that of the French or the British. In fact, the writings of Scottish historians like William Robertson and of Voltaire and his circle in France had a formative influence on the ideas of the rising German intelligentsia. Perhaps their thinking soared higher and their orientation was more idealistic than that of their counterparts in the Western countries because their social situation in a relatively underdeveloped country with a very exclusive upper class of courtiers and nobles was more confined. But their sense of living in an advanced and continually progressing age was for a time almost as strong as that of the rising middle-class intelligentsia of other European countries.

When Schiller painted the development of humankind on a broad canvas in his inaugural lecture 'What is, and to what end do we study, universal history?', he gave what was more or less the standard view of the enlightened intellectual avant-garde of his time. The year was 1789. Soon afterwards, fear of revolutionary violence and upheavals began to fall like a shadow over the thinking of Europeans and to cloud their hopes for a better future, just as happened again in the twentieth century under the influence of the violent upheavals of new revolutions. But in Schiller's lecture the hopes were still untarnished by fear.

Schiller could still note with confidence the fact that human 'culture' had advanced, that one could see it clearly if one compared one's own ordinary mode of living with that of simpler societies. He spoke of the roughness and cruelty of the life of many simpler societies, of the repulsiveness of some of its aspects which arouses in us, as he said, either disgust or pity. He went on to remind his listeners that they were indebted to past ages and distant regions, that all these 'highly dissimilar periods of humankind' had contributed to *their* culture, just as 'the most distant parts of the world' were contributing at present to their comforts. And he justified the study of universal history with the argument that the concatenation of events which had led to the circumstances of the generations living today could only be understood when it was recognised, to quote his own words, that:

> A long chain of events interlocking as causes and effects, stretches from the present moment right back to the beginnings of the human race.[3]

His grasp of the factual connections, like that of many of his middle-class contemporaries, was not yet disturbed and confused, as is the case today, by the growth of an immensely large and rapidly growing body of detailed knowledge to which the overall picture has to stand up.

The meaning of terms like 'culture' and 'civilisation' was in the eighteenth century attuned to this overall vision. Today the term 'culture' can be applied to less and to more developed societies regardless of their stage of development, and the use of the term 'civilisation' appears to be moving in the same direction. People speak of the 'culture' of Australian aborigines as well as of the 'culture' of the Renaissance and of the 'civilisation' of neolithic hunters as well as that of nineteenth-century England or France.

In Schiller's time things were different. If one spoke in Germany of 'culture' (*Kultur*) – or in France of *civilité* or *civilisation* – one had in mind a general framework which took account of the development of humanity or of particular societies from a less to a more advanced stage. As spokesmen of rising social strata, the middle-class intelligentsia of that period looked with hope and confidence to a better future. And as the future advance of society was important to them, they had the emotional impetus to notice and to single out for attention the advances which had already been made by humanity in the past. Many of their concepts, particularly those which, like 'culture' and 'civilisation', were related to their 'we-image', reflected this deeply development-orientated and dynamic character of their attitudes and basic beliefs.

Not less characteristic was the use made of these and other related concepts as code words for what was then a new outlook on history conceived by spokesmen of the rising middle classes. Voltaire and others initiated a type of history writing which was intended to correct, and to oppose, the dominant type of writing at the time – the 'political history' which placed in the centre of attention the deeds of princes and courtiers, the conflicts and alliances of states, the actions of diplomats and of great military leaders, in short, the history of the aristocratic ruling sections of absolutist states.

It was quite decisive for the position and self-image of the German middle-class elites that the tradition of history writing most clearly opposed to 'political history' became known as 'cultural history' (*Kulturgeschichte*). For many members of the educated German middle classes, 'culture' continued to represent a realm of retreat and of freedom from the unsatisfactory pressures of a state which accorded them the position of second-class citizens by comparison with the privileged nobility and denied them access to most of the leading positions in the state and to the responsibilities, power and prestige associated with these positions. Withdrawal into the non-political realm of culture made it possible for them to maintain an attitude of reserve, often highly critical reserve, towards the existing social order without embarking on any active opposition to the regime itself and without any overt conflict with its representatives. This was one of the possible solutions which could be chosen in order to cope with the cardinal dilemma of many middle classes, of which that of the modernising, but still feudaloid and semi-autocratic Germany of the nineteenth and early twentieth centuries was only one variant. Any determined and active opposition against this regime and its princely and aristocratic ruling groups on the part of middle-class groups was made difficult by the fear that they might endanger their own elevated position in relation to the lower orders by upsetting the existing regime through a fight against the elevated position of the higher orders. This fear often paralysed them.

There were two main avenues along which the middle-class groups could seek relief from the pressures of this dilemma. They could identify with the regime in spite of its oppressive and humiliating aspects. That was the road which sections of the German middle classes took in increasing numbers after 1870. Or they could, as before, retreat into the non-political area of 'culture' which provided compensatory chances of creativeness, interest and enjoyment and which enabled them to keep intact their 'inner freedom', the integrity of their own person and their pride. This was the road usually chosen by historians and other representatives of the educated German middle classes whose temper and conviction was what one might call 'liberal', though this term comprised beliefs of a variety of different shades. Their often quite considerable distaste for the political regime in which they lived was eased and their political willpower sank into passive resignation, because no reasonably safe way of altering the regime was in sight.

At the turn of the twentieth century the controversy between representatives of the two types of history flared up once more. It showed very clearly the continuity of the role of 'culture' in the development of German society as a protective and often productive sanctuary of middle-class people who, without active opposition, remained critical of the regime, while their opponents were historians representative of the other road open to the educated German middle classes; they had not only come to terms with the state in which they lived; they identified themselves with it and found in it their ideal.[4]

Yet compared with earlier, the antithesis had broadened. It now no longer lay between 'culture' (*Kultur*) as a representative symbol for fields in which educated middle-class people could find their own sense of achievement and fulfilment, and 'civilisation' (*Zivilisation*) as a symbol of the world of princes, courts and the ruling upper classes. It was rather between 'culture', still the preserve of educated middle classes with humanist ideals, and the state which, in its highest regions, remained the preserve of aristocratic upper classes skilled in political strategy, diplomacy and good manners and who, in the eyes of men from the humanist middle-class elites, often lacked true 'culture'. Even at the turn of the twentieth century, the newly united German empire (*Reich*) was not only divided along class lines, but also along lines derived from the traditional estate order which gave men of noble descent distinct legal or customary privileges by virtue of their birth.

The humanist middle-class scholars' advocacy of 'cultural history' in preference to political history, moreover, indicated – in a small way – the manner in which constructive withdrawal into the non-political realm of culture, like many other positions hemmed in by social stratification of a comparatively rigid kind, selectively opened and selectively blocked the outlook of the people concerned. The prioritisation of humanist values, as opposed to national ones, was still stressed, though more hesitantly than a hundred years before – 'the state is only a part of human culture, *the most important aspect perhaps*' – and the awareness of the narrowness of a type of history writing which selected above all the activities of princes, state legislation and diplomacy, wars, power politics and related topics for attention, was quite unambiguous. However, while sections of these elites still remained aloof from the state and continued to hold humanistic ideals such as 'culture' in the direct line of succession of the classical thinkers and poets of Germany with strong, though strictly inactive, undercurrents of criticism of Germany's ruling classes, others, gradually increasing in power, became reconciled to the secondary role allotted to the leading sections of the middle classes in the newly unified empire as junior partners of the still highly exclusive and highly class-conscious ruling nobility. The frustration and resentment inherent in such a position found expression in their case, not in relation to their social superiors, with whom as representatives of nation and empire they came, in a general way, to identify themselves, but rather in relation to all those social formations who were inferior to them in status or power; among the latter were the humanist or liberal sections of the German middle classes, particularly the humanist intelligentsia.

The controversy over the respective merits of 'cultural history' and 'political history' was one of many symptoms of the antagonism between the two rival groups in the middle-class intelligentsia. It also marked the turning point in their fortunes. Gradually, the nationalist sections became stronger, the humanist sections weaker; the latter in turn became more nationalistic; that is to say, they too gave a higher place to an ideal image of state and nation in their self-image and their scale of values, though they still tried to reconcile it with wider humanist and moral ideals. The other more radical sections of the German nationalist intelligentsia made no such attempt. Although the conservative nationalist sections of the middle classes in other countries often attempted to fuse humanist and moralist with nationalist ideals, the comparable sections of the German middle classes rejected the compromise. They turned often with an air of triumph against the humanist and moral ideals of the rising middle classes as ideals whose falsehood had been unmasked.

From humanist to nationalist middle-class elites.

A general trend, then, can be observed in the outlook of the middle classes of most European countries between the eighteenth and twentieth centuries. This trend consisted in a shift in priority from humanist and moral ideals and values applicable to people in general to nationalist ideals, which placed an ideal image of country and nation above general human and moral ideals in one's scale of values. Almost everywhere in Europe, the intellectual elites of the rising eighteenth-century middle classes shared a general belief in moral principles, in the rights of human beings as such and in the natural progress of humanity. They were forward-looking. Even if they were to some extent assimilated in outlook and manners by the ruling court aristocracy – as they were in France – and, up to a point, accepted the established belief of the ruling groups that their own age surpassed in civility and civilisation all previous ages of humans, they – the middle-class intelligentsia – at the same time took it for granted that the conditions of humanity would further improve in the future. And the better future, symbolised by the concept of 'progress', assumed in their beliefs the character of an ideal towards which one could strive and for which one could struggle with complete confidence in its eventual realisation.

When, in one European country after another, men, and later women, of middle-class descent rose to power and increasingly shared with, or altogether took over from, the traditional aristocratic ruling classes the reins of government in their societies, and when the leading middle-class sections established themselves more and more as their societies' most powerful groups, forward-looking beliefs and ideals – the hope for a better future – lost their former significance for them. The concept of 'progress' as the symbol of an overall aim, as an ideal, lost status and prestige among the middle-class intelligentsia of the countries where middle-class groups joined or replaced aristocratic groups as the ruling groups of their countries. It was no longer the auspicious symbol of a better future suffused by the glow of strong positive feelings. Instead, an idealised image of their nation moved into the centre of their self-image, their social beliefs and their scale of values. Once they had risen to the position of ruling classes, their leading sections and their intellectual elites, like those of other ruling groups, increasingly founded their ideal image of themselves on the past rather than on the future. The emotional satisfactions derived from looking forward gave way to emotional satisfactions derived from looking back. The core of their we-image and their we-ideal was formed by an image of their national tradition and heritage. Just as aristocratic groups had based their pride and their claim to a special value on their family's ancestry, so, as their successors, the leading sections of the industrial middle classes – gradually in conjunction with those of the industrial working classes wherever the latter, too, had reached a ruling position – increasingly based their pride and their claim to a special value either on their nation's ancestry or on seemingly unchanging national achievements, characteristics and values. An ideal image of themselves as the nation moved to the highest place in their public scale of values; it won precedence over the older humanistic and moralistic ideals, triumphing over them in case of conflict, and, pervaded by strong positive feelings, became the centrepiece of their system of social beliefs.

It was in connection with this change in outlook, with this shift in emotional emphasis from the future to the past and the present, from the belief in change for the better to the belief in the unchanging value of national characteristics and traditions and with the corresponding change in the whole climate of opinion of middle-class intelligentsias that took place in the highly developed European societies between the eighteenth and the early twentieth centuries, that concepts such as 'civilisation' and 'culture' changed from concepts referring to processes – to progressive developments – into concepts referring to unchanging states. While serving initially, each in its own way, as symbols of the we-image of forward-looking groups who found the emotionally most satisfying justification for their self-image and their pride in general humanist and moral values and in their contribution to the continued progress of humanity, they now came more and more to serve as symbols of the we-image of groups who found the emotionally most satisfying justification for their self-image and their pride in the past achievements of their collective ancestors, in their nation's immutable heritage and tradition. But in the late nineteenth and early twentieth centuries when the term 'culture' was increasingly used in the sense of 'national culture', the humanist and moral connotations associated with it at an earlier stage in its career faded into the background and finally disappeared.

The duality of codes within the nation-state

The question of what happens to the traditions – or, one might say, to the 'culture' – of a class in such a case has perhaps not been sufficiently considered. As long as one fails to take the wider problem into account, as long as one does not consider as a basic feature of *all* European societies the changes which occur in the traditions and attitudes of lower-class elites when – whether gradually or suddenly – they move up into the position of a ruling class, one will not be able clearly to determine the distinguishing features of this development in particular societies.

Individually, men of middle-class descent had risen to high positions frequently enough prior to the nineteenth and twentieth centuries. But, in accordance with the structure of dynastic state societies, they were more or less absorbed into the traditions of the ruling classes of their societies. In most cases they rose to high positions in the service of a prince. Rising in his service they became courtiers; they dressed like courtiers; they adopted the manners and outlook of courtiers. Rising individually they left, as it were, the traditions of their own class; they became more or less assimilated to the traditions of the ruling classes and their elites and the dividing line between them and the middle class became almost as marked as that between this class and courtiers of aristocratic descent

But from the late eighteenth and nineteenth centuries onwards the problem which rising middle-class elites had to face was different. In these centuries, the rise of middle-class men into high positions in the state was no longer a matter of the rise of individual people or of families which in one or two generations left their class and became assimilated into another. In these centuries the former middle classes themselves were rising in status and in power. If people in that phase of the development of society moved into the highest positions of the state, it no longer meant that they moved into a different class, that they sooner or later abandoned the tradition, the outlook, the code of conduct of their own class and assimilated themselves to those of a higher class. It meant that they occupied the highest positions in the state without abandoning their status, their outlook, their code of conduct, in short their 'culture' as persons of the middle classes.

Thus, when elite groups from the former 'middle classes' in that phase of the development of societies moved into the position of ruling elites, two traditions or 'cultures' which had before developed in relatively separate social compartments, in social strata whose contacts and communications with each other were not very close (although the degree of separatedness varied greatly from society to society), were brought into very much closer contact; they merged or rather, since they were in a number of aspects hardly compatible, they collided often enough within one and the same person.

When the former middle classes rose as such into the position of ruling classes, their representatives, who entered the commanding positions of the state, were exposed to experiences, particularly in the field of inter-state relations, which had formerly been accessible mainly to people in the tradition of the nobility and court. They were exposed to these experiences without abandoning their middle-class traditions and their middle-class code of conduct. It was difficult to apply this code, which had originated in the more limited world of pre-industrial artisan and trading communities and of the elites descended from them, to some of the new experiences as ruling elites of a state. Especially in inter-state relations they were faced with types of conduct to which it was difficult to apply their own code of morality. It was in this field above all – though by no means only – that they drew, in their capacity as ruling groups, on the models provided by the 'culture' of the former ruling groups, on a code which for want of a better label one might call 'Machiavellian'. For, in this sphere the belief in the pursuit of unrestrained self-interest as the leading principle of conduct, checked only by the fear of the greater power or the greater skill of potential opponents, which had dominated the politics of the leading dynasties and the leading aristocratic groups of different states in their relations with each other, had left a heritage of mutual fears and suspicions in inter-state relations.[5]

The aristocratic tradition of inter-state relations – the tradition which had its origins among the warrior classes of Europe and which was perpetuated by nobles whose beliefs and values were those of military men – certainly did not fit the traditions, beliefs and values of the pre-industrial and early industrial middle classes. What happened in fact was that the leading groups of the industrial classes to some extent absorbed the dynastic and aristocratic traditions in this field. They tried to combine the belief in their traditional egalitarian and humanist code of norms – in the moral code which excluded violence and implied a fundamental identification with all human beings – with the belief that in the relations between states unrestrained self-interest must prevail. Thus they entered into, and perpetuated, the vicious circle of mutual fears and suspicions which, in inter-state relations, had existed before, and which must exist in human relations everywhere as long as those forming a particular figuration with each other do not agree on, and do not maintain effectively among themselves, a common code of norms.

However, when the middle classes moved into the position of ruling classes and middle-class elites came to occupy the commanding positions of society, they did not simply take over the aristocratic heritage. They did not simply make the tradition of unrestrained pursuit of self-interest, backed by military means, and of mutual fears and suspicions in inter-state relations, their own without changing it to a considerable extent in the process. By assimilating it they altered the dynastic tradition. Until the eighteenth century, the aristocratic code of valour and honour was the common code of the ruling classes in most European states. As in the case of duelling, noblemen and gentlemen who encountered each other as opponents in the case of war might do their utmost to defeat and even to kill the men on the other side; but even the use of physical force, even violence and killing were, within limits, subject to a code of honour and valour which military officers on both sides shared with each other. Wars, like duels, were the affairs of gentlemen; they did not destroy the fairly highly developed esprit de corps, the 'we-feeling' of military officers on opposite sides in their capacity as gentlemen or noblemen, as members of the same 'estate'. On balance this 'we-feeling' of the pre-revolutionary upper classes of Europe, which surpassed the frontiers of states, was probably stronger than any 'we-feeling' – any feeling of identity – which men of these upper classes had with the lower classes of their own country. Their attachment to their own state did not yet have the character of an attachment to their nation. With few exceptions national sentiments were alien to the noblemen of Europe prior to the French Revolution and in some countries for a long time after it They were, of course, conscious of being French, English, German or Russian noblemen and gentlemen. But before the rise of commercial or industrial middle classes and their elites, the 'we-feelings' of local groups in relation to their locality, region or country were, in societies whose stratification had the character of a hierarchy of estates rather than of classes, in no way equivalent to national solidarity feelings. One cannot quite understand the specific characteristics of nationalist values and belief systems as sociological data unless one has a clear understanding of their connection with a specific stage of social development and, therefore, with a specific type of social structure. It was only in class-societies, not in estate-societies, that the identity feelings of the ruling elites and in course of time those of wider strata, too, acquired the specific stamp of national feelings.

It can be seen very clearly in what way identity feelings changed in European states when, whether gradually or abruptly, ruling elites descended from the middle classes replaced those descended from the traditional aristocratic upper classes.[6] On balance, their identification with their own compatriots became stronger, that with men of the same class and standing in other countries weaker. This change in the pattern of people's 'we-and-they-feelings', of identification and exclusion, was one of the principal conditions of the development of nationalist sentiments, values and beliefs. As Sieyès's treatise and other revolutionary pronouncements indicated, sentiments, values and beliefs centred on the image of the nation were from early on associated with the self-image of middle classes – and somewhat later also of working classes – which were on the point of claiming, or actually ascending into, the commanding positions of a state.

That the middle-class elites saw themselves, when they came to occupy the ruling positions of the state, not only as leading groups of a country or a state, but also of a nation, influenced their conduct in inter-state relations. In one sense they simply took over the code of princes, the Machiavellian code of power politics. The continuity is unmistakable. However, in the course of becoming a middle-class code, the Machiavellian code was also significantly transformed. In its original form it was a code of conduct primarily tailored for a prince in his relations with other princes. Now it became a code primarily applied to the conduct of the affairs of a nation-state in its relations with other nation-states. The development implied change as well as continuity.

One can get a glimpse of both if one compares the manner in which Machiavelli presented the policy of unrestrained self-interest as the principle for the rulers of states in inter-state relations and the manner in which essentially the same policy was, centuries later in the twentieth century, usually presented by national elites. Machiavelli's policy prescriptions,[7] were of a highly practical nature. He explained what he believed was the best way in which a prince could hold his own in the jungle of inter-state relations. As an experienced servant of rulers he gave the rulers of states, some of whom he knew personally, practical advice.

When power politics came to be pursued in the name of a nation, certain basic aspects of the figuration which states formed with each other remained unaltered. In that case, too, the ruling groups of interdependent and yet sovereign state organisations pursued in relation to each other policies of uncontrolled and apparently uncontrollable self-interest which induced, and were in turn induced by, mutual fears and suspicions; these were at the same time the main checks to the unlimited pursuit of self-interest by any individual state. But power politics, pursued in the name of a nation and not of a prince, could no longer be conceived of and represented as the policy of or for a person. They were politics in the name of a collectivity which was so large that the majority of its members did not and could not know each other.

Power politics remained largely unchanged but the shift from thinking about them in terms of a sovereign person to thinking about them in terms of a sovereign collectivity had curious consequences It was easier to speak about matters of policy unemotionally in practical and realistic terms to, and about, princes than it was to do the same in relation to a sovereign collectivity. Both the sovereign prince and the sovereign people required, for the execution of any policy undertaken for them or in their name, a measure of emotional attachment on the part of those helping to execute the policy or acting in their name. But in the first case, the feelings of loyalty and attachment were still feelings from person to person. In the second case, the emotional bonds had to some extent a different character. They were to a much higher degree symbolic attachments – attachments to symbols of the collectivity. These symbols could be of many types. But among them verbal symbols played a special role. Whatever form they took, these symbols for a collectivity and its various aspects became focal points for the emotional bonding of persons to the collectivity, and appeared to endow the collectivity itself with a peculiar quality; they endowed it, one might say, with a numinous existence of its own outside and above the individuals who formed it – with a kind of holiness formerly associated mainly with super-human beings.

It is a mark of democratisation processes which has perhaps not found the attention it deserves that, in the course of these processes, whether they result in a multi-party or a one-party state, a parliamentary or a dictatorial regime, these numinous qualities and the corresponding emotions are attached by people to the societies they themselves form with each other. In simpler societies, according to Durkheim's suggestion, these emotional bonds of individuals with the collectivity they form crystallise and organise themselves around figures or images of gods or ancestors – of beings of more or less super-human stature; whatever other functions they may have, they also have that of emotion-laden symbols of a we-group. Compared with simpler societies, the nation-states of the nineteenth and twentieth centuries are large and extremely populous. Moreover, the factual bonds of millions of individuals belonging to the same society, their interlinking through the occupational division of labour, through integration within the same framework of governmental and administrative organisations and in many other ways, are much more complex, much more elusive from the point of view of most of the individuals who form these gigantic social organisations, than the interlinking of people in simpler societies. Unless educational levels are very advanced, the factual interdependencies of the individuals living in highly differentiated industrial nation-states remain at the most half understood – they are often obscure and incomprehensible for most of their members. So, the emotional bonds of individuals with the collectivity which they form with each other crystallise and organise themselves around common symbols which do not require any factual explanations, which can and must be regarded as absolute values which are not to be questioned and which form focal points of a common belief system. To call them into question – to cast doubt on the common belief in one's own sovereign collectivity as a high, if not the highest possible, value means deviancy, a breach of trust; it can lead one to become an ostracised outsider if nothing worse.

Most of the sovereign interdependent nation-states, which together form the balance of power-figuration in the twentieth century, produce a twofold code of norms whose demands are inherently contradictory: a moral code descended from that of rising sections of the *tiers état*, egalitarian in character, and whose highest value is 'man' – the human individual as such; and a nationalist code descended from the Machiavellian code of princes and ruling aristocracies, inegalitarian in character, and whose highest value is a collectivity – the state, the country, the nation to which an individual belongs. The continuity of a Machiavellian ethos in inter-state relations is simply understandable, almost irrespective of the social characteristics and traditions of the ruling elites, in terms of the fact that these relations themselves continue to remain a sphere of social life in which none of the interdependent social units can be sure that others will not ultimately resort to the use of physical force in order to pursue their supposed interests. However, the continuity in the self-perpetuating beliefs and code of conduct linking the strategy of princes and aristo-cratic ruling elites in inter-state affairs to that of the middle- or working-class elites of twentieth-century nation-states was not absolute. It left room for specific changes. The most noticeable of these was the change in the character of the postulate that, in inter-state relations, the interests of one's own state ought to be regarded as the decisive consideration overruling all others. This originated as a simple practical maxim of princes and their ministers, or of aristocratic ruling elites with a privileged position, who regarded their state and the mass of its subjects as a kind of possession and themselves as the hub of the state. However, with the increasing democratisation of state societies and with the corresponding nationalisation of the outlook and sentiments of most of the individuals who formed them, this practical maxim became a categorical imperative with deep roots not only in the feelings of these individuals, but also in their conscience, their I-and-we image, their I-and-we-ideal.

In nineteenth- and twentieth-century state societies, people are thus brought up with dis-positions to act in accordance with at least two major codes of norms which are in some respects incompatible with each other. The preservation, integrity and interests of the state society, of their own sovereign collectivity and all it stands for are assimilated by each individual as part of his or her habitus, as a guiding principle of action which in certain situations can and must override all others. At the same time, however, they are brought up with a humanist, egalitarian or moral code, whose supreme value overriding all others is the individual human being as such. Both become, in the usual language, 'internalised', or perhaps one should simply say 'individualised'. They become facets of the individual's own conscience. To break either of these two codes can expose an individual in appropriate situations to punishment not only from others, but also from himself or herself in the form of guilt feelings, of a 'bad conscience'.

The development of a dual and inherently contradictory code of norms is one of the common features of all countries which have undergone the transformation from an aristocratic-dynastic into a more democratic national state. The contradictions, conflicts and tensions inherent in this development may come into the open and become very acute only in specific situations, above all in national emergencies such as wars. But even as a latent determinant of action, even in times of peace, a dual code of norms of this type has very considerable influence on the attitudes of individuals and on the conduct of affairs. It accounts for a specific polarisation of political ideals. It enables some groups to lay greater stress in their programmes on the values of the nationalist creed and of the warrior tradition without necessarily completely abandoning those of the humanist, egalitarian moral tradition. The stress of others is the reverse, in a great variety of combinations. It makes it possible for different individuals, in accordance with their social position, to link their attitudes, their personality structure with a group whether it stands more towards the centre or towards one or other pole of the spectrum. The whole figuration itself, the alignment of groups of people somewhere between these two poles, is a common feature of all societies of this type.

The nationalism of the nation-state

One can understand better the confluence of change and continuity in the development which led from the original Machiavellian code to its sublimation as part of a nationalist belief system if one considers the change in the focus of emotional attachments from living princes to impersonal symbols of a hallowed collectivity. In a world of dynastic states, particularly of monarchical states ruled more or less autocratically, a policy of unrestrained self-interest in inter-state relations was a personal policy of rulers who, either by birth or by their own military and political achievements, stood in the line of succession of a warrior tradition. The code they followed in inter-state relations was largely an extension of the code which they followed in personal relations. There was no high barrier, no sharp dividing line between the two – no basic contradiction between personal or private and public or state morality. What had once been the principle of a practical and, one might say, reasonably realistic strategy for the conduct of princes in inter-state affairs changed its emotional colour when it became a strategy of nations or, more specifically, of their ruling elites. The realistic aspects of the traditional warrior code which sowed mistrust and fear between ruling groups, just as, conversely, it grew out of mistrust and fear between them, fused with the mystique of a nationalist creed which thousands could believe in as something absolute without asking questions.

It is easy to see why this belief in the 'nation' as a sacrosanct we-ideal arose in an age of highly differentiated mass societies with conscript armies and an increasing involvement of the total population in conflicts with other mass societies. In that situation simple drill and obedience to a prince or a military commander were not enough to ensure a country's success in a power struggle with others. Under these conditions it was necessary that all citizens were, in addition to any external compulsion, also compelled by their own conscience and their own ideals, by a fervently held belief or, in other words, by a compulsion they exercised upon themselves individually, to subordinate their individual needs to those of the collectivity, the country or the nation, and if necessary to lay down their lives. It was necessary that the individual members of all these relatively highly differentiated mass societies of the twentieth century should be motivated by an unquestionable belief in the value of the society they formed with each other, of the 'nation'; for it was not always possible to explain in factual terms the merits of the society for those whose services or whose lives were demanded.

Although the primary impulse for the formation of nationalism as a belief system came from the inter-state sphere, whether from common fear for the integrity and survival of one's own society or the common wish for an increase in its power, status and prestige in relation to other sovereign societies, a nationalist creed could also serve as an instrument of rule and domination, or attempted domination, by a small group over others. One of the basic characteristics of industrial state societies at the stage of development reached in the nineteenth and twentieth centuries is the simultaneity of, on the one hand, a growing inter-dependence of all social classes and, on the other, of standing tensions between the leading working-class and middle-class groups. Many subsidiary tensions between different occu-pational groups cluster around this main axis of tension usually represented by that between employers' federations and trade unions. In this situation the appeal to national sentiments and loyalties, which had taken firm roots in all classes for a variety of reasons, particularly connected with wars and the advancement of education through state-controlled schools and armies, could be used within a society as a lever for fostering sectional interests by one or another of the leading groups. As is well known they were used in this manner in a number of countries, Germany among them, mainly by discontented middle-class groups.

Nationalist belief and value systems in highly developed countries with relatively high standards of living are usually backwards-looking creeds. They are used in societies of this type with the aim of preserving the established order, even if the social movement rallied in the name of the national heritage and its virtues in fact aims at overthrowing the existing order. If that is done, it is usually in the name of the restoration of the past, of the unchanging heritage of the nation. In short, the character of nationalist ideas can hardly be understood if it is deduced from the study of these ideas alone as they may appear in books by philosophers or other prominent writers, in other words if they are studied in accordance with the traditions of the 'history of ideas'. Their succession in time is not simply due to the fact that authors of one generation read, as a matter of course, books written by authors of previous generations and develop further, approvingly or critically, the ideas of previous authors without reference to the development and to the structural peculiarities of the societies where these books are written and read. Nor are the nationalist ideas of prominent writers the 'cause' of 'nationalism'. In a latent or manifest form, nationalism constitutes one of the most powerful, perhaps *the* most powerful, social beliefs of the nineteenth and twentieth centuries. Book ideas constitute, to use an apt if well-worn simile, only the tip of an iceberg. They are the most articulate manifestations of a process during which national sentiments and a national ethos spread sooner or later through the whole of a society. Unless one asks what changes in the structure of state societies account for the change from an expression of loyalties and of solidarity feelings in terms of an attachment to princes – *Vive le Roi!* – to an expression of loyalties and solidarity feelings in terms of a nation – *Vive la France* – in society at large, one cannot assess the role which publications of a nationalist intelligentsia have in the nationalisation of ethos and sentiment of the great mass of indi-viduals who form these societies.

Nationalism, even in a preliminary sociological analysis, is thus revealed as a specific social phenomenon characteristic of large industrial state societies at the level of develop-ment reached by the nineteenth and twentieth centuries. It is related to, and yet clearly distinct from, group beliefs representing the attachment and solidarity of individuals in relation to collectivities such as villages, towns, principalities or kingdoms in earlier stages of social development. It is a question of a belief of a characteristically secular kind. That is, it can be sustained without justification through super-human agencies; it approximates to the types of belief and ethos which Max Weber called 'inner worldly'. It presupposes a high degree of democratisation of societies in the sociological, not in the political sense of the word: if social barriers between groups of different social power and rank are too high – as they are, for instance, in estate societies with a hereditary nobility or in dynastic states with a very steep power gradient between princes and subjects – individual feelings of attachment, of solidarity and obligation in relation to a state society have a different character from that expressed in the form of a nationalist ethos.

A nationalist ethos implies a sense of solidarity and obligation, not simply with regard to particular persons or a single person in a ruling position as such, but with regard to a sovereign collectivity which the individual concerned himself or herself forms with thousands or millions of others, which, here and now, is organised as a state – or which according to the beliefs of the people concerned will be so in the future – and the attachment to which is mediated through special symbols, some of which can be persons. These symbols and the collectivity for which they stand attract to themselves strong positive emotions of the type usually called love. The collectivity is experienced and the symbols are represented as something apart from, something holier and higher than, the individuals concerned. Collectivities which generate a nationalist ethos are structured in such a way that the individuals who form them can experience them – more specifically their emotion-laden symbols – as representatives of themselves. The love for one's nation is never only a love for persons or groups of whom one says 'You'; it is always also the love of a collectivity to which one can refer as 'We'. Whatever else it may be, it is also a form of self-love.

The image of a nation experienced by an individual who forms part of that nation, therefore, is also a constituent of that person's self-image. The virtue, the value, the meaningfulness of the nation are also his or her own. Current sociological and social psychological theories, in so far as they are concerned with such problems at all, offer for reflections on phenomena of this kind the concept of identification. However, it is a concept which is not wholly appropriate to what one actually observes in this case. The concept of identification makes it appear that the individual is here and the nation is there; it implies that 'individual' and 'nation' are two different entities separated in space. Since nations consist of individuals, and individuals who live in the more developed twentieth-century state societies belong, in the majority of cases, unambiguously to a nation, a conceptualisation which evokes the picture of two different entities separated in space, like mother and child, does not fit the facts.

Relationships of this type can be adequately expressed only in terms of personal pronouns. An individual does not only have an ego-image and an ego-ideal, but also a we-image and a we-ideal. It is a central aspect of the nationalisation of individual ethos and sentiment, which can be observed empirically in nineteenth- and twentieth-century industrial state societies, that the image of these state societies, represented, among others, by verbal symbols such as 'nation', form an integral part of the we-images and the we-ideals of most of the individuals who form with each other societies of this type. This, in short, is one of the many instances of correspondence between specific types of social structure and specific types of personality structure. A member of a differentiated twentieth-century industrial nation-state who makes statements in which he or she uses an adjectival form of the name of his or her country as an attribute of him or herself – 'I am French', 'I am American', 'I am Russian' – expresses in most cases much more than: 'I have been born in this particular country' or 'I have a passport of this particular country'. For the bulk of the individuals reared in a state society of this type such a statement carries with it a reference to their nation and to personal characteristics and values at the same time. It is a statement about both himself/herself perceived as an 'I' *vis-à-vis* others to whom he or she refers in communications as 'you', 'he' or 'she' and himself/herself perceived as constituent of one of the collectivities to which he or she refers in thought and sentiment as 'we' *vis-à-vis* others which are to him/her 'you' or 'they'. To say 'I am Russian, American, French', or whatever, usually implies 'I and we believe in specific values and ideas', 'I and we are suspicious and feel more or less antagonistic in relation to members of this or that other nation state', 'I as well as we have attachments and obligations in relation to these symbols and the collectivity for which they stand'. Moreover, the image of this 'we' forms an integral part of the personality organisation of the individual who in these cases uses the pronouns 'I' and 'We' with reference to himself or herself.[8]

Thus, for the purposes of a sociological enquiry one has to standardise a term which can be used without undertones of either disapproval or approval. One requires a term indicating the specific scale of values, the specific type of sentiments, beliefs and ideals by means of which, in the more industrialised state societies of the nineteenth and twentieth centuries, individuals attach themselves to the sovereign society which they form with each other. What is needed is a unified term, a clear conceptual instrument for registering the common structural properties of that type of emotional bonding, belief and personality organisation which sooner or later appears, not just in one or another but in all industrial nation-states of the developmental level of the nineteenth and twentieth centuries. And since substantives ending with the syllable 'ism', adjectives ending with the syllable 'ist' are the accepted linguistic expressions for social belief systems of this kind, and for the personality structures connected with them, the common language offers for sociological standardisation as a unified concept mainly the choice between the two terms 'patriotism' and 'nationalism'. On balance, the latter seems preferable as a standard sociological term; it is more flexible; one can form with its help easily understandable derivatives with a process character such as 'nationalisation of sentiments and thoughts'. It is in that sense, cleansed of undertones of approval or disapproval, that it is being used here. It is simply intended to refer to one aspect of an overall transformation which specific state societies, in conjunction with the balance of power within a specific figuration of interdependent societies, underwent during a specific period of time. It refers to a social belief system which, latently or acutely, raises the state society, the sovereign collectivity to which its members belong, to the position of a supreme value to which all other values can and sometimes must be subordinated.

As one of the great secular social beliefs of nineteenth- and twentieth-century societies, nationalism distinguishes itself in certain respects from the other great social beliefs of the time, such as conservatism and communism, liberalism and socialism The latter gain their primary impetus from the changing balance of power within particular state societies and irradiate inter-state relations only secondarily. Nationalism gains its primary impetus from the changing balance of power among different state societies and irradiates only secondarily the tensions and conflicts among different social strata within them. And although the ideals and beliefs associated with the polarisation of interdependent classes within one and the same state society blend in a variety of ways with the nationalist beliefs which arise primarily from the polarisation of interdependent states within their balance of power-figuration, in the long run the impact of the latter on the direction of politics is more decisive and continuous. Societies may differ with regard to the beliefs and ideals which guide their ruling elites in their intra-state politics; but they all have in common the nationalisation of ethos and sentiment, of we-attachment and we-image of most of the individuals who form them. As is easy to see, this nationalisation of ethos and sentiment takes place sooner or later in all modernising countries at the nineteenth- and twentieth-century level regardless of the social complexion of their ruling elites.

Notes

1 The following text originated as a reworking of the first chapter of *The Civilizing Process*, Vol. I, *The History of Manners* (Oxford: Blackwell, 1978), 'On the Sociogenesis of the Concepts "Civilisation" and "Culture"', pp. 1–50.
2 See Elias's discussion of 'process reduction' as an afliction of modern sociology in *What is Sociology?*, London, Hutchinson and New York, Columbia University Press, 1978, p. 111ff.; see also his castigation of the related but more general 'Retreat of Sociologists into the Present', Theory, Culture and Society, 4 (2–3) 1987: 223–47. [Translators' note.]
3 Friedrich Schiller, 'Was Heist und zu welchen Ende studiert man Universalgeschichte?' [What does universal history mean, and why does one study it?], in *Schillers Werke* [The Works of Schiller], Nationalausgabe, Vol.17, Weimer, 1970, p. 367ff.
4 See E. Gothein, 'The Tasks of the History of Culture', in *Die Aufgabe der Kulturegeschichte*, Leipzig, 1889, for the non-political humanist direction, and Dietrich Schaffer, *Deutsches National Bewusstein im Lichte der Geschichte*, Jena, 1884, for the nationalist direction.
5 Cf. Norbert Elias, *The Civilizing Process*, Vol. II. The 'Machiavellian code of control' was a code of honour, of civility and good manners, of expediency and diplomacy which even in its application to members of one and the same society included the use of violence providing it was used in a gentlemanly manner, for instance in the form of duelling. To some extent, the code of honour and civility which ruled relations of nobleman and gentleman within the dynastic states also ruled the relations between members of the upper classes of different states. It even tempered to a certain degree the tradtional conduct of inter-state relations where princes and their aristocratic representatives – forming with each other a balance of power configuration which for them was uncontrollable as well as inescapable – used in a Machiavellian manner deception, violence or any other device which they thought might help them to get the better of others without moral scruples and restraints as a matter of course, as long as they were not afraid of defeat and humiliation from the hands of a more powerful prince. In their case, in the case of dynastic states with ruling elites dominated by nobles, few if any contradictions existed between the code of rules they observed among themselves within one and the same state and the code they observed in inter-state relations.
6 Particularly strong expressions of this change in identity feelings can be clearly observed during the French Revolution. One of the best known literary expressions of this transition to a value and belief system which lifts the image of the nation to the highest rank can be found in E. J. Sieyès, *What is the Third Estate?*, first published 1789, here quoted in the translation by M. Blondel, London, 1963. A characteristic expression of the new stress on the nation is this: (p. 124):

> The nation is prior to everything. It is the source of everything. Its will is always legal; indeed it is the law itself. Prior to and above the nation, there is only the natural law.

Sieyès represents the rising middle classes in the literal sense of the word, the classes in the middle between the privileged estates – in France, the nobility and the clergy – and 'the poor' who did not earn enough to contribute to the upkeep of the state. Theoretically Sieyès still held firmly to the ideal of the equality of all human beings which was used as a weapon of the rising middle classes in their struggle with the privileged estates above them. But in practice, in his proposals for the new constitution he wanted to limit the right to vote for the national assembly to those citizens who could contribute at least three livres a year in taxes. The main front on which Sieyès as representative of the 'classes in the middle' fought, though, was in the revolutionary situation the front against the privileged ruling classes, against kings, nobles and clergy (p. 57): 'What then is "The Third Estate"? All; but an all that is fettered and oppressed.' Sentences such as this show clearly how the beginnings of an identification with the 'nation' already heralded specific changes in the emotional atmosphere. One encountered here – in an age whose mode of thinking in many areas was becoming more realistic or 'rational' and less emotional – the rise of a new mystique, related not to 'nature' but to 'society', the rise of a new belief system centred on an ideal image of one's own nation, a compound of fact and fantasy. The difference in atmosphere becomes particularly clear if one compares these and other expressions of the rising nationalist belief system with the attitudes of authors such as Machiavelli to the relations between dynastic states which were not yet conceived as nations.

7 In a chapter of *The Prince* which has the heading 'In what manner Princes should keep their faith', Machiavelli wrote:

> You must know, therefore, that there are two ways of carrying on a contest; the one by law and the other by force. The first is practised by men, and the other by animals; and as the first is often insufficient, it becomes necessary to resort to the second.
>
> A prince then should know how to employ the nature of man and that of beasts as well. This was figuratively taught by ancient writers, who relate how Achilles and many other princes were given to Chiron the centaur to be nurtured, and how they were trained under his tutorship; which fable means nothing else than that their preceptor combined the qualities of the man and the beast, and that a prince, to succeed, will have to employ both the one and the other nature, as the one without the other cannot produce lasting results.
>
> It being necessary then for a prince to know well how to employ the nature of the beasts, he should be able to assume both that of the fox and that of the lion; for whilst the latter cannot escape the traps laid for him, the former cannot defend himself against the wolves. A prince should be a fox, to know the traps and snares; and a lion, to be able to frighten the wolves; for those who simply hold to the nature of the lion do not understand their business.
>
> A sagacious prince then cannot and should not fulfil his pledges when their observance is contrary to his interest, and when the causes that induced him to pledge his faith no longer exist. If men were all good, then indeed this precept would be bad; but as men are naturally bad, and will not observe their faith towards you, you must, in the same way, not observe yours to them; and no prince ever yet lacked legitimate reasons with which to colour his want of good faith. Innumerable modern examples could be given of this; and it could easily be shown how many treaties of peace, and how many engagements, have been made null and void by the faithlessness of princes; and he who has best known how to play the fox has ever been the most successful

(From *The Living Thoughts of Machiavelli*, Cassell, London, 1942, pp. 65–66.)

8 Nationalism, as an expression of love towards, pride in, and identification with a particular we-unit, is different from the apparently similar ties of traditional aristocratic groups. Bismarck for instance is often taken as the prototype of German nationalism. In fact his love was directed in the first instance to King and country, not to the German nation as a symbolic representation of the mass of the German people as a whole – although, since he lived in a period of transition, he had to pay belated lip-service to it as an ideal when the need arose.

INDEX